REASON IN CONTROVERSY

On General Argumentation

Second Edition

REASON IN CONTROVERSY

On General Argumentation
Second Edition

Glen E. Mills
Northwestern University

ALLYN AND BACON, INC.

PREFACE

THIS BOOK AND THE COURSE IN WHICH IT WAS DEVELOPED HAVE BEEN
based upon the assumption that a worthwhile contribution to the
education of many college students can be made by a course in argumentation. Such a course would provide systematic instruction in the
analysis of controversial statements, the accumulation and the testing
of evidence, the drawing and the criticism of arguments, the questions
of logical and ethical responsibility, the procedures of attack and defense, the logical arrangement of ideas, the social import of advocacy,
the effective presentation of their views, and the evaluation of argumentative essays and speeches.

Classroom experiences, suggestions from professional colleagues,
and the author's reactions to recent writings in this field have resulted
in some substantial revisions to the first edition of this book. Much
more attention has been paid in this edition to definitions of basic
concepts such as argumentation, debate, and proof. Where differences
of opinion on theoretical matters are deemed important, they are reported and documented. However, if these reviews of the literature are

not used in the course, a reader may skip them and proceed directly to this writer's views which follow. The chapter on the logic of argument has been recast to provide several ways, from the classical to the contemporary, to diagram arguments. Finally, a new, short chapter on the evaluation of argumentative discourse has been added.

Five specimens for use in applying the principles of argumentation are provided in Appendixes A to E. They include case outlines, a college oration on responsible advocacy, a championship tournament debate, an essay on Presidential campaign debating, and an exchange between an editor and a letter-writer.

G. E. M.

CONTENTS

1   Introduction to Argumentation   1

2   Basic Definitions   13

3   Logical and Ethical Responsibilities   47

4   Propositions: Bases of Controversy   69

5   Analysis: A Crucial Process   89

6   Investigation   115

7   Evidence   137

8   Argument: Structures, Kinds, and Tests   173

9   Other Forms of Support   205

10   Case Construction   221

11   Attack and Defense   253

12   Presentation of Argument   289

13   Evaluating Argument   307

Appendix A—Case Outlines   311

Appendix B—Responsibility and Rhetoric   335

Appendix C—Championship Debate   339

Appendix D—TV and the Elections   371

Appendix E—Editorial Followed by Letter to Editor   379

CHAPTER I

INTRODUCTION TO ARGUMENTATION

IN A COMPARATIVELY FREE SOCIETY THERE IS RARELY A SHORTAGE OF public controversies on which the citizenry is asked to pass judgment. The specific subjects vary with time and place, but these editorial headlines called attention to complaints which were salient at the time of this writing: "Restore Amateurism to Intercollegiate Athletics," "Let Students Help Select Dean of Students," "Pass Gun Control Bill," "Get Out of Viet Nam," "Abolish H. U. A. C.," "Support Subscription T. V.," "Make Social Security Voluntary," "Legalize Abortion," and "Adopt Pass or No-Credit Grading." How to deal on a verbal level with controversial matters such as these is the concern of this book.

For more than sixty years the titles of textbooks and courses in this subject have typically included the words *argumentation* and *debate*. The historical explanation of this phenomenon will be given later in this chapter under "Argumentation as an Academic Discipline." For the present it will suffice merely to state that the newer emphasis upon a less specialized treatment of the subject suggests the appropriateness of a different title.

Reason in Controversy came to mind for the obvious reason that this study is intended to deal with reasoned discourse as presumedly the most civilized human expression in a conflictive situation. We know that controversy, which is here taken to mean an exchange of opposing views on a problem of mutual interest to the contending parties, can entail many combinations of rational, nonrational, and irrational remarks; and we believe, according to the basic documents of our society, that rational problem-solving behavior is preferable. Even those of us whose reasoning often takes the form of rationalizing profess to prefer rational behavior. This inconsistency stems from our ability either to think our way to a conclusion or to invent plausible reasons for a conclusion which we previously reached impulsively.

In response to this inconsistency some persons question the historic Greek notion, "Man is a rational animal," calling it possibly "more a prayer than a proposition." An existentialist, it is claimed, would not agree that rationality is the essence of man. Our advice to students to be rational is alleged to be prescriptive in terms of a value judgment which is assumed rather than proved.[1]

If one does not espouse existentialism, and takes the Greek view to mean that man, as distinguished from other forms of life, is *capable* of reason, it seems "reasonable" to argue that one defensible "reason for being reasonable" is that such behavior is uniquely human. A practical reason is that decisions which one arrives at critically seem better to withstand the scrutiny by others.

SOCIAL CONTEXT ON THIS SUBJECT

Ideals of a Democracy

Before we can relate the principles of argumentation to the philosophical tenets of our social order, we must state what we believe to be the relevant ideals of our democracy. One is that individuals will participate in making decisions. This is the essence of self-government. Another is the faith that man, if sufficiently well informed and in communication with his fellows, can solve social problems. Thus education and communication are of great importance, because if one cannot hear or understand what others say, or if they cannot hear or understand him, there can be no dialogue, and democracy loses its meaning, as

[1] R. L. Scott, "Some Implications of Existentialism for Rhetoric," *Central States Speech Journal*, XV, No. 4 (1964), 267–278.

Robert M. Hutchins has said.[2] A third ideal is that the dialogue will not cease. As Alexander Meiklejohn put it,[3] the basic need of free discussion is not that everyone shall speak but that everything worth saying shall be said. Another ideal is that we can have majority rule coupled with a respect for minority views, even though some persons argue that the two are mutually exclusive. The hard fact is that the persons on the winning side who try to silence the minority are revealing their contempt for the democratic ideal. This thought suggests the fifth ideal, the right of dissent. But this implies more than protection against arbitrary power; it means that no one may be barred from expressing views which some say are false or unwise. When people govern themselves, it is they alone who must judge falsehood or folly. In Judge Learned Hand's view, the privilege of free speech rests upon the assumption that there is no proposition so uniformly believed that it is beyond challenge or debate. In other words, in the end it is "worse to suppress dissent than to run the risk of heresy."[4]

Though these ideals sound familiar and are subject to much lip-service, they constantly face serious threats. One of these threats stems from the failures of education and of communication on some occasions to achieve the ideal expressed above. Germany under the Weimar Republic, for instance, had a high literacy rate, ample publication, a tradition of scholarship, and a scheme of proportional representation, but these could not prevail against the emergent dictatorship of Hitler. And this can happen elsewhere. Education can become trivial, and the communication media can become exclusively purveyors of entertainment or of propaganda. The dialogue which is the essence of a free society may practically cease because the citizens either have nothing to say or have no place to say it.

Another threat, probably a consequence of the first, involves the development of authoritarian leadership behind a democratic disguise consisting of the forms, rituals, slogans, and other symbols of a free society. At all levels of human organization, from a small, local group to a major nation-state, we have seen leaders make a mockery of parliamentary procedure, the ballot, constitutions, and labels such as "democratic," "people's," and "peace-loving."

A third threat to our cherished ideals comes about through the

[2] "Is Democracy Possible?" *Saturday Review*, February 21, 1959.
[3] "Everything Worth Saying Should Be Said," *New York Times Magazine*, July 18, 1948.
[4] *Saturday Review*, March 15, 1958, p. 17.

desire for "efficiency" in the face of the amazing complexity and number of problems which citizens are expected to solve. One is sorely tempted to give up and turn the whole business over to administrators and bureaucrats. This attitude of resignation becomes understandable when we realize that the mass of technical information on many public problems makes it unlikely that there can be a fully informed citizen. Because thorough debating takes much time, because none can become fully informed, and because the analogy of the New England town meeting cannot apply to our large, heterogeneous, industrial, bureaucratic society, it is argued that the most we should hope for is a condition of order, efficiency, and some semblance of civil rights.

Fourth in our list of threats is the widespread fear of unpopular opinions and the resulting temptation to deny them a forum. A case in point was the reaction to a paid advertisement in the Chicago *Daily News* which sought support for the defense of a man who had been indicted under the Smith Act. A letter writer contended that the accused should have his hearing in court but not in "an American newspaper worthy of the name." The editor replied that his paper did not favor jailing people solely for their ideas, however perverted, and that the issue of civil liberty was so fundamental that the defense was entitled to appeal for public support. Perhaps the most familiar type of case is that of the school- and college teachers who have been reprimanded or discharged for exposing young minds to "controversial subjects." This verbal subterfuge scarcely conceals the fact that the real objection is to the disclosure that there is a view other than the prevailing opinion. One is reminded of the futile attempt which was made to prohibit intercollegiate debating of the recognition of Red China a few years ago. As if these instances were insufficient to make the point, we can recall local, statewide, and nationwide agitations to ban allegedly subversive books or authors such as Carl Sandburg, Archibald MacLeish, and "Robin Hood." "We try to avoid all controversial pieces of literature," said a school superintendent.[5] As several interpreters of the First Amendment have pointed out, we will be fit to govern ourselves only if we have faced everything that can be said in favor of or against our institutions. Unabridged freedom of public discussion and debate on public policy has been called the rock on which our government stands.

The fifth threat to democratic ideals is the fear of community

[5] Committee on Freedom of Speech, Speech Association of America, "Freedom of Speech Newsletter," No. 11 (1967).

decision. It is fomented by those who seek sources of wisdom other than the people of the community debating and deciding together. Some would limit the area in which the citizens have the right to choose what is to be preserved, changed, or abolished. There are individuals and groups that seek the uncritical preservation of their cherished values, institutions, activities, and ideas. They try to prevent the critical scrutiny of the status quo by limiting the authority of the community.

Finally, there is a threat to democratic ideals when ideas are falsified and people are thereby exploited. This moral problem arises when public persuaders either adapt ideas to people in ways which distort the content of the ideas or adjust people to ideas in ways which paralyze the public will. Opponents of the League of Nations who misrepresented the voting procedures to mislead Americans were guilty of the first, while those who try to silence any dissenter by claiming he is "opening the door for our enemy" are guilty of the second practice.

Relevance of Argumentation to Democratic Ideals

Little needs to be said on the point that the study and practice of argumentation can contribute to the perpetuation and improvement of dialogue. As we increase understanding of and enthusiasm for discussion and debate, we stimulate exercise of free speech. This is the best way to prevent the triumph of censors and propagandists. As Walter Lippmann puts it:

> For in the absence of debate unrestricted utterance leads to the degradation of opinion. By a kind of Gresham's Law the more rational is overcome by the less rational, and the opinions that will prevail will be those which are held most ardently by those with the most passionate will. For that reason the freedom to speak can never be maintained by objecting to interference with the liberty of the press, of printing, of broadcasting, of the screen. It can be maintained only by promoting debate.[6]

But mere freedom of speech is not enough; there must be thoughtful and responsible speech. Widespread indulgence in irrational or unethical communication is not consistent with our democratic ideals. Hence the importance of critical thinking and the ethics of advocacy which are expounded in this book. If our deliberations are according to

---

[6] W. Lippmann, *Essays in the Public Philosophy* (Boston: Little, Brown and Co., 1955), pp. 129–130.

Lippmann's hope, they must involve commitment, dialogue, information, testing, and decision.[7]

A significant part of thoughtful and responsible speech occurs in
the expression of dissenting opinions. These expressions are essential to
the continued existence of a free society, and argumentation serves to
instruct persons in formulating them or in replying to them. But three
conditions must be met before reasoned controversy can take place:
existing differences among men's reasoned interpretations, judgments,
predictions, and the like; a tendency to try to influence others' views
short of violent means; a willingness of the parties to use reasoned
discourse, to submit their views to reasoned criticism, and to accept
superior arguments.[8] In a particular instance, these conditions were met
in a debate between a trucking company president and a spokesman for
the Teamsters Union before a voting audience of 527 employees who,
after hearing both sides, voted against affiliation.[9]

In the instance of political debating, which increased in popularity
during the presidential campaign of 1960, there is an opportunity for
argumentation to play a part in civic education. When the voters learn
to demand competent argument from campaigners, the political debates
will help to clarify positions, reveal issues, arouse interest, provide
opportunities to evaluate candidates, and reduce the amount of "hot
air." However, as we observed in the 1960 Kennedy-Nixon campaign,
merely calling a televised joint appearance a "debate" does not produce
these desirable outcomes. The works of Homer, Thucydides, and Seneca
the Elder tell of debate in ancient Greece and Rome. Government
by public debate existed in ancient Athens, and in Cicero's day there
was public debating, albeit hazardous, in Rome.

The importance of educating the young people in particular for
democratic participation has been mentioned by Aristotle ("the fate of
empires depends upon it"), Thomas Jefferson, and many others. As
Admiral Rickover argued, public debate is needed to clarify issues, but
this contest will often deteriorate into mere quarreling when the
uneducated confront the educated, because the former cannot argue on
the level of facts and ideas, so they stoop to personal vilification instead.[10]

[7] R. Monroe, "Renewal of a Public Philosophy: Role of Teachers of Speech,"
The Speech Teacher, XVI, No. 1 (1967), pp. 38–46.

[8] G. R. Miller and T. R. Nilsen (eds.), *Perspectives on Argumentation* (Chicago: Scott, Foresman & Co., 1966), pp. 16–17.

[9] *Chicago Daily News*, April 13, 1966.

[10] "The World of the Uneducated," *Saturday Evening Post*, November 28,
1959.

The relevance of argumentation to democratic ideals can be shown, finally, by demonstrating the humanistic character of the process. Argumentation qualifies as humanistic for four reasons: man in general is an arguing creature; as a means of social control, argumentation provides a freedom of choice which commands, threats, and brainwashing do not; nonargumentative procedures bypass the individual; a completely closed mind shuts one off from the human race.

For the doctrine of argumentation to be meaningful in the social context described above, it must be predicated upon certain assumptions. The first of these four is that a case can be made for either side of a controversial judgment. Proof in this context means adducing evidence and reasoning sufficient to establish a reasonable degree of probability in favor of the position taken. By this means ideas are democratically tested.

It is assumed, secondly, that ". . . truth and justice are by nature more powerful than their opposites . . . ," as Aristotle put it. Elaborating on this notion, he continued, ". . . speaking broadly, what is true and preferable is by nature always easier to prove, and more convincing" (*Rhetoric*, 1355a). A more familiar version of the indestructibility of right ideas is to be found in Goethe's statement that nothing is so powerful as an idea whose time has come. Similarly comforting is Bryant's line, "Truth crushed to earth shall rise again."[11] In some specific cases, this idea is scarcely reassuring, because the individuals concerned are afraid they won't live to see the day. Aristotle did not set a time limit or give any other qualifications which life's experiences have taught us to add. We know that despots have ruled for decades, that some murderers are never caught, that innocent men have been imprisoned or executed, and that some wrongs have been righted only after long delay.[12] However, Aristotle did not say that truth could be counted on to win by itself; he explained that one function of rhetoric was to prevent the triumph of fraud and injustice. But in order for debate or persuasion to perform this function, the society must be one which permits free competition among ideas.

A third assumption is that deliberative decisions are preferable to emotional reactions, impulsive snap judgments, and trial-and-error procedures. Commitments which develop from rational, logical thought are ethically defensible and generally are more enduring. Obviously this assumption, like most of the doctrine of argumentation, is predicated

[11] William Cullen Bryant, "The Battle Field," Stanza 9.
[12] E. S. Gardner, "Trial By Jury," *Chicago Daily News* (*This Week Magazine*), January 27, 1967, pp. 4–5.

upon the prior assumption that man is a rational being, at least potentially. This reservation is suggested by the statement that often in times past men have preferred fighting for freedom to thinking about it. There may be better ways to establish good on earth than by fighting for it, but they can be found only by making rational decisions.[13]

Even if it is deemed necessary, in the interest of persuasion, to motivate the acceptance of a decision, it is better to begin with a logically adequate case and then to add the so-called emotional appeals. This is the meaning of the fourth assumption, which is that affective appeals work best when they supplement the logical ones which were discussed under the third assumption. It is pointless to ignore the fact that reason, emotion, and imagination function as a configuration in the human personality. To omit the rational element of persuasion is to violate the ethical principle which holds that an appeal should not circumvent the critical thinking process. That would, by definition, result in propaganda.

ARGUMENTATION IN GENERAL EDUCATION

Specific Topics Involved

It is assumed to be self-evident that there is a place in the general education of most college students for an academic experience which includes systematic instruction in the analysis of controversial statements, the accumulation and the testing of evidence, the making and the criticism of inferences, the questions of logical responsibility, the making of value judgments, the application of ethical standards to decisions, the procedures of intellectual attack and defense, the logical marshaling of ideas, the social import of advocacy, and the effective communication of one's views. This is what argumentation is about.

But there are students as well as some school- and college teachers and administrators to whom the place of argumentation in general education is not self-evident. Apparently they do not know that critical thinking as a defense against "hidden persuaders" and the related question of what is ethical in persuasion are major topics in this study.

---

[13] For an existential view of rationality, see first footnote in this book.

One writer on liberal education who understood argumentation said that the fundamental equipment of a liberally educated person requires three parts: the Arm of Information, the Arm of Operative Logic, and the Arm of Imagination.[14]

Some Essential Attitudes and Beliefs

Our notions about the ethics of advocacy are of basic importance; they influence much of what we think or do as students, teachers, and practitioners of the art. This book supports the view that free competition among ideas should take place in order to facilitate an honest search for wise conclusions. Putting the idea negatively, one might say that the central purpose of argumentation is *not* to teach persons how to get ahead of their fellows in the struggle for personal gain. Nor is it to sanction the catering to ignorance, bias, or irrationality by stressing audience acceptability of evidence and reasoning at the expense of logical adequacy or substantive accuracy! As one writer on the ethics of argumentation put it, ethical behavior in a free society is guided by considerations of truth, human welfare, and rationality.[15]

This ethical commitment implies an attitude of open-mindedness, at least to the point of being tolerant toward different ideas and objective enough to admit the possibility of one's own error. The possessor of this attitude will try to analyze why he thinks as he does and what makes the other fellow think differently about a controversial subject. He would not say, "I may have my faults, but being wrong isn't one of them." Nor would he retort, "I didn't say there aren't two sides to every dispute; I merely said I wouldn't listen to yours."

A belief in the constructive uses of disagreement is an obvious corollary of the preceding point. Intelligently expressed disagreement can often move us to reexamine our beliefs and feelings. This is a symptom of growth; we do not learn from sycophants. Today this advice applies to both men and women, but it was not always so. In the early days of Radcliffe, when Professor Copeland of Harvard was asked if he would teach argumentation to the young ladies, he is reported to have

[14] H. H. Hudson, *Educating Liberally* (Stanford University, California: Stanford University Press, 1945), pp. 10 ff.
[15] S. G. Rives, "Ethical Argumentation," *Journal of the American Forensic Association*, I, No. 3 (1964), 79–85. Also see G. G. Grisez, "The Concept of Appropriateness: Ethical Considerations in Persuasive Argument," *Journal of the American Forensic Association*, II, No. 2 (1965), 53–58.

answered, "How deplorable for women to become apt in argument. We can't obliterate a natural tendency, but why cultivate it?"

A fourth essential attitude or belief is needed to cope with the popular notion that argumentative communication is futile because "facts speak for themselves." The folly of this misconception was shown in a feature story titled "Great Health Discoveries Wasted." It cited five widely known facts about life-and-death matters which have not spoken effectively on their own behalf: after the Salk polio vaccine had been widely available for six years, at least half of our children under five years of age had not been immunized; antibiotic treatment can often prevent the recurrence of rheumatic fever, yet thousands of cases are not so treated and hence recur; simple tests for certain diseases which produce forty per cent of the cases of blindness could practically eliminate those sources, but thousands are blinded yearly by cataracts, glaucoma, and diabetes; automobile seat belts could save an estimated 5,500 lives annually, yet only a few motorists use them; fluoridation of city water is a demonstrated success in reducing tooth decay by two-thirds in young people, but only one-third of the persons using central water sources have been afforded this boon. Obviously these facts need some help in reaching and influencing people.

Fifth, a reasonable confidence in one's own ability to think is an essential attitude to develop. But this is difficult in our time, as Albert Schweitzer has explained.[16] The influences of what a person hears and reads, the examples of his associates, and the pressures from the organizations which claim his loyalty tend to make him doubt his own thinking ability and thereby make him receptive to the "truth" which a so-called authority hands down. One who would be a truly educated person must successfully resist this erosion of the self.

Finally, it is well to understand not only the uses of argumentation but also its limitations. Controversy as a method of reaching decisions is said to have four limits: it is indecisive (no final solution); it is bilateral; it is verbal; it deals with means rather than ends (in an ultimate sense, presumably).[17]

When argumentation is so taught and learned that it contributes to the development of these attitudes and beliefs, its claim to a place in general education cannot be denied.

[16] Charles R. Joy (ed.), *Albert Schweitzer: An Anthology* (Boston: Beacon Press, 1947).

[17] D. Ehninger, "Limits of Controversy," *Speech Teacher*, September, 1966, pp. 180–185.

QUESTIONS

1. What is meant by "general education," and what is the relevance of argumentation to it?
2. For what reasons might one call argumentation and debate "techniques of a free society"?
3. Suppose someone says, "Those who live by their appetites suffer for ignoring their reason; those who live by their reason suffer for ignoring their appetites; only a few are wise or lucky enough to keep a creative tension between these forces." What has this to do with footnotes 1 and 13?
4. Discuss the bearing of Appendix B upon this chapter.

EXERCISES

1. Discuss, or prepare oral reports on, the implications of the John Stuart Mill "Essay on Liberty" in relation to this chapter. For instance, dare we go as far with freedom of speech as he proposes?
2. Report in class on your observation of argumentation in use in a city council meeting, a legislature, or a business meeting of an organization.
3. Do you think John Milton, in *Areopagitica* (1644), placed too much value upon certain liberties when he wrote: "Give me the liberty to know, to utter, and to argue freely according to conscience, above all liberties."
4. How has debate served in the decision-making process in the White House? See T. C. Sorensen, *Decision-Making in the White House: The Olive Branch Or the Arrows* (New York: Columbia University Press, 1963), p. 59.
5. Read "Yankee Lawyer Go Home," *New York Times*, March 12, 1967, p. 8E. Comment on its relevance to topics in Chapter I.

CHAPTER 2

BASIC DEFINITIONS

Of the many key concepts that require definition, only three will be given extended treatment at this time. They are argumentation, debate, and proof. The several interpretations of each concept which a scholarly student can find in the literature will be explained and documented, and the implications of each view will be explored. The purpose of this unusual approach is not to declare which are "right" and which are "wrong" but rather to facilitate thoughtful choices among the possibilities.

ARGUMENTATION

Traditionally, four forms of discourse (narration, description, exposition, and argumentation) have been discussed in textbooks on composition. It may be helpful to review briefly the meaning of argumentation in this context.

After the cause of death was found to have been homicide by person or persons unknown, the officers of the law continued their investigation until they found a suspect who was subsequently tried for first degree murder. The proof was such that the jury brought in a verdict of guilty, and the judge sentenced the convict to death in the electric chair.

This specimen of discourse is mostly narration; it relates a series of events as in a story. In a fictional work, the plot is developed by narration. In ancient times narration meant the statement of facts in a given case, but today we think of narration as a compositional element which can be used in speech or writing for the purpose of relating a succession of events. Illustrations are probably the most familiar narrative materials in speeches and essays.

The sound of footsteps outside his cell made him feel certain that his time had come. Though dazed by fear, he sat up on his bunk as the guards and other prison officials came to escort him to the execution chamber. Down the long, gray corridor he moved as if in a dream.

Description, which predominates in the foregoing paragraph, involves the recording of sensory impressions. We say "predominates" because one kind of discourse rarely occurs in pure form. For example, description is often combined with narration to make more interesting composition. Speakers and writers use description to reveal the appearance, attributes, or the nature of objects, scenes, persons, and experiences of many sorts.

What is capital punishment? It is the legal application of the death penalty for certain serious crimes. Historically it has taken several forms, including electrocution, hanging, shooting, gassing, decapitation, and burning.

Exposition, in this case by definition, appears in the preceding paragraph. This third traditional form of discourse explains or informs, yet it often appears in persuasive communication, as do narration and description. Exposition is used to achieve clarity by explaining, defining, and perhaps evaluating. It is concerned with the nature, the scope and the relations, but not the truth or falsity, of ideas. When exposition is associated with things rather than with abstract ideas, it relates to processes, functions, and parts in relation to those things.

Capital punishment should be abolished wherever it exists, because it is based upon the discredited notion of retribution and because it is ineffective as a deterrent to crime.

No doubt this is a specimen of argumentation; it has logical structure and rhetorical content conjoined to serve an advocatory purpose. This example happens to contain two arguments, each of which, in its simplest aspect, consists of two statements: a conclusion and a supporting reason. Under a microcosmic sort of analysis, the arguments become: (1) Capital punishment should be abolished wherever it exists, because it is based upon the discredited notion of retribution, and (2) capital punishment should be abolished wherever it exists, because it is ineffective as a deterrent to crime.

The use of argumentation to influence others is inherently risky in that failure is possible. Real argument, according to this view, maintains personal relationships; consequently, it is claimed that threats, commands which imply threats, and bald assertions of fact are degenerate forms of argument.[1]

But argumentation seldom appears in pure form; it often includes narration, description, and exposition in the interest of effective style. Even so, we classify discourse as argumentative if the central purpose appears to be the advocacy of a controversial conclusion or the criticism of ideas. For the moment we shall consider only the first purpose, that of advocacy.

In this broad, traditional sense only, argumentation would necessarily be classified as a part of persuasion; but, as a later exposition will explain, our professional usage has for academic purposes narrowed the concept of argumentation to that part of persuasive communication in which reasoned discourse is the principal form of support. This definition in no way denies or deplores the occurrence of emotional and personal proofs in advocacy, but it does imply the existence of a method for placing such proofs in a logical framework to give them some semblance of rigor. Thus we explain that argumentation is the form of discourse used in solving problems with a deliberative method.

As an Analytical-Critical Instrument

Discourse which we classify as argumentative, advocatory, or suasory has been analyzed, described, criticized, evaluated, and judged in terms of many criteria or standards. In this context, analysis and description are closely related; they are used to emphasize the content of the discourse. The last three terms—criticism, evaluation, and judgment—are roughly synonymous and have to do with the appraisal of the discourse by an "outside" party.

Any one of the several analytical-critical instruments is a way to

---

[1] M. Natanson and H. W. Johnstone, Jr. (eds.), *Philosophy, Rhetoric and Argumentation* (University Park: Pennsylvania State University Press, 1965), p. 2.

get at two broad questions: What was said in the arguments? According to a given set of standards, how well was it said? The simplest and least sophisticated approaches to critical analysis involve unorganized assortments of items such as "correct" grammar, apparent sincerity, signs of "common sense" and knowledge, acceptability of the speaker's views to the observer, and the like. Such criteria are not altogether irrelevant, but they do not enable one to evaluate the intellectual merit of the presentation.

To a serious student of this subject, a sound argument is one that can stand appropriate criticism. A few systems of criticism, the appropriateness of which will be discussed later, will be only briefly identified here. One is traditionally rhetorical, based upon Aristotle,[2] Whately,[3] and others. Another old system, the syllogistic, is concerned only with formal validity in relation to the rules of the syllogism.[4] In modern times the dramatistic conception of rhetoric by Kenneth Burke[5] has attracted considerable attention, and the professional reactions have ranged between "remarkably insightful" and "obscurantist." The most recent—some say "faddish"—system to influence the newer literature of argumentation is the Toulmin "layout of arguments."[6] Finally, there is an approach to rhetorical criticism which stems from phenomenological psychology.[7] Using this approach, a critic would examine the images constructed by the persuader as well as the methods employed. The "things to look for" would include (1) value judgments in the discourse and in the audience, (2) the strategy used in achieving identification of values if a difference existed, (3) the treatment of physical reality and the reactions thereto, (4) the use of supporting material in developing cognitive structuring, and the audience interpretation of it, (5) the image-making uses of language, (6) the audience image (ethos) of the speaker, and (7) the reciprocal action of the speech and the climate of opinion.

In this specialized study of argumentation, the more sophisticated

[2] L. Cooper (trans.), *The Rhetoric of Aristotle* (New York: D. Appleton and Co., 1932).

[3] R. Whately, *Elements of Rhetoric* (Cambridge: Jas. Munroe and Co., 1834).

[4] See representative college textbooks in logic.

[5] M. Hochmuth, "Kenneth Burke and the 'New Rhetoric'," *Quarterly Journal of Speech*, XXXVIII, No. 1 (1952), 133–144.

[6] S. Toulmin, *The Uses of Argument* (Cambridge, England: Cambridge University Press, 1958), Chap. III.

[7] R. B. Gregg, "A Phenomenologically Oriented Approach to Rhetorical Criticism," *Central States Speech Journal*, XVII, No. 2 (1966), 89.

kinds of evaluation involve us as critics in raising discerning questions about what the arguer is trying to prove, what he must do to prove it, and how well or ill he fares. Principles have to do with probability, presumption, burden of proof, burden of rebuttal, analysis, evidence, attack and defense, and related matters will, in subsequent chapters, be explained as elements of an analytical-critical instrument. The use of such an instrument in evaluating or judging advocatory discourse will be treated briefly under "Kinds of Debate" in Chapter 3, and in greater detail in Chapter 13.

Frequently a critic of argument will express his judgment in argumentative form, because it is a cogent way to marshal the reasons for his critical position. Take for instance the Frankel review of Senator Fulbright's book *The Arrogance of Power*.[8] The reviewer reports at considerable length the author's affirmative case on a proposition of policy, including serious evils and an eight-point plan, and then gives his own critique which resembles a negative case against the Senator's stand on the Viet Nam question.

Perhaps the greatest claim that can be made for the kind of analytical-critical instrument we have been considering is its value in critical thinking, whether one is speaking, listening, writing, reading, or meditating. With such an instrument one can evaluate the writing and the speaking of others, either in single presentations or in debates, and one can test his own reasoning with a sort of internal dialogue or deliberation. A way to do this is to imagine oneself on the opposing side of each argument which comes to mind. Self-testing is important because an individual has occasions to justify his behavior to himself as well as to others. Then, when actual opposition is present, one will more likely be able to make a case, defend it, and test the opposing case. This outcome stems from the fact that argumentation as an analytical-critical instrument explains what must be proved or disproved.

Such rigorous testing of arguments with critical instruments tends to make controversy self-corrective, which means that one side is less likely to win by trickery (as in propaganda) or by default (as in censorship). The resulting critical deliberation is characterized by the testing of evidence, motives, values, assumptions, inferences, and the like. A decision so arrived at is said to be more reliable, more flexible, and more human.[9]

[8] *The New York Times*, January 22, 1967, Book Reviews, p. 1.
[9] D. Ehninger and W. Brockriede, *Decision by Debate* (New York: Dodd, Mead and Co., 1963), pp. 3–4. Compare pp. 100, 168, 186, 203.

In Relation to Persuasion

Is argumentation theoretically related to persuasion, and if so, how closely? This is one of the vexed questions in the literature of this subject. As we shall observe, the answers span a continuum including separateness, part-to-whole relationships, and overlapping.

The doctrine of separateness is predicated upon the idea that there are two modes of rational decision making (logical and psychological), and that the former includes argumentation and argumentative analysis. "Argumentation itself does not seek to persuade anybody of anything." It "functions to discover and formulate the requirements of proof for a proposition or a conclusion."[10] Argumentative analysis is said to be independent of the advocate and the audience. The advocate, accordingly, uses these findings plus psychological proofs to persuade.

When the foregoing statement of separateness is viewed in a broader context than a single page, it comes close to saying that argumentation is the *logos* (logical proof) of persuasion. This popular, traditional view means that argumentation is that part of persuasion which includes evidence, reasoning, and the other so-called logical aspects. A book which unequivocally takes this position defines argument as the use of logic to influence others. In fact, the terms *logos* and *the logical mode of persuasion* are used explicitly. Finally, according to that source, logic is the science, while argumentation is the art, of persuasion.[11]

Nearby on this continuum of definitions is to be found the view that argumentation is mainly or principally the *logos* of persuasion. "Argumentation is the art and science of using primarily logical appeals to secure decisions," is the way one author puts it. He adds that although argumentation may use extralogical appeals, the major emphasis is upon logical reasoning, while persuasion gives priority to the extralogical appeals.[12] This definition would place argumentation within the boundaries of rhetoric if we were to agree that the rhetorical process functions "at its best for the exposition and dissemination of ideas in

[10] R. R. Windes and A. Hastings, *Argumentation and Advocacy* (New York: Random House, Inc., 1965), p. 24. Compare pp. 207 and 235.

[11] R. Huber, *Influencing Through Argument* (New York: David McKay Co., 1963), pp. 4–6.

[12] A. Freeley, *Argumentation and Debate* (Belmont, California: Wadsworth Publishing Co., 1966), pp. 2, 7.

the wielding of public opinion, with the ethical and pathetic modes of proof in ancillary relations to the logical . . ."[13]

There is also a definition which treats argumentation and persuasion, or reasoned discourse and motive appeal, as coordinate terms. Reasoned discourse and motive appeal can coincide, it is explained, because "reasoned discourse is one form for presenting motive appeals." This is premised on the explanation that "emotional proofs are concerned with the content of a unit of discourse, and that logical proof is concerned with its form."[14] Two other writers seem to be thinking of these terms as being coordinate when they state that persuasion is one of three meanings of argument: ". . . the process of employing any number of instances of reasoning to influence beliefs."[15] Finally, there is an explanation which, at the outset, treats the equivalents of logic and emotion as coordinate parts of a process, but the concluding pronouncement on the evaluation of the logical argument places argumentation *within* the field of persuasion. According to this theory, persuasion involves relating a proposition ("object concept") to a stable attitude ("motivational concept") by means of a logical argument ("concept association"), and this linkage "must be evaluated from the point of view of the audience rather than from that of the critic."[16]

It is but a short step, so to speak, to the implication that argumentation is mainly concerned with persuasion. "Proof is the process of securing belief in one statement by relating it to another statement already believed," according to two authors. Argumentation, in their view, serves to judge whether beliefs are "healthy" and valid, but "The concept of proof is meaningless when divorced from the person to whom the proof is offered."[17] As we shall see in relation to "Definitions of Proof," it is one thing to say that argumentation is persuasive, but it is quite another to specify to whom. Most writers ignore the latter, but some by implication seem to say "just anybody."

[13] D. C. Bryant, "Rhetoric: Its Functions and Scope," *Philosophy, Rhetoric and Argumentation*, ed. M. Natanson and H. W. Johnstone, Jr., p. 50.

[14] E. Knepprath and T. Clevenger, Jr., "Reasoned Discourse and Motive Appeals in Selected Political Speeches," *Quarterly Journal of Speech*, LI, No. 2 (1965), 154–156.

[15] W. R. Fisher and E. M. Sayles, "The Nature and Functions of Argument," in *Perspectives on Argumentation*, G. R. Miller and T. R. Nilsen, eds. (Chicago: Scott, Foresman and Co., 1966), pp. 3–4. Compare p. 20.

[16] G. L. Cronkhite, "Logic, Emotion, and the Paradigm of Persuasion," *Quarterly Journal of Speech*, L, No. 1 (1964), 13–18.

[17] Ehninger and Brockriede, *Decision by Debate*, pp. 99, 201–203.

Some years ago our professional literature dichotomized argumentation (to convince) and persuasion (to persuade). Seemingly there was no widespread doubt that they were distinct concepts and processes. In recent decades, however, there have been many doubters, probably because of the decline of faculty psychology and the rise of monistic psychology. But the dichotomizers have not been vanquished; a reputable philosopher has recently set out a basis for distinguishing between conviction and persuasion. To convince, he explains, implies no risk of the self; it is manipulation without commitment. To persuade, however, does risk the self and does imply commitment.[18]

These simple diagrams borrowed from formal logic will suggest three broad categories of asserted relationships between argumentation and persuasion:

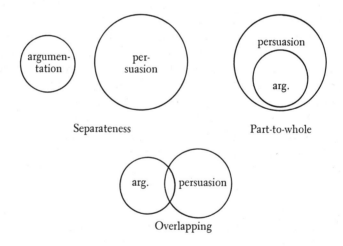

Separateness Part-to-whole

Overlapping

---

[18] Natanson and Johnstone, *Philosophy, Rhetoric and Argumentation*, p. 18.

According to one writer in the "overlapping" school of thought on this problem, argumentation is part of, as well as a check on, persuasion, especially when argumentation is used in debate: ". . . argumentation is concerned mainly with the conditions of *justifiable* [italics mine] belief." The merit of an argument is not to be measured solely in terms of persuasiveness; a valid argument may not gain popular approval, while an invalid one may.[19] A shift in this direction may also be seen upon comparing 1951 and 1964 editions of a standard work. In the former, argumentation is defined as "the art or activity by which one person, through the use of reasoned discourse, seeks to get other persons to believe or to do what he wants . . ."[20] In the latter edition, the definition is broadened by adding to the *logos* of persuasion an analytical-critical dimension, so that argumentation is viewed "as a method of analysis and reasoning designed to provide acceptable bases for belief and action."[21] The questions of acceptability to whom and on what basis are not answered in this short definition; they are treated either implicitly or explicitly in the subsequent exposition.

More will be said of the relationships between argumentation and persuasion in the next section, "As an Academic Discipline"; but in terms of theoretical implications of the most familiar definitions, a few concluding remarks are in order. Since argumentation serves analytical and critical functions which are not used to effect persuasion, and since, as we shall soon see, argumentation has derived its principles from dialectic and logic as well as rhetoric, it seems proper to conclude that the process called argumentation is more than a logical part of persuasion. In fact, if argumentation were defined as persuasion, its so-called logic would have to be judged in terms of its persuasive effect instead of some external standard of reasonableness. But when argumentation is taken to be a kind of science of proof, it can be used to test the reasoning in a persuasive communication, because, as we saw earlier, it embodies more or less objective standards of critical analysis.

In conclusion, how shall we define argumentation in terms of its relationship to persuasion? For the reasons given above, the definition which emphasizes the partial overlapping of these concepts (third diagram) is preferred here.

[19] J. H. McBath, ed., *Argumentation and Debate, Principles and Practices* (New York: Holt, Rinehart and Winston, Inc., 1963), p. 8.

[20] J. H. McBurney, J. M. O'Neill, and G. E. Mills, *Argumentation and Debate: Techniques of a Free Society* (New York: The Macmillan Co., 1951), p. 1.

[21] J. H. McBurney and G. E. Mills, *Argumentation and Debate: Techniques of a Free Society* (New York: The Macmillan Co., 1964), p. 1.

As an Academic Discipline

As it is understood today, the collegiate subject called argumentation is probably not much more than a century old. While it is true that Archbishop Whately referred to his Elements of Rhetoric (1828) as "argumentative composition"[22] and made landmark contributions to the theory of the subject, it would be inaccurate to say that the academic subject of argumentation dates from his work. Among the earliest specialized textbooks or manuals were Rowton's How To Conduct a Debate (c. 1840), Holyoake's Public Speaking and Debate (1853), and McElligott's The American Debater (1855). Probably the most influential college textbook in terms of defining the scope of the subject was George Pierce Baker's Principles of Argumentation (1895), which he developed while teaching a pioneer course at Harvard College. Some of the early credit-bearing courses in argumentation were brought into college curricula in response to requests by intercollegiate debaters for systematic faculty assistance in preparing for contests. Thus the close linkage of argumentation and debate came about quite naturally. This circumstance plus the early popularity of the course with prelegal students may explain why so many courses and textbooks in argumentation have stressed the applications of the subject to school debating and courtroom pleading.

Nowadays this subject includes considerably more than the theory and principles of debate; ". . . it refers especially to the body of logical and rhetorical concepts and principles that underlie reasoned controversy,"[23] according to one source. Another says the concepts of this eclectic discipline have been drawn from logic, rhetoric, and psychology [of belief].[24] The growing influence of behavioral science upon this subject, particularly on the topics of audience analysis and motivation, shows the popularity of the notion that argumentation should be persuasion-oriented.[25] This book treats popular persuasion as a peripheral matter in Chapter 9, but it reinstates to a central position some principles of dialectic, the long-neglected method of argument.[26]

[22] Whately, Elements of Rhetoric, p. 5.
[23] Miller and Nilsen, Perspectives . . . , p. 4.
[24] Ehninger and Brockriede, Decision . . . , p. 28.
[25] Miller and Nilsen, Perspectives . . . , Chap. V; McBath, Argumentation . . . , Chap. VIII; and Freeley, Argumentation . . . chaps. XVIII, XIX.
[26] E. L. Hunt, "Dialectic: A Neglected Method of Argument," Quarterly Journal of Speech Education, VII (1921), 221–232.

Although argumentation as a distinct subject is comparatively new, its parent disciplines, rhetoric and dialectic, date back at least twenty-four centuries. According to Aristotle, whose *Rhetoric* has been placed at 330–322 B.C., rhetoric was concerned with persuasive discourse, usually in the form of oratory. According to Cooper's translation, Aristotle defined rhetoric as the faculty or power of discovering in the particular case what are the available means of persuasion. The principles of this ancient liberal art were generalized by observing and analyzing the persuasive oratory of the popular speakers in the legislative and judicial assemblies of that time.

Classical rhetoric embodied a broad range of advice, only a part of which has central relevance to argumentation. For Aristotle, rhetoric was mainly concerned with deliberation about matters having two possible alternatives. Certainty was not to be its province. Aristotle's intellectual mode of proof was *logos* (probability and signs in enthymematic form, or conclusions and reasons), from which we derive much of our doctrine on analysis, evidence, and reasoning.

Ethical (*ethos*) and emotional (*pathos*) forms of support are not core concepts in argumentation as they are in the broader field of persuasion in general; but when argumentation is viewed as a part of persuasion, these forms of support must be considered. Ethical proof originally meant the persuasive impact of the speaker's personality, that is, the impressions of character, intelligence, and goodwill which the listeners received during the speaker's presentation. Now, one's status or prior reputation is included among the constituents of ethical proof. Emotional proof, including appeals to values and goals as well as to the familiar emotional states, is likewise more clearly identified with the theory of persuasion than with that of argumentation. These nonlogical appeals *can be* treated logically if they are posited as premises, and if their consequences are inferred.

However, these three modes of proof (logical, ethical, emotional) are not discrete in real life. In fact, they were not so conceived by Aristotle. Thought and emotion were not completely separated; he used the enthymeme mainly for logical argument, but in treating emotional argument he wrote of discovering materials for enthymemes which would put listeners into a receptive state of feeling. An example of an argument embodying all three forms of support would be one which is perceived as being substantively sound, emotionally satisfying, and coming from a credible source.

But rhetoric is not the only parent discipline of argumentation;

there is its ancient counterpart, dialectic. This tool of intellectual criticism was originally the art of disputation by question and answer. Socrates used it to reveal the inadequacy of popular beliefs. He did so, not by stating a contention supported by evidence, as in rhetoric, but by asking a series of questions in which each successive one was based upon the respondent's previous reply. In short, each answer served either as evidence or as a logical premise for the questioner's next step. Socrates spent much of his time asking one question, "What do you mean?"— often to the discomfort of his contemporaries, as we see in Plato's *Dialogues*. He deflated humbug and ironically tested accepted notions which could not stand honest logical criticism.[27]

As method, dialectic was an investigative procedure to establish truth about doubtful propositions. It was used prior to rhetoric in a given problem situation to establish certain evaluative terms such as *just, good, fact, cause, effect,* and the like. Each dialectical term required an opposite for its definition. Next, the rhetorical process would be used to espouse one of the contraries in the dialectic. For this reason it is said that dialectic is for understanding, while rhetoric is for actualization.[28] At this stage there is no judgment or decision by a third party.

We have said that dialectic, in its ancient usage, was intended to establish truth. Strictly speaking, dialectic as well as rhetoric can attain no more than probability. It uses formal logic and deals in universals; therefore, it can achieve high probability, because it admits the debatable only in the assumption of its premises. Rhetoric, on the other hand, uses probability in method as well as in premises.[29]

Viewing ancient dialectic and rhetoric ideally, one could say that there can be no honest rhetoric without a preceding dialectic.[30] Thus it is no wonder that a would-be propagandist fears dialectic; he prefers to prevent an honest examination of alternatives.

So much for classical dialectic. There have been other varieties during the past twenty-odd centuries, but they will not be set out here. For the nonce we shall merely note that modern cross-examination in court and in school debate evolved from earlier dialectics. More will be said of this in Chapter 11.

Most readers of this book quite properly think of argumentation

[27] M. White, "New Horizons in Philosophy," *Central States Speech Journal*, XII, No. 3 (1961), 189.
[28] Natanson and Johnstone, *Philosophy, Rhetoric and Argumentation*, p. 76.
[29] *Ibid.*, p. 39.
[30] *Ibid.*, p. 79.

as an undergraduate subject, but there may be some interest in learning that it is also a research field. Two broad categories of studies have been done, the historical-critical and the quantitative. Research which is historical-critical describes, explains, and evaluates the phenomena. There have been histories of debate (*A Century of Debating at Northwestern University*), studies of various theoretical constructs (*A Reformulation of the Modes of Reasoning in Argumentation*), evolutionary studies of concepts (*The Place of the Enthymeme in Rhetorical Theory*), investigations of landmark theorists (*John Ward's Theory of Rhetoric*), textual criticisms (*The Great Debates*), studies of debaters (*The Forensic Speaking of Clarence Darrow*), and critical analyses of debates (*The Debate on the Atomic Test Ban Treaty*).[31]

Quantitative research, including the descriptive and the experimental, has been in the minority in this field, but it is growing. Descriptive studies have included surveys of current practices in school debating, tabulations of evidence used in tournament debates, and content analyses of transcribed debates. Experimental studies have been concerned with the effectiveness of evidence, the influence of arrangement upon impact, factors in debate judging, effects of debating upon critical thinking ability, and other phenomena which can be controlled, manipulated, and measured.[32]

In sum, we may define argumentation as an academic discipline which deals with the analysis, synthesis, and criticism of predominantly reasoned discourse on controversial ideas. It is no ivory-tower study; its concern is with how persons operate in an important aspect of life. However, we recognize that although man argues, he is not concerned with the theory of argumentation unless he has studied it. These principles are applied in order to discover proof requirements of an assertion or to make a case for or against it. Argumentation is concerned mainly with advocacy and, to a lesser degree, with inquiry. In this latter sense it teaches analysis for personal understanding, whether or not one advocates or perceives advocacy. Perhaps the foremost educational goal of this subject is the improvement in critical thinking ability so that persons will demand more of themselves and of others in the conduct of controversies. To this end are directed the explanations of the core concepts of argumentation: proof requirements of a thesis, propositions,

[31] P. J. Dovre, "Historical-Critical Research in Debate," *Journal of the American Forensic Association*, II, No. 2 (1965), 72–79.

[32] K. E. Andersen, "Quantitative Research in Debate," *Journal of the American Forensic Association*, III, No. 3 (1966), 112–115.

analysis, investigation, evidence, reasoning, cases, attack and defense, cross-examination, and evaluation.

Topics such as explanation, ethos, motivation, composition, and delivery are treated herein as secondary rather than main concepts. The reasons for this are two: (1) Such treatment is consistent with the definition of the subject in this work. (2) The secondary topics are often the principal concerns of other courses. Thus the use one chooses to make of each concept or topic will depend on his definition of argumentation and the relationships of this course to others in the curriculum.

DEBATE

In Relation to Argumentation

When persons think of argumentation as theory and consider debate as an application of that theory by contending parties to a controversy, there is not much likelihood of their regarding argumentation and debate as synonyms. The body of theory and principles called argumentation pertains to both oral and written discourse and to both one-sided and multisided presentations. Debate is two-sided or bilateral, as we shall see.

While it may be that argumentation and debate are not often mistaken as synonyms, there remain five theoretically serious questions concerning definitions or characterizations of debate: Is it persuasion? Is it inquiry? Must it be judged by an "outsider"? Is it cooperative, or is it competitive? Must it be structured? These currently controversial questions will now be discussed.

In Relation to Persuasion and Propaganda

One reputable writer with long experience in this field places the psychology of persuasion among the central topics of argumentation and, by implication, of debate as well. He goes on to state unequivocally the "ability to persuade an audience" is part of the art of debate.[33] A more recent source seems to say that the end of argumentation is persuasion, but debate is not specifically mentioned, nor is the critical ability of the audience. A whole chapter discusses "Motivation in Argument," and another says that most arguments fall between the extremes of persuasiveness and logical adequacy.[34] Another recent book shows a central tendency to include the persuasion of audiences in the definition of debate: contending parties appeal to a third party for decision; all three modes of proof (*ethos, logos, pathos*) are used; acceptance or belief is the criterion, and only occasionally is a *critical* audience specified.[35] The last book to be cited on this point unequivocally explains that the purpose of debate, meaning a school contest, is to convince a third party of the logical tenability of a position. Although the available means may range from sound reasons to "clubbing someone over the head," as the author puts it, the nonlogical forms of support are outside the scope of his work. Thus a critical audience is obviously assumed.[36]

Others agree that some degree or level of persuasion is involved in debate, but they add an informative dimension, which is variously termed education,[37] understanding,[38] and inquiry.[39] Adlai Stevenson expressed a stronger view of this sort when he explained to this writer that in political debate he was more interested in educating the electorate on the issues than in persuading them to vote for him.

His philosophy was clearly antithetical to the definition of debate as either one-sided persuasion or as propaganda. If we define both persuasion and propaganda as one-sided presentations, and if we further define propaganda as the least ethical variety of persuasion, we must conclude that debate, which is two-sided and requires an opportunity for attack and defense, stands in sharp contrast to propaganda and is quite unlike one-sided persuasion. Debate demands critical thinking, while popular persuasion typically avoids deliberation. Finally, unilateral popular per-

[33] A. C. Baird, *Argumentation, Discussion, and Debate* (New York: McGraw-Hill Book Co., 1950), pp. 214–234 and 312.

[34] Miller and Nilsen, *Perspectives* . . ., pp. 110–128 and 181.

[35] Ehninger and Brockriede, *Decision* . . ., pp. 9–10, but compare 201–203 and 99.

[36] A. N. Kruger, *Modern Debate: Its Logic and Strategy* (New York: McGraw-Hill Book Co., 1960), pp. 113–114.

[37] McBath, *Argumentation* . . ., p. 6.

[38] E. R. Moulton, *The Dynamics of Debate* (New York: Harcourt, Brace and World, 1966), pp. 4–5.

[39] Ehninger and Brockriede, *Decision.* . . .

suasion easily becomes propaganda, whereas bilateral (two-sided) persuasion, being akin to debate, cannot degenerate into propaganda.[40]

Persuasion as treated above refers to audiences, but are debaters expected to persuade or convince each other? For years we have heard the complaint that, since school debaters can't convince each other, the activity is unrealistic. The implicit assumption is that competing advocates should try to change each other's minds. A recent book on group dynamics[41] echoes this notion by stating that people do not ordinarily engage in serious debate on a direct clash of interests unless they hope to exert influence upon the other side. And Anatol Rapoport, in his *Fights, Games, and Debates*, prefers to define debate as a clash which cannot be resolved rationally but in which the object is to convince your opponent. Rapoport acknowledges reality for a moment when he concedes that the more common objective of debate is the influencing of "some bystander." In a political campaign debate, this so-called bystander may be millions of voters. A few questions will elaborate this misconception: Did Webster try to convince Hayne? Did Lincoln try to convince Douglas? Did Darrow try to convince Bryan? Did Kennedy try to convince Nixon?

Two coauthors probe this question by distinguishing between "internal" and "external" methods for making group decisions critically. "Internal" means that the group members by themselves or without outside adjudication settle a question by using dialectic or discussion. Their "external" method involves a third party who judges, and this process they define as debate.[42] One serious theoretical difficulty with their dichotomy is that parliamentary deliberation, which is a major member of their so-called internal class, is better defined as debate unless one believes, as those authors assert, that an outside arbitrator is a necessary part of any debate.

In answer to the question "Do debaters try to convince each other?" the best answer is "Sometimes." When two or more committed persons dispute without an audience, they may hope to influence each other, but they are more likely merely to clarify for each other the grounds for their differences. When some undecided individuals are added to the group, the hopes of effecting persuasion become more

[40] These distinctions are verbalized by most contemporary works on the subject.
[41] D. C. Barnlund and F. S. Haiman, *The Dynamics of Discussion* (Boston: Houghton Mifflin Co., 1960), p. 49.
[42] Ehninger and Brockriede, *Decision* . . . , pp. 7–10.

realistic. The latter is the more significant condition in terms of impact upon events.

In Relation to Inquiry and Advocacy

Four conceptions of the relationships among debate, inquiry, and advocacy can be found in the literature: (1) Debate is investigation (inquiry), not propagation. (2) Debate is both inquiry and advocacy. (3) Advocacy, including debate, is essentially unlike inquiry. (4) Debate and discussion (a form of inquiry) are complementary processes whose differences can be visualized on several continua.

Debate is said by some to be an instrument of investigation rather than of propagation, because its end and method are critical. Unlike "psychic hucksters" and their ilk, ". . . the debater does not seek conviction regardless of the terms." He is said to be more concerned that decisions be reflective and his method correct than any particular end be achieved. If he were interested in results, it is claimed, he would not have chosen debate as his mode. A debater, according to this view, renounces "short-circuit" devices when he chooses to debate.[43]

It is one thing to say that debate *ought* to be a kind of inquiry, but it is quite another to assert that it therefore *is*. In relation to what actually happens in all four kinds of debate, there is more prescription than description in the claim that debate is investigation, not propagation.[44] A more descriptive statement would be that debate is sometimes investigative and sometimes not, but one would be loath to adopt this view if he were persuaded by certain writers that an advocate is likely to be a "psychic huckster." While warning against the public persuaders' tricks, these writers use a familiar one, namely, the application of polar terms—"good" words for their side and "bad" ones for the other. "Investigator" and "propagandist" are the polar terms between which there is no choice for a debater unless we torture a definition of "investigator" to make it mean "advocate." To the claim that he who is interested in the result will not choose to debate, one needs only to point out that he who propagates a controversial idea may not have begun with any intention to debate, but when his case is attacked, he must debate or face defeat. Therefore, if he is interested in the result,

---

43 *Ibid.*, p. 18.
44 See first footnote in Chapter 1.

he will have to debate. Then, contrary to what the prescription stated, there would be a debater with an interest in the result.

But this is not to say that there is no investigative element in debate. Investigation of some sort usually precedes advocacy, and debate often serves the function of inquiry. Participants and observers alike have been known to learn from the confrontation of opposing arguments. By modifying the definition of debate in a way that is not accepted here, it is even possible to say that debate can be inquiry (deliberation) in *one* person's mind. Arguments for and against a proposition may, in this sense, be used by one person to decide a question by himself.[45]

A second conception of the relationships among debate, inquiry, and advocacy is that debate is both inquiry and advocacy. Debaters aim "to educate or persuade . . . (They) present their hypotheses to the scrutiny of informed opponents . . . Productive inquiry is encouraged by the intellectual competition of debate . . ." The end of inquiry may be served in any of four ways: by debaters' contributing to each other's information, by the generation of new ideas, by the exposing of errors, and by the encouragement of fresh analysis.[46] For at least one of our fellow citizens the Kennedy-Nixon debates served neither to inform nor to persuade. "The debates didn't help me," she complained. "They were always contradicting each other."

Advocacy, including debate, is essentially unlike inquiry, according to a third conceptualization of these relationships. In his landmark exposition of this point, Whately considered both the advocate-audience relationship and the advocate's attitude toward preparation.

. . . Reasoning may be considered as applicable to two purposes . . . the *ascertainment* of the truth by investigation (inquiry) and the *establishment* of it to the satisfaction of *another* (proof). . . . The process of *investigation* must be supposed completed, and certain conclusions arrived at by that process, before he (advocate) begins to *prove* the justness of those conclusions. And in doing this, he will not always find it expedient to adhere to the same course of reasoning by which his own discoveries were originally made; other arguments may occur to him afterwards, more clear, or more concise, or better adapted to the understanding of those he addresses . . .

If a man begins (as is too plainly a frequent mode of proceeding) by hastily adopting, or strongly leaning to some opinion, which suits his inclination, or which is sanctioned by some authority that he blindly venerates, and then studies with the utmost diligence, not as an Investigator of Truth,

45 Freeley, *Argumentation* . . . , p. 2.
46 McBath, *Argumentation* . . . , pp. 6–7 and 11–12.

but as an Advocate labouring to prove his point, his talents and his researches, whatever effect they may produce in making converts to his notions, will avail nothing in enlightening his own judgment, and securing him from error.[47]

Competitive advocacy is often decried on the ground that it does not, or perhaps cannot, discover truth. Even if an individual who asserts this can define truth or could recognize a discovered truth if it were revealed to him, he may experience many disappointments if he expects debates often to provide such revelations. Writers from Aristotle to the present have distinguished between inquiry, or the ascertainment of truth, and the advocacy or proof of that truth to the satisfaction of others.

Another way to approach the dissimilarity of inquiry and advocacy is through the juxtaposition of discussion and debate as problem-solving methods. The important differences in the thought processes which are involved have been explained by many scholars since Sellars (1925), Rignano (1927), Schiller (1930), and Dewey (1933).[48] According to this school of thought, discussion requires reflective thinking, which involves working from a question toward a solution not known in advance. This process is inquiry. Debate requires intentional thinking, which proceeds from a desired solution (proposition) to the grounds for its support. This process is advocacy. Even though inquiry and advocacy are not strictly dichotomous, their differences are worthy of note.

Some discussion enthusiasts in the early thirties went so far with their dichotomization of discussion and debate as to equate their polar terms with good and evil, respectively. In some writings, "debate" and "debater" were pejorative words. Sometimes those discussants would become advocates on the affirmative side of the proposition that debate was educationally undesirable, but their paradoxical behavior seemed not to trouble them.

Finally, the fourth view of the relationships among debate, inquiry, and advocacy is that debate and discussion (an obvious form of inquiry) are complementary processes whose differences can be shown on several continua. Following the excesses of the early theorists and popularizers of discussion, several writers took a more philosophical position. On the inquiry-advocacy continuum, the reflective thinking-intentional reasoning continuum, and the cooperation-competition continuum, they

---

[47] Whately, *Elements of Rhetoric*, pp. 5–7.
[48] J. H. McBurney and K. G. Hance, *Discussion in Human Affairs* (New York: Harper and Bros., 1950), pp. 4–5; also *Reason in Controversy*, Chap. 8.

placed discussion closer to the first term in each pair, and debate closer to the second. In this more modern school of thought the identification of differences in degree and kind was not an expression of preference for either discussion or debate; it was an attempt to describe.

Actually, the theorists who formulated the foregoing doctrine had observed that in many real-life situations one cannot draw a sharp distinction between discussion and debate. A situation which begins as a discussion can become a debate if an issue divides the group into irreconcilable sides. Conversely two sides which start to debate can sometimes be brought together through a reflective-thinking process. Even when the pattern and the spirit of the group communication are clearly definable as inquiry rather than advocacy, there are or should be some applications of argumentation within that framework, particularly in the testing of the proposed solutions. More will be said of this in a later chapter on investigation.

This leads to the point that in the utilization of oral communication for problem solving, discussion must sometimes give way to debate or possibly persuasion. Occasions for this shift include the following: when an honest disagreement cannot be resolved by the discussion method, when some persons either cannot or will not discuss, when a large assembly has to act, and when time is short.

In Relation to Decision

Must a debate be judged or decided in some way? An impressive array of expert opinions can be cited to support the belief that judgment or decision is an essential element in any definition of debate. According to this view, if a presentation of opposing arguments is not judged or decided, it is not a debate. "Debaters present their hypotheses to the scrutiny of informed opponents, appealing beyond themselves for judgment," writes one expert.[49] Another states that, excepting the instances of so-called debate in one person's mind (deliberation), debaters try to secure decisions from others.[50] A third version, although limited by implication to legislative debate on propositions of policy, treats advocacy "as a rational means through which free society resolves its public controversies and reaches decisions as to matters of public policy."[51]

[49] McBath, *Argumentation* . . . , p. 7.
[50] Freeley, *Argumentation* . . . , p. 2.
[51] Windes and Hastings, *Argumentation* . . . , p. 5.

One author of the previously cited work which distinguishes between internal and external methods of deliberation explains that controversy as a method of deciding conflicting claims is characterized by reasoned discourse, confrontation, and assent from either one party (in discussion or dialectic) or from a neutral agency (in debate). This outside judge may be, for example, a board, a judge, a jury, an executive, or the voters.[52]

Some say that school, educational, or academic debate, as it is variously identified, should be judged, because decisions serve to motivate students to do their best to win.[53] This familiar argument implies what anyone experienced in the activity knows to be the case, namely, that nondecision school debates can and do occur. If there are no critic judges, and if no audience vote is taken, there can be no verifiable decision. Indeed, if no vote is taken, who can be sure there was even a covert decision? The audience may have perceived the debate as entertainment.

In conclusion, the position of this writer is that political, legislative, and judicial debates (all defined in Chapter 3) are judged, that school debates most often are judged but need not be, and that philosophical debates are mostly for understanding rather than decision.

In Relation to Behavior of Debaters

Does debate imply, by definition, that those who engage in it are always contentious? William Hazlitt, the essayist, explained the error in this opinion when he said that the main purposes of conversation among friends are to learn the views of others and to see what they think of yours. These ends are thwarted by contentious persons who "get up a thesis upon every topic" as if they were in a debating society. Indulging in vigorous argument is equally unwise when one is in the presence of a closed mind. "It is impossible," said Dean Swift, "to reason a man out of something he has not been reasoned into." The trouble is that a dogmatist when opposed grows more extreme, more heated, and increasingly abusive.

Unsophisticated disputants often behave as if they believe it is

[52] D. Ehninger, "Limits of Controversy," *Speech Teacher*, September, 1966, pp. 180–185.
[53] See Kruger, *Modern Debate* . . . , p. 361.

necessary to become disagreeable when they disagree with someone. G. K. Chesterton put it this way: "People generally quarrel because they cannot argue." Another man said to his opponent in debate, "Sir, you raise your voice when you should reinforce your argument." The point, of course, is that one should be able to disagree without being disagreeable. But this, too, can be carried to such an extreme that competent spokesmen for opposing sides of controversial questions are sometimes asked by moderators to act as if their differences were slight and easily smoothed over. Both extremes, belligerency and pseudo-agreement, are inimical to worthwhile debating.

Does a definition of debate entail competition or cooperation, or some of each? For approximately thirty years in the literature of this field, the word "cooperation" was associated with discussion, while "competition" was associated with debate. In recent years a few theorists have defined debate as "a cooperative enterprise."[54] Anyone who calls debate competitive is confusing means and ends, they charge. They define debate as competition within a cooperative (procedural) framework for the purpose of testing alternatives.[55] In the short-range view, debaters in political, legislative, judicial, and educational contexts seem to compete to win, according to one way of looking at debate. But the larger purpose of the "game," as one critic puts it, is to achieve cooperative ends through the technique of competition.[56]

If, in the adversary system of our courts, the opposing counsel were as cooperative as this critic says they ought to be, they would investigate together or at least exchange evidence. That procedure would be more congenial to the Russian system than to the English or the American. But the "game" notion requires special attention. This expounder of it does mention the dissimilarity of the "training-ground" debate and the "real-life thing," but he proceeds to classify all debates as games. The definition of "game" which seems to have the sanction of general usage is "amusement or sport conducted according to rules." However, according to this critic's proposed definition and classification, all of these events are games: trials at law, legislative deliberations, political campaigns, collegiate "bull sessions," prizefighting, and football. This almost limitless extension of the meanings of "game," the mixing of the literal and the metaphorical usages, and the shifting from the descriptive *is* to

---

[54] Ehninger and Brockriede, *Decision* . . . , pp. 19–21.

[55] McBath, *Argumentation* . . . ; p. 12.

[56] F. S. Haiman, "A Critical View of the Game of Forensics," *Journal of the American Forensic Association*, I, No. 2 (1964), 62–66.

the prescriptive *ought* constitute some sort of "game" in their own right.

In sum, what shall we say about the definition of debate in relation to the attitudes and the general behavior of debaters? On the first topic there is consensus: debaters need not be habitually contentious. There are times and places for debate, and there are some that are unsuitable; but when disagreement is to be verbalized, it does not call for disagreeableness.

On the second topic, cooperation *vs.* competition, the answer is complex. For reasons that have been set out, it is an oversimplification to identify debate primarily with inquiry and cooperation, and only incidentally with advocacy and competition. Qualifiers such as "For whom?" and "In what circumstances?" are needed. When a local League of Women Voters invites the rival mayoralty candidates to debate in a meeting, the confrontation is likely to be inquiry for the members but competitive advocacy for the candidates. In a societal sense, the debate and its related interactions can be classified as a mode of inquiry consisting of competitive advocacy conducted according to predetermined procedures for purposes of enlightenment and/or decision.

In this connection it may be helpful to think of several levels of cooperation and competition on a sort of continuum, ranging from perfect cooperation through independent action to extreme competition. The phenomenon we label "discussion, inquiry, and cooperation" and the one we call "debate, advocacy, and competition" will not always occupy the fixed places on that continuum. Each can be moved toward one end or the other in terms of the goals, attitudes, and procedures that are dominant at any given instant. How we label the discourse when it is finished should depend upon the central tendency in respect to the goals sought, the attitudes of the participants, and the procedures followed.

The reader may have noticed that the books in which cooperation and inquiry are emphasized in the introductory chapters have incomparably more space devoted to the principles and the procedures of competitive advocacy. True, advocacy does not occur in a vacuum, but a definition of debate can reasonably be expected to comport with reality. It is realistic to recognize the respects in which debate involves cooperation and inquiry, but it is still more so to realize that a debater can more competently serve his purpose if he has functional knowledge of the principles and procedures of competitive advocacy.

In Relation to Procedure

It is generally agreed that debate is defined as a subclass of controversy, and all agree that pro and con presentations are made. There is, however, diversity of opinion on three other questions: (1) Must the discourse be oral, or may it be written as well? (2) Must debate be formal, that is, structured by rules? (3) Must there be a physical confrontation?

On the question of the requirement that the discourse in debate be oral, four categories of answers were found among thirteen books. The orientation of most of the books toward school or academic debate may be a biasing influence. Be that as it may, the little survey showed, in this writer's opinion, that three[57] stipulated oral discourse only, four[58] implied oral discourse, five[59] said the discourse is usually or typically oral, and one[60] apparently did not say. Two conclusions seem to be justified: (1) One who says "debate" to professionals in this field is likely to be understood to mean "oral discourse," and (2) one who wishes to communicate a different meaning will be well advised to add the qualifiers "written" or "oral and written," for instance.

Must a debate be formal in terms of structure and rules? Eleven books, most of which are oriented toward academic debate, were consulted on this point. Six[61] stipulated some formality, three[62] implied it, one[63] mentioned both the formal and the informal, and one[64] said

[57] W. C. Shaw, *The Art of Debate* (Boston: Allyn and Bacon, 1922), p. 2; Moulton, *Dynamics* . . . , p. 4; Kruger, *Modern Debate* (on school debate).

[58] Freeley, *Argumentation* . . . , p. 2; McBath, *Argumentation* . . . , pp. 3–12; J. J. Auer, "Counterfeit Debates" in *The Great Debates*, S. Kraus (ed.) (Bloomington: Indiana University Press, 1962), pp. 146–148; Huber, *Influencing* . . . , p. 9.

[59] Baird, *Argumentation* . . . , p. 309; G. R. Capp and T. R. Capp, *Principles of Argumentation and Debate* (Englewood Cliffs, N.J.: Prentice-Hall, Inc., 1965); R. H. Wagner, *Handbook of Argumentation* (New York: Thomas Nelson and Sons, 1936), p. 118; Windes and Hastings, *Argumentation* . . . , pp. 27–28; McBurney and Mills, *Argumentation* . . . , p. 4.

[60] Ehninger and Brockriede, *Decision* . . .

[61] Moulton, *Dynamics* . . . , p. 4; Baird, *Argumentation, Discussion, and Debate*, p. 308; Shaw, *Art of Debate*, p. 2; Wagner, *Handbook* . . . , p. 118; Kruger, *Modern Debate* . . . (school only); Auer, "Counterfeit Debates," pp. 146–148, but "matched contestants" is a questionable criterion.

[62] Freeley, *Argumentation* . . . , p. 2; McBath, *Argumentation* . . . , pp. 3–12; Ehninger and Brockriede, *Decision* . . .

[63] Windes and Hastings, *Argumentation* . . . , pp. 26–27.

[64] McBurney and Mills, *Argumentation* . . . , p. 4.

formality is not required for an encounter to be called a debate. Again two generalizations appear warranted: (1) The word "debate" in our literature is typically taken to imply a structured situation governed by rules or conventions, and (2) a second meaning, which is not conditioned by forensic and parliamentary experiences, includes not only the most formal presentations but also informal conversations which on other counts qualify as debates. When the second meaning is intended, the modifier "informal" should suffice to designate the unstructured debate.

Must there be a physical confrontation in debate? Of the thirteen sources consulted, two[65] said "yes" explicitly, five[66] agreed implicitly, one[67] said it is not essential, and five made no commitment. Actually the "no comment" category has additional books, but they are not included because they make no comment upon any of these procedural questions. It may be that some writers omit this topic because they assume that confrontation is an obvious element of debate, or perhaps they have not thought of it at all. In any case, there is no clear mandate. The position of this book is that face-to-face confrontation is the typical case, but there can be debate without it. In the history of public address we speak of the continuing debate on states' rights since 1787.

After considering the preceding exposition of six ways to define debate, one is less likely to be satisfied with a one-sentence definition, despite its beguiling simplicity and ease of memorization. Brief summaries of the six aspects of definition follow.

1. In relation to argumentation, debate is a specialized branch which is concerned with bilateral discourse in controversy.

2. Because of its bilaterality a completed debate cannot qualify as persuasion, even though in some cases each side has attempted persuasion. Further, because the decision, if any is sought, must be a critical one, any persuasion which either side attempts cannot be of the popular sort. While there may be some doubt about the debaters' persuading an audience, there is serious doubt that debaters persuade each other.

3. Debate is related both to inquiry and to advocacy in that debaters inquire before they advocate, and for listeners and readers the function is often informative; however, the debaters' presentations are

---

[65] Kruger, *Modern Debate* . . . (school debate); Auer, "Counterfeit Debates."
[66] Freeley, *Argumentation* . . . , p. 2; McBath (ed.), *Argumentation* . . . , pp. 3–12; Windes and Hastings, *Argumentation* . . . , pp. 191–192; Baird, *Argumentation* . . . , p. 308; Wagner, *Handbook* . . . , p. 118.
[67] McBurney and Mills, *Argumentation* . . . , p. 4.

advocatory. The interrelationships of discussion, debate, and persuasion are instructive on this point.

4. Debate is related to decision but not on the one-to-one basis that some assert. Decision by a third party is hardly a necessary part of a definition of debate.

5. Two observations were made concerning the behavior of debaters: disagreement need not entail disagreeableness, and both cooperation and competition are required.

6. Finally, in relation to procedure, three pairs of generalizations were made: "debate" usually means oral discourse, but the addition of "written" will identify the exceptions; a debate is presumed to be structured, but the adjective "informal" will denote exceptions; physical confrontation is the typical debate situation, but it is not the only one.

PROOF

Perhaps the most nearly standard, traditional definitions state that proof means evidence and/or premises plus reasoning to support a conclusion or claim. According to this view, evidence alone is not proof; there must also be interpretative inference. Thus one might say that an advocate has submitted, as proof of his claim that inflation is a problem in need of solution, the facts on reduced consumer purchasing power and rising costs of government during recent wars, plus an economic principle which holds that these phenomena often lead to harmful consequences.

When proof is defined in relation to rhetoric as persuasion, the function of an argument is to establish proof, and that implies enough evidence and reasoning to create belief. Logical proof alone does not always suffice; oftentimes ethical proof (evidences of the speaker's credibility) and pathetic (emotional) proof are required.

These simple explanations of proof conceal more than they reveal. They do not come to grips with the basic issues, nor do they candidly explicate the complex implications of any definition. What is implied if we define proof in terms of what some unspecified listeners or readers will believe? And what is implied if we define it in terms of some critical standard? In the sections which follow, five conceptions of proof will be discussed: as need-fulfillment, as consonance with a climate of opinion, as empirical verifiability, as logical demonstration, and as a combination of substantive and structural factors to satisfy disinterested, intelligently critical listeners or readers.

As Need-Fulfillment

This definition relates to the psychology of the individual rather than the group. If one has a psychological need to believe a particular idea, he will uncritically accept someone's presentation of it as proof. "Desire, wish, or feeling can cause a person to believe and accept. . . ."[68] For instance, some persons seem eager to accept as conclusive proof any unsupported assertion that "the international Communist conspiracy" is responsible for any given act of protest. Writing on "proving a theory and getting it accepted," a philosopher of ethics draws a distinction which delineates the objection to equating proof and belief.[69]

His remarks about "proving" something to a lunatic apply in a lesser degree to the "proving" of something to a closed mind. In the case of a bigot, for example, there appears to be a psychological need to reject ideas which threaten those he needs to believe. He may be unable to believe that any African has at least normal intelligence, that any American Indian has ambition, or that any slum-dweller aspires to a better life through his own efforts.

When a teacher urges students of this subject to adapt their advocatory remarks to the beliefs of their audiences, does this mean that an advocate should "prove" what the audience wants to believe? It does not. Rather, as one book explains, it means that he must find among the beliefs of his audience a starting point for his argument if it is to be convincing. But the ease with which one can slip from this position to the equation of proof and persuasion can be seen in the same book. The authors cite two concepts of proof (". . . in relation to the most objective logical requirements . . ." and ". . . in terms of what will convince a particular audience . . ."), and they choose the latter as the ultimate test.[70]

---

[68] Miller and Nilsen, *Perspectives* . . . , p. 52.
[69] Paul Edwards, *The Logic of Moral Discourse* (Glencoe: The Free Press, 1955), pp. 25–28.
[70] Windes and Hastings, *Argumentation* . . . , pp. 207–210.

As Consonance With Climate of Opinion

This definition is socio-psychological in viewpoint. Several writers assert, with little or no qualification, that belief is proof. The consonance-with-opinion doctrine is unequivocally stated in one book as follows: "Proof is the process of securing belief in one statement by relating it to another statement already believed."[71] Later in the same work we read that evidence is whatever the audience thinks is evidence.[72] Again, each reader or listener decides for himself how strong or weak any proof is.[73] Putting it another way, the same authors state that proof is deficient only when the recipient believes it is deficient.[74] And finally, "The concept of proof is meaningless when divorced from the person to whom the proof is offered."[75] Another author modifies this view ever so slightly to state that belief does not make a false statement true, but audience acceptance is an essential characteristic of proof.[76]

Proof is also defined as almost unqualified belief, or whatever supporting material a given audience situation requires: "When the belief of listeners is obtained, the communicator has proved his case. This is the goal of all persuasion . . . Proof is the process of using evidence to secure belief in an idea or statement."[77] There is a trace of limitation on this doctrine: evidence can be tested by the communicator and by the auditors.[78]

A single citation will indicate implicatively that some writers who occasionally adopt the consonance-with-opinion conception of proof do recognize that belief is not the sole criterion of proof: "The fact that United States policy in Viet Nam moved in a direction opposite that advocated by faculty critics is *one* [italics mine] reason for considering the movement a failure."[79]

Even some physical scientists have been so limited by prevailing

[71] Ehninger and Brockriede, *Decision . . .* , p. 99.
[72] *Ibid.*, p. 100.
[73] *Ibid.*, p. 168.
[74] *Ibid.*, p. 186.
[75] *Ibid.*, p. 203.
[76] E. G. Bormann, "An Empirical Approach to Certain Concepts of Logical Proof," *Central States Speech Journal*, XII, No. 2 (1961), 85–91.
[77] E. P. Bettinghaus, *Message Preparation: The Nature of Proof* (Indianapolis: The Bobbs-Merrill Co., 1966), p. 5.
[78] *Ibid.*, pp. 42–43.
[79] H. Martin, "The Rhetoric of Academic Protest," *Central States Speech Journal*, XVII, No. 4 (1966), 248.

opinion that they refused to accept proofs which were not consonant with it. A Dutch scientist in 1857 was severely criticized by his peers for his article on the arrangement of atoms in space. Later he received the first Nobel Prize in chemistry. Sir Isaac Newton once "demonstrated" mathematically the "impossibility" of manned flight, and Lord Kelvin "disproved" the theory of evolution.

As Empirical Verifiability

I am concerned with what makes empirical propositions true, and with the definition of "truth" as applied to such propositions. Empirical propositions, except when their subject matter happens to be linguistic, are true in virtue of occurrences which are not linguistic . . . Empiricism, in agreement with common sense, holds that a verbal statement may be confirmed or confuted by an observation, provided it is a statement which is significant and is not one of logic.[80]

In the sciences, empirical verifiability means confirmation by experiment and observation, but in common parlance it means proof by reference to experience. Verification can be either direct or indirect. The shape of the earth has become directly verifiable in the Space Age, but the exact language of Patrick Henry's "Liberty or Death" speech remains indirectly verifiable. Evidence, according to an empirical view, consists of facts and true statements of fact. In view of this limitation, it may be that empirical verifiability is an impractical standard of proof in many rhetorical situations, such as speeches containing value judgments on morals, taste, and the like.

As Logical Demonstration

More will be said of logic under "Reasoning" (Chapter 8), but for the present a brief introduction to logic will suffice to show what proof by logical demonstration means. To a specialist in it, logic is an abstract, formal science of structure which exhibits and analyzes the relations permitting valid inference. It is abstract in that it deals with skeletal patterns which fit any actual materials of fact or imagination in existence or in thought. It is on a level of abstraction at least twice removed from life facts concerning persons, places, things, and ideas.

[80] B. Russell, *An Inquiry into Meaning and Truth* (London: G. Allen and Unwin, 1940), pp. 18–19.

It is formal because a logician is interested in general laws or forms of all inference. Nonformal science works through experience to determine whether certain statements are in reality true, while a formal science, such as logic or geometry, deduces theorems from definitions and assumptions or postulates. Formal science has a hypothetical element, that is, if the assumptions and definitions are true, so are the theorems. Plane geometry, as systematized by Euclid (c. 300 B.C.), is another formal discipline. Physical sciences are nonformal in their laboratory operations, but they are clearly formal in deducing theorems from assumptions.

Structure in logic refers to the interrelations of the parts of the whole, as in this example:

There are four bonds in your investment portfolio (A, B, C, D).

A yields more than B,
B yields more than C,
C yields more than D; therefore
A yields more than D.

A second example will show the logical symbols for simple relationships:

p) If we reduce tariffs,
q) imports will increase,
r) exports will rise,
s) internal prosperity will develop.

If p, then q;
if q, then r;
if r, then s. Therefore,
if p, then s.

The intermediate steps are usually omitted in ordinary discourse, just as one of the three in the following syllogism would be:

All mammals are vertebrates.
All dogs are mammals.
All dogs are vertebrates.

In short, any proof by logical demonstration is based upon the inevitability of a conclusion in a closed system of discourse. However, two or three limitations merit careful attention: (1) If one critic is right, there are ambiguities in the syllogism.[81] (2) An argument may be formally valid but materially false. (3) An argument may meet logical requirements but fail to influence anyone.

[81] S. E. Toulmin, *The Uses of Argument* (London: Cambridge University Press, 1958), pp. 107–113.

As Combination of Substantive and Structural Factors to Satisfy Disinterested, Intelligently Critical Listeners or Readers

In this fifth definition of proof we have what is essentially a blending of the third and fourth plus the qualification that any resulting persuasion may be of a restricted sort. This is admittedly an ideal which cannot be spelled out with the specificity of the rules of the syllogism, and it is not egilitarian in its social philosophy. According to this way of looking at it, proof is that combination of reliable knowledge and valid inference which can meet the expectations of intelligently critical listeners or readers. This means that persons who are normally critical would be excluded from this category in cases of biasing personal interest in the outcome.

Some writers express or imply this definition of proof without emphasizing any component such as content or form. Commenting upon evidence and reasoning, one states: "Proof may be defined as that which causes a reasonable person to assent to a proposition."[82] Another explains that assent, meaning justifiable belief, is sought in debate. Influence is not the sole measure of merit; critical deliberation is also to be considered.[83] The revised edition of a long-established work explicitly states the doctrine of a balance of substantive and structural factors.[84] Finally, another revised edition discusses proof as "good reasons" to convince those who decide, and the priority of logical appeals is stipulated.[85]

One book will serve to exemplify the fifth definition but with strong emphasis upon logical demonstration: Proof shows [to whom?] ". . . that a proposition is true by virtue of its being the consequence of one or more propositions which are themselves true."[86] Proof is a relative concept in that it extends from the conclusive (inevitable or certain) to the extremely doubtful. The midpoint called "probably true" is said to merit belief until "probably false" looks better. The emphasis upon logical proof to convince critical persons comes out clearly in the assertion that logical proof and expert testimony are "the only basis of belief of thinking people." *Ethos* and *pathos* are excluded from consideration.

---

[82] Wagner, *Handbook* . . . , p. 27.
[83] McBath, *Argumentation* . . . , pp. 8–9.
[84] McBurney and Mills, *Argumentation* . . . , pp. 2–3.
[85] Freeley, *Argumentation* . . . , pp. 7 and 30.
[86] Kruger, *Modern Debate* . . . , pp. 125–131.

A somewhat different stance is taken by two sources which, while they appear to lean toward this fifth definition of proof, also partially accept the first four. One sets out two conceptions of proof: to gain acceptance or rejection (persuasion), and to evoke in listeners certain kinds of thought processes or decision-making responses by presenting a rational case in form and content. A preference for the latter is implied when it is said of argumentation that ". . . its major contribution is to create constructive critics who will, through their criticism and arguing, raise the level of public controversy."[87] Some ambivalence appears in the second work in this group. At times a critical standard is stressed, and at others the rhetoric of persuasion. We read that the findings of argumentative analysis may be used to influence others, but this is not the central purpose of argumentation. The main concern is with the proof requirements of propositions, or how to find proper reasons for accepting conclusions as probably true. But elsewhere in the same source we read: "In this chapter we will define 'proof' as 'that which causes an audience to believe or accept a conclusion as true on the basis of the evidence and reasoning presented by the advocate'." This is followed by quotations from the rhetoric of persuasion.[88]

Finally, there is a point of view which shows some trace of this fifth definition of proof within the context of an almost unqualified "belief" criterion of proof. In a passage which is the exception to the otherwise unqualified espousal of the "belief" criterion of proof, one contemporary source states: "A unit of proof will not convince a *critical* [italics mine] listener or reader unless it is based on evidence he will believe."[89]

Another way of expressing the fifth definition of proof (substance and structure to satisfy disinterested, intelligently critical observers) is to say that it requires of an argument the ability to stand up under appropriate criticism, as previously mentioned under "As an Analytical-Critical Instrument." The canons of such criticism are the "core" concepts of argumentation which are discussed in subsequent chapters. These items of a critical instrument will be applied to several models including the syllogistic (syllogism, sorites, epicheireme), the canons of induction, and the Toulmin layout of arguments (Chapter 8).

When one adopts the fifth definition of proof, what becomes of the audience's relation to proof? How much can we stress critical appraisal and still deal with flesh-and-blood controversy? What happens

[87] Miller and Nilsen, *Perspectives* . . . , pp. 20 and 181.
[88] Windes and Hastings, *Argumentation* . . . , pp. 24, 97, and 207.
[89] Ehninger and Brockriede, *Decision* . . . , p. 169.

to the critical faculty under impassioned oratory and crowd psychology? How much adaptation to an audience is consonant with this lofty conception of proof? The answer to the first question is self-evident; if a given audience is not disinterested and not intelligently critical, proof in the present sense may be of no interest, even if persuasion occurs. Ideally, we can apply critical appraisal to real-life controversies for educational purposes in the hope that the learners will come to demand better proof from advocates who try to influence them. This answer relates also to the question of the impact of demagoguery. With respect to the ethical question of adaptation to an audience, the criterion of understanding takes precedence over persuasion. If this hope is vain, we have been deluding ourselves about the values of mass education.

This fifth definition of proof will be related to four other basic concepts of argumentation (presumption, burden of proof, probability, and burden of proceeding) in Chapter 3.

QUESTIONS

1. Explain what is meant by "argumentation as a critical apparatus."
2. In what respect are rhetoric and dialectic the parent disciplines of argumentation? Why are logic and psychology not so treated here?
3. What might be the consequences of defining argumentation as merely a part of persuasion? Or as a form of cooperative inquiry? See R. L. Scott, "On Viewing Rhetoric As Epistemic," *Central States Speech Journal*, XVIII, No. 1 (1967), 13.
4. In what circumstances might real-life debaters reasonably expect to convince each other?
5. What has a person's philosophical orientation (existentialism or any other) to do with his conception of argumentation?
6. On what contemporary topics might scholars of argumentation do research?
7. Discuss the implications or consequences of ignoring some of the six aspects of a definition of debate.
8. H. S. Leonard, *Principles of Right Reason* (New York: Henry Holt and Co., 1957), pp. 412–414, states six uses of arguments: to record an inference, to serve as a testing device for inferences, as a tool of inference, as

an instrument of persuasion, to exhibit an implication (if . . . then), and to serve as a component in the method of hypothesis and verification. Relate this to the notion that argumentation is merely a part of persuasion.

EXERCISES

1. Give an example of the placing of emotional or personal proofs into a logical framework for the purpose of imposing some rigor upon the arguments.
2. Select a short specimen of argumentative discourse such as an editorial, a letter to the editor, or a printed speech. Apply as best you can at this stage the evaluative criteria listed under "Critical Apparatus" in this chapter.
3. Report on the following article in relation to the idea that persuasion can become propaganda much more easily than debate can: T. R. Nilsen, "Free Speech, Persuasion, and the Democratic Process," *Quarterly Journal of Speech*, XLIV, No. 3 (1958), 235–243.
4. Choose a proposition (controversial conclusion) and a side, describe a real or an imaginary audience, and explain in general terms what each of the five conceptions of proof would require of you in that situation.
5. How would you suggest going about the task of changing some Indian's attitude toward *suttee* (immolation of a widow on the pyre of her dead husband) by verbal means? What part might argumentation, as herein defined, play?
6. Apply the procedure of Exercise 5 to the smoking habit of your contemporaries.
7. Apply the above procedure to a campaign to increase the use of automobile seat belts.

CHAPTER 3

LOGICAL AND ETHICAL

RESPONSIBILITIES

Freedom of speech is of central importance to our study, but it does not stand alone. The philosophy of this work holds that an advocate has basic responsibilities to be informed, to be thoughtful, to be socially aware, and to behave ethically; one might say, "An advocate has the ethical responsibility to talk sense."

The aspects of an advocate's logical and ethical responsibilities will now be discussed. Although they may be treated separately for instructional purposes, they are interrelated in practice.

ASPECTS OF LOGICAL RESPONSIBILITY

Probability

Under "Definitions of Proof" we considered five points of view, all of which have direct bearing upon the degrees of proof which can be achieved or may be demanded. These degrees of proof range from uncritical belief to objective verifiability. The crucial difference between

[47]

these two is that objective verifiability is by far the better source of reliable knowledge. It is more nearly free of the biasing effects of ignorance and wishful thinking.

Perhaps this difference can be shown in relation to the vernacular words for the degrees of proof: possible, plausible, probable, and certain. *Possible* usually means "it could be." One would, at most, accept a possibly valid statement as a tentative hypothesis subject to further scrutiny. The possibility is reliably so if objectively verified, but not if belief by the gullible is the standard. *Plausible* conveys some likelihood of credibility. Its lowest level is characterized by what the gullible will accept. Plausibility is a matter of belief, not verification. *Probable*, in everyday English, means more likely true than false. Probability can be established by objective methods, but when it is thought of in terms of belief, it means little more than plausibility. *Certain* designates the highest degree of proof when objectively verified; but when certainty is strictly a function of belief, its reliability may vary from nil to considerable. In a closed system of discourse such as plane geometry or formal logic, a kind of certainty can be achieved, However, in the so-called exact sciences, certainty is not generally asserted today. Heinsenberg's uncertainty principle, which came from a physical finding of quantum mechanics, implies that a physicist cannot show by experiment any more than a probable prediction, because the improbable may still happen.[1]

A few of the contemporary textbooks in argumentation use the same four vernacular words to distinguish four degrees of proof, while most of the sources omit this topic altogether. There is one recent book, however, which sets out four meanings of probability in a unique way: (1) probability between the sentence and the world, as in "Red China will start a war against the U.S.A."; (2) probability within the sentence, as in "Chicago Democrats usually vote the party ticket"; (3) probability between the reasons and the conclusion, as in the induction, "Swede 1 is blond, Swede 2 is blond, etc., therefore, Swedes tend to be blond"; (4) probability indicating a degree of certainty on the part of the advocate in his predictive statement.[2]

In the study of argumentation we are concerned with probability as a rhetorical concept, but preferably not in the original sense. More than

---

[1] D. Bergamini, "The Language of Science," *The Reporter*, March 31, 1960, p. 38.

[2] J. Ray and H. Zavos, "Reasoning and Argument: Some Special Problems and Types," in *Perspectives* . . . , Miller and Nilsen, pp. 80–88; see Chap. 8, *Reason in Controversy*.

a century before Aristotle wrote his monumental *Rhetoric*, Corax in Syracuse taught successful pleading for fees, thereby incurring Plato's contempt. In his sophistic orientation, Corax taught that an orator need not search for truth but only for a way to make an idea plausible to an audience. His principal invention was the "probability" argument which achieved only plausibility, but he prospered by giving clever, practical advice.[3]

But even though our standards are higher than those of the Sophists, they are still less exacting than those of modern physical scientists. For example, probability in science does not bear on only one case. The word has no operational meaning except in relation to frequency of occurrence in numerous situations. But as a *minimal* rhetorical goal, probability may mean as little as plausibility and bear upon a single case. The position of this book is that an intelligent person should demand something better than the minimum.

Some level of probability is all we can hope to achieve, because the human behavior about which we deliberate belongs in the class of uncertainties. We argue about matters which appear to admit of two possibilities: expedient or inexpedient, just or unjust, wise or foolish, etc. In each case we advocate a view which we think is true for the most part or as a general rule. The inherent reason is that probability statements cannot reliably predict a specific instance; they indicate a trend on a long-run basis. In practical affairs we must bet on the odds, as it were.

Probability in argumentation is rarely mathematical; it is expressed in the somewhat vague language of relations. Words such as *probably, likely, highly probable,* and their antonyms are typical choices. Fractions or percentages are, of course, more precise than adverbs, but they are less often applicable. In view of these observations, a student of argumentation should heed these hints. (1) Express the claimed degree of probability candidly, avoiding extravagances such as "beyond a shadow of doubt" (2) Do enough research so that the highest potential degree of proof can be asserted. (3) Whenever feasible, express the degree of probability as a numerical estimate. If we think of probability as meaning more than mere plausibility to the gullible, we must offer proof sufficient to satisfy a critical thinker that our view is the preferable one. The establishment of probability as defined above is both an ethical and a logical responsibility.

[3] B. Smith, "Corax and Probability," *Quarterly Journal of Speech*, VII (1921), 13–42.

Presumption

As a legal convention, presumption is extremely important in the Anglo-American tradition. Even though the legal usage is not our main concern here, it does help us to appreciate the significance of presumption. The law presumes certain things to be true until evidence and argument sufficient to overcome the presumption are introduced. Presumptions vary in strength, as we can see in these examples: innocence of the accused until guilt is proved, sanity until otherwise is proved, ownership implied by possession, validity of a will, survivorship of someone in a common disaster, and presumption of death after a certain period of absence.

There have been violations of this principle in "trial by mass media (newspaper, radio, television)", because this treatment creates a presumption of guilt before a hearing or a trial. Branding a person "questionable" or "controversial" has led to lawsuits over loss of employment stemming from such branding. Some businessmen have found themselves without the benefit of presumption in their dealings with regulatory agencies. Processed food which contains additives to color, flavor, or preserve it is no longer presumed to be safe; it must be proved to be so. On some occasions when firms are charged with criminal offenses in the regulatory field, the traditional presumption of innocence is replaced by the doctrine of absolute criminal liability.[4]

Presumption as a rhetorical convention was introduced and expounded at length by Whately in 1828.[5] His formulation has been so influential in the literature of argumentation that it will be summarized here before the later views are reported. He began by stressing the importance of an advocate's knowing and pointing out to the hearer at the outset where the presumption lies and to which party the burden of proof belongs. This matter is often overlooked, he continues, even though the character of the proceedings depends upon it. One who has a presumption in his favor is analogous to a body of troops in a fortress. Why sally forth and give up your advantage? When accused it is better to make a simple denial which challenges the accuser to make his case.

Presumption in favor of a supposition means such a preoccupation of

---

[4] G. O. W. Mueller, "Ambushed Businessmen," *Wall Street Journal*, October 23, 1961.

[5] R. Whately, *Elements of Rhetoric* (Cambridge: Jas. Munroe and Co., 1834), pp. 73–80.

the ground that the supposition must stand until overthrown by sufficient proof. In legal proceedings, for instance, anyone who is on trial is presumed innocent until found otherwise through due process. This does not imply innocence or even its likelihood; it simply means that the accused need not open the proceedings with a defense of his own innocence.

Whately explains that there are presumptions in favor of every existing institution, the harmlessness of every book as well as every person, and the prevailing opinion on any subject until a charge is proved. Christianity, the Reformation, and the episcopacy now have presumption on their side, but such was not the case when each originated.

Finally, he explains that a presumption may be rebutted by an opposite presumption. One who urges the removal of an existing restriction seemingly enjoys no presumption, but he may argue, "True, but there is another presumption which rebuts the former: every restriction is in itself an evil; and therefore there is a presumption in favor of its removal, unless it can be shown necessary for prevention of some greater evil. I am not bound to allege any specific inconvenience; if the restriction is unnecessary, that is reason enough for its abolition. Its defenders, therefore, are fairly called on to prove its necessity."

What does Whately's traditional theory mean in terms of controversies about what should be done, what is true, and what is good? If it is proposed that a college now on the quarterly calendar should adopt a trimester plan, the presumption favors the quarterly arrangement at that institution. If the proponents of change merely say, "Let's change to the trimester plan," the defenders of the quarterly system need not reply, because the presumption in their favor has not been overcome by that unsupported assertion. A reply in defense of the status quo is called for only after the advocates of change have made a case.

In a situation involving a contest between two ways of doing something, as in the quarterly vs. trimester case, it is easy to see which party has the presumption at the outset. But in controversies about what is true and what is good, the placement of presumption is less clear. The traditional doctrine holds that presumption favors prevailing belief at the beginning of the controversy. If one were to assert that the earth was round when all about him believed it to be flat, the presumption would favor the "flat" side. If a minority in a materialistic society asserts that materialism is an unworthy philosophy of life, the presumption favors the materialists in the beginning. In these examples we can observe that a presumption is an advanced starting point or a precedural convention which identifies the party which occupies the disputed ground at the outset and therefore does not have to make the first move.

It has been observed that most of the contemporary writing on presumption in argumentation is in the Whately tradition. An examination of eight textbooks copyrighted in the sixties reveals that six present the Whately doctrine: two briefly report it,[6] two quote from it and add modern illustrations,[7] one cites it and adds "natural" and "artificial" (assigned) presumptions,[8] and one adapts it to academic debate exclusively.[9] Of the two which are less clearly indebted to Whately, one is concerned solely with propositions of policy, especially in academic debate,[10] while the other has only five or six lines on presumption.[11]

Do impersonal factors determine the placement of presumption, or does public opinion? Until recently there were three views on this problem. One holds that a general presumption is placed without regard for audience opinion. Thus the status quo would be given the initial benefit of presumption even if the audience were opposed to it. As long as unregulated child labor was the status quo, it enjoyed a presumption despite any unfavorable public opinion which may have existed. A second view is that a general presumption is determined by a favorable public opinion. According to this interpretation, there is a presumption in favor of the majority opinion on a given question. Majority opinion, however, varies enormously among audiences, and the measurements of range and intensity are difficult to perform, complicating the issue. Finally, there is the notion that specific presumptions are determined in relation to individual opinions in specific audiences. Thus some listeners or readers would entertain a presumption in favor of the status quo, while others would initially favor a change. This view is geared directly to the notion that belief equals proof.

The difficulty in these disparate views results from a confusion of a procedural convention and the tactics of popular persuasion. The second interpretation has not prevailed because it is less dependable and

[6] Windes and Hastings, *Argumentation* . . . , pp. 75–77; O. Bauer, *Fundamentals of Debate: Theory and Practice* (Chicago: Scott, Foresman and Co., 1966) pp. 3–4, 16, and 31.

[7] A. Freeley, *Argumentation* . . . , pp. 30–34; McBurney and Mills, *Argumentation* . . . , pp. 18–19.

[8] Ehninger and Brockriede, *Decision* . . . , pp. 83–84.

[9] McBath, *Argumentation* . . . , pp. 105–107.

[10] Kruger, *Modern Debate* . . . , pp. 40–43 and 127.

[11] W. R. Fisher and E. M. Sayles, "The Nature and Functions of Argument," in *Perspectives* . . . , Miller and Nilsen, p. 18.

is potentially more troublesome. It is better to have a nonevaluative convention which enables the parties to determine what ground is in dispute. This is the reason for defining presumption as Cronkhite has proposed. He explains that much recent controversy over this matter stems from the need to reconcile three kinds of burden against which a presumption may stand: the burden to support what one asserts, the burden to oppose the inertia of the status quo, and the burden to oppose audience consensus. In relation to academic debate there is no need to change the principle that presumption resides with the status quo, because practically all intercollegiate debating is done on propositions of policy (resolutions calling for a change in our way of doing something). But in controversy in general, the least confusing principle or rule, according to Cronkhite, is "He who asserts must prove,"

regardless of whether the assertion attacks or defends the *status quo*, regardless of whether the *status quo* can be identified, and regardless of whether the proposition is one of fact, value, or policy.[12]

Thus anyone standing in opposition to the assertion has the presumption at the outset.

Burden of Proof

As the immediately preceding paragraph indicates, the burden of proof stands opposite the presumption. These two concepts are, figuratively speaking, two sides of a coin. Once a dissatisfied party starts a controversy by stating his complaint, we know that he has the burden of proof, and we locate the presumption on the side that initially needs to say no more than "Why?" "Prove it," or an equivalent expression. The recent textbooks are in general agreement on the meaning of burden of proof. Their treatments echo Whately, but several of them limit their scope to academic debate on propositions of policy.

As a *legal* convention, burden of proof means the responsibility of the prosecution or the plaintiff to proceed first and make a case. That burden in a criminal case is "proof beyond reasonable doubt," while in a civil action it is "proof by mere preponderance of evidence." In a larger sense, burden of proof is more than a procedural rule; it is a time-tested device to protect the integrity of the individual. Were it not for this

[12] G. Cronkhite, "The Locus of Presumption," *Central States Speech Journal*, XVII, No. 4 (1966), 270–276.

protection, anyone might be continually harrassed and called upon to answer irresponsible and unsupported accusations. Under this protection, the accused may stand upon his presumption and say to the accuser, "Prove it." This seems at times to aid the "obviously guilty," but, as Sir William Blackstone once said, "'It is better that ten guilty persons escape than that one innocent suffer.'"

Burden of proof means the risk of the proposition, and it entails on the part of the affirmative the duty to affirm the issues. This is another way of saying that the affirmative has the responsibility to submit a prima facie case (as defined in Chapter 10). Failure to affirm *one* contested issue usually means defeat for the prosecution or the plaintiff, especially in a trial before a judge or judges. For instance, the Justice Department lawyers tried for nearly three years to prove seventeen investment banks guilty of a conspiracy to monopolize the securities business, but all they could show was some parallel behavior. When a deliberate conspiracy could not be proved, Judge Medina ruled that the defense did not have to present its side. Similarly, in the DuPont-General Motors case, Judge La Buy ruled that the Government failed to prove conspiracy to restrain trade. Finally, in the Crest Theater case, Justice Clark spoke for the majority in ruling that proof of parallel business behavior does not also prove conspiratorial agreement. Thus the affirmatives failed by losing *one* issue. They did not make prima facie cases.

The legal concept of burden of proof is sometimes hard for laymen to understand. For instance, there was the case of a juror in a murder trial who, despite the judge's instructions to vote "not guilty" or "guilty of first-degree murder," voted "second-degree murder" because she had some doubts about the prisoner's guilt. In effect this juror gave the affirmative a partial victory for proving part of its case. Her confusion about burden of proof becomes more comprehensible when we observe how it operates in the regulatory field. After six airlines made a mutual-aid pact to minimize losses due to strikes, the Civil Aeronautics Board challenged them to prove that their pact would not reduce competition in that industry. Most of us would assume that the burden of proof belonged on the accuser's side.

Perhaps it is just as well that our main concern is with burden of proof as a convention in argumentation as distinguished from a legal one. There are, however, five points of similarity between the two: the extent of the burden varies somewhat with circumstances; in the event of a negative counterproposition, each side is responsible for proving its own case; the affirmative must preponderate to win, whereas the negative needs only to balance the affirmative; each side in turn must maintain its burden of proceeding, as explained below; the burden of proof on the original proposition is on the affirmative and does not shift to the negative.

But placing the burden of proof on the affirmative does not relieve the negative of responsibility. The opponents of a proposition of policy have several strategic options, as we shall see under "Cases," but each kind of negative case entails some responsibility to make arguments. The negative may elect to show that the present situation is not so bad as the affirmative alleges, or it may show faults in the affirmative plan, or it may support an alternative proposal or counterproposition. Suppose that the affirmative calls for statehood for Puerto Rico. The negative has four or five choices, depending on how they are defined, but the three most likely ones are: (1) to argue that the present status of Puerto Rico creates no hardship, (2) to contend that statehood would bring more troubles than benefits, or (3) to propose independence for Puerto Rico.

What happens to the burden of proof when the negative offers a counterproposition? One writer, having found conflicting views on this question in eleven books published before 1961, attempted to clarify the matter.[13] Without getting into the details of judging an academic debate at this time, we might examine his proposed reformulation of theory in relation to general argumentation. He first cites some references which say that the affirmative has *the* burden of proof on the original proposition throughout the debate, that the negative has *a* burden of proof on its counterproposition, and that the affirmative's burden is the greater. But next he cites one reference which says the negative must support a claim that its plan is the better. Thus he concludes that when the two rival plans are in equipoise, the affirmative has met its responsibility.

The last two sentences are open to question on several counts. In the "five points of similarity" listed three paragraphs back, it was explained that the affirmative must preponderate. Next, the assertion that the negative must claim superiority for its plan is mistaken. It is the affirmative that must be prepared to show that a situation needs a remedy and that a plan expressed or implied in the proposition is the best solution. Otherwise the affirmative could not cope with any counterproposition the negative might offer. The object of the negative is to

---

[13] W. Thompson, "The Effect of a Counterplan Upon the Burden of Proof," *Central States Speech Journal*, XIII, No. 5 (1962), 247–252.

block the affirmative case. Thus, if the negative plan is "just as good" as the affirmative's, the affirmative has not entirely met its burden of proof, but the negative has met its responsibility.

Even assuming that the tie situation should occur, which is unlikely, there are two additional objections to the proposed new rule on burden of proof. One is the appeal to the jurisprudential analogy which would have academic debate governed by one kind of courtroom practice. The second is the doubtful premise that burden of proof and prima facie case are less important to good debating than reasoning, issues, evidence, attack and defense, and language are. While it is true that some persons make a fetish of the prima facie case, we should recognize that analysis, evidence, and reasoning are used to build a case; and if it is not logically adequate, there is some inadequacy in the three elements which comprise it as well as at least half of the customary criteria for judging a school debate.

The position of this work is that, in the event of a counterproposition (a plan so inconsistent with the affirmative's that they dare not accept it), each side is responsible for proving its own case, but the affirmative must preponderate, if ever so slightly, to win. In the event of a so-called tie, the negative will have discharged its burden, but the affirmative will not have discharged the burden of proof on the main proposition. Four contemporary textbooks disagree with this view; they require the negative counterproposition in academic debate to be shown superior to the affirmative plan.[14]

In short, burden of proof is here taken to mean the logical and ethical responsibility adequately to affirm any assertion which turns out to be controversial. Such assertions (propositions) typically but not necessarily oppose existing institutions, prevalent beliefs, cultural norms, or some other sort of status quo. Adequate affirmation usually means a primia facie case, because proof is here taken to mean that substance and structure sufficient to satisfy disinterested, intelligently critical observers.[15]

A few instances will illustrate the location of the burden of proof. As in the case of presumption, it is important to know how its opposite is located. The sides and their responsibilities are determined by this means. If someone is dissatisfied with the quarterly calendar at his institution, he may accept the burden to advocate the trimester or some

---

[14] McBath, Argumentation . . . , p. 116; Freeley, Argumentation . . . , p. 213; Ehninger and Brockriede, Decision . . . , p. 244; Windes and Hastings, Argumentation . . . , p. 77.

[15] See "Definitions of Proof" in Chapter I.

other scheme. Similarly, anyone who alleges that Mr. X is a Communist or something else that is locally disliked has the burden of proof until the fact becomes established. Suspicion, as in "Where there's smoke there's fire," does not relieve the asserter of his logical and ethical responsibility. Thus a person who makes any charge, accusation, complaint, or the like has the burden of proof if anyone chooses to question his claim. The "if" clause is added because it is idle to speak of burden of proof if nobody shows the slightest interest in the assertion.

Burden of Proceeding

Last among the basic responsibilities of advocates in a controversy is the burden of proceeding. It is also known as the burden of rebuttal or the burden of going forward with the argument. In judicial cases this responsibility can be enforced by the presiding judge, while in general argumentation it is done less formally and sometimes less strictly by adversaries or by listeners and readers. An example will show how the burden of proceeding appeared in a public controversy over the charge that the management of a county hospital was poor. The complainant (affirmative) made a case by arguing: (1) that poor hospital management could be measured by certain criteria such as research activities of the staff, training facilities, range of services, reputation among physicians, and overcrowding, and (2) that the hospital in question deserved a poor rating on those counts. Since these matters were developed by evidence and reasoning, we should say that the affirmative met its responsibility known as the burden of proof, thereby undermining the presumption which favored the negative before the dispute began. At this juncture the burden of proceeding has been shifted to the negative side. Now suppose the negative replies by showing that the criteria are improper, or, even if they are proper, that the hospital does not rate poorly in terms of them. At this point the burden of proceeding has been shifted back to the affirmative.

This exchange could go on indefinitely, but enough has been reported to warrant some generalizations about the burden of proceeding. One is that this responsibility can shift and does so in a good debate. As we saw above, after an affirmative has discharged its burden of proof by giving a logically adequate case, the negative is under obligation to reply in an attempt to balance the affirmative case or possibly to outweigh it. If it succeeds in doing either, the burden of proceeding shifts to the affirmative. Then the affirmative has to overpower the negative rejoinder or fall behind at this point. A second observation is that the number of shifts of this responsibility is limited only by existing rules, the persistence of the contestants, the resolution of the problem, or the patience of those who could stop the exchange. We know that the number of "turns" is arbitrarily determined by rules in some legislative assemblies and in most judicial and school debates.

In the customary tournament format, an academic debate proceeds according to a set order of speeches: first affirmative constructive speech, first negative constructive speech, second affirmative construction speech, second negative constructive speech, first negative rebuttal speech, first affirmative rebuttal speech, second negative rebuttal speech, and second affirmative rebuttal speech. Because of the rules of the contest, the first negative constructive speaker has the burden of proceeding whether the first affirmative has made an adequate case or not. The burden of proceeding shifts from side to side, starting with the first negative constructive, who usually follows the presentation of somewhat more than the first half of the affirmative team's case. The second affirmative constructive speech completes the case. Shifts in the burden of proceeding follow a set pattern in academic debate. The negative may not delay its reply until the affirmative case is complete; the first speaker's portion of the affirmative's case must be answered forthwith.

Some textbooks omit this topic, but those that treat it are in general agreement on how it should be discussed. One exception to this consensus is the assertion that the burden of going forward starts with the affirmative and calls upon that side to discharge its burden of proof with a prima facie case.[16] It will be recalled that the consensus places the burden of rebuttal (or of proceeding) upon the negative initially, but not until the affirmative has either made a logically adequate case or has done as much toward that goal as the rules or conventions of the situation require.

ETHICAL RESPONSIBILITY
OF AN ADVOCATE

Whether an advocate communicates in a political campaign, a deliberative assembly, a philosophical dispute, a courtroom, or a school

---

[16] Ehninger and Brockriede, *Decision* . . . , pp. 85–87.

debate—whether he seeks a critical decision or a popular vote—he has an ethical responsibility to give the cause the representation it deserves. This means that once he espouses the cause, he is under a moral obligation to make the best case he can in terms of the assumptions, evidence, and reasoning which are both available and legitimate. One writer distinguishes between the responsibility for the consequences of the advocated proposition and the responsibility for the method of argument he employs.[17]

Obviously this principle rules out the philosophy of "win at any cost" or "victory by fair means or foul." The use of fallacious stratagems, lies, misquotations, and the suppression of evidence is reprehensible, according to this view, and letting someone get away with such behavior is deplorable. Debate is designed to expose such deficiencies in proof, as we shall see in the materials on the tests of evidence, the tests of reasoning, and the tactics of attack and defense. It is not difficult to detect defects in proof, but it is quite another matter to establish culpable intent.

Much of what is said about the ethical responsibility to represent a cause competently stems from the adversary system which characterizes trial procedures in the Western world. The prosecutor or the lawyer for the plaintiff is supposed to try his best, and so is his opponent. From this clash we expect justice to emerge.[18] So important is this clash situation deemed to be that the court will appoint counsel if someone cannot pay for his own, and any case, however unpopular in the community, is supposedly assured of representation. This latter point was forcefully illustrated by the efforts of Robert Servatius to defend Adolph Eichmann in an Israeli court against charges of responsibility for the massacre of millions of Jews during Hitler's regime.

But our system doesn't always work this way.[19] Some legal scholars have pointed out that occasional cases go unrepresented or poorly represented either because of the poverty of the defendant or the unpopularity of his side. Unpopular cases sometimes fail to attract lawyers at any price because of the fear of social and economic reprisals stemming from the typical citizen's inability to distinguish between the offense charged and the constitutional guaranty of defense. And some-

[17] T. R. Nilsen, "Ethics and Argument," in *Perspectives* . . . , Miller and Nilsen, p. 181.

[18] See Joseph N. Welch, "Should a Lawyer Defend a Guilty Man?" *This Week Magazine*, December 6, 1959, p. 9.

[19] See last Exercise in Chapter 1.

times local feeling runs so high that the excesses of zealous prosecutors go unchecked. For instance, in 1967 the United States Supreme Court upset the 1955 conviction of an alleged rape-murderer, who was once within seven hours of the electric chair, on the ground that "the prosecution deliberately misrepresented the truth."[20] It seems reasonable to conclude from this evidence that society, as well as the advocates, has an ethical responsibility here.

This ethical responsibility of an advocate to represent his cause the best he can is similar to his logical responsibility, which is to secure a commitment based on intellectually defensible grounds. Even though he starts with emotionally toned assumptions and value judgments, he should expound their logical consequences in a form of proof. In the instance of value judgments it is important to take account of their hierarchy of salience or importance to those concerned. Some values rank above others, as when social status takes precedence over thrift as an end to be served by the purchase of a house, a car, or a television set. One's philosophy of proof affects ethical responsibility, too. If popular persuasion is the accepted goal, the ethical problem is potentially great, because it is so easy to salve one's conscience with the assurance that the end justifies the means. More will be said of both logical and ethical responsibilities in relation to the several kinds of debate.

KINDS OF DEBATE

Debate has here been defined at some length in order to take account of six aspects of the phenomenon. This type of discourse occurs in a variety of settings, each of which affects the procedures, goals, and responsibilities of the parties in discernible ways; therefore, it seems useful to classify debates as political, legislative, philosophical, judicial, and academic. These class names are useful but not necessarily mutually exclusive or all-inclusive. Even so, one can explain each kind and particularize the ethical and logical responsibilities of the participants. But first it is worth noting that all five kinds involve the ethical responsibility to make the best case one can in terms of available and legitimate assumptions, evidence, and reasoning.

[20] *Chicago Daily News*, February 13, 1967.

Political Debate

Political or campaign debate takes place when rival candidates contend for nomination or election, and when controversial public questions are referred to the citizenry for decision. In this kind there are the fewest procedural regulations. What few limitations there are can be seen in the laws relating to elections and libel and slander.

Often the demands in terms of probability, presumption, burden of proof, and burden of proceeding are less rigorous than they are in the other kinds of debate. True, the objective is a decision, but it is typically sought with the use of popular persuasion rather than rigorous argumentation. When rival spokesmen do not confront each other on the same platform or in the same publication, there are only some listeners' or readers' critical faculties to satisfy. Obviously there is nothing so salutary as the presence of a competent adversary. When a confrontation of peers occurs, the ethical and logical responsibilities are more likely to be met, because each rival fears the exposure of his weakness.

The Lincoln-Douglas and the Kennedy-Nixon political debates are familiar, at least by name, to many persons. It is generally agreed among those who know the debates well that the latter were inferior to the former. It must be conceded, however, that the 1960 debates started a fad among rival candidates at all levels to debate for the approval of the voters.

Legislative Debate

Deliberate assemblies use legislative debate in reaching decisions on matters of policy concerning which motions are made. Many think of Congress as the place where legislative debating goes on. They are correct, but they would be equally right in naming countless other situations, down to the lowliest local committee meeting. One relationship between political and legislative debate can be a source of embarrassment to a politician; he may make a promise while campaigning, but after election he may not be able to make good on it.

Legislative debate in the United States Senate is not strictly structured, and some say it is not really debate, but one student of the process who thinks it is makes four analytical points about it: (1) The opening, expository stages serve to inform the members concerning the bill before the Senate. (2) Senate debate can be used to attract public attention to a measure, to allow time for opinions to change, to delay action, and so on. (3) Senate debate enables the minority to record its opposition in the *Congressional Record*. (4) It cannot always be interpreted as functional persuasion, because there is no telling what determines the final vote.[21]

Writing on public speaking and the legislative process in the California legislature, an observer lists six ways in which speech operates: direct persuasion, expository persuasion, personal persuasion, speaking for the outside audience, achieving long-range attitude formation, and serving to perfect the legislation.[22]

While it is true that some legislative debating is incredibly poor according to our critical standards, the fact is that speakers in situations where parliamentary procedure is involved find it more difficult to ignore the burden of proof and the burden of proceeding than participants in political debates which involve no confrontation. Space does not permit an adequate explanation of parliamentary procedure or rules of order at this time, but there are specialized, standard works on the subject.[23]

Philosophical Debate

Most of us will agree, once we think about it, that there are many informal, decisionless controversies in real life which cannot be classified as political, legislative, judicial, or school debates. Every college generation as far back as we have heard of has engaged in informal discussions and debates about more or less philosophical questions such as "Is politics a worthwhile career?" "Are grades overrated?" "Is the administration paternalistic?" and the old standbys, religion and sex. Frequently the controversies deal with value judgments, and understanding more often than victory is the goal.

[21] E. Cain, "Debate in Modern Politics: The United States Senate," The American Forensic Association *Register*, XI, No. 1 (1963), 1–6.

[22] H. E. Knepprath, "Speech In the Legislative Process," *Today's Speech*, XIV, No. 4 (1966), 13–16.

[23] See P. A. Carmack, "Evolution in Parliamentary Procedure," *Speech Teacher*, XI (1962), 26–39; A. F. Sturgis, *Standard Code of Parliamentary Procedure* (New York: McGraw-Hill Book Co., 1950); H. M. Roberts, *Rules of Order*, Revised (Chicago: Scott, Foresman and Co., 1951); J. F. O'Brien, *Parliamentary Law for the Layman* . . . , (New York: Harper and Bros., 1952).

Strictly speaking, philosophical argumentation is more closely related to dialectic than it is to the persuasive applications of argumentation.[24] The use of philosophical debate to classify the many miscellaneous controversies which would not be so considered by a philosopher is justified on the ground that it meets a need and apparently does no harm.

When a dialectical give-and-take involves good minds, there is a testing of the consequences of premises which might profitably take place more often in the other four kinds of debate. From this observation we may readily infer that the burden of proceeding is well taken care of, even though the placement of presumption and burden of proof may not be clear to the participants.

Judicial Debate

What the ancients called forensic speaking is the judicial debate which today takes place in courts of law. Contrary to the impression gained by many "whodunit" addicts, this kind of debating, which takes a small fraction of the time of the typical law firm, is concerned with such matters as facts, laws, and decisions.

Of all the kinds of debate, this one is the most demanding with respect to evidence, presumption, burden of proof, and burden of proceeding. There are rules governing all of these matters, and judges are expected to enforce them. It is unfortunate that many persons think these rules apply in the same way to the other four kinds of debate. We hear them say, "You couldn't prove that in court." The obvious reply is that we aren't in court when we participate in nonlegal debates.

Most legal controversies are on so-called questions of fact, but there are some of value judgments and policy decisions. The two sides in this adversary situation are, as previously stated, the plaintiff (in civil actions) or the prosecution (in criminal actions) and the defendant. These correspond to affirmative and negative, respectively. Decisions are rendered by judges or juries.

There are occasions when judicial debating takes on the character of another kind. Andrew Hamilton, Thomas Erskine, and Clarence Darrow excelled in modifying a forensic situation (whether the facts fit a legal definition of a crime) into a deliberative one (whether the

---

[24] M. Natanson, "Rhetoric and Philosophical Argumentation," *Quarterly Journal of Speech*, XLVIII (1962), 24–30.

accused should be declared guilty).[25] In terms of the next chapter, this is akin to shifting from a proposition of legal fact to one of policy.

Academic Debate

When the word "debate" is mentioned to students who have heard of academic or school debate, they typically assume that the tournament variety is meant. They are less accustomed to thinking of judicial and philosophical encounters as debates. This association or argumentation with school debate dates back to the establishment of the first collegiate courses in argumentation, as we noted in Chapter 1.

School debates can be structured so as to simulate any of the other four kinds. In fact, the educational version is intended to prepare students for participation in the real-life kinds of debate. However, because of this educational aim, the canons of criticism and the type of decision rendered are unlike those in real-life situations. More will be said of this later, but for the present it is well to know that school debates are often judged by critics who apply criteria of excellence instead of voting for the side they agree with.

As we should expect, the presence of a critic-judge and presumably skilled opponents tends to make the participants more careful in their handling of the ethical and logical responsibilities which have been discussed in this chapter. Perhaps the similarity to judicial debate is exaggerated in current practice,[26] but that can be corrected in time.

Although this textbook is not intended as a how-to-debate manual for tournament competitors, it seems appropriate to treat briefly three topics which are of some general interest. In fact, the first two are certain to bear upon the general students' study, practice, and evaluation of debate. The third may relate to the oral practice exercises. These topics are strategy, unethical practices, and some varieties of academic debate.

Strategy has interested military men, players of games, merchandisers, lawyers, lovers, politicians, and debaters for centuries, but it was not until 1922 that a prominent collegiate textbook on argumentation

[25] J. W. Bowers, "Deliberative Speech in a Forensic Context: Andrew Hamilton at the Peter Zenger Trial," *Central States Speech Journal*, XVI, No. 3 (1965), 164–172.

[26] J. L. Robinson, "Are We 'Overlegalizing' School Debate?" *The Speech Teacher*, IX (1960), pp. 109–115.

and debate featured a chapter on strategy.[27] Shaw defines it by saying, "Strategy in debate, like strategy in war, consists in arranging and directing one's forces in such a way as to gain an unexpected advantage over an adversary in respect to the conditions of fighting." Some of his ten devices are "Retreat," "Evading Traps," "Withholding Reserves," "Skirmishing," and "Bottling Up the Enemy." In 1940 a former school debater wrote a short, sophistic book on this subject. "This information is so valuable," he wrote, "that we were too selfish to publish it while in school."[28] Among his thirty-odd stratagems are "You Can Prove Anything," "Splitting Hairs," "Some Good Fallacies To Try Sometime," "Getting Between Your Opponent and the Truth," "The Resurrection of the Dead," and "Waving the Red Flag."

Tricks such as these involve questions of ethical responsibility which are recurrent for directors and debaters. A survey among college debaters revealed the practices which they rejected as unethical, the practices they said occurred often, and those they thought wise to use. The five practices most opposed by the subjects involved the misuse of evidence: manufacturing evidence, violating the intention of a quotation, changing the source, misrepresenting the significance of an item, and misrepresenting the competence of a source. The debaters' estimates of the occurrence of practices involving ethical considerations ranked these as the most frequent: scouting of possible opponents' cases, misquoting opponents, appealing to judges' known prejudices, misrepresenting the significance of an item of proof, and using a trick case. Finally, the practices endorsed as wise include scouting, appealing to prejudice, misquoting, and using a trick case.[29] Apparently misquoting an opponent is slightly rejected, often occurring, and a rather wise stratagem, according to these data.

When some debate instructors were surveyed on similar questions, they disagreed on what practices to label unethical, but more than half said sixteen practices were either questionable or downright unethical. Three practices concerned the coaches' doing the debaters' work (research, case outlining, and speech writing), two involved scouting, three were sharp practices with evidence and definitions, three indicated bad

[27] Shaw, *The Art of Debate*, pp. 365–402.

[28] R. E. Harlan, Jr., *Strategic Debating* (Boston: Chapman and Grimes, 1940), p. 9.

[29] C. E. Larson and K. Giffin," Ethical Considerations in the Attitudes and Practices of College Debaters," *Journal of the American Forensic Association*, I, No. 3 (1964), 86–90.

platform manners, three represented crafty maneuvers (delayed refutation, stalling in cross-examination, and raising new issues in rebuttal), and two indicated the professional incompetence of some judges (giving legislative votes or voting for a friend's team).[30]

Two published studies of the actual practices of intercollegiate debaters in the use of evidence shed additional light on this serious problem of ethical responsibility of advocates. One study reports on 100 citations of evidence by sixteen debaters in four intercollegiate tournament debates. Fifty were validly represented, forty-two were unverifiable, five were either misrepresented or violated in context, and three were either manufactured or quoted from nonexistent sources.[31] Another analysis of transcribed material shows that in a final debate of the West Point Tournament, twenty-six unethical abuses of evidence were found among seventy-one citations. These included three outright fabrications and twenty-three misrepresentations.[32] Some of the apparent dishonesty stemmed from the uncritical use of evidence cards which had been carelessly or dishonestly prepared by less experienced members of the debate squads.

Several varieties of academic debate are available for use on platforms, on television, and in the classroom. Specific details on speaking orders, time limits, and other procedural matters can be found in the several modern textbooks which have been cited thus far.[33] Perhaps the most widely used varieties are the traditional, the cross-examination, the direct-clash, the parliamentary, and the short forms for television or classroom exercises.

[30] D. Klopf and J. McCroskey, "Ethical Practices in Debate," *Journal of the American Forensic Association*, I, No. 1 (1964), 13–16.

[31] See footnote 29.

[32] R. P. Newman and K. R. Sanders, "A Study In the Integrity of Evidence," *Journal of the American Forensic Association*, II, No. 1 (1965), 7–13.

[33] McBurney and Mills, *Argumentation* . . . , pp. 340–344 and 349–354; Bauer, *Fundamentals* . . . , pp. 9–10 and 82–84; McBath, *Argumentation* . . . , pp. 285–292 and 296–299; Freeley, *Argumentation* . . . , pp. 325–330.

QUESTIONS

1. What is involved when one says, "A lawyer should not defend a guilty person?"

   What if he has been found guilty in court, or what if his so-called "guilt" is merely a public opinion?

   What if the defense counsel tries to prove innocence? Or what if he only *tests* the prosecutor's case?

2. What went wrong with the probability inferences in this anecdote? When Joe and Bill came back to school after Christmas, each noticed that the other was wearing a new watch. They fell to guessing and arguing about the comparative prices of their gifts, and they agreed to settle the dispute by checking prices at a local store. They agreed that the man who "won" i.e., had the more expensive watch, would give his to the "loser." Both men reasoned thus: "My chances of winning or of losing are even. If I win, I shall be poorer by the price of my watch; but if I lose, I am certain to gain a more expensive watch. Hence the bet is advantageous to me."

3. An article in the April 1960 *Reader's Digest* urged the abolition of professional boxing, alleging that fights are "fixed" and that unsavory characters actually control the business behind "front men." The Illinois Athletic Commission subpoenaed the author to substantiate his allegations. Was that action proper in relation to the doctrine of presumption and burden of proof?

4. Suppose that the proponents of fluoridation of the water supply in Bumpkin Center argue that the natural fluoride in the local water is insufficient to retard tooth decay in children, and that the artificial fluoridation of that water supply would reduce decay and introduce no harmful side-effects. They quote endorsements by the American Dental Association, the American Medical Association, and the U.S. Public Health Service. They also cite the studies conducted in Grand Rapids, Newburgh, Brantford, Jacksonville, Evanston, and elsewhere. In fact, they refer to 8,500 separate research reports which support the belief that fluoridation can prevent tooth decay and is harmless to public health. Should this suffice to discharge the burden of proof for the time being? If so, what must the opposition do to discharge its burden of proceeding? However, if the affirmative case above is judged to be logically inadequate, what more is needed to make it adequate?

5. In connection with the controversy over automobile-safety legislation, an editorial contributed this blockbuster: "American auto manufacturers

have an outstanding engineering record, and say what you will they already build the safest cars in the world." (*Wall Street Journal*, February 3, 1967.) Comment upon this claim in relation to the logical and the ethical responsibilities of the writer.

6. Early in 1967, Tennessee was the only state in the Union that had a state law prohibiting the teaching of evolution. Suppose that someone desired to move about the country stirring up controversies about the teaching of evolution. For what sort of assertion on the subject would he have had the burden of proof in Tennessee? In some other state?

7. It is common knowledge that the advocate with the greater popularity, reputation, or presentational skill often is the more persuasive. Why do you think this is not explained in this chapter?

EXERCISES

1. Read "Trial By Newspaper" in the February, 1949, *Scientific American*. Discuss its implications for the concepts treated in this chapter (ethical responsibility, probability, presumption, burden of proof, etc.).

2. Select for comment a current controversy or one in the Appendixes. How well do the advocates meet their ethical responsibilities?

3. Choose a controversy as in Exercise 2 above. Who had the presumption and who had the burden of proof at the outset? Evaluate the work of the two sides in terms of discharging the burden of proof and the burden of proceeding. If the last speaker or writer in your specimen debate could be followed by a new opponent, what would you have that new opponent say?

4. One or more students might be assigned to read one of the Lincoln-Douglas debates in P. M. Angle, ed., *Created Equal?* (Chicago: University of Chicago Press, 1958). Others might be assigned to read some of the four Kennedy-Nixon encounters in S. Kraus (ed.) *The Great Debates* (Bloomington: Indiana University Press, 1962). After the reviews have been heard, the class might profitably discuss the comparative merits of these specimens of political debate.

5. Read the Welch item cited in footnote No. 18, if available, and compare his view of the adversary system with that of D. Dressler, "Trial by Combat in American Courts," *Harper's Magazine*, Vol. 222, No. 1331 (1961), pp. 31–36.

6. According to the 1929 Warsaw convention, international airlines are presumed at fault in any crash and must bear the legal burden of proving otherwise. Comment on this in relation to the doctrine of presumption and burden of proof as set out in this chapter.

CHAPTER 4

PROPOSITIONS:

BASES OF CONTROVERSY

IN RESPONSE TO A TENSION-PRODUCING SITUATION, A DISSATISFIED PARTY might complain, "Why doesn't somebody *do* something about thieves and confidence men who pose as door-to-door solicitors?" Either a unilateral presentation or a debate must be *about* something, and that "something" is best expressed as a proposition. But in order to have a fruitful deliberation, the proposition must clearly state what the complainant has in mind. The "do something" question as stated above is an unsatisfactory basis of a controversy. It would be better, for instance, to demand legislation to license solicitors and door-to-door salesmen. Then all would know what is being proposed to meet a specific problem.

There are many controversies about what happened, what a present state of affairs is, and what value judgment befits a given situation. Not all controversies are about doing something. A few best-selling books either stirred up or popularized controversies in one year: *Unsafe at Any Speed, Rush to Judgment, Human Sexual Response, Between the Wars, Vinland Maps, Flying Saucers—Serious Business,* and *Death of a President.* Questions on financial pages posed these bases of controversies in the business community: "It advertising an economic waste?" "Should we outlaw trading stamps?" "Are labor unions too powerful?" "Have corporate mergers gone too far?" "Are stock exchanges gambling casinos?"

FORMS AND DEFINITIONS

Forms of Statement

In political or campaign debating, the subject or the basis of the controversy is usually implied; it can be inferred from the nature of the speaking or writing. Typically it is something like one of these: "Mr. X should be nominated (or elected)," or "Vote 'yes' on the bond issue." In court (judicial) proceedings, the basis of the controversy is usually stated in the form of the prosecutor's charge or the plaintiff's complaint. In school debates, the basis is almost always given explicit statement in the form of a resolution which has for more than sixty years been called a proposition: "*Resolved,* That the school-attendance requirement in Illinois should be raised to age seventeen." In legislative debates, the bases may be expressed in motions, bills, ordinances, and resolutions as illustrated below. Finally, in philosophical debates, the bases are not always exactly verbalized, but when they are, they are likely to be statements of opinion, questions, or phrases: "Self-reliance is an antiquated notion." "Should one practice Emerson's idea of self-reliance?" "Self-reliance as a personal philosophy."

MOTION

Mr. Chairman, I move that the report of the nominating committee be accepted.

BILL

Be it enacted by the Senate and the House of Representatives of the United States of America in Congress assembled, That . . .

ORDINANCE

It shall be unlawful for any person to show or exhibit, or cause to be shown or exhibited, any moving picture which is immoral or obscene, salacious or teaches false ethics, or which contains nakedness or suggestive dress, prolonged passionate love scenes, or scenes making crime, drunkenness or the use of narcotics attractive, or which depicts the commission of crime, the white-slave traffic or resistance to police authority, or scenes that are unduly horrible.

RESOLUTION (long form)

WHEREAS, The membership of the Association is confident that federal support, through the School Assistance Act of 1961, can be provided without federal control; and

WHEREAS, The survival and growth of our democratic way of life depend upon the quality of public education, and the people of this country desire and deserve high quality education for all children and youth consistent with the enduring ideals and aspirations of our nation; and

WHEREAS, The unprecedented increases in enrollment have created urgent needs for more classrooms, facilities and an increasing supply and qualified teachers; and

WHEREAS, Only four per cent of the gross national product is now being spent for education; and

WHEREAS, The Association recognizes the imperative need for additional finances for research and experimentation in education at the federal, state, and local levels; and

WHEREAS, Many states and local school districts have reached the point of saturation in financing public education; and

WHEREAS, We believe that this bill is sound and strong because it is only a money bill and does not attempt to settle other issues such as desegregation and the place of financial aid for parochial and other private schools; therefore, be it

RESOLVED, That the Association go on record as strongly supporting the School Assistance Act of 1961 (HR4970) and make its support known to the President of the United States, the Secretary of Health, Education, and Welfare, and to other appropriate persons.

Proposition Defined

"Proposition" is variously defined in dictionaries: something proposed, an indecent proposal, an undertaking, a logical expression in which the predicate says something true or false about the subject, a mathematical problem to be solved, and in rhetoric a subject to be discussed. Books on argumentation have pretty generally agreed for many years that the assertion which expresses the basis of a controversy shall be called a proposition. It may appear in any of the forms mentioned above.

It has been properly contended that a statement of a controversial judgment is not a proposition in a logical or a grammatical sense. Defining "proposition" by authority of several logic textbooks, one writer concludes that a debate resolution cannot be a proposition but must be a hypothesis.[1] Granted, it would be simpler for us if the "founding fathers" of argumentation had devised a wholly new set of names for their concepts. Instead, they borrowed and modified some terms from logic, law, rhetoric, dialectic, pedagogy, and other disciplines. The result, as viewed over a span of three-quarters of a century, has been quite satisfactory. It could be even better if all who communicate about argumentation would use the word "proposition" in the sense that it is defined here, rather than vainly insisting one discipline use the lexicon of another. It would also be helpful if writers and speakers on argumentation and debate would resist the temptation to use "topic" and "question" as precise equivalents of "proposition."

Two other definitions are of interest because of difficulties they pose. Whately's "judgment expressed in words"[2] is too general for argumentation, because there are many judgments which are not bases of controversy. This definition appeared in his book on logic. A recent work defines a proposition as "a conclusion about a controversy, a conclusion believed by the advocate and a conclusion the advocate wishes to persuade others to accept."[3] The last two of the three elements are open to reservations: academic debaters need not believe their proposition, and, as was explained earlier, persuasion is not always the object.

IMPORTANCE OF ISOLATING PROPOSITIONS

Essential in Analysis

While making oral or written preparations, an advocate needs to isolate the essence of the controversy and to state it in a proposition. If

[1] D. W. Shepard, "Logical Propositions and Debate Resolutions," *Central States Speech Journal*, XI (1960), 186–190.

[2] R. Whately, *Elements of Logic* (Boston: James Munroe and Company, 1843), p. 74.

[3] Windes and Hastings, *Argumentation* . . . , pp. 35–36.

the statement is only a catch phrase instead of a complete thought, he cannot satisfactorily define the terms, find the issues, determine his side and his proof responsibilities, or select his evidence and arguments. In sum, he cannot realistically expect to make the best possible case for his side if he hasn't clearly formulated the basis of the controversy.

When evaluating the advocacy of others, which is one of the principal uses of argumentation, it is again necessary to express the basis of the controversy in a complete sentence rather than a phrase. Before this can be done, it is necessary to ask whether the communicator is dissatisfied and consequently is initiating or joining in starting a controversy. If so, that party is on the affirmative side, and the proposition should express his view. Occasionally this determination is hard to make, because the author was not clear, or he argued more than one proposition, or the exact nature of the status quo is in doubt. The specimen below will serve to illustrate some of these problems.

"MAIL-ORDER FILTH"

In asking Congress for stronger laws to curb "mail-order filth," Postmaster General Summerfield also said that effective action will require the cooperation of an aroused citizenry.

That is a point which needs to be emphasized. Citizen cooperation is necessary to effective law enforcement; in the case of "mail-order filth," it is an absolute must. For these purveyors of pornography are preying on school age children, and it is the parents who can spot the stuff and turn it over to the postal authorities.

If the citizenry needs any arousing, Summerfield certainly painted a shocking picture of conditions as they now exist. "The sales volume of mail-order obscenity has doubled in the last five years," he told Senator Kefauver's subcommittee on juvenile delinquency. "Unless vigorously checked, it can double again over the next four years." In most cases, he added, the material is not ordered by the children but is sent to them because they happen to land on a mailing list.

Congress should strengthen the laws. The moral fiber of the nation's youth is endangered. And no one should be misled by what Summerfield called "pious cries of 'censorship,' 'freedom of the press,' 'civil liberties' and so forth." Liberty is not license.

Give the Post Office Department the weapons with which to fight those vile creatures who reap huge profits by using the mails to peddle obscenity.[4]

According to this editorial, the Postmaster General had stated a proposition which called upon Congress to enact legislation to curb "mail order filth." Apparently the Post Office Department would thereby receive additional authority to regulate the content of the mails.

[4] *The Salt Lake Tribune,* August 31, 1959.

This editorial joined the Postmaster General on the affirmative side, but in so doing it seemed to advocate a primary proposition and a secondary one. Before getting to the call for Congressional action, which was the intended proposition, the writer argued at greater length for a proposition calling for citizen cooperation. Of course the two are related, perhaps even vitally, but the matters of arrangement, style, and relative emphasis should not mislead the reader with respect to the proposition.

Although a proposition for debate contains one central idea, its support typically requires several subpropositions, otherwise known as points in partition. It is the business of analysis to find them, but this is difficult in the instance of a vague proposition. Thus it is necessary to isolate and state explicitly the proposition which will serve as the basis of the controversy.

Other Functions of Propositions

The importance of identifying or stating a proposition is attributable to the significant functions which it serves. These are not discrete or mutually exclusive functions, but each has enough meaning to justify its inclusion. First among these is to verbalize explicitly the basis of the controversy, be it a conviction or merely a kind of hypothesis offered for testing. A proposition should serve this purpose regardless of the formality or the informality of its statement. Thus a speaker or a writer is well advised to state the proposition for his own use, even if he does not announce it, because without it an intelligent discourse is unlikely. An explicit statement is even more necessary when both sides are to be represented on the same occasion; a controversy can rarely be kept on the point otherwise.

Another function of a proposition is to express the affirmative stand, thereby naming the sides and placing the presumption and the burden of proof. (The reader is referred to "presumption" and "burden of proof" in Chapter 3 and to a section on "Wording a proposition" near the end of this chapter.)

Finally, and this may be another way of expressing the preceding function, a proposition asserts a claim for acceptance. Anyone who offers a motion or a hypothesis for debate may phrase it, but he has a responsibility to make it clear. Should he fail to state his claim clearly, fairly, and reasonably, the negative may raise an objection, in no wise to be considered quibbling. The functions of a proposition, you can therefore see, are closely related to the problems of wording, which will be discussed a few pages hence.

KINDS OF PROPOSITIONS

Importance of Classification

A student might guess that the naming and classifying of propositions is a mere technicality, the purpose of which is to increase his burden. He might also conclude, after consulting several textbooks, that the names were chosen for reasons of personal taste rather than function. These are a few of the class names for propositions which he could find: fact, value, policy, belief, explanation, definition, theoretically sound, action, judgment, and variants of some of these. Both cynical views are mistaken. We classify propositions, not for whimsical reasons, but for analytic ones. We need to know what the potential issues are, as Chapter 5 explains, and we can more expeditiously analyze a proposition to discover its issues once we know what kind of proposition we are dealing with. Such is the consensus of the literature.

To this widely held opinion there is one dissenting view. We do not distinguish among kinds of propositions for purposes of analysis or because of differing proof requirements, according to one writer. "The choice of a given type of proposition is a rhetorical device designed to prepare the audience for a particular type of argument," he claims.[5] Some criticisms of this opinion will here be developed in relation to the kinds of propositions and in the next chapter in relation to analyzing those propositions. It will be explained and argued that the kind of proposition has a great deal to do with the analysis and the proof requirements of a given proposition.

Evolution of Classifications

Perhaps a historical perspective on this matter of classifying propositions will help to clarify the differences of opinion in our literature.

[5] G. Cronkhite, "Propositions of Past and Future Fact and Value: A Proposed Classification," *Journal of the American Forensic Association*, III, No. 1 (1966), 11–16.

Baker and Huntington in 1905[6] named no types of propositions, but they distinguished between conviction and persuasion as intentions of advocates. In effect, they classified propositions in terms of intent. In 1917, Foster devoted eleven pages to the phrasing of propositions, but it was not until 1932 that he classified propositions into fact and policy or principle.[7] Thus it appears that Shaw in 1922 was the first major writer to name the propositions of fact and of policy.[8] This was an innovation because it based a classification upon the nature of the matter in dispute rather than upon the intentions of the advocates. O'Neill, Laycock, and Scales followed Shaw's lead in 1927,[9] and a year later Baird used the same two and added a third, "advocated as theoretically sound," which resembles the "value" proposition of today.[10] In later editions he adopted the prevailing fact-policy dichotomy, which remained in vogue until Wagner in 1938 modified Baird's original tripartite scheme into fact (true or false), value (assess the worth), and policy (action).[11]

These three kinds of propositions are discussed in seven of eleven textbooks published since 1960.[12] The four books in the minority express as many classifications. Kruger uses a fourfold classification: fact (past, present, future), value, policy, and explanation ("The Versailles Treaty was largely responsible for Hitler's rise . . .").[13] Ehninger and Brockreide use fact, value, policy, and definition ("Equal" in "separate but equal" means . . .").[14] Windes and Hastings use two broad kinds, belief (description, establishing existence, and value judgments) and action (same as policy).[15] Miller and Nilsen have fact and value.[16]

Two articles in the journals propose additional schemes of classifi-

[6] G. P. Baker and H. B. Huntington, The Principles of Argumentation (Boston: Ginn and Co., 1905).

[7] W. T. Foster, Argumentation and Debating (Boston: Houghton Mifflin Co., 1932), p. 13.

[8] Shaw, The Art of Debate, pp. 20–21.

[9] J. M. O'Neill, C. Laycock, and R. L. Scales, Argumentation and Debating (New York: The Macmillan Co., 1927), p. 19.

[10] A. C. Baird, Public Discussion and Debate (Boston: Ginn and Co., 1928), pp. 41–42.

[11] Wagner, Handbook . . . , pp. 15–16.

[12] McBurney and Mills, Argumentation . . . , pp. 30–31; McBath, Argumentation . . . , pp. 49–50; Bauer, Fundamentals . . . , pp. 2–3; Freeley, Argumentation . . . , pp. 38–39; Moulton, Dynamics . . . , pp. 58–59; Capp and Capp, Argumentation . . . , pp. 55–56; Huber, Influencing . . . , pp. 17–19.

[13] Kruger, Modern Debate pp. 14–17.

[14] Ehninger and Brockriede, Decision . . . , pp. 218–228.

[15] Windes and Hastings, Argumentation . . . , pp. 53 and 218–226.

[16] Miller and Nilsen, Perspectives . . . , pp. 36–37.

cation. Terris prefers two kinds of propositions, of judgment (fact or value) and of policy.[17] His classification preceded the similar one immediately above. One difficulty in naming one kind "a judgment" is that *all* propositions for debate are judgments. The most recent classification, that by Cronkhite, represents the most noticeable deviation from the norm.[18] After deciding that value and policy are essentially alike, he arrives at four kinds of propositions: past or present fact, future fact, past or present value, and future value. One obviously important premise in this pattern of thought is that the temporal dimension is more important than others have believed it to be. This is doubtful. It is quite possible to have philosophical debates on timeless propositions of value which, when projected into the future, involve no call for action. Thus there is reason to reject the unqualified claim that what we know as a proposition of policy is only one of future value. "The United States should extend diplomatic recognition to Red China" is Cronkhite's example of "future value." It is alleged that this sort of proposition assigns or implies a value term and assumes a future resembling the past. On the contrary, the affirmative on Chinese recognition more often predicts a future essentially different from the past. It is further claimed that this proposition involves propositions of future fact, past fact, and audience values. It would be more accurate to say that a proposition of policy involves issues concerning facts, values, and so forth. This was explained at least as early as 1951,[19] when it was shown that the sequence of propositions (fact, value, policy) is based upon developmental complexity. The first is the simplest; it involves definition and classification. The second is more complex; it goes beyond the first and into criteria and their application. The last, which calls for action, includes the scope of the first two and goes beyond into matters of expediency, practicality, and the like.

Perhaps the pivotal premise in the proposed reformulation is that there is a greater difference between fact and value than between value and policy. Let us examine the propositions which allegedly illustrate this. The stated proposition of fact claims that an act harms others, that is, causes suffering for innocent persons. The stated proposition of value claims that the same act is immoral. Now suppose we substitute "is harmful" for "harms others." Only the level of abstraction is altered,

---

[17] W. F. Terris, "The Classification of the Argumentative Proposition," *Quarterly Journal of Speech*, XLIX, No. 3 (1963), 266–273.

[18] See footnote 5.

[19] McBurney, O'Neill, and Mills, *Argumentation* . . . , pp. 23–24.

but now the two propositions are alike; they assign the value terms "harmful" and "immoral," respectively. It has also been claimed that propositions of value focus on criteria, while propositions of fact focus on showing that the object of judgment matches the criteria. If we waive propositions of legal fact in which crimes and similar terms are already defined, this claim is as often wrong as right. Issues of definition-classification and of criteria-application are potential in propositions of fact and of value, respectively, and they are closely related. In fact, if we define criteria and application broadly enough, we can force *all* propositions into a single class and thereby reduce this whole business to an absurdity. This, of course, would seriously interfere with the analysis of propositions. (See Chapter 5.)

What is the upshot of this historical-critical survey? It seems as if some defensible scheme of classification should be forthcoming. In the light of what has been said, one could defend these classifications: fact-value-policy, belief-action, nonpolicy-policy, and perhaps judgment-policy. The choice for the purposes of this book is fact-value-policy, not only because it is the most familiar but also because it serves to call appropriate attention to the frequently slighted proposition of value.

Propositions of Fact

Four subtypes comprise this category. In each there is a considerable element of definition and classification. These four are legal fact, past fact, present fact, and future fact or prediction. In every case of a debatable proposition of fact, the asserted claim is not yet a fact; it is merely an *alleged* fact.

The first subtype is the proposition of fact in legal proceedings. Strictly speaking, "fact" implies objective verifiability as in the instance of the charge that A's wound was made by B's gun. But when it is contended that a committed act is definable as a felony, we have the additional problem of definition and classification, which involves inference beyond raw fact. If the proposition asserts that the committed act was justified, we have added a value dimension. Finally, if the case turns upon the question of whether capital punishment should be employed, a policy dimension has been added. Returning to the simplest form of the legal proposition of fact, we can observe that definition and classification are involved. In each case there are two basic questions:

What did the party in question do? Is it definable as loitering, slander, or whatever the allegation stated?

Z Company is engaging in an unfair labor practice.
John Dough's Bakery is violating the health ordinance.
X injured Y's professional reputation by slandering him.
Federal intervention in local school affairs is unconstitutional.
Mr. X is (allegedly) guilty of grand theft.

A second subtype is the proposition of past fact. It asserts a controversial claim concerning a past event. Its analysis involves two questions similar to those immediately above: What would be required to establish the alleged fact? Do our available data meet this requirement?

President Lincoln's party was split over the purpose of the war.
Bacon wrote some of the literature attributed to Shakespeare.
A Russian invented the airplane.
Lack of securities regulation was a minor factor in the Great Depression.
The Norse were first to reach North America.

Third among the subcategories of definition and classification is the proposition of present fact. It makes a controversial claim concerning a current situation. Here we would ask the same preliminary analytical questions that are given for the past-fact propositions above.

"Obscene" in the municipal censorship ordinance means "immoral in the opinion of the ordinary person."
The party in power is responsible for the civil disorders.
Many businessmen really do not want free enterprise.
Crime comics induce juvenile delinquency.
Moral standards are in a decline.

A fourth subtype is the proposition of future fact, better known as a prediction. Again we would ask what evidence would be necessary to make the prediction probably true, and whether we have such evidence. These are specimen predictions:

Deficit financing will result in an accelerated growth rate in our economy.
Extensive broadening of the Social Security system will socialize the United States.
Mass education at the collegiate level will reduce the quality of higher education.

The current trend in the financial support of science and technology by government and foundations will retard the comparative growth of the other disciplines.

An increase in the prime rate of interest will retard business growth.

Propositions of Value

Evaluative claims involve criteria and their application. The appropriate analytical questions ask what criteria or standards apply and whether the matter in question meets those criteria. In this kind of proposition, as distinguished from most of the above examples, the criteria are subjectively determined. Notice, however, that propositions of fact and those of value are sometimes similar, and they are analyzed in nearly the same way. These are mainly evaluative claims:

The military draft is unfair.
Categorical prohibition of abortion is inhumane.
Materialism is an unworthy philosophy of life.
Big-time football is out of place on a university campus.
The U.N. is not worth its cost to us.

Propositions of Policy

In legislative and school debating, and perhaps in political debating, this kind of proposition predominates. It calls for a change of policy; it proposes some action. Typically the word "should" is used, as we see in the specimens below. This word implies that the action *could* be taken, but not that it will be taken.

A proposition of policy is, generally speaking, more complex than the others. The simplest, but not necessarily the easiest, involves the proof of a factual claim. Above this in complexity is the subtype which involves not only facts but also standards of judgment. The proposition of policy involves facts and values, but it extends into expediency, practicality, and action. These are typical specimens:

The Federal Government should subsidize the higher education of superior students.

Fraternity pledging should be deferred until the sophomore year.
Athletic grants-in-aid should be abolished.
School marks should be "pass" and "no credit."
Peace-keeping activities should be conducted by the U.N. exclusively.

SOURCES OF PROPOSITIONS

Propositions are formulated and expressed by persons who wish either to advocate a controversial point of view or to set it out as a kind of hypothesis to be tested. The question of source actually asks under what circumstances a person or a group becomes identified with a proposition. Some propositions arise from disputes over what the facts are, still more from interpretations of accepted evidence, and obviously a great many from differences in values.

One source is the situation in which a problem gives rise to one or more proposed solutions in a group meeting. When this happens, motions or their equivalents are debated. This is true whether the problem comes up in a regular meeting, or whether the group has been formed ad hoc in response to the problem. While the General Assembly of the National Council of Churches was considering what stand it should take on war and peace, several resolutions were proposed, debated, amended, and either passed or defeated. One resolution or proposition called for widespread debate by the American people on the questions of overseas military commitments. This is typical of the way propositions develop in meetings.

Another source of a proposition might be an individual's reaction to a disturbance of his equilibrium, so to speak. A citizen might be so irritated by a sound truck during a political campaign that he would attend the local council meeting and demand the passage of an ordinance to ban such advertising. Or an aggrieved party might bring suit against someone for libel, for instance. Two liberal theologians in South Africa sued a conservative theologian for libel on the ground that he had injured them by accusing them of seeking to overthrow the existing order in league with the World Council of Churches, black African "barbarism," and the Communists. What started as a proposition of legal fact soon became a debate on church policy and, even more fundamentally, a theological dispute over social gospel *vs.* fundamentalism.[20]

A third source might be the circumstances of employment or one's involvement in some activity. In this situation the proposition, and perhaps even one's side, would probably be assigned. When an advertising agent or a lawyer is retained by a client, the proposition and the side are not matters of independent choice; they are imposed by circumstances. Both the proposition and the side are likewise imposed upon anyone who is made a defendant in a legal action. In school debating, the propositions are in most situations selected by national committees. The individual director may cast one of hundreds of votes, but his student debaters may have no direct voice in the selection process.

This explanation of sources of propositions does not imply that the basis of a specific controversy arises suddenly, although it may. More often than not there is a developmental process. Take the case of a person who reads on page one of a Chicago daily newspaper these two headlines: "We Are World's Richest City" and "Rats Killed Baby, His Mother Insists." If the reader is actively concerned with such situations, he may brood about it, communicate with others, and perhaps try to stir up organized effort of some sort. Causes will be imputed, remedies will be proposed, and discussions and debates will take place. Perhaps the mass media will take up the controversy, and a large following may develop. What began as a local proposition may reach state or even national forums.

SELECTION OF A PROPOSITION

Whenever a person has a choice of problem areas or of stated propositions, he has at his disposal several criteria to guide his choice. At this stage, before the wording of propositions has been discussed, the selection of a proposition refers in the main to the business of selecting a problem area in which a resolution will be framed. For our present purpose, four broadly stated criteria will suffice.

One is that the problem should be worthy of debate, that is,

[20] *The New York Times*, March 19, 1967.

controversial and significant or interesting. It is not worthwhile to select a problem which is likely to produce emotional ravings or shallow speculations. More satisfaction stems from a controversy which calls forth the best efforts of the participants.

Another criterion is that the problem be suited to the advocate's interests, information, and convictions. A speaker or a writer is well advised to select a problem area or a stated proposition from the fields in which his background enables him to communicate something worthy of attention. School debaters, of course, have to develop a specific background *after* the proposition has been given to them. If the official proposition doesn't suit a student, and if there is no alternative, he may drop out of the activity.

The third standard is that the problem or the proposition be potentially interesting to the intended audience. This implies audience analysis and adaptation to discover what is timely, ego-involving, and comprehensible. In addition, the affirmation of one of these questions is likely to indicate the interest value of a proposition: Is it possible to solve? Is it possible to convince some persons of this? Is it possible to stimulate critical thinking about this? The last question is especially relevant in the instance of a philosophical proposition.

Finally, the problem or proposition should be adaptable to the occasion. As is the case with any subject for whatever purpose, there are common-sense criteria of appropriateness. While it is possible that the same problem area or specific proposition would be adaptable to a classroom exercise, an intercollegiate debate, or a public lecture, it is probable that one choice would not be equally wise in all three situations. Then too, some kinds of propositions (such as policy) are better suited than others to certain kinds of debates (such as philosophical or political). The legislative context typically calls for a policy proposition, the judicial calls most often for a factual determination, the philosophical calls for a debate on values, and the school debate is almost always based upon a proposition of policy. If the speaking time or the space in print is limited, the scope of the proposition has to be considered, too.

When an official, national proposition is being selected for high school or college and university debaters, somewhat different criteria are used. These eight are representative: (1) It should involve and interest the students. (2) It should be nationally controversial. (3) Two sides should have equal opportunities for arguments. (4) Ample evidence should be available. (5) Its key terms should be in the language of subject-matter experts. (6) It should have ample substance for a season.

(7) The status quo should be unlikely to change during the season.
(8) The subject should be single.

WORDING A PROPOSITION

When an individual has an opportunity to verbalize the proposition to which he expects to address himself, he should observe several principles, here grouped under four headings; clarity of language, correct placement of burden of proof, limited scope, and the effect of amendment.

Clarity of language means that the locution avoids vague or ambiguous terms, has no question-begging words, indicates the kind of proposition, and achieves plainness without the loss of accuracy. A vague term has many meanings, while an ambiguous one has two. Note the lack of clarity in this proposition from an editorial: "What our colleges need is more emphasis upon the laboratory and the library rather than intercollegiate athletics." Another violation of clarity consists of the use of question-begging term as in this specimen: "The unfair income tax law should be repealed." A supposition (unfair) which should be proved by the affirmative is assumed to have been proved. Clarity is also served by phrasing a proposition so as to indicate its kind, and consequently the appropriate analysis. Note the difficulty in classifying this proposition: "America needs men like Robinson Crusoe." Are these two statements the same kind of proposition: "Teacher May *is* guilty of misconduct," and "Teacher May *should be declared* guilty of misconduct"? Finally, there is the problem of achieving plainness without losing accuracy. In the following propositions we have apparent plainness which is actually vagueness: "The U.S.A. needs her allies more than they need her"; "Washington was greater than Lincoln." Although perfect clarity is seldom if ever achieved, it is reasonably approximated in his statement: "The membership dues of this club should be increased from the current two dollars per month to three dollars per month."

Correct placement of burden of proof is, as we have seen before, a matter of immense importance in the conduct of a controversy. Since the affirmative speaks in the proposition, this statement must clearly express the affirmative's claim and thereby define its responsibility for proof. As we noted in Chapter 3, there are three kinds of burden: to oppose the status quo, to oppose audience consensus, and to support what one asserts. The first kind, which is the traditional one in academic debate, affects the wording of a proposition in ways which will now be explained.

According to the traditional view, calling one side "affirmative" does not suffice to make it so; it may be merely the *nominal* affirmative as distinguished from the *actual* affirmative. In many situations the actual affirmative is the party that will be dissatisfied if the situation in question remains as it is. Thus the proposition must express the actual affirmative's view by calling for a change in belief or action. If the proposition says we should retain the Social Security system, the side saying "Yes" is merely the nominal affirmative, because it is not calling for a change. These propositions involve improper or highly questionable placement of burden of proof: "Socialism and democracy are incompatible," and "Monogamy is natural and desirable." They are wrong because the nominal affirmative is the actual negative, that is, the side saying "yes" has no burden of proof. No change from the prevailing belief or the cultural norm in our society is being urged. The proposition about socialism would place the burden of proof upon the affirmative (both nominal and actual) if the wording were something like this: "America could realize her democratic ideals through socialism." The proposition about monogamy should, for the same reason, be changed to something like this: "Monogamy is an unnatural (or undesirable) custom." Note the option of either of two single ideas.

When confronted with a situation in which the status quo is indeterminate, as it occasionally is outside of academic and judicial debate, an advocate who asserts a controversial claim automatically assumes the burden of proof.[21] With the exposition of these two views we conclude the matter of wording a proposition so as to place the burden of proof on the affirmative.

A third principle of correct phrasing holds that a proposition should be limited in scope. Undoubtedly the best general rule is to express one idea in a simple sentence. Imagine the difficulties you would face in arguing either side of this two-idea proposition: "Ivy College should adopt an honor system and a trimester calendar." A certain editorial gave a student some trouble when he was attempting to isolate the proposition. He justifiably thought the proposition was calling for

[21] See footnote 12 in Chapter 2.

the passage of a bill to ban "mail-order filth" from the mails when he read: "Give the Post Office Department the legal weapon with which to fight those vile creatures. . . ." However, the bulk of the editorial argued that parents should take more notice of what their children read. Two propositions were being argued at once. The legal remedy and parental vigilance could have been made major points under a definitely phrased, but rather broad, proposition such as: "Parents and the Congress should join forces in combating mail-order filth."

Lastly, on this matter of wording, there is the question of the status of a proposition which has been changed by amendment. In parliamentary deliberations this is done by adding, deleting, substituting, and the like. The result is a *new* proposition, regardless of how much or how little it resembles the original motion. A slight change will not affect the sides, but a major one might. Take the case of Magnolia Normal, which is on the semester calendar. If the proposition called for a change to the trimester calendar, an amendment substituting "quarter" for "trimester" could make a real difference in the choice of sides and in the nature of their cases.

QUESTIONS

1. Evaluate these propositions as if they were to be used in academic debate:
   a. The United Nations is an ineffective agency for maintaining collective security.
   b. Marriage is undesirable for undergraduates.
   c. The price of the affluent society is not worth paying.
   d. Good government is better than self-government.
   e. Democratic socialism is the best answer to communism.
   f. Evanston should legalize 3.2 beer and off-track betting.

2. Carlyle (*On Heroes, Hero-Worship, and the Heroic in History*) said that men of genius played causative roles in history, whereas Tolstoy (*War and Peace*) argued that leaders of men did not really have free will to influence events. What is the proposition here? Or are there two or more? If so, what are they? What kind is each? What kind or kinds of debate could take place on it or them?

3. On the matter of military examination of the Civil War, Roland wrote, in *Albert Sidney Johnston and the Shiloh Campaign*: "Many historians

have attempted to expurgate Grant for the cardinal sin of permitting himself to be out-generaled and surprised by his opponent at Shiloh. They point out that Grant had recommended . . . a bolder strategy which, if adopted, would have made impossible the Battle of Shiloh. This does not, however, excuse Grant for the gross misjudgment as to Confederate capabilities and intentions, nor relieve him of the responsibility of protecting his command against surprise . . ." Catton, in *Grant Moves South*, however, wrote: "General Buell remarks that Grant is very seldom seen in reports of the Shiloh fight and implies broadly that the Army commander was very inert. Actually, there are few Civil War battles in which once gets so many glimpses of a commanding general going about his business so energetically and competently." What is the proposition if one takes the two statements to be a debate? What kind is it? What kind or kinds of debate might be held on it?

4. What proposition or propositions come to mind when you observe on one page of a metropolitan daily newspaper at least ten advertisements containing captions such as these: "Short on Cash? Bankrupt? Bad Credit? Just Turned 21? Try Our Credit Plan"; "Bad Credit Our Specialty"; "Repossessed? Short on Cash? We Finance You on Premises"; "Bankrupt? We Finance Anyone!"

5. Discuss some of the above propositions (Questions 1–4) in terms of (a) the functions served, (b) their likely sources, (c) their suitability as measured by the four criteria of selection, and (d) the suitability of their wording.

6. An advocate needs a clear wording of proposition for his own guidance before he communicates, and sooner or later his audience should understand what his proposition is, but early disclosure of the proposition may not be persuasive. What should the advocate do? Is there an ethical issue here?

EXERCISES

1. Select an editorial, a letter to the editor, or a short printed speech. State its proposition. What kind is it? Evaluate the composition on the basis of the ease or difficulty in isolating the proposition and in classifying it.

2. On a specified number of these general subjects, compose one proposition of each kind:
   a. Labor-management relations
   b. International relations

    c. Intercollegiate athletics

    d. Cheating in school.

3. The class (or each subgroup thereof) will select a problem and word a proposition on it for use in later exercises. In this way the exercises will build toward something more meaningful than would result from unrelated assignments.

4. Report critically on one or more items in the Appendixes, using topics similar to those in Question 5 in the preceding section. In addition, word the proposition if it isn't stated in print, and classify it.

5. Before the U.S. Senate confirmed the peace treaty in 1899, the debate was on the proposition: The U.S. should acquire the Philippines. After confirmation on February 6, 1899, the proposition became: The U.S. should relinquish the Philippines.[22] Why did a scholar so explain the situation? How did the change affect the sides the debaters were on? Identify a comparable situation in the recent past.

[22] W. Lashley, "The Debate Over Imperialism in the United States, 1898–1900" (Doctoral dissertation, Northwestern University, 1966).

CHAPTER 5

ANALYSIS:

A CRUCIAL PROCESS

IN ARGUMENTATION THEORY, ANALYSIS IS THE PROCESS OF DETERMINING what a proposition means and of finding the controversial questions which must be answered if the deliberation is to be critical and thorough. Speakers and writers are more likely to meet their logical and ethical responsibilities if they perform this process competently. Listeners and readers also use analysis if they are intelligently critical.

This is a crucial process in the context of the philosophy of this book. However, given a persuasion-oriented philosophy, audience analysis would take precedence over substantive analysis. The conception of analysis which governs this chapter is based upon several assumptions: analysis is the most intellectual facet of argumentation; it is a continuous process; it can be done in a variety of ways; it is rarely definitive.[1] In sum, analysis plays a vital role in building a case, in attacking a case, in defending a case, and in evaluating or criticizing a case, but first it guides the investigative process.

Perhaps a bit more needs to be said concerning the connection between analysis and the burdens or responsibilities of the parties to a controversy. This will be treated by commenting upon some possible or actual misconceptions, one of which is the notion that the affirmative may with impunity interpret a proposition as it pleases. The

---

[1] See Windes and Hastings, *Argumentation* . . . , pp. 62–64.

principle which was explained in Chapter 3 holds that anyone who espouses a cause has an ethical obligation to make the best case he can in terms of the assumptions, evidence, and reasoning which are both available and *legitimate*. The only effective remedy in response to a trick case is a firm objection by the opposition or anyone else who is in a position to express himself.

A second misconception or misunderstanding concerns the responsibility of the negative for the issues. One book explains that each side must make good its claims, which is the accepted view, but it adds that each side must find the issues which are vital questions that must be answered in favor of a side in order to win.[2] If this statement means that the negative must negate all potential issues, it is wrong. It is the affirmative that must be prepared to affirm all potential issues. More will be said of this under "Kinds of Issues."

Finally, what kinds of issues are required by each kind of proposition? In one book the issues and claims are classified as *definitive* (for definition), *designative* (for fact), *evaluative* (for value), and *actuative* (for policy). According to this formulation, propositions of fact and of value required definitive and designative issues, while propositions of policy required definitive, designative, and evaluative issues.[3] One difficulty with this vocabulary is that it does not seem to allow for an evaluative issue in a proposition of value or for an actuative issue in a proposition of policy. The explanation of the increasing-complexity order of propositions in Chapter 4 is intended as an alternative to this seemingly obtuse formulation.

There are several important, specific benefits of analysis: the saving of time because of spending it only on essentials, the prevention of surprise attacks by an opponent, the guidance of one's preparation, the providing of questions to evaluate the relevance of one's materials, and the clarification of the basis of the controversy for all interested parties. This takes time, but it is time well spent. Fools rush in, as the saying goes, but wise men stop to analyze and investigate a proposition before they argue either side of it. In terms of strictly logical considerations, an advocate would confine himself to the controversial topics within his subject, but in the interest of popular persuasion he would discover and make use of the points of agreement as well. For example, most questions of public policy in this country must be considered on two levels: one is what would be best under ideal conditions; the other is what is expedient in relation to the voting interest involved.

[2] Ehninger and Brockriede, *Decision* . . . , p. 211.
[3] *Ibid.*, pp. 102 and 218–219.

Thus far we have considered the uses of analysis in case construction, attack, and defense. However, analysis is a crucial process in the arbitration or in the evaluation of a dispute. For instance, in a labor-management dispute it is necessary to isolate the issues before any fruitful bargaining can take place. The chairman of a fact-finding panel in a lengthy steel strike once remarked that the mediators could not work effectively until the issues were etched out, and he complained that this process could take many days.

POSSIBLE STEPS INVOLVED

Determination of the Kind of Proposition

Perhaps the first analytical step should be the determination of the kind of proposition one is dealing with. A speaker or a writer should verbalize and classify his proposition in order that he can estimate the nature of his responsibilities. A listener or a reader, on the other hand, should perform the same process for the purpose of estimating the demands he will make upon the advocate. This can be difficult, because speakers and writers occasionally think so fuzzily or express themselves so vaguely that the proposition is difficult to isolate and classify. An editorial, a letter to an editor, or an oral comment may seem to argue two or more propositions. In one instance the proposition seemed at first to claim that there is "a moral revolution calling the old codes into question," but later it became "morals have declined among college students." Another proposition seemed at first to oppose teachers' joining unions, but it later turned out to be a negative reply to an affirmative claim that some teachers oppose unions for a snobbish reason. This shift from policy to fact affected the proof responsibilities considerably.

Definition and Interpretation

What does the proposition mean? When anyone originates a proposition, he presumably intends to communicate about it. In order to accomplish this he tries to make his proposition convey his intent to those whom he addresses. If, on the other hand, an advocate is assigned a proposition, he has an obligation to interpret the intent of its source. Such obvious advice is sometimes needed, because, as we noted earlier, some persons who claim expertness in argumentation say that an affirmative spokesman may interpret a proposition however he wishes. One objection to this permissive doctrine is the likelihood of resultant futility in a deliberation on "Alice-in-Wonderland" language. Even if an advocate likes to practice intentional ambiguity, which is a fallacious stratagem, he has an obligation to use language which facilitates understanding.

This entails more than looking it up in a dictionary. Many writers advise us to begin with a sort of mental inventory of what we know and think about the problem in question. This personal background is a resource that is often overlooked. For instance, suppose one were to advocate one side of a proposal to enact open-occupancy legislation in a given state. After discovering precisely what the proposal stipulates, he who conducts a mental inventory will, in effect, ask himself what he knows about the racial question in housing, what he has heard or read about it, what he honestly feels about the matter, how he might react if he were in the situation of those who would be most affected by the change, and what his own special philosophy in relation to this problem actually is.

This leads to a consideration of the other major methods of definition, some of which may in some kinds of propositions reveal the issues. The familiar methods include synonym, classification, etymology, illustration, negation, criteria, and operational description. A synonym is a word or phrase whose meaning approximates that of the word being defined, as in using "disengage" for "extricate." Definition by classification is accomplished either by showing how the item to be defined belongs to a larger class of related items or by placing it on a continuum. Thus an atomic device could be classified as a weaponry, and its differences from conventional weapons would be pointed out. Sometimes the etymology of a term throws some light on its meaning, but the dynamic character of a living language renders the historical approach a bit risky. *Parlay* may have come from *paro*, meaning *pair*, but not all pairs are parlays. Definition by negation involves stating what something is not: "When I speak of courage, I don't mean foolhardiness." When a case in point is cited, the definition is by illustration: "If you seek the meaning of humility, consider the life of Lincoln." In defining by criteria, one sets out the conditions under which a given term is appropriate: "A valid contract requires an offer and an acceptance."

Finally, an operational definition tells how something works: "A Fair Employment Practices Commission would help to enforce the law by. . . ." Regardless of the methods of definition which one uses, the context or setting in which the term occurs is an important variable.

Perhaps one of the most important, yet the most often ignored, of the aspects of definition and interpretation is the statement of the advocate's philosophical position and its related assumptions. Suppose one urges that Congress expand the coverage of Social Security to include many more aspects of health, education, and general welfare. Does he favor or oppose the *direction* of the ongoing social change, or does he favor or oppose only the *rate* of that change? Does he oppose the value assumptions underlying the proposal, or does he favor them? An unpublished study has associated these questions with the classification of speeches as reactionary, conservative, liberal, and radical.[4]

Three illustrations will show how assumptions operate. In the Social Security proposition, one value assumption might be that the achievement of a higher minimum standard of general welfare in the United States is more important than any considerations of financial cost, bureaucracy, or impairment of self-reliance. The other side might value self-reliance, a balanced budget, and minimal governmental control of local matters. Two assumptions of the Federal Reserve System which underlie our national monetary policy are: (1) that money, in order to maintain its value, should be backed by something of value; and (2) that the monetary system should be able to expand and contract as the demand requires. Finally, in the debate between the champions of free press and those of fair trials, the rival assumptions practically tell the whole story. One side assumes the inviolability of the public's right to know, while the other holds that the right of the accused to a fair trial must take precedence.

When the contending sides in a controversy fail to reveal their intentions, define their terms, state their philosophical positions, or disclose their assumptions, the debate is not likely to be intellectually satisfying. Some say that Republicans and Democrats are often indistinguishable and that their political debates are consequently dull. The reason is that they dispute about tactics instead of getting to the roots of the problems. Perhaps they do so because most of their listeners and readers do not demand better of them.

[4] B. L. Brock, "A Definition of Four Political Positions and a Description of Their Rhetorical Characteristics" (Doctoral dissertation, Northwestern University, 1965).

Background of the Controversy

This step is both analytical and investigative. Although it treated in this chapter on analysis, it could be discussed in the following one on investigation. It is taken up here because the nature of a controversy depends in a large measure upon the circumstances of its origin and the reasons for its present importance. These matters of origin and development aid one in interpreting a proposition, and that is essential to analysis.

Suppose a person were to participate in a debate on the proposal to adopt the city manager form of government in his home town. He would want to learn what kinds of local government have been tried and what some qualified obserers have said about their virtues and faults. In particular he would be well advised to examine most carefully the experiences of that town and others with the mayor-and-council format, which is the most common. Next he would trace the origin and development of the manager form of local government, paying particular attention to the experiences of towns similar to his which have this arrangement. Then he would want to study the history of city government in order to observe trends. Is the manager form the coming thing, or is it merely a passing fad?

Next he would bring the background survey right down to the present time and ask what are the immediate causes of the controversy. Typically it would be a situation which is sufficiently disturbing to prompt someone to challenge a prevailing belief, a current practice, or an existing institution. The disclosure of gross mismanagement of a city's finances may lead to the demand for a professional city manager. Deaths in the ring or on the field often prompt individuals or groups to urge the abolition or the closer regulation of contact sports. Disclosures of greedy behavior have been known to give rise to propositions calling for a change in our values. An examination of precipitating causes such as these may help one to locate the issues. At the very least it will provide an advocate with some attention-getting material.

Finding Issues

If any one part of the analytical process accounts for its being crucial, it is that of finding issues. From the definition of issues one can judge that finding them in a proposition is the most important step in the preparation of a case or in the critical analysis of someone else's case. Preliminary analysis yields only tentative issues which must subsequently be refined through further investigation and analysis. The number of issues thereby arrived at will vary as to propositions; some will have one or two, while others will have three, four, five, or more. The remaining sections of this chapter will deal with the nature and the kinds of issues, the ways to find issues in each kind of proposition, and the effects of special situations upon the use of issues.

NATURE AND KINDS OF ISSUES

Issues Defined

Some writers say an issue is any question the affirmative must affirm. This definition doesn't explain *why* a certain question must be affirmed and it doesn't stipulate any *negative* obligation. Others say issues are points of disagreement between persuader and persuadee, but what if argumentation is used without persuasive intent? Still others, who are more numerous, define issues as points of clash between affirmative and negative cases, or as questions which express differences of opinion between the two sides. Generally speaking, this is a usable definition, except that it presupposes the existence of cases on both sides. What if someone is going to *originate* a controversy? He needs a method of finding the potential points of clash before they become actual. Or what if one wishes to analyze critically a debate which has taken place, and it turns out that the participants did not meet their logical responsibilities? If the critic considers as issues only those points on which a clash occurred, he will of necessity ignore any potential issues which did not become actual, and he cannot judge whether a case is prima facie or logically adequate. More will be said about the kinds of issues in the next section.

Two uses of the word *issues* in the mass media of communication illustrate the difference between the meaning intended here and a confusion of it. An example of the first use occurred in an editorial (on Title Seven of the Taft-Hartley Act amendments)[5] which answered

[5] *Salt Lake City Tribune*, August 26, 1959, p. 16.

three issues: Will it handle "no-man's-land" labor cases? Will it bar secondary boycotts? Will it ban organizational picketing? These areas were said to be "of vital concern," which is one way to characterize issues. A less helpful usage occurred on the evening of July 28, 1960, when candidate Nixon told an interviewer that he hoped the televised debates between himself and candidate Kennedy would not merely show who was the better debater but would show who could better handle the issues. In the context of this course on argumentation, the better debater *is* the one who better handles the issues.

In view of these considerations, it seems advisable to define issues in more detail. One part of such a definition here offered states that an issue is an inherent and vital *question* within a proposition: inherent because it exists inseparably and inevitably within a proposition, and vital because it is crucial or essential to the meaning of that proposition. A second part of the definition follows in consequence of the first: each issue must be affirmed unless it is waived or admitted by the negative, and at least one issue must be denied by the negative. The imperative *must* is not an overstatement if we assume that each side will be held to its logical and ethical responsibilities. The reason for the interrogative (question) form is that the affirmative must say "yes" to each issue and the negative must say "no" to the issues it chooses to contest.

Kinds of Issues

Issues are often classified as potential, stock, waived or admitted, and actual. Potential issues are all of the issues which are possible in a given proposition. They are to be found, not selected, and they are the same for both sides of the controversy. However, the affirmative can be held responsible for every one, while the negative may limit its own responsibility to as few as one if it chooses, according to the standard of logical responsibility. If the standard of popular persuasion were applied here, we should have to say that the listeners or readers would determine the number of issues which either side would have to answer. Shoddy analysis often satisfies the "results" criterion.

Benjamin Franklin and several authors of argumentation textbooks have advised us to locate potential issues by listing all of the affirmative points that have been made, doing likewise with negative points, and then observing where the lists clash. This will reveal the actual issues in a controversy which has taken place, but it is less reliable as a method of finding potential issues before a controversy begins. For example, suppose we wanted to find the potential issues in a Senate debate on a bill to increase the regulation of the securities markets. If some potential issues were not brought up, our list of pro and con points would not reveal them. In this particular controversy nobody raised the potential issue concerning the wisdom of checking the sharp increase in consumer debt. This was explained under the previous section, "Issues Defined."

Stock issues are potential issues in a preliminary, generalized form. They are preliminary in that they are used early in the analytical process, and they are general in statement because they are intended to apply to all propositions of a given type. Thus at the beginning of his analysis of a proposition of policy, an advocate might use stock issues such as these: Are there serious, inherent evils in the status quo? Is the affirmative plan the best solution? Stock issues would be worded differently for other kinds of propositions.

Although this "formula" approach to analysis is in some ways convenient, some limitations should be noted.[6] Since this approach is stereotyped or cut-and-dried, it does not say anything about the subject matter of the particular proposition. Suppose the proposition calls for an honor system at Igloo U. We don't say anything specific about the system or the school when we ask a stock question about "serious, inherent evils in the status quo," but we do get some guidance in framing the desired, specific questions about the proposition. Perhaps the greatest risk in using stock-issue analysis is that it will become a poor substitute for original thinking.

These objections have been answered by several explanations,[7] one of which is that stock issues are intended to be used only as broad questions which serve as guide lines to suggest areas for further study. Thus they are not the end of analysis. They don't commit anyone to a position before he has studied the proposition thoroughly. They are not intended as substitutes for thinking. That not all stock issues become actual issues is not remarkable. Some potential issues, whether stated in stock form or otherwise, do not necessarily become contested. Also, in the later stages of analysis, the stock issues take on qualifiers such as the degree of need, the details of a plan, or the nature of benefits. Finally, the "need-plan-benefits" matters need not be handled in three separate

[6] R. P. Newman, "Analysis and Issues—A Study of Doctrine," *Central States Speech Journal*, XIII, No. 1 (1961), 43.
[7] R. Nadeau, "In Defense of Deliberative Stock Issues," *Central States Speech Journal*, XIII, No. 2 (1962), 142.

units; they may be developed in a series of "need-plan-benefit" topics, as we shall see in the discussion of Cases.

Waived or admitted issues are those which are subtracted from the list of potential issues by action of the negative side. This necessarily follows from the fact that the negative *may* require the affirmative to affirm every potential issue. In practice, though, the negative side often contests fewer than all of the potential issues, mostly on account of considerations of time, interest, and vulnerability. Perhaps the most familiar instance of admission occurs when the negative side on a proposition of policy concedes some cause for action ("need") but offers a rival solution (counterproposition). Once an issue is waived or admitted, it ceases to be an issue in that particular debate.

Actual issues are, therefore, those which remain in contention after waivers and admissions have been subtracted from the list of potential issues. Actual issues are also called "ultimate," "real," and "issues of the debate." They are the key questions on which the sides clash. In fact, the best way to find the points of clash in an actual controversy which has taken place or is going on is to make parallel outlines of the two sides, placing opposing points directly opposite each other, and leaving blank spaces opposite those points which are not attacked. Critic judges of school debates typically do this. However, this method is not so useful in the analysis of a proposition which has not yet been debated. Below is a specimen of the clash-outline method of locating the actual issues in a debate that has been going on. The proposition, as of 1961, called for the amendment of the Illinois Banking Act to allow banks to open branches in their own trade areas.

AFFIRMATIVE POINTS	NEGATIVE POINTS
Business development is retarded by inadequate banking facilities.	Chicago is a net exporter of bank loans.
Individuals are inconvenienced by a shortage of banks.	Very few communities are more than a few minutes from a bank.
Only large banks can provide specialized services.	
	Branches cost more than independent local units to operate.
Chicago banks are losing business because of having no branches.	
It would not lead to monopoly.	It would create a monopoly.

The actual issues were: (1) Is the present arrangement of banks in the Chicago are unable to render satisfactory service? (2) Would branch banking avoid the danger of monopoly? Again, note the interrogative form.

ISSUES IN PROPOSITIONS OF FACT

Four subtypes will be distinguished: legal fact, past fact, present fact, and future fact or prediction. In a sense, "fact" may be a misnomer, because inferences are involved, and the claims are *alleged* to be verifiable *sometime*. It will be recalled that we are dealing with probability, not certainty.

As noted in Chapter 4, consideration of two basic questions will help to delineate the issues in a legal-fact proposition: What did the party in question do? Is the act definable as the offense which is charged? Suppose the proposition is Z *Company is engaging in an unfair labor practice*. The potential issues would be questions to which the affirmative would have to say "yes": (1) Did Z Company campaign against the union organizers? (2) Is this activity prohibited by the National Labor Relations Act? In a criminal case, the definition of murder, arson, or assault is not debatable; the statutes say what first-degree murder is, for instance. The potential issues concern what someone allegedly did and whether the definition fits the facts.

In a proposition of past fact that is nonlegal, there are similar potential issues. Two exploratory questions will serve to get at them: What would be required to establish the alleged fact? Do our available data meet this requirement? Suppose the proposition were *President Lincoln's party was split over the purpose of the war*. Again the potential issues would appear as questions which the affirmative would have the burden to affirm: (1) Were there in the Republican Party in 1864 two or more views of the purpose of the war? (2) Were those differences sufficiently serious to be called a "split"? Or suppose the proposition were *Dean Doe destroyed student government at Flunkout U*. There might be as many as five potential issues: (1) Did student government function at Flunkout prior to the alleged action? (2) Did Dean Doe do something which impaired student government there? (3) Did he do it alone or principally? (4) Did his action result in the termination of student government? (5) Was this act the main cause?

Propositions of present fact call for the same sort of preliminary, analytical questions. These questions are, in a way, similar to stock issues. A familiar proposition of present fact is *Crime comics induce juvenile delinquency*. Again two broad questions will help to get at the issues: What would be required to prove this claimed connection? Do the available data suffice to do this? Actually, this controversy could be resolved more satisfactorily through social science research than through debate, but we may still have to debate it. Can a correlation between the consumption of crime comics and the incidence of juvenile crimes be shown? Must a causal connection be shown? Can it be shown? Or would the showing of a crime-suggesting context meet the affirmative's responsibility? When the House of Representatives was deciding how to punish a reelected member, Adam Clayton Powell of Harlem, a syndicated columnist explained his analysis of the controversy. There were three moral issues, in his view: Is Powell getting what he deserves? Are his sins so much worse than those of some colleagues that he should be singled out for punishment? Is race a significant factor?[8]

Propositions of future fact (prediction) involve a similar preliminary analysis which can be accomplished by asking the same two questions that were used in the three preceding subtypes. Suppose the proposition is *Mass education at the collegiate level will reduce the quality of higher education*. After asking the preliminary questions mentioned above, one would arrive at tentative statements of potential issues somewhat like these: (1) Must standards be lowered for some when larger numbers are admitted to college? (2) Will the lowering of standards for some students result in the reduction in the quality of higher education?

Before leaving the so-called factual subtypes of nonpolicy propositions and moving on to those of evaluation, it might be prudent to observe that facts and values are sometimes closely interrelated. This is true, contrary to popular belief, even in science, as Dr. Conant points out.[9] He explains that science is not neutral in regard to value judgments. For instance, research scientists and practitioners in the medical sciences operate on the basis of these values: that life is preferable to death, that good health is important, and that each person has a kind of sanctity which requires that life be saved whenever possible. These value judgments serve as implied premises in medical discourse.

[8] C. T. Rowan, "Racism a Factor in Powell Action," *Chicago Daily News*, January 17, 1967, p. 16.

[9] J. B. Conant, "The Scientist in Our Unique Society, *Atlantic*, 181, No. 3 (1948), p. 49.

ISSUES IN PROPOSITIONS OF VALUE

The preliminary, analytical questions which would be useful in the search for potential issues in a proposition of value might be phrased this way: Upon what criteria should the evaluation be based? How well does the matter to be evaluated measure up to these criteria? Suppose the proposition is *Resolved, That big-time football is out of place on a university campus.* The analytical questions can now be phrased more specifically: Under what conditions might we decide that an activity is out of place on a campus? Does big-time football qualify under these criteria? In the next analytical stage one would state pairs of criteria-and-application questions somewhat like these: (1) Is an activity out of place on a campus if it is not academically oriented? (1′) Does big-time football lack an academic orientation? (2) Is it out of place if it becomes an end in itself? (2′) Is big-time football an end in itself? (3) Is it out of place if it exploits the participants? (3′) Does big-time football exploit its players? Or take the proposition that *installment buying is harmful to the public interest.* Again several pairs of criteria-and-application questions will suggest approaches to issues: (1) Is a scheme of consumer finance harmful if it contributes to inflation? (1′) Does installment buying contribute to inflation? (2) Is a scheme . . . harmful if it encourages many persons to live beyond their means? (2′) Does installment buying encourage many persons to live beyond their means? Further study, as explained in the next chapter, may lead to a further refinement of these potential issues.

Before leaving the propositions of value we might at least raise a few relevant philosophical questions: What are the human values? Where do we get them? Why are they believed to be good? There are many values, some of the highest of which are love, truth, beauty, self-realization, in *our* culture. We get our values through our cultural heritage. They became a part of the cultural heritage because of the social good which they served. Through the centuries man learned to value good relations within his social units, because he perceived the unpleasant effect of dissension, disruption, and the like. But the reasons *why* certain values are believed in are in dispute. Some say that values are not rationally derived; they are arbitrary postulates. Others contend that human nature determines the norms, in other words, that the pursuit of certain values is conducive to psychological well-being. Finally, there is a metaphysical view, which is that the highest values are inherent in the character of being.

In analysis of a problem in which two or more values are in conflict, it might be well to determine which values are operating, in what rank or order the persons concerned seem to hold them, and why the parties hold certain values. This procedure has obvious uses in persuasion, but it also serves in the reasoned development of the implications or consequences of any value judgments which are used as postulates or premises for argument. In philosophical debates we should expect to use this sort of analysis, but we should find it useful also in a proposition like the one above on big-time football. What if one had to choose either school spirit or intellectual stimulation for top priority in his hierarchy of values? Is this a real choice? If so, which would he choose, and why? These questions serve to illustrate the functioning of values.

ISSUES IN PROPOSITIONS OF POLICY

Much of the literature of argumentation has stressed the analysis of propositions of policy, often to the point of giving no instruction on the analysis of the other kinds. The authors' concern for the interests of academic and possibly legislative debate has accounted for the widespread discussion of stock-issue patterns of analysis. These and other formulations are best used as guides or suggestions, not as "cookie cutters."

Stasis or Status

Although the elaboration of stereotyped formulas for the analysis of propositions of policy in academic debate is a twentieth-century phenomenon, the roots of these procedures date back to *stasis* and *status* in ancient Greek and Roman rhetoric, respectively. Instead of going to the works of Aristotle, Quintilian, and other classical sources, we shall consult the work of a recent American scholar who set out to adapt the ancient doctrine to modern "debate before a deliberative assembly."[10] This limitation plus the Procrustean-bed modification of value proposi-

[10] L. S. Hultzén, "Status in Deliberative Analysis," in *The Rhetorical Idiom*, D. C. Bryant (ed.) (Ithaca, N. Y.: Cornell University Press, 1958), pp. 97–123.

tions into fact, and the changing of propositions of fact and of value
into mere issues within propositions of policy made this reformulation
possible. The result is four stock issues and at least nine subissues:

Ill (Something wrong in the status quo?)
    Conjecture (existence of facts)
    Definition (classifiable as "need")
    Quality (degree; how bad?)
Blame (Caused by a reformable condition?)
    Same three subissues to get at scapegoat,
    remediability, etc.
Cure (Will plan meet need?)
    Same subissues to get at removal of causes,
    achievement of benefits, etc.
Cost (Would cure be worth its cost?)
    Same subissues to get at new evils, counter-
    proposition, etc.

Quite recently a young scholar has adapted the concept of *stasis* to
take account of *status quo, need, comparative-advantages,* and *burden
of proof* as they are explained in this and a few other recent publications. Writing on *status* and *need* in propositions of policy, Mader[11]
remarks that *status in time* is but one of the possible positions. It deals
with conditions that exist. Such a proposition offers a fundamental
change, as in discontinuing foreign aid, recognizing Red China, and
nationalizing basic industries. But there are propositions that call for
lesser changes; they involve extending and continuing something that
might otherwise be reduced or terminated. In such cases the *status quo*
may not be the "fixed point" or *status*. When the *status quo* is the
"fixed point," the affirmative must show an inherent need for a fundamental change; but when it is not, the affirmative must show "need" in
terms of principle. Adapting this to the comparative-advantages case, an
affirmative would argue that if there is a better solution, it should be
adopted, even if there is no desperate need for a change.

Three illustrations are offered by Mader in explication of his thesis.
On the proposition that the Federal government should guarantee an
opportunity for higher education to all qualified high school graduates,
affirmatives typically argued a need for such a guarantee and that the
Federal government was the best agency. Negatives typically opposed
either or both of these points. However, in terms of the explanation

[11] T. F. Mader, "The Inherent Need to Analyze *Stasis*," *Journal of the
American Forensic Association,* IV, No. 1 (1967), 13–20.

above, neither side should argue that the *amount* of money is crucial; both sides should argue federal involvement in principle, even if there is some aid in the *status quo*. The second proposition asks that law-enforcement agencies in the United States be given greater freedom in the investigation and prosecution of crime. Precisely what was the *status quo*? Giving Congress the power to set aside Supreme Court decisions does not answer the proposition. Negatives sometimes argued that police already had enough power but did not know how to use it, in which case the negative speakers should have opposed added power, even if the Supreme Court later granted it. Some debaters tried to limit their burden by interpreting "crime" as "organized crime." What these debaters should have done, according to this view of *status*, was to stress the philosophical issue of individual *vs.* societal rights. (More Locke and Hobbes and less R. Kennedy and J. Edgar Hoover.) A direct confrontation between law-and-order champions and civil-rights advocates would then occur. The third proposition asserts that the requirement of membership in a labor organization as a condition of employment should be illegal. Here the *status quo* was still more confused; some states had right-to-work laws, and some did not. In a state that had such a law, the affirmative could not propose a change; they defended the *status quo*. The wording of this proposition required the negative to oppose right-to-work laws; but in states that already had such laws, the negative sounded like an affirmative calling for a change. Both sides would have been better off to argue the philosophy of compulsory unionism. This view is consistent with the newer conception of presumption and burden of proof described in Chapter 3.

Shaw's Survey of Proof

Some traces of the classical concept of *stasis* can be found in Baker and Huntington, *Principles of Argumentation*, 1905, but the most extensive elaboration of the idea appeared in 1922 in Shaw's *Art of Debate*. Using Edmund Burke's celebrated speech "On Conciliation with the American Colonies" as a specimen, Shaw[12] found four issues: (1) Is some change from the present policy of taxation necessary to restore peace in America? (2) Would Burke's policy of conciliation restore peace in America? (3) Would Burke's policy of conciliation

---

[12] Shaw, *The Art of Debate*, pp. 201–202.

introduce new and worse evils? (4) Would any other policy be more satisfactory than Burke's policy of conciliation?

Before coming to these issues, which resemble the stock issues we have discussed, Shaw diagrammed under "Surveying the Proof" a fifteen-step procedure (including negative counterproposition) for use with a proposition of policy:

Phases 1–4 represent the affirmative constructive case. Phases 5–7 represent a negative case of attacking the affirmative's plan. Phases 8–11 represent a negative counterproposition case. Phases 12–15 represent the affirmative attack upon the counterproposition. Dotted lines represent comparisons such as "better than" or "worse than."

Stock Issues Today

Nowadays the stock-issue analysis of a proposition of policy typically begins with questions such as these: Is there a need for a fundamental change from the present policy? Would the affirmative's plan remedy the serious, inherent difficulties in the status quo? Would the new plan avoid new and worse problems? Sometimes, in order to cope with possible counterpropositions, the third stock issue is changed to this: Is the affirmative plan the best answer to the problem? Details of wording will vary in terms of the sub-type of proposition of policy one is dealing with—a whole new policy, a substitution of one for another, or the cessation of a current policy. The first might call for the establishment of a community college where no college has existed; the second might call for a change from the quarterly calendar to the semester; the third might call for the abolishment of capital punishment where it now exists.

Let us analyze the second proposition of policy by modifying the stock issues into more meaningful potential issues and by stating some potential subissues which our research has turned up:

    I. Are there important shortcomings in the quarterly division of the academic year?
       A. Do quarter-length courses sacrifice some comprehensiveness in the students' grasp of the subjects?
       B. Do they give too little opportunity for independent study between meetings?
       C. Do they aggravate the problems of academic adjustment?
       D. Do the frequent starts and stops break the continuity of learning?

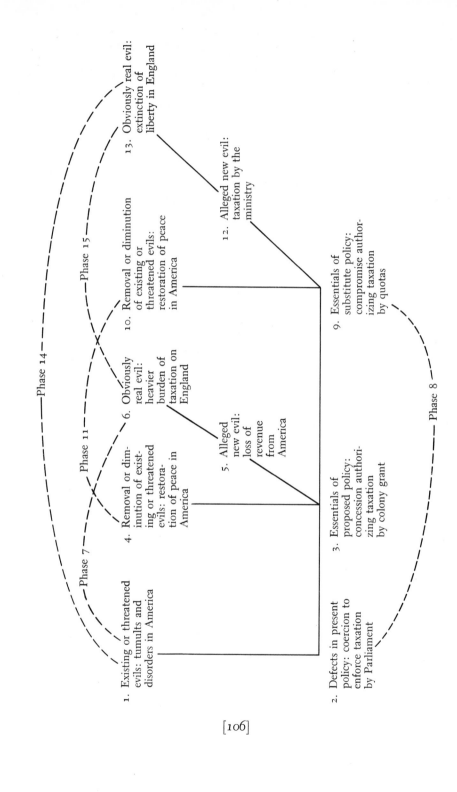

1. Existing or threatened evils: tumults and disorders in America

2. Defects in present policy: coercion to enforce taxation by Parliament

3. Essentials of proposed policy: concession authorizing taxation by colony grant

4. Removal or diminution of existing or threatened evils: restoration of peace in America

5. Alleged new evil: loss of revenue from America

6. Obviously real evil: heavier burden of taxation on England

9. Essentials of substitute policy: compromise authorizing taxation by quotas

10. Removal or diminution of existing or threatened evils: restoration of peace in America

12. Alleged new evil: taxation by the ministry

13. Obviously real evil: extinction of liberty in England

Phase 7

Phase 8

Phase 11

Phase 14

Phase 15

II. Would the change to a semester calendar remedy these short-comings?
   A. Would semester courses provide more comprehensive treatment of each subject?
   B. Would they allow for more independent work?
   C. Would they give more time for academic adjustment?
   D. Would they provide more continuity of study?
III. Would the semester plan be the best solution?
   A. Would it suit our purposes better than some trimester plan?
   B. Would it be better than some other alternative?
   C. Could it be adopted without serious inconvenience?

When the shortcomings of the *status quo* are not serious, and when only modest claims can be made for the benefits of the proposed change, we can use the comparative-advantages approach instead of the outline above. Actually, an advocate who would try to make a "crying-shame" argument about the "evils" of the quarterly calendar would be suspected of exaggerating. More will be said of this in the chapter on "Cases."

In a survey of the use of stock issues in an intercollegiate debate tournament, some findings were made concerning the relative importance of five so-called stock issues. On a maximum scale of ten, "Need" scored 7.87, "Workability" 7.34, "Solution" 6.37, "Disadvantages" 5.78, and "Counterproposition" 0.65.[13] The first item has to do with the problem, but the next four deal with solution. Among the last four there is apparent overlapping, a condition which suggests that these are not four discrete issues after all.

EFFECTS OF SPECIAL SITUATIONS

In this section we shall consider the relationships between issues and each of four special situations: a negative counterproposition case, a choice between a critical and a popular decision, the partitioning of a case, and the use of the Toulmin layout.

[13] K. Giffin and K. Magill, "Stock Issues in Tournament Debates," *Central States Speech Journal*, XII, No. 1 (1960), 27–32.

Negative Counterproposition

Let us suppose that our proposition calls for statehood for Puerto Rico. If the negative concedes that the present status is not the best but urges a substitute solution in the form of national independence for Puerto Rico, we have a counterproposition. Each side in this situation has a responsibility to prove its own case. The affirmative has *the* burden of proof on the statehood proposal, but the negative has what we could call *a* burden of proof on national independence.

Does this change the issues? It does not; the counterplan fits under the issue which asks whether the affirmative proposal is the best answer to the problem. Instead of saying, "No, because of its drawbacks," the negative says, "No, because our plan is better." Thus the substitute acts as an obstacle to the affirmation on at least one issue. If this obstacle blocks the affirmative on one issue, that is enough to defeat the affirmative case, at least insofar as the logic of the controversy is concerned.

Should the negative counterplan then be adopted? This is not a necessary implication, because the alternative was advanced merely to challenge the affirmative's claim that statehood would be the best solution. We should expect to debate a proposition calling for national independence before there would be ample grounds for adopting that solution. A parallel situation occurs in a criminal trial when the defense contends that someone other than the accused did the deed. The new suspect is not thereby proved guilty; he is entitled to his own trial, and he goes into it with a presumption of innocence. The confusion of theory on this point was treated in Chapter 3 under the effect of a counterproposition upon burden of proof.

Popular vs. Critical Decision

The kind of decision an advocate seeks will affect his analysis in one major respect: it will prompt him to emphasize either the analysis of the audience or the analysis of the subject. A writer on legal evidence was getting at a point like this when he wrote, "The risk of not having persuaded the jury is one thing; the duty of producing evidence sufficient to cause the court to submit the case to the jury is a very different matter.[14] A practical politician is thinking of audience analysis

[14] H. W. Humble, *Principles of the Law of Evidence with Cases for Discussion* (Chicago: Callaghan and Co., 1934), p .25.

and a popular decision when he advises, "You can talk all campaign long on an issue, but if the public isn't interested in it, you've wasted your time." But an idealist in politics would insist upon trying to *educate* the voters on issues which he thought were important, even if initial public interest were lacking.

Two modern textbooks epitomize the difference between these two views on analysis. The first[15] says an advocate analyzes the audience as well as the proposition for the purpose of discovering persuasive points. Applying this doctrine to rhetorical criticism, another writer[16] explained that spokesmen for political protest movements have been generally unsuccessful because they failed adequately to adapt to specific desires and experiences of the voters. Instead, they dealt in abstract, theoretical terms of the federal deficit while the voters wanted jobs, better prices, etc. The second of the modern textbooks[17] espouses the nearly opposite view, namely, that analysis should disregard the beliefs of the debaters and the audience. The latter of these two conceptions of analysis is much more likely to result in logically adequate cases, or proof which is not equated with belief. This point, which was developed at some length under definitions of proof in Chapter 2, does not mean that analysis with an audience in mind is improper. After all, ideas, and people must be adjusted to each other if behavioral change is desired. However, *substantive* analysis is the greater concern of argumentation.

Partitioning a Case

Analysis has presumably been completed when an advocate sets down his points in partition. These are the main "talking points," which will be treated later under "Cases." The reason for mentioning the partitioning of a case at this juncture is that the relationships between issues and points in partition are frequently misunderstood.

Issues are inherent, vital questions, *all* of which the affirmative must be prepared to affirm, and *some* of which the negative must negate. Points in partition are declarative sentences which answer issues affirmatively or negatively. These points may closely resemble the issues in number and form, but they may also differ widely. An issue is vital,

---

15 C. S. Mudd and M. O. Sillars, *Speech Content and Communication* (San Francisco: Chandler Publishing Co., 1962), p. 42.
16 H. P. Kerr, "The Rhetoric of Political Protest," *Quarterly Journal of Speech*, XLV, No. 2 (1959), 146.
17 Ehninger and Brockriede, *Decision* . . . , p. 233.

but a point in partition is not so important unless it is the only answer which one side gives to an actual issue. Earlier in this chapter, under "Issues in Propositions of Fact," five potential issues were ascribed to the proposition concerning Dean Doe and student government. Note that the points in partition can be fewer: (1) Dean Doe suspended the constitution of student government at Flywheel Tech.; (2) this action made it impossible for the active organization to continue. These two main points plus their supporting subpoints could be made to answer all five issues. Or consider the proposition on installment buying under "Issues in Propositions of Value." Four or more potential issues were isolated, but there might be as many as five points in partition, each one in the form of a declarative sentence to answer an issue. It is more likely, however, that subpoints would be used to cover some issues and that three points in partition would suffice: (1) Installment buying harmfully contributes to inflation. (2) It harmfully encourages many of us to live beyond our means. (3) These faults outweigh any claimed advantages.

The Toulmin Layout

Early in Chapter 2, under "Argumentation As an Analytical-Critical Instrument," the Toulmin contribution was listed as the most recent of the influential items in the literature. Here, under "Analysis," it will be explained in some detail. Later, in relation to reasoning, it will be applied to the kinds and structures of argument.

Prior to this point we have considered the gross aspects of analysis: classifying the proposition, defining and interpreting it, exploring its background, and finding its issues. Next we shall take up the finer aspects of analysis—the examination of individual arguments, be they ours or someone else's. Toulmin's "layout of arguments"[18] will be offered as one model for this purpose. The criticisms of this model will be deferred until Chapter 8.

When analyzing arguments sentence by sentence in order to judge their merits and defects, one may follow either the geometric or the legal model. Since Aristotle developed the syllogism, the microstructure of arguments has been oversimplified according to the geometric analogy into minor premise, major premise, and conclusion. What we need to consider, according to Toulmin, is that legal arguments, and many

[18] Toulmin, *Uses of Argument*, pp. 94–145.

others for that matter, are quite complex. Hence the legal or jurisprudential analogy suggests a more suitable model. Let us see how it
works.

What may be involved when an arguer backs up a claim? C is the
Claim or conclusion to be supported. D represents Data or facts cited as
the basis of the Claim. These are appealed to explicitly, as are questions
of fact in court. The Data step answers the question, "What do you
have to go on?" W stands for Warrant, step, or bridge. It is appealed to
implicitly, like questions of law in court. It answers the question, "How
did you get there?" Thus far, the model is essentially a categorical
syllogism, but other kinds will be taken into account later: D = minor
premise, W = major premise, and C = conclusion.

(D) Taiwan's leaders vow to ——→ So (C) Nationalist China
      invade China mainland | cannot qualify as peace-
                                       loving
                     Since (W)
Any government that threatens another cannot be called peace-loving

But what if the Data and the Warrant do not suffice to show the
conclusion to be necessary, but only probable? We then add a Qualifier,
Q, before Claim. Further, if the conclusion is not inescapably true,
there must be exceptions or reservations to it. The Toulmin model
provides the R for Reservations, or "Rebuttal" as he named it. This
model then needs a final step: the Backing, B, which provides the
authority for the Warrant. Starting with the Data, Warrant, and Claim
as given above, we shall add Qualifier, Reservation, and Backing:

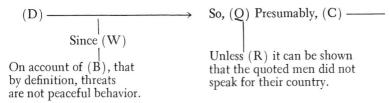

(D) ——————————→ So, (Q) Presumably, (C) ———
        |
     Since (W)
        | Unless (R) it can be shown
On account of (B), that   that the quoted men did not
by definition, threats   speak for their country.
are not peaceful behavior.

This model makes no provision for either testing or backing the
Data step. Thus one must say, "If the Taiwan leaders vow . . . , then,
presumably . . . " But one who wants to make a stronger argument
than "if . . . then" needs the equivalent of a Backing step under Data
to verify the assertion that the Taiwan leaders *did* vow to invade China.

QUESTIONS

1. Evaluate this definition: "Analysis is the process of finding a central idea or a group of central ideas."

2. Would it be reasonable to define stock issues as "analytical arguments that are used to investigate the materials of proof on both sides of the proposition?"

3. Comment upon the conception of analysis which this statement implies: "Debaters in this generation must measure ideas in terms of the needs and values of the next generation as opposed to the present desire for lower taxes, etc."

4. A proposed amendment which would extend Swiss female suffrage to the federal level stirred up a lively controversy. The affirmative points were: (a) Progress demands that Switzerland not lag behind the rest of the world. (b) The traditional rule discriminates unfairly against women. (c) Swiss women are politically mature. The negative points were: (a) Swiss women have not voted in the past. (b) Women are emotional. (c) Women are not interested in politics. (d) They don't understand complex Swiss politics. (e) Disunity in the home might ensue. (f) Loss of femininity might result.

   What actual issue or issues does the "clash" technique yield? Which of the above points are main points, and which are subordinate? Which are required for a critical decision, and which for a popular one?

5. Analysis has been explained as a process which is essential to any advocate who wishes to meet his ethical and logical responsibilities. Discuss that view in relation to this statement attributed to a campus politician: "When you go to a house to speak, don't talk about issues, especially if they are controversial [What other kind is there?], or even yourself. Concentrate on complimenting someone outstanding in the house. They'll remember you because they'll think you're interested in them."

6. The *Saturday Review* of February 22, 1958, gave this summary of "clash points" between the pro's and con's of "Pay TV":

   a) The minority should have the opportunity to decide what it is willing to pay for.

   a) Presentation of programs for which a charge is made would be "fencing off the best for the carriage trade."

   b) Free TV will still have the bulk of viewing time.

   b) Pay TV can succeed only by "cannibalizing free television."

c) Nobody can determine what the outcome might be without trial.

d) Pay TV would provide a source of competition from which everybody would benefit.

c) Trial performances would give "pay interests a golden opportunity to infiltrate."

d) The "best programs would inevitably go over to pay television, should a successful nationwide system be established."

What actual issues are involved here? Are any potential issues not used?

7. Why doesn't the negative have to negate as many issues as the affirmative has to affirm?

EXERCISES

1. Analyze a printed argument such as a speech or an essay selected from an Appendix or elsewhere. Report in outline form on these topics: (a) Statement of proposition. (b) Kind of proposition. (c) Side taken by author. (d) Whether he had presumption or burden of proof. (e) Evaluation of proposition in terms of the criteria of selection and of phrasing. (f) Potential issues. (g) Issue or issues treated here. (h) Expressed or implied assumptions. And (i) Point or points in partition.

2. Analyze a proposition for use in your own future oral or written discourses. Report in topical form your analytical steps such as these: (a) Statement of proposition. (b) Classification of proposition. (c) Choice of side. (d) Obligation in terms of presumption or of burden of proof. (e) Evaluation or proposition in relation to criteria of selection and of phrasing. (f) Define and interpret it. (g) Sketch its history. (h) Cite reason for present controversy. (i) List potential issues. (j) State admissions or waivers if you are negative and wish to omit anything. (k) List any expressed or implied assumptions. And (l) Set out your intended points in partition.

3. Prepare an oral or written report on the debate on stock issues which can be located through footnotes 6 and 7 in this chapter.

4. Apply the Shaw diagram, or as much of it as is applicable, to a debate in an Appendix or in a collection of school debates.

5. Criticize the analysis which is apparent in the college oration in Appendix C.

6. Apply the Toulmin layout to selected specimens of argument from the Appendix debate. Set up the framework for D, C, W, Q, B, and R. Write in the parts that are explicitly stated. Finally, place in parentheses the unstated parts which would be needed to complete the model. What does this analysis enable you to say in evaluation of the argument or chain of arguments?

CHAPTER 6

INVESTIGATION

IN THE CONTEXT OF ARGUMENTATION, INVESTIGATION IS THE PROCESS OF accumulating information about a proposition. Sometimes it involves no more than looking up a few magazine articles or conversing with some friends, but it may also be a long and arduous inquiry which can properly be called research. Within this broad range there are several investigative procedures, including thinking, observing, reading, listening, discussion, interviewing, corresponding, brainstorming, and recording the results of these activities. Directions on the utilization of these procedures will be given shortly.

When should investigation take place? Is it not the same process as analysis? These related questions can be answered by saying that analysis is the process of determining the meaning of a proposition and discovering its issues, while investigation is the closely related process of finding materials with which to develop the points which will answer those issues. Thus it follows that *a studious advocate typically alternates between analysis and investigation.* When he already has his proposition, he begins with a preliminary analysis which will direct his study, next he seeks material on the tentative issues, then he sharpens the issues in the light of greater knowledge, and finally he continues his investigation as guided by these more specifically worded issues. In other words, analysis tells him what he must be prepared to argue, and investigation provides the material with which to do it.

The importance of investigation is obvious, or at least it should be. Readers and listeners who have any claim to rationality expect an advocate to know what he is arguing about. When he does not, he risks exposure. Such was the experience of a letter writer who attacked the scientists who helped with the American missile program and then praised "scientists like Einstein who refuse to prostitute their genius to perfecting methods of exterminating life . . ." The editor's reply reminded the writer that Einstein signed the letter that persuaded President Franklin Roosevelt to order top priority for the development of the first A-bomb.

It is useful to distinguish between original and unoriginal investigation. The former is firsthand inquiry as in the personal observation discussed below. Unoriginal investigation is by far the more popular with students who prepare arguments. It means the use of reports made by others who did the research. On subjects other than strictly local or personal matters it is usually wise to concentrate on unoriginal investigation after the preliminary stages.

Investigation may also be classified as direct or indirect. Direct preparation is the kind most of us think of; it is the thought and study which an advocate undertakes after he knows what his proposition is and perhaps when he will argue it. Students who "go out for debate" and lawyers who accept cases are obliged to do direct preparation. Indirect investigation may take place over a long period of time and without reference to a specific use. It actually means one's background of knowledge and experience. The value of this kind of investigation is pointed out in a later section, "Following Current Affairs."

Thorough investigation means work, which is to say that it requires time, energy, skill, patience, and, in a word, self-discipline. Consequently it is to be expected that some persons will try the easy shortcuts. But when they do, they fall short of meeting their ethical and logical responsibilities. The harm may be slight when a student does inadequate investigation for one classroom exercise, but it is a cause for alarm when police detectives detain a suspect for prolonged "grilling," an undisciplined, sloppy substitute for efficient criminal investigation. This point about taking time for research calls to mind the remark attributed to Warden Duffy of San Quentin: "Our debating teams go against the colleges and usually win. Why do they? Well, I always say, they have more time for research."

THINKING AND OBSERVING

A speaker's or a writer's own background may be his best potential resource, but it is often overlooked. To prevent this mistake, an advocate should begin his investigation with a mental inventory of what he knows and thinks about the proposition. It is wise to take ample time to survey one's own knowledge and ideas before rushing to a library. Some of the general hints which experienced persons have given are: Ask guiding questions like those in the study outline below; recall pertinent experiences; determine meanings of words and ideas; set up tests and classifications of material. This process of mental inventory pertains to both analysis and investigation.

If, as is often the case, previous personal experience is not enough, it may be supplemented with original investigation. This is firsthand inquiry, which may include field trips and experiments. A newspaper feature writer who planned a series on the sharp practices of some used-car dealers and their finance companies sent some assistants out to make deals at some suspected lots. Through this procedure he turned up some cases in which the interest on installment contracts ranged between 139 and 275 percent. Not only did he obtain striking evidence; it is doubtful that he could have found it by other means. In a quite different area of human concern there are cases of certain state legislators being moved from indifference to advocacy by a tour of a substandard state mental hospital. The point is that, however useful reading is, it is no substitute for thinking and firsthand observation.

When observing, reading, interviewing, or in any other conceivable manner investigating a proposition, a person is occasionally tempted to "see" what he wants to see or to refuse to see what he finds unpleasant. An Iranian (Persian) writer has pointed to the tendency of many Westerners to romanticize as the "Wisdom of the East" the "stale philosophies" of the past. The tragic results, he argues, include our ignoring the serious problems of underdeveloped countries and actually "helping to perpetuate Eastern backwardness."[1]

In all phases of investigation—thinking, observing, reading, interview-

[1] F. M. Esfandiary, "The Mystical West Puzzles the Practical East," *New York Times Magazine*, Feb. 5, 1967, pp. 22–23.

ing, discussing, and the like—a guiding plan is at least useful if not indispensable. When surveying personal ideas or making observations, one should ask analytical questions, record impressions, and make allowances for one's own limitations in terms of selective perception, imperfect recall, and amateurishness in general. The first major step in the making of a guiding plan is taken when an individual performs the preliminary analysis as explained in Chapter 5. Once he defines the proposition and discovers the potential issues, he has some guidelines to follow. From this stage he can move on to the construction of a study guide or discussion outline of the sort illustrated in the final section of this chapter.

A true story of scholarly sleuthing will serve to illustrate the importance of systematic questioning and observing. For more than a half century some Viking lore enthusiasts had accepted as authentic the Kensington stone which a Minnesota farmer allegedly found in 1898. The stone bore runic inscriptions relating the adventures of a band of Norsemen in 1362. It could not be a fake, the believers said, because the farmer was almost unlettered and had no books to guide him. However, one scholar in Germanic languages, sensing some peculiarities in the inscription, determined to test his hypothesis that the late farmer had perpetrated a hoax. He engaged a professor of Norse from a nearby college to visit the farm, then occupied by the "discoverer's" sons. This visit yielded the contents of the old farmer's scrapbook and the knowledge that he owned a Swedish encyclopedia. Next it was learned by interviewing old neighbors that the uneducated farmer was considered to be intelligent and had often expressed his wish to fool the experts. In the four pages on runes in the encyclopedia there was enough information to enable anyone to compose the Kensington stone inscription. The characters on the stone were exact copies of those in the book; in fact, the farmer had even copied the mistakes. His old scrapbook revealed the practice exercises which he worked on while perfecting his technique.

FOLLOWING CURRENT AFFAIRS

Students who try to keep up on current affairs read with some regularity a few representative samples of daily newspapers, weekly news summaries, and monthly or quarterly journals of opinion. Three newspapers among the many possible choices are noteworthy in their categories: *New York Times, Christian Science Monitor,* and *Wall Street Journal.* Most familiar of the weekly publications are *Time, Newsweek, U.S. News and World Report,* and *Facts on File.* Depending upon his specific research interest, a student would be likely to use some of these periodical publications as well: *Reporter, Business Week, Congressional Record, Harper's, Atlantic, New Republic, Nation, Fortune, Monthly Labor Review, Congressional Digest, American Economic Review, Foreign Affairs, Editorial Research Reports,* and *Annals of the American Academy of Political and Social Science.*

Suppose that you are working on the general subject of wage and price controls administered by the national government. Before getting down to particulars, read for general background in the main subject and in the bordering subjects as well. One of the first lessons a novice has to learn—often the hard way—is that an advocate has to read more than the minimum material for one speech or essay. On the economic-controls proposition, begin by looking up the topic in an encyclopedia, some economics books, the periodical indexes, and the general guides (especially Winchell's) in the following section. Find out what the controls are, how they work, when they originated, what they have accomplished, and what people have said about them. Look into bordering subjects such as the economic philosophies (R. L. Heilbroner, *The Worldly Philosophers*), public administration, supply and demand, and the like. Seek out some critical articles in journals of opinion and the professional journals in economics and political science.

When you progress beyond these preliminaries, go to the primary sources of information. It is better, for example, to quote from the opinion of the Supreme Court than to rely solely upon a newspaper columnist's version of that decision. If you want to cite what Senator X said about economic controls during the debate on a bill, look it up in the *Congressional Record.* Experienced scholars know the hazards of relying upon secondary sources such as newspapers, magazines, biographies, textbooks, and handbooks. Particular care must be exercised when quoting from condensations in popular magazines. They are the most likely to distort the original, however honest the editors' intentions may be.

This comment offers the further advice to read with an alert, open, and inquiring mind. Analyze and evaluate the purported facts and the opinions. Systematic instructions on this process are given under "Tests of Evidence" in the next chapter. Perhaps the hardest advice to follow concerns the keeping of an open mind. This does not mean a state of indecision; it implies that an advocate will consider views in addition to the one he favors at the outset. The practical value of this attitude stems from the fact that a debater who is broadly prepared is better able to conduct attack and defense. He knows what to expect.

USING LIBRARY RESOURCES[2]

Reference Works

Until library resources become extensively automated, and perhaps even afterward, any student who investigates a proposition with sufficient thoroughness will need to know how to find what he needs in a library. The research tools and procedures explained here will not soon be rendered obsolete by microfilm cameras, computers, and mechanical selection devices combined into information retrieval systems.[3]

General guides to reference works are designed to help the investigator to locate the more specific reference works. The first choice should be Constance Winchell's *Guide to Reference Books,* with its supplements, to answer the question, "Where can I find something on . . . ?" It also gives helpful hints on how to look up information. Three other guides are *Subject Guide to Reference Books* by Herbert Hirshberg, *Basic Reference Sources* by Louis Shores, and *Guide to Reference Material* by Arthur J. Walford.

Guides to newspapers and periodicals include *British Union—Catalogue of Periodicals,* N. W. Ayer and Son's *Directory of Newspapers and Periodicals* (by state, city, and title in the United States, Canada, and territories), Ulrich's *Periodical Directory* (worldwide and by subject), and the *Union List of Serials* (kept up-to-date by *New Serial Titles*).

Periodical indexes, including *Readers' Guide,* are numerous and

[2] The author gratefully acknowledges the professional advice given by George M. Bailey, Executive Secretary, Association of College and Research Libraries. Information leaflets prepared by the Deering Library staff have been used extensively here.

[3] See R. B. Downs, *How To Do Library Research* (Urbana: University of Illinois Press, 1966).

cover a wide variety of interests. The standard items are listed here alphabetically.

> An Index to Book Reviews in the Humanities
> Art Index (1929–date)
> Bibliographie der Deutschen Zeitschriften-literatur (1876–date; German index to German periodicals)
> Bibliographie der Fremdsprachigen Zeitschriften-literatur (1911–date; a German index to non-German periodicals)
> Biography Index (1946–date; biographical material in books and magazines)
> Book Review Digest (1910–date; an index to book reviews)
> Canadian Index (1931–date; for Canadian periodicals)
> Cumulative Book Index (1898–date; for books in English)
> Education Index (1929–date)
> Essay and General Literature Index (1900–date; for essays in collections, book chapters, etc.)
> International Index (1920–date; humanities and social sciences)
> Magazine Subject Index and Dramatic Index (1907–49; American and British)
> Poole's Index (1802–1906; general)
> Pais (1915–date; economics, political science, public administration)
> Publishers' Weekly (1872–date; for new U.S. books)
> Readers' Guide to Periodical Literature (1900–date; general)
> Subject Index to Periodicals (1915–16, 1926–date; British)

Newspaper indexes enable one to locate newspaper materials on specific subjects and by names of writers. After locating the date of a story in the New York Times, one could consult other papers of the same or approximate dates. The four principal newspaper indexes are those of the New York Times (1913–date), London Times (1790–date), Christian Science Monitor, and Wall Street Journal (December, 1957–date).

Bibliographies are lists of source materials on specific subjects. Such lists may be classified according to types of material such as books, periodicals, documents, recordings, etc. They may also be annotated, which means that the nature of the contents is indicated under each entry. The two most important bibliographies of bibliography are Besterman's World Bibliography of Bibliographies and the Bibliographic Index. There are many specialized subject bibliographies such as The Cambridge Bibliography of English Literature, "American Bibliography" in PMLA (publications of The Modern Language Association of America), Writings in American History, Year's Work in Modern Language Studies, and The International Bibliography of Political

Science. National and trade bibliographies such as the *Cumulative Book Index* and the *British National Bibliography*, the *National Union Catalogue* of the Library of Congress, the catalogs of the British Museum and the Bibliothèque Nationale, and the later edition of the British Museum catalog are available in the larger libraries. See also Winchell's *Guide to Reference Books*, 19 ff.

Biographical reference works will be useful to students of argumentation when they need to look up the qualifications of experts whom they intend to quote. The following are the most widely known:

> *Allgemeine Deutsche Biographie* (Germans no longer living)
> *Biographé Universelle* (universal)
> *Contemporary Authors*
> *Current Biographies* (universal)
> *Dictionary of American Biography* (Americans no longer living)
> *Dictionnaire de Biographie Française* (Frenchmen no longer living)
> *Dictionary of National Biography* (Englishmen no longer living)
> *Neue Deutsche Biographie* (Germans no longer living)
> *Nouvelle Biographie Generale* (universal)
> *Who's Who* (living Englishmen)
> *Who Was Who* (Englishmen no longer living)
> *Who Was Who in America* (Americans no longer living)
> *Who's Who in America* (living Americans)

In addition to the above, there are biographical references for other nationalities, regions of the United States, and subject specialties. Among these are *Who's Who in the Midwest, Who's Who in American Education, Directory of American Scholars, American Men of Science,* and *Who Knows—and What.*

Encyclopedias, yearbooks, dictionaries, directories, and statistical compilations are numerous and cover most subjects, countries, and languages. Encyclopedias are good for general background. Best known among the general encyclopedias used by college people are the *Britannica,* the *Americana,* the *New International,* and *Colliers'.* Specialized encyclopedias are available in social sciences, education, government, social reform, and other fields of interest. Yearbooks containing information on events in specific years include *World Almanac, Statesman's Yearbook, Information Please Almanac, American Yearbook, New International Yearbook, Statistical Abstract of the United States, Commerce Yearbook, Statistical Yearbook of the United Nations,* and *Demographic Yearbook of the United Nations.* General dictionaries, especially the unabridged, contain such information as usage, derivation, pronunciation, place geography, weights and measures, colleges, or holidays. The data on postal rates and foreign exchange are likely to be out of date. *Webster's, Funk and Wagnalls, American College Dictionary,* and *Oxford* are the best known. Law, medicine, and other specialized fields have their own dictionaries.

Government documents contain important source material for many propositions. The *Congressional Record* and records of committee hearings are perhaps the best known. Publications of foreign, state, and local governments are also included in this category of government documents, as are the many items issued by the United Nations and its specialized agencies. Guides to U.S. government publications include *United States Government Publications* by Boyd and Rips and *Manual of Government Publications* by E. S. Brown. The U.S. Government Printing Office is the source of the *Documents Catalogue* and the *U.S. Government Publications: Monthly Catalogue.*

Pamphlets on a vast number of subjects are available in the larger collections, some of which have upwards of forty thousand items. Two guides to consult are the *Vertical File Index* and *Public Affairs Pamphlets*. Since much of this kind of material is issued by interest groups, it is useful to know that the names and addresses of organizations can be found in *Guide to Public Affairs Organizations, World Almanac,* and the U.S. Chamber of Commerce *Trade and Professional Associations of the United States.* A critical reader will make allowance for the fact that a pamphlet or a leaflet issued by an interest group may be intended to promote that interest.

Theses and dissertations are not often used by persons who are developing arguments, but this does not imply that they should not be included as potential sources of evidence. *Dissertation Abstracts,* a monthly publication, is the best current listing in abstract form of the dissertations of 117 universities. *Index to American Doctoral Dissertations* serves as an annual index to *Dissertation Abstracts* and as a continuation of *Doctoral Dissertations Accepted by American Universities.*

Interlibrary loan and microfilm have expanded the resources of individual libraries without adding much bulk to any one. Some years ago a researcher had to travel to a library which held something he wished to consult, then interlibrary loan enabled him to borrow such things by paying the postage. Today, thanks to regional library associations and the development of copying machines which reduce the size of the material, the distant resources can be brought to the investigator. Microfilm, microprint, microcards, and photocopy are familiar to most scholars and librarians. Guides to this sort of material include the *Union List of Microfilms* and the *Guide to Microfilms in Print*. Dissertations are available through University Microfilms.

Card Catalogs

In the libraries which will be used by many students of this subject, each card catalog is divided into a general catalog and a serial catalog. Cards are filed alphabetically in the sliding trays according to the system explained below.

General catalog books will be found under their authors' names, or, when no author is given, under the title. The author may be a person (Milton, John), a society or institution (Speech Association of America), or a branch of government (Department of Labor). In addition to the author card there are entries for titles, subjects, and secondary authors. These are interfiled with the author cards.

Subject headings appear at the top of a card in red, or in black underlined in red. A subject will be put under the most specific term applying to it, that is, the subject "oak trees" will be under "Oak," not "Trees." Proper names may also appear as subjects (Lee, Robert E.). Cross references are used when it is necessary to refer from a variant form of a subject to the form used in the catalog (Organic chemistry, see Chemistry, organic), and when referring from one subject heading to other headings under which related material may be found (Architecture, see also Building). Cross references are filed at the end of a subject. A list of subject headings with the appropriate cross references may be found in the U.S. Library of Congress, Subject Cataloging Division, *Subject Headings*. . . .

Titles appear on title cards which are made for works having distinctive titles, such as belles-lettres, anonymous works, and collections. They are generally not made for biographical works which have as their title the subject of the biography, or for works with commonly used phrases such as "A history of . . ." or "A study of. . . ." Look under the subject heading when neither the author nor the title of a book is known.

Cross references, such as those used with subjects, are often necessary to refer from variant forms of an author's name, editions of a work, titles, and translations of a work, to the form used in the catalog. Cross references also are used to refer the user of the general catalog to the serial catalog for fuller information concerning the library's holdings of a particular series or serial. In case there are branch or cooperating libraries, there will be cross-reference cards for items in those places. Special cards are inserted for new accessions, removals, and new orders.

On pages 126 and 127 are specimens of cards in general card catalogs: the first five are for personal authors; the last five are for corporate bodies as authors.

Serial catalogs contain cards for bound periodicals and society publications which are issued in numbered series. Magazines are generally found under their titles, such as *Atlantic Monthly* or *Journal of Higher Education*. Many serials, however, can be found only by looking under the name of the issuing organization, as in the case of the *Proceedings* of the National Education Association. Cards in this catalog indicate which volumes and numbers of a given serial are held by the library. In most cases the recent issues are shelved in a periodical room, but they are listed in the serial catalog. There are no subject cards in this catalog. On page 129 are five specimens of serial catalog cards.

INTERVIEWS AND CORRESPONDENCE

An advocate who is in the investigative stage of his preparation may find it useful to consult with experts in person or by correspondence. We shall consider first the interview in some detail and then apply many of the principles to correspondence as well.

Interviews are used for the purpose of asking knowledgeable persons what they know or think about specific matters in relation to the interviewer's proposition. Students often consult professors, government officials, commentators, and others who seem to qualify either as sources of evidence or as guides to research. Thus it should be obvious that an interview requires more purpose and plan than a social conversation does. But when it is well managed, an interview may yield expert opinion, new facts, different insights, and hints on further research. One step in good management is advance preparation in the form of composing some opening questions, making an appointment, and keeping it promptly. Next, the interviewer should avoid imposing upon the interviewee. This involves investigating elsewhere first so that naive questions will not be asked, and it means that the interrogation will be

CROSS REFERENCE TO RELATED SUBJECT

Literature, Modern. History and criticism see also
Baroque literature

TITLE ADDED ENTRY

809   Ishmael
B163i   Baird, James.
         Ishmael. Baltimore, Johns Hopkins
         Press, 1956.
         xxviii,445p. 24cm.
         Bibliographical footnotes.

SUBJECT ADDED ENTRY, PERSON AS
SUBJECT

809   Melville, Herman, 1819–1891
B163i   Baird, James.
         Ishmael. Baltimore, Johns Hopkins
         Press, 1956.
         xxviii,445p. 24cm.
         Bibliographical footnotes.

SUBJECT ADDED ENTRY, IN RED
OR UNDERLINED IN RED

809   Literature, Modern. History and criti-
B163i   cism, Baird James
         Ishmael. Baltimore, John Hopkins
         Press, 1956.
         xxviii,445p. 24cm.
         Bibliographical footnotes.

MAIN ENTRY

809   Baird, James.
B163i   Ishmael. Baltimore, John Hopkins
         Press, 1956.
         xxviii,445p. 24cm.
         Bibliographical footnotes.

         1. Literature, Modern. Hist. & crit.
         2. Primitivism in literature. 3. Symbol-
         ism in literature. 4. Melville, Herman,
         1819–1891. 5. Religion, Primitive. I.
         Title.

CROSS REFERENCE FROM ALTERNATE
FORM OF AUTHOR
Museum of Fine Arts, Boston
see
Boston. Museum of Fine Arts.

TITLE ADDED ENTRY
L741.64   The artist & the book, 1860–1960
B747a   Boston. Museum of Fine Arts.
The artist & the book, 1860–1960,
in western Europe and the United
States. Boston, Museum of Fine Arts;
[Cambridge] Harvard College Library,
Dept. of Printing and Graphic Arts
[1961]
232p. illus.(part col.) 29cm.

AUTHOR ADDED ENTRY
L741.64   Harvard University. Library. Dept. of
B747a   Graphic Arts
Boston. Museum of Fine Arts.
The artist & the book, 1860–1960,
in western Europe and the United
States. Boston, Museum of Fine Arts;
[Cambridge] Harvard College Library,
Dept. of Printing and Graphic Arts
[1961]
232p. illus.(part col.) 29cm.

SUBJECT ADDED ENTRY, IN RED
OR UNDERLINED IN RED
L741.64   Illustrated books. Exhibitions
B747a   Boston, Museum of Fine Arts.
The artist & the book, 1860–1960,
in western Europe and the United
States. Boston, Museum of Fine Arts;
[Cambridge] Harvard College Library,
Dept. of Printing and Graphic Arts
[1961]
232p. illus.(part col.) 29cm.

MAIN ENTRY
L741.64   Boston. Museum of Fine Arts.
B747a   The artist & the book, 1860–1960,
in western Europe and the United
States. Boston, Museum of Fine Arts;
[Cambridge] Harvard College Library,
Dept. of Printing and Graphic Arts
[1961]
232p. illus.(part. col.) 29cm.
"Exhibition held at the Museum of
Fine Arts, Boston, May 4–July 16, 1961."
Bibliography: p.222–227.
1. Illustrated books. Exhibitions.
I. Harvard University. Library. Dept.
of Graphic Arts. II. Title.

[127]

CROSS REFERENCE TO SERIAL CATALOG
FROM GENERAL CATALOG
AFRICANA
960.5   Northwestern University, Evanston,
N879   Ill. African studies.

For full record see Serial catalog
at beginning of Main catalog.

CARD 2 FOR SERIES SHOWING CONTENTS
AFRICANA
960.5   Northwestern University, Evanston,
N879   Ill. African studies . . . (Card
2)
Contents.
no.1. Herskovits, M.J. Dahomean
narrative. [1958]
no.2. Cohen, A. British policy in
changing

MAIN ENTRY FOR SERIES
AFRICANA
960.5   Northwestern University, Evanston,
N879   Ill. African studies, no.1—
[1958]—
Evanston.

CROSS REFERENCE TO SERIAL CATALOG
FROM GENERAL CATALOG
Lo51   New statesman; the week-end re-
N553   view.
For full record see Serial catalog
at beginning of Main catalog.

MAIN ENTRY FOR PERIODICAL
Lo51   New statesman; the week-end re-
N553   view. v.1–36, Apr.12, 1913–Feb.
21, 1931; new ser., v.1–Feb.28,
1931—
London.

Title varies: Apr.12, 1913–Feb.
21, 1931, The New statesman; a
weekly review of politics and literature; Feb.28, 1931–June 29, 1957,
The New statesman and nation.
See next card

brief, to the point, and courteous. Finally, before the interview takes place, it is wise to learn about the interviewee. This includes reading what he has written on the subject.

When the conversation gets under way, focus upon his area of special competence; presumably that is the reason for the visit. Get him to talk while you listen. Avoid the temptation to debate with him or to press him for a conclusion on the whole proposition. Finally, take notes and ask permission to quote, if that is what you intend to do with his testimony.

Much the same advice applies to correspondence, including questionnaires. This procedure is actually a substitute for interviewing. Probably the best advice is that letters and questionnaires should be used sparingly if at all. If they are used, they should ask about specific evidence, sources, and the like. Use library sources first, and above all, don't reveal your ignorance with a request like this: "Please send me everything you have about speech."

Sometimes a well-designed survey questionnaire is the only feasible instrument. When the General Faculty Committee of Northwestern University was discussing the probable faculty preference for fringe benefits as opposed to the equivalent in take-home pay, there seemed to be no other suitable way to find the answer. Accordingly a questionnaire was carefully designed and administered, and the results were analyzed and interpreted. The finding was in favor of increased fringe benefits, and the administration acted accordingly.

RECORDING NOTES

General Hints

While there is little doubt about the desirability of recording some sort of notes, there is some question about which system is best. Perhaps there is no single, best system, but there is a worst one which we shall call the makeshift or casual system. This judgment stems from the observation that there are distinct advantages in the systematic recording of research notes: it assembles in usable form the materials for essays, speeches, and debates; it facilitates the exchange of information; it prevents the loss of ideas and sources.

Assuming that the systematic recording of *some* notes is desirable, there is still the question of *what* or *how much* to record. A few students record too much—or at least too much that will be practically useless. They need to develop more discrimination. Others, and they seem to be the more numerous, record too little. Precisely how much is enough one cannot say in advance. The nature and the amount of the notes will vary in relation to the complexity of the subject, the investigator's acquaintance with it, the time available for study, and the importance of the occasion for which he is preparing. A survey of the advice on logical responsibility (Chapter 3), analysis (Chapter 5), and evidence (Chapter 7) will provide guidance on what and how much to study and record.

File cards and loose-leaf notebooks are by far the most satisfactory for the storage of notes. Among school debaters and many other library researchers, the 4 × 6 cards seem to be the most popular. They can be moved about easily as the need arises. Of course this advantage holds only if the investigator places just one item on a card and includes enough information about it. This information, in the instance of an evidence card, includes the topic involved, the authority and his qualifications (for opinion evidence), the quotation or paraphrase, and the documentation which would enable any interested person to look up the citation. Ideally, each card should contain enough information to defend its evidence against the likely attacks. See "Types of Notes" below.

Accuracy in recording is of prime importance. If a reader or a listener finds out that someone's words have been misquoted or that a figure is wrong, he is likely to discount everything else that advocate says. Use quotation marks for direct quotations, and plainly identify omissions, condensations, and paraphrases. Copyreading for accuracy can best be done by two persons, one to read aloud from the card and the other to follow the original.

As soon as one accumulates a few cards he is likely to sense the need for a filing system. Suppose he has a box of 4 × 6 cards with raised dividers and a table of contents inside the lid. If he groups his cards by topics or likely points of clash, and if he writes key words and documentation at the top of each card, he can easily find what he wants. These evidence cards are to be used in building a case, in attacking a case, and in defending a case. Variations of this filing system have stood the test of countless school debates in which the speakers needed to select the right cards in a hurry.

In 1966 a new commercial venture introduced a filing system using digital computer cards which can be notched and cut so as to facilitate rapid and complete retrieval by topics.

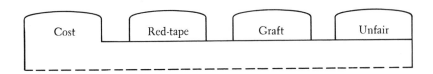

Types of Notes

Bibliography cards or sheets, preferably the former during the investigative stage, are useful in keeping a record of the worthwhile sources. To this end the following items are included: indentification of the reference (person's name, title of article and magazine or book, publication date, pages used), place of storage (general library, law library, closed reserve, stacks, reference room, etc.), and annotation (what is in it, and of what use to one side or both sides). The identification of the reference comes first.

> Geo. L. Bach, Prof. & Head, Econ. Dept., Carnegie Tech.
>
> *Economics: An Intro. to Analysis & Policy*
> N.Y., Prentice-Hall, 1954
>
> Business Reading Room
>
> Book VII, pp. 547–617.
>
> Ch. 31—Monetary policy . . .
> Ch. 32—Fiscal Policy . . .
> Ch. 33—Anti-Monopoly Measures . . .
>
> Affirmative on liberal, planned fiscal policy.

Evidence cards, including those which contain ideas for attack and defense, are often drawn from the sources recorded on bibliography cards. Since the "General Hints" above cover all but the illustration of evidence cards, the following specimens will suffice. The first is for a direct quotation, and the second is for a paraphrase or a précis:

Increased industrial output of CM nations.

Robert L. Heilbroner, *The Making of Economic Society*, p. 191

Ed. at Harvard and New School for Social Research; author of economic history, *The Worldly Philosophers*.

"The Common Market is still in the process of achieving many of these goals, although it is well ahead of its timetable. Already, however, it has led to a remarkable increase in European production. By the early 1960's, industrial production has more than doubled, and agricultural output has risen by a third. Over the entire decade, Western Europe's rate of growth has exceeded by 50% that of the United States, and most important of all, for the first time the standard of living for the middle and working classes of Europe has begun to resemble that of America."

Food pollution from testing

"Iodine-131 in Fallout: a Public Health Problem," *Consumer's Reports*, XVII (September, 1962), p. 447.

A leading periodical devoted to making available objective research data. Completely unbiased politically.

(Précis)

No. of micromicrocuries per liter of milk: The Radiation Protection Guide for Iodine-131 for children is 100 micromicrocuries per day over a year's time. Yet, in May 1962 Wichita, Kansas, averaged 220 micromicrocuries per day; Kansas City, 200 per day; Minneapolis, 120 per day. In June, 1962, Kansas City was up to 240 per day; Wichita was still above safe levels with 130 per day. In the same month, Spokane, Washington, averaged 350 micromicrocuries per day and in July, 1962, Salt Lake City averaged 650 micromicrocuries per day. If these present high levels continue, our milk supply will actually endanger our children's health.

DISCUSSION

In the preceding sections of this chapter it has been assumed that the investigator has a stated proposition with which to work. But now let us suppose a situation in which some persons discover a common interest in a problem which has not yet been verbalized. What can they do? Where should they begin? Their investigative problem can be handled with a modification of the Dewey formulation of reflective thinking.[4] But before they can use this procedure they must express their problem in question form. It could be something like this: What should be done to provide a higher minimum of educational opportunity in this country? Then they can develop an expanded version of this sketchy outline:

    I. Define and delimit the problem
       A. What is the general problem?
       B. How much of it will we consider?
       C. What do the terms mean?
    II. Analyze the problem
       A. What are signs of problem?
       B. Why do these signs exist?
       C. By what criteria should proposals be judged?
    III. Offer solutions
       A. Explain solution "A."
       B. Explain solution "B," etc.

By the time the discussants have moved through the third of the five possible steps, they are likely to choose either of two courses: to continue the reflective deliberation until one solution is agreed upon, or to move into a parliamentary context and reach a decision through debating. The latter has often occurred with the question of how to improve educational opportunity. Federal aid in some form usually comes into contention. In this kind of situation we see how discussion can serve to develop a proposition. This is obviously one of the investigative functions of discussion.

The second investigative function of discussion is to assist in planning a case. In this setting, however, discussion undergoes changes in attitude, purpose, and possibly method. Here the idea changes from

---

[4] See J. H. McBurney and K. G. Hance, *Discussion in Human Affairs* (New York: Harper and Bros., 1950), pp. 65–80.

"What should be done to provide a higher minimum of educational opportunity in this country?" to "How can we prove that our scheme of federal aid is the best solution?" Even so, the individual contributions need not be advanced in the spirit of controversy; they can be expressed in explanatory form. If each speaker in the conference, "skull session," or brainstorming period explains what arguments he thinks would be good and how he so decided, then the colleagues can understand him and in turn explain why and how they agree or disagree with him. In this way some of the valuable features of reflective group deliberation are preserved. This outcome is even more likely if each contributed idea for the case is advanced as a hypothesis without personal commitment or ego involvement.

BRAINSTORMING

Writing on the "very latest vogues he has been through in the discussion movement," Murphy[5] attributes the naming and the popularizing of this variety to an advertising executive, A. F. Osborn, around 1939. Starting with the twenties and moving toward the recent past, one can list several vogues: forum discussion, panels and symposia, the Dewey five-step, Korzybski's version of semantics, brainstorming, group dynamics, and so on. Each has had its devotees, and all have added to our understanding.

In relation to preparation for advocacy, brainstorming is an informal, permissive kind of discussion which has been found to have some value in turning up leads to definitions, interpretations, issues, evidence, arguments, cases, and strategic approaches. This procedure is not intended to provide the actual evidence or to evaluate the resulting ideas. It is an exploratory technique.

Although only two recent textbooks on argumentation offer any appreciable material on this technique, it does seem to be worthy of some attention.[6] Six principles of procedure appear in the literature: (1) Express anything that comes to mind. No idea is "too wild." (2)

---

[5] R. Murphy, "Shop Talk," *Quarterly Journal of Speech*, XLIII, No 3 (1957), 337–340.

[6] A. Freeley, *Argumentation* . . . , pp. 169–175; E. Moulton, *Dynamics* . . . , pp. 13–24.

Quantity is desired. Keep the ideas coming. (3) Suspend judgment. Do not criticize the suggestions as they are made. (4) Contribute, combine, blend, and try to improve upon the ideas. (5) Select participants so as to avoid pecking-order problems due to rank or status. (6) There is no set pattern or outline except as dictated by the subject and a possible time limit.

Finally, there are several topics or devices that have been suggested as means to the end of creative thinking: borrow or adjust, seek new twists, magnify, minify, eliminate, rearrange, reverse, and combine suggestions. Suppose we have a small group of students preparing to debate on federal subsidy for the performing arts. Conversation on the first topic might go something like this: "What are the performing arts?" "Acting, singing, dancing, and playing instruments, I suppose." "Well, if actors qualify, why not the writers and directors who make their performances possible?" "And why not technical theatre people, too?" "Is painting a performing art?" "No, that's more like sculpture and architecture." "Then we had better cut out 'performing' if we want to encourage all of the fine arts." This gives only a suggestive glimpse of the way in which a so-called free-wheeling discussion can function in the analysis and the investigation of a proposition.

QUESTIONS

1. Define these terms so as to distinguish among them: investigation, research, analysis.
2. Why start with a self-inventory and possibly observation? Illustrate with a proposition.
3. Do you agree with the widespread claim that undergraduates have no time to read newspapers or magazines?
4. In order to locate newspaper accounts of the NATO conference held on a certain date, which reference work should be consulted first?
5. What if "magazine" were substituted for "newspaper" in question 4?
6. Is it not a contradiction in terms to speak of a group of advocates discussing ways to prove a predetermined proposition?
7. With how much confidence can one assert that the printed record in the *Congressional Record* is an exact report of what a member of Congress said?

EXERCISES

(Covering investigation plus a review of analysis)
1. As a *speaker*, report orally for three to four minutes on these items:
   A. Statement of a controversial problem
   B. Statement of your proposition based upon "A"
   C. Classification of that proposition
   D. List of potential issues in question form
   E. Stipulation of any waived or admitted issues
   F. Issues on which you would contend
   G. Point or points in partition on which you would build your case
   H. Kinds of material needed to support "G"
   I. Sources for material (Sketch an investigative procedure.)
2. As a *writer*, submit the equivalent of Exercise 1 in outline form.
3. As a *reader or a listener*, submit this version of Exercise 1 in outline form, except that you will use the text of someone else's argument (in Appendix or elsewhere):
   A. State his proposition.
   B. Classify it.
   C. List his actual issues.
   D. List any potential issues not used.
   E. State his points in partition.
   F. Are these points, if well supported, sufficient to discharge the advocate's ethical and logical responsibilities?
   G. How thoroughly did the advocate apparently conduct his investigation? Did he seem to know enough about his proposition? Explain your evaluation.
4. This is an assignment in the investigation of a proposition of one type. Either an oral or a written composition may be based upon this exercise on a later occasion. First, you will think through the steps of Exercise 2 at the end of Chapter 5 as they apply to your proposition for this lesson. That analysis will guide your reading. Second, you will prepare five cards for bibliography. Third, you will prepare twenty evidence cards which will be used in the next oral or written lessons. Finally, you will hand in the cards, but some students will be asked to demonstrate by reading some cards or copying one or two on the board.

CHAPTER 7

EVIDENCE

WAS THERE A CONSPIRACY TO ASSASSINATE PRESIDENT KENNEDY? IS MARI-juana habit-forming? Are lung cancer and heart disease traceable to heavy cigarette smoking? Did North Viet Nam act militarily in South Viet Nam prior to the American involvement there? Answers to these and countless other questions require evidence if anyone is sufficiently interested to ask, "What do you have to go on?" or "How do you know?"

When advocates prepare systematically, their analysis and investigation lead to the accumulation and the testing of evidence which they expect to use in support of their points. But before we get into the so-called technicalities of evidence, we should try to decide what evidence is. A dictionary definition is inadequate, because it broadly characterizes evidence as that which tends to prove or that which serves as a ground for belief. Legal definitions are appropriate for judicial contexts but sometimes not for purposes of general argumentation. Evidence in court consists of testimony, documents, precedents, and things which, if admitted by the presiding judge, are offered in support of a point in question. In other words, legal evidence is informative material, acceptable to those who are to judge, which is offered by an advocate to buttress his own inferences. In both the legal and the nonlegal settings, evidence is called the raw material of proof, because evidence plus inference equals proof. These two ingredients of proof differ in that evidence is independent of and external to the advocate; it is not of his own invention, which means that he did not "make it up." However, the acceptability of his evidence to either persuadees or critics will be treated under "Tests."

There is general agreement that evidence in general argumentation includes the raw materials of proof which have not been contrived by the advocate himself, but beyond this there is no consensus. In fact, there are at least five distinguishable definitions in the contemporary literature of argumentation theory. One school of though limits evidence to "statements of fact," although judgmental statements do sometimes serve as evidence in changing belief.[1] Another includes "facts and opinions as to facts," and it helpfully reminds us that evidence is in the substantive fields about which we argue.[2] A third agrees that facts and opinions are included, but it adds that these data are not invented by the advocate and that enough detail must be given to establish the independence of that invention to the satisfaction of the audience.[3] One of the persuasion-oriented books defines evidence as data intended to induce belief, by which it means testimony of statistics or of authoritative opinion.[4] Finally, there are definitions which stress factual statements and sometimes admit authoritative statements, but the crucial element is belief or acceptance by those to whom the material is offered as evidence. ". . . any matter of fact used in gaining the belief or changing attitudes of others," is the way one writer puts it.[5] Another source defines evidence as information to which a proof appeals (factual foundation, data, etc.), but it must be germane and be believed by listeners or readers. The "factual" character of the evidence depends upon the "opinion" of the audience, it is claimed.[6] The last writer in this group sets out two definitions, the first of which includes "available pertinent facts plus available pertinent true statements of fact." But this is too restrictive to accommodate what actually passes for evidence; therefore, a second and wider definition includes: (1) "authoritative advice and statement acceptable to the audience," (2) "available facts,"

[1] Bettinghaus, *Message Preparation* . . . , pp. 9–12, 44, 82.
[2] Windes and Hastings, *Argumentation* . . . , pp. 97 and 105.
[3] McBath (ed), *Argumentation* . . . , pp. 145–146.
[4] Miller and Nilsen, *Perspectives* . . . , pp. 25 and 37.
[5] Huber, *Influencing* . . . , p. 94.
[6] Ehninger and Brockriede, *Decision* . . . , pp. 99–100.

(3) "all available statements of fact, true and false, that the audience believes," and (4) "statements of value, ethics, and taste that the audience accepts as starting places for the argument."[7]

For the purposes of general argumentation, let us define evidence as factual statements, objects not created by the advocate, and opinions of persons other than the advocate which are offered in support of his claims. Factual statements or empirical data consist of presumably verifiable information on the occurrence, existence, classification or character of phenomena. These data are sometimes statistically expressed and sometimes not. Opinions of persons other than the advocate will be discussed under "Legal Classification" and "Tests," wherein a distinction between ordinary and expert opinion will be drawn. In this category we should also place the admissions of a respondent in a dialectical (cross-examination) situation. Our present distinction between factual statements and statements of opinion is neat and convenient, but it is not universally applicable. Allegedly factual statements sometimes turn out to be expressions of opinion, and misguided ones at that. Objects not created by the speaker or writer will be defined in more detail under "real evidence," but for the present we shall merely mention that material things such as weapons, burglar tools, ladders, eye glasses, and articles of clothing have often been offered as real evidence.

THEORETICAL IMPORTANCE

In theoretical writings on rhetoric and argumentation we find three principal reasons for using evidence in argumentative discourse: it adds probative force, it tends to increase the credibility of the communicator, and it may add emotional impact. Probative force means logical and substantive adequacy which the ancients treated under *logos* in rhetorical theory. The contribution of evidence to probative force can be seen in the fact that a controversial statement which is not evidenced is potentially a fallacy of unsupported assertion. When we say that the use of evidence enhances the credibility (*ethos*) of the communicator, we

[7] Bormann, "An Empirical Approach . . .," *Central States Speech Journal*, XII, No. 2 (1961), 90–91.

mean that a writer or a speaker in a controversial situation makes his statements more believable when he supports them with material other than his own. If the advocate is not a prestigious source in his own right, he may improve his acceptability by quoting from esteemed sources. Thus a student speaking on a common market for the Western Hemisphere might improve his persuasiveness by citing the testimony of recognized authorities in international trade and finance. Exceptions to this principle are likely to occur when one tries to influence closed minds, wishful thinkers, and the like. On the other hand, when an advocate addresses critical thinkers, his *ethos* is automatically enhanced when his arguments are judged to have probative force. In saying that evidence may add emotional impact to the message, we mean that some affective reaction is practically inevitable. It may be a mild emotional impact as in the case of a friendly attitude toward the source of evidence which the advocate is using, or it may be a strong one as in the instance of revulsion at the sight of an atrocity photograph. The point is that the use of evidence which may stimulate emotional reaction is not categorically unethical; we must weigh the factors of relevance and taste, for example, to determine whether the argument is *ad populum* or not.

When discussing the persuasiveness of evidence we once again get into the troublesome distinction between proof and belief. Those writers who focus upon the "behavioral effects" of evidence do not specify *upon whom*. Only one example will be cited here, because the basic issue has been extensively treated in the definition of proof: ". . . the function of evidence in argument is to induce belief [just anyone's?],[8] not necessarily to aid in communicating truth or establishing fact." This source then refers to Nazi propaganda as having met the "results" criterion of successful persuasion.[9]

Although the theory of argumentation attributes much importance to evidence, it does not say that all factual statements and inferences require such support. Matters of common notoriety, for instance, need not be evidenced. This situation is analogous to judicial notice in law, but the critical listener or reader would do well to test any statement prefaced by potentially question-begging language such as "We all know that . . ." or some beguiling equivalent. Finally, waived or admitted matters need not be proved either in court or elsewhere. More will be said about the *practical* importance of evidence near the end of this chapter.

[8] Italics mine.
[9] Miller and Nilsen, *Perspectives* . . . , pp. 26–27.

COMMON FORMS

Textbooks on argumentation and on the law of evidence present a variety of the common forms of evidence. A few listings will be mentioned, with the note that the forms that evidence may take constitute a less important topic than the classifications of evidence which appear in the next section. There are two reasons for this: the classifications include the forms; and the tests, especially in legal settings, are more directly related to the classes of evidence. In law the common forms include oral testimony, testimony by deposition, documentary evidence, and real evidence. In the literature of persuasion the simplest listing of the common forms includes personal observation and observation by others, either trained or untrained.[10] One of the newer books on academic debating lists two common forms: facts (statistics, examples, and analogy) and expert opinions.[11] Whether there is a confusion of evidence and reasoning in the "fact" category here is worthy of scrutiny. Five common forms are listed in another recent book: factual examples, statistics, opinions of authorities, testimony of lay witnesses, and documents, legal papers, and the like.[12] One of the listings of common forms of evidence is distinctive in adding judicial notice and in subdividing the "documents" category. Its six categories are judicial notice, public records, public written material, private written material, personal testimony, and inspection.[13] Finally, there is a list of five common forms, the last two of which are seldom mentioned specifically: witness, document, relics, recordings, and pictorializations.[14]

After noting these differences of opinion, one may raise two questions: "Which common forms should one consider?" and "What difference does it make?" It is not here claimed that there is only one "right" listing of the common forms of evidence. Instead, these six forms which have been derived eclectically from the preceding survey are suggested: judicial notice, documents, witnesses, objects, pictures, and recordings.

---

[10] E. Abernathy, *The Advocate* (New York: David McKay Co., 1964), pp. 23–25.
[11] Capp and Capp, *Principles* . . . , pp. 105–109.
[12] Huber, *Influencing* . . . , pp. 94–97.
[13] Freeley, *Argumentation* . . . , pp. 74–77.
[14] P. Brandes in McBath, *Argumentation* . . . , pp. 153–159.

Whether any scheme of classification makes a difference can be answered best by putting it to the test of practicality.

Judicial notice is a legal term for the court's allowing an item to be used as a premise for an argument without its being evidenced. Actually there are three circumstances when evidence in the usual sense is not used in a judicial situation: when an item is admitted by the adversary's pleading, when it is stipulated by parties to be true without proof, and when it is a matter of common knowledge or common notoriety. However, these admitted, stipulated, or commonly known items cannot be taken for granted and ignored; they must be cited as starting points of arguments, just as if they were evidence. This is why judicial notice may be taken as a common form of evidence, at least in general argumentation. To illustrate, one might state without proof that a private business enterprise is intended to be financially profitable, that smoking near combustibles is hazardous, that specific drugs are addictive, and so on.

Documents are of many subtypes, three of which are official public records, public printed matter, and private written matter. All are written by someone other than the advocate himself. Official public records, which are kept by governmental agencies, include statute books, ordinances, minutes, deeds, and vital statistics. The *Congressional Record* is perhaps the most familiar. These official public records are usually reliable sources of factual data, but all sorts of personal remarks clutter up some public records. Public printed matter is familiar to all. Books, newspapers, and magazines, all of which were treated under "Reading" in Chapter 6 belong in this group. Private written matter includes material which was written for private use but which may sometime become public, as in the instances of wills, contracts, diaries, correspondence, and company books.

Witnesses give personal testimony either orally or by deposition. Oral testimony is given under oath in legal and quasi-legal cases, but it also appears as reports in nonlegal meetings. The distinguishing characteristic of this form of evidence is the physical presence of the source before the audience. This makes cross-examination possible. We are familiar with the situation in which a witness is called to the stand to testify in a trial. The deposition is a sworn statement taken by a court stenographer from a witness who will not appear in court. The obvious weakness of this form of evidence is the impossibility of cross-examination. In general argumentation, personal testimony by witnesses is less rigorously tested than in court. For instance, in a campus meeting on

Parents' Day, a dean argued that students have more serious interests than their parents' student generation had. In support of his point he called upon several students, faculty men, and personnel administrators to report their impressions and to answer questions from the floor.

Physical objects, by definition, provide the stuff of concreteness in a presentation. In the legal classification this form of evidence is known as real, demonstrative, or of inspection. More will be said of real evidence later, but for the present we shall discuss the other two names for it. Demonstrative evidence involves someone's showing how something works, while evidence of inspection means that the speaker gives the listeners something to look over. From the fundamentalist-modernist religious debate of the 1920's we get an interesting specimen of the object as a form of evidence. According to an article titled "Monkey in Pulpit—Which?" a fundamentalist preacher in Montana brought into his pulpit a chattering monkey in support of his argument against evolution. "The presence of the monkey in the pulpit is supposed to have proved something, and it did, but possibly not what the Rev. Mr. _____anticipated."[15] From real and fictional murder trials we know about real evidence such as weapons, clothing, and miscellaneous personal effects, but some of it is not as real as claimed. The dark stains on the clothing of one convicted murderer proved to be paint, not blood.

Pictorial representations are typically referred to as visual aids rather than a form of evidence. Still photographs, movies, video tape, charts, diagrams, graphs, drawings, and mock-ups are familiar varieties of this form of evidence. With the growth of television has come an increasing awareness of the part that visual aids can play in entertaining and persuading vast audiences. In the absence of precise measurement of this effectiveness there has been substituted an abundance of guesswork which has resulted in a flood of apparently ridiculous visual commercials. On the other side it must be conceded that some psychological studies have indicated the persuasive superiority of a visually augmented verbal message. The risks of doctored evidence apply to the visual form as well as the others. The printed decision of an appealed case involving infringement of a trademark shows the crucial nature of this form of evidence in the case at hand:

Picture or graphic representation used in association with word may serve as coaching device to indicate how word is to be pronounced; hence,

[15] *Christian Century*, XLI, 39 (1924), 1245.

presence of two mountains on label stimulates person looking at label to pro-
nounce "Rocké" thereon as "Rocky" as in "Rocky Mountains."[16]

Recordings are more likely to be used in nonlegal situations not
covered by the rules of evidence. At present most courts do not admit,
and most states do not allow, wiretapping or other kinds of electronic
eavesdropping. But there are nonjudicial situations in which recorded
sounds are the best evidence that the sounds were made. Tape recordings of business conferences and interviews are cases in point. The
extent to which the presence of the recorder causes speakers to modify
their remarks is, of course, a question of some importance. Of potentially even greater importance is the possibility of tampering with a
recording by editing in various ways.

CLASSIFICATIONS

Schemes of classification of evidence which appear in writings on
argumentation have been considerably influenced by legal practice.
Probably the simplest formulation in our literature is one that names
two classes: testimony of statistical data and testimony composed of
authority-based assertions.[17] Another has five classes, one of which is
stated as a pair: direct or circumstantial, negative, reluctant, real, and
created.[18] Seven pairs of classes which, except for the omission of
admissible-inadmissible and ordinary-expert, are like those given in this
book appear in another recent work.[19] The six pairs of classes and two
single classes in a recent revision are standard except for the altered
wording in the first two, the omission of direct-circumstantial, willing-
reluctant, and positive, and the addition of "evidence aliunde," which
means one item of evidence that serves to explain another. In debating
the atomic test-ban treaty in the Senate, for instance, one item of evi-

---

[16] District Court, D. Colorado. Coopers, Inc. *vs.* Rocky Mountain Textile,
Inc., No. 6170. Decided Nov. 12, 1959. Member of winning law firm wrote to this
writer as follows: "The court decided in our favor and, as you will note, handed
down a rule incorporating your theory that a picture may serve as a coaching device
to indicate how a word should be pronounced. This is a novel and important rule of
law and I believe the first one in the country."

[17] Miller and Nilsen, *Perspectives* . . . , pp. 37–47.

[18] Bettinghaus, *Message Preparation* . . . , pp. 44–51.

[19] Ehninger and Brockriede, *Decision* . . . , pp. 110–115.

dence concerned the amount of fallout, while another, interpretative item was an expert's opinion on how much fallout is tolerable. This latter item would be called "aliunde," in case the distinction seems to be worth making.

A four-point classification based upon the fields of endeavor in which evidence is used in distinctive ways is the contribution of a recent textbook.[20] According to this schema, evidence can be historical, scientific, journalistic, or legal. Those who try conscientiously to report or interpret the past have occasion to find, test, and use evidence. Professor Gordon Craig, a Stanford University historian, lists many of the materials which may serve as historical evidence:

> . . . The historian generally finds, if he is imaginative enough, that he has lots of material to work with. As it marches through history, the human species leaves an incredible clutter behind it: Charters and treaties, political constitutions and manifestoes, speeches and newspaper editorials, trade indices and bills of lading, the proceedings of scientific and fraternal societies and the tables of organization of military units, school curricula and municipal sanitary codes, inscriptions on gravestones and labels on bottles, agricultural instruments and inventions that never worked, diplomatic notes and poems of commemoration, begging letters, dunning letters, love letters, Sears Roebuck catalogs, music hall songs and bad plays, self-congratulatory autobiographies and doctored diaries and, most recently, tape-recorded interviews with witnesses to this, that or the other.
>
> Once he has accumulated this mass of stuff . . . the historian has to wade through it and mull over it and take notes on it and fret about it and check bits of it against each other and try to reconcile parts of it that don't agree. With it he plays an endless . . . detective game . . . he looks for truth and, knowing that the job he does will all have to be done again by later historians, he tries to establish a true record of man's past.[21]

Scientific evidence comes from the findings of investigators in life sciences, physical sciences, behavioral sciences, and the like. This kind of evidence is called for when controversial questions such as these come up: Can atomic explosions be detected at great distances? How does smoking affect health? Which drugs are addictive? Does pornography induce criminal behavior? Would our agricultural methods work in India? What effect will open-occupancy legislation have upon the economics of real estate?

Journalistic evidence is the most familiar to the average person: "I see by the paper that so-and-so did thus-and-so." After the passage of

20 Windes and Hastings, *Argumentation* . . . , pp. 106–147.
21 "Some Reflections on the Historian's Job and His Audience," *Key Reporter*, XXXII, No. 1 (1966), 2–3.

time, some journalistic evidence becomes historical evidence. In either case the characteristic, potential weaknesses of this kind of evidence are well worth noting. More will be said of this in relation to tests of evidence, but for the present these will be listed: selection and interpretation, inaccuracy, slanting, fabrication, and news management. In 1967, for instance, there were charges of a "credibility gap" which stemmed from the suspicion that news was being "managed" to create a favorable impression of our military and civilian operations in Viet Nam.

Legal evidence will not be treated specifically nor in detail here, but in the classification which follows the names will be borrowed from the law. The principal difference between this treatment and that given in law books lies in the lesser stress which will be given to testimony, documents, precedents, and things, especially the last two, in general argumentation. The main reason for the lesser emphasis is that most students of general argumentation do not have occasions to make all of the distinctions important to lawyers and judges. The following nine pairs of categories have been adapted from legal practice because they are generally serviceable, and pre-law students will find the introduction instructive. It is important to notice that an individual item of evidence can be classified according to one-half of each of the nine pairs of categories.

Admissible or Inadmissible

In one sense this dichotomy has a null class; if some material is not admitted in evidence, it is actually not evidence in that case. If it is not admitted, it need not be classified in terms of the following pairs of categories. The general reason for rules on this point is to screen potential evidence so as to exclude that which would not aid in the decision-making process. There are two broad rules of exclusion: objections to the form in which a question is put to a witness (coaching or leading), and objections to the substance of the evidence sought (irrelevant, immaterial, and incompetent). In addition to the one general reason for rules of exclusion there are four particular reasons: they make for a more orderly presentation of cases; they save time by allowing only that evidence which bears upon the issues before the court; they aim to have evidence authenticated before the jury is permitted to ponder it; they preserve the privileged status of some communications, such as those between physician and patient, priest and penitent, lawyer and client, and husband and wife.

Rules of evidence exist only in judicial settings, although "ground rules" may be established by assemblies, debate leagues, and the like. Legal rules are obviously too complex for other situations. However, a person of integrity, judgment, and taste can profitably apply some of these standards to his own evidence and to that of others who seek his approval.

Original or Hearsay

In nonlegal usage these might be named primary and secondary, respectively. Original evidence comes directly from the primary source: the eyewitness himself, the researcher who made the finding, the expert who looked into the matter, or the document in question. Hearsay, on the other hand, is secondary and somewhat suspect, although it is under certain conditions admissible. Sometimes it is the only evidence available. An oral report of the contents of a document or a senator's version of the President's opinion on a pending bill would be classified as hearsay.

For purposes of general argumentation, five principles will serve to guide our use of hearsay evidence: its use is entirely proper if it is the best available; readable hearsay should not be stigmatized because of the shoddy hearsay which some persons use; the intermediary should be checked for reliability; public records and public written material which students use extensively are acceptable because their public nature stands in lieu of cross-examination; hearsay testimony given before the controversy arose is generally given more credence than that which is given during the debate. When these principles are followed, the use of hearsay evidence or secondary sources need not be a cause of embarrassment.

Direct or Circumstantial

Direct evidence applies, without the need of any mediating inference, to the precise point in issue. Statistical data on employment, production, consumer spending, bank deposits, consumer debt, and interest rates, for instance, can be used as direct evidence on the health of the domestic economy. A more obvious instance of direct evidence would be the testimony of an eyewitness who reports that Mr. X was standing at a specific spot when Mr. Y's car struck him. This would be direct evidence if the point in issue were the whereabouts of the victim at the moment of impact.

Circumstantial evidence involves a set of facts other than those in issue which, when coupled with an inference, tend to support the point in issue. Circumstantial evidence abounds in criminal trials because wrongdoers rarely invite witnesses. Also, on the suspected connection between cigarette smoking and lung cancer and heart disease, the evidence is thus far circumstantial. An apocryphal story relates a Chicago judge's embarrassing experience with this kind of evidence outside his courtroom. After lunching in a restaurant, the judge absent-mindedly picked up another customer's umbrella and started toward the door, whereupon the owner rushed up to retrieve his property. After apologizing for his mistake, the judge returned to his office. When it was time to commute to his home, he decided to take some of his family's umbrellas which had been accumulating at one end of his daily trip. Aboard the commuter train the man whose umbrella the judge had picked up at noon noticed the judge carrying several umbrellas. "Had a good day, didn't you?" he quipped.

Although direct evidence is often preferable, we should recognize that it may be unreliable because of faulty perception by a witness, inaccurate reporting by him, or intentional misrepresentation. And, as one should expect, circumstantial evidence may be misleading because of fallacious inferences which may be drawn from it. For these reasons it is advisable, whenever possible, to use the two kinds in combination. If they corroborate each other, the result is a stronger argument.

Ordinary or Expert

When classified by source, evidence may be termed ordinary or expert. According to law, an ordinary witness may testify to facts, not opinions. This rule stems from the fact that an ordinary witness is, by definition, without qualifications in the disputed matter. He is supposed to report observation rather than inference, but these are easily confused. A cross-examining lawyer had this in mind when he admonished a witness to tell what he saw and omit what he thought. "I can't talk without thinking," replied the witness, "I'm not a lawyer."

In general argumentation, opinions of laymen, as in opinion polls, are often cited. Ordinary evidence may also be seen in the testimony of a student who testifies before the Discipline Committee that he saw another student copying someone's paper. When an ordinary witness is quoted, one should ask whether he is giving a fact or an opinion, and whether it meets the appropriate tests as explained below.

Expert opinion evidence is, as the name indicates, an expression of a judgment by one whose training and experience qualify him as an authority on the subject at hand. Social science testimony was used on both sides in the public school segregation cases before the Supreme Court.[22] Experts in this field include specialists in sociology, psychology, anthropology, political science, economics, psychiatry, history, and law. Experts disagree on bygone events as well as on current controversies, as we see in this century-old topic. "Almost from the day when armed conflict began," wrote T. Harry Williams in *Lincoln and the Radicals*, "the Radical and Conservative factions of the Republican Party clashed over the purpose of the War. Lincoln and the moderates attempted to make the restoration of the union the sole objective . . . against this mild program the radicals inveighed, ranted and sneered." In *Lincoln Reconsidered*, however, Ronald states: "To picture Lincoln at swords' points with the Radical leaders of his own party . . . is an error. It is also a reflection of the naive view of the nature of American politics."

Since qualified experts disagree, and since self-styled authorities exist in profusion, what is a student to do? Unfortunately there are too few persons like Mr. A. P. Herbert who once stood for Parliament. He stated his platform on several leading issues of the day, but under Agriculture he confessed, "I know nothing whatsoever about agriculture." Have we heard any of our politicians disclaiming expertness on any subjects lately? Specific tests for ordinary and expert evidence, as well as for other kinds, will be set out in the next main division of this chapter.

Written or Unwritten

These categories of evidence are based upon form. In court the unwritten evidence is mostly the oral testimony of witnesses, and it is

[22] D. B. Strother, "Polemics and the Reversal of the 'Separate But Equal' Doctrine," *Quarterly Journal of Speech*, XLIX, No. 1 (1963), 50–56.

often the larger part of the total evidence. In the other formal situations such as legislative and school debate, most advocates use written evidence, while in the countless, informal advocatory situations the use of experts' oral comments in hearsay form is commonplace. For purposes of general argumentation we may conclude that written evidence can be authenticated more easily and is generally preferable in nonlegal situations.

Real or Personal

Needless repetition can be avoided if we refer to "Witnesses" and "Objects" under "Common Forms" in this chapter. It will suffice to say that real evidence includes tangible objects, while personal evidence means information given by a person or persons. An interesting but inconclusive use of real evidence occurred in a school debate on the detrimental character of chain stores. A student shopped in an independent store and a chain store for identical groceries and displayed two market baskets with their respective sales slips for the purpose of demonstrating a price differential. This would have been personal evidence if the shopper had reported his experience without bringing the groceries. Some of the tests explained below might well be applied to real evidence as well as to the personal evidence to which they so clearly apply.

Preappointed or Casual

Material which is created and kept for future use in proving something is called preappointed evidence. Most of us have or will have firsthand acquaintance with contracts, deeds, notes, and wills, all of which are preappointed and stand ready to be used as evidence if the need should arise. If a student asks the manager of a local television station what he thinks of a particular regulation by the Federal Communications Commission, and if that student plans to quote the source in a speech against that regulation, he is dealing with preappointed evidence.

A comment which is spoken or written without intending it for use as evidence in the future is called casual evidence when it is subsequently employed in proof. Thus if a student were to describe to his roommate the appearance of a man he had seen emerging from a darkened store, that testimony would become casual evidence if it were later used in a burglary trial. One is tempted to place greater trust in this kind because there is less suspicion of bias or self-serving intent. However, this kind of remark may have been made in an offhand, careless manner. For these reasons evaluation should involve more than snap judgment; it calls for careful application of appropriate tests of evidence.

Willing or Reluctant

A distinction similar to the one immediately above is occasionally made between the willing or eager and the reluctant or unwilling witness. This is akin to the test of moral qualification for the reason that the motivation of the witness has a considerable bearing upon the reliability of his evidence. Someone who dislikes college students in general is likely to testify willingly against one who is charged with a traffic violation. However, a friend of the accused is likely to be reluctant in that situation. A reluctant witness may not be hiding anything; he may simply be timid. At the other extreme, a willing witness may be pleasantly cooperative, but he may be acting out of self-interest, such as the desire for vengeance. As a classification this has little usefulness, and as a test it is less significant than several others.

Positive or Negative

Negative evidence is the name given to the so-called testimony of silence, which means a significant absence of evidence to the contrary. It implies that a statement is true because it cannot be proved false. Failure to find cheaters on a relief roll would be negative evidence of lack of graft. Similarly one might conclude that a library does not own a specific book if there is no entry for it in the card catalog. Potential weaknesses of this kind of evidence, if we may call it such, are apparent.

Most of what we have treated as evidence is positive, meaning it directly supports a contention. Since all evidence, strictly speaking, is positive, we rarely use the name. When, in a rare circumstance, the absence of contrary evidence is used as proof, we use the adjective "negative." In all other cases neither of these two modifiers is used; we simply use the word "evidence" alone or modify it with "hearsay," "circumstantial," or some other class name.

TESTS

If we assume the importance of evidence in most argumentation, our next concern should be with the dependability of that evidence. Whether we speak, listen, read, or write, we have a stake in the quality of the evidence used. Ths is why a critical thinker tests the evidence in any matter of interest to him, whether it be his own evidence, that of an opponent, or that of an advocate who seeks his belief. If we wish to behave as rationally as possible, we will demand that the evidence approximate the probable truth, a condition which implies the achievement of as much verifiability as possible. Thus we will beware of evidence which is unclear, false, doubtful, or from a questionable source. We should at the same time realize that facts are not easy to observe correctly, report objectively, or verify reliably. In the interest of critical thinking the following tests of evidence are named and explained. The two major classes of tests are those of substance and of sources, while the four lesser classes are those of investigative method, of reporting, of documentation, and (except in popular persuasion, where it is the major test) of audience acceptability. Obviously there is overlapping especially between audience acceptability and some of the other tests of evidence.

Of Substance

Substantive tests of evidence are intended to insure that the material is relevant to the point in question, significant in its impact, and able to achieve probative force without raising extraneous questions.

Honesty is rarely given as a substantive test of evidence, although some of the traditional tests imply it. The criterion of honesty is specifically stated and placed in first position for two reasons: wise decisions cannot be based upon falsehood, and lying is sufficiently widespread to warrant specific attention. Two cases will illustrate this principle. In one, the Federal Trade Commission charged that a televised commercial purporting to prove the clearness of one brand of automobile glass was actually filmed through an open window. In the other, the official spokesmen for several countries in the Security Council of the United Nations lied while arguing about the Arab-Israeli war in June, 1967.

Recency of evidence is not always important, but at times it is crucial. One dealing with current, changing events must be alert to the risks of outdated evidence. Last year's fact may be this year's fiction. Old statistics and quoted opinions from persons who have since changed their minds have embarrassed many an advocate. The unkindest cut of all occurs when, in reply to your evidence, your opponent quotes substantially different information given by your own source at a later date. In theological debates, however, there is much less emphasis upon recency and sufficiency of evidence: recency, because the Scriptures have been available for centuries, and authorities from the first to the twentieth centuries are equally credible; sufficiency because the number is much less important than the acceptability of the interpreters.

Relevance may be either legal or logical. Legal relevance is a test which excludes some logically relevant evidence which might mislead a jury or unduly complicate the case. But in general argumentation our greater concern is for logical relevance, which exists when evidence supports the point in connection with which it is used. This test is intended to discourage the raising of side issues like those which muddied the Army-McCarthy hearings in 1954.[23] Practically no tests were applied there; the committee admitted nearly all of the evidence and entertained all issues which anyone chose to raise. The result was a mixture of show, inquiry, trial, and policy debate.

Internal consistency as a test of the substance of the evidence means that one asks, "Is the evidence consistent within itself?" Evidence that is self-contradictory would seem to be the weakest kind imaginable, but it sometimes goes undetected, probably because of a complicated message and uncritical listening or reading. The following are three shortened versions of internally inconsistent evidential state-

[23] F. W. Haberman, *et al.*, "Views on the Army-McCarthy Hearings," *Quarterly Journal of Speech*, XLI, No. 1 (1955), 1–18.

ments which were not detected by college students:[24] (1) Non-Jewish teachers have never properly taught Jewish children the fundamentals of their religion, but proper instruction of this sort has been found in a few cases. (2) All students received religious instruction, but some, including those who were opposed to it, did not. (3) The program was discontinued in 1956, but it is still being conducted. No doubt these flaws would have been noticed by most of the experimental subjects if the above statements had been taken from context and listed under the caption, "Is there anything wrong with these statements?" But propagandists do not give us this much help.

Internal inconsistencies are searched for by the sleuths who examine important documents for evidence of forgery. At least fifty questioned-document examiners are employed by the Federal agencies, and some metropolitan police departments have sections in which these experts examine signatures, watermarks on stationery, type faces, and ink. Since the Supreme Court rulings have affected the practice of interrogating suspects and the use of confessions, the internal-consistency test of evidence has grown in importance.

External consistency of evidence is determined by comparing the item in question with similar material from another source. Is the evidence in question consistent with known fact? Is it consistent with human experience? In other words, is it verifiable in terms of outside criteria? Consider the case of the female worker in a workshop for the blind who testified that a male fellow worker had window-peeped at her. In a more serious vein were the McCarthy charges of communism in the State Department, which Professor Hart found to be at variance with the facts in fifty specific instances.[25] In 1967 an independent citizens' group alleged that a survey of drug prices conducted by the American Medical Association was inaccurate because the findings were incompatible with those of a survey conducted by the citizens' group. The alleged external inconsistency was in the price differential between generic and brand-name drugs when used in filling prescriptions. The A.M.A. survey showed that prescribing drugs generically rather than by brand names did not guarantee a lower consumer cost, whereas the survey by the citizens' committee found that not once had the tradename product been cheaper than the generic.[26]

[24] W. R. Dresser, "Studies of the Effects of 'Satisfactory' and 'Unsatisfactory' Evidence in a Speech of Advocacy" (Doctoral dissertation, Northwestern University, 1962).

[25] H. Hart, "McCarthyism versus Democracy," *New Republic*, CXXVI (1952), 12.

[26] *The New York Times*, May 28, 1967, p. 62.

Sufficiency of evidence is such a variable test that only a few, broad comments can be made about it. Some claims are acceptable without evidence, some require only a little, and still others require an abundance of evidence. Then too, the quality of evidence is more important than mere quantity. Let it suffice to generalize that multiple sources tend to be better than single ones, that the selection ought to be representative, and that "card-stacking" should be avoided. To take a specific example, should we conclude that a drunkometer test administered by highway police is sufficient evidence to convict a motorist of drunken driving? The criterion is a certain concentration of alcohol in the breath or the blood, despite the fact that persons vary enormously in their tolerance levels. Our second case is one of too much evidence. It concerns a young Englishman who vowed that he loved his girl so much he could not live without her. Apparently she did not believe him, because he took his life after writing a note which said in part, "She will believe me now, but it's a hard way of proving my love, don't you think?"

Comparative quality as a test of evidence includes what lawyers know as the "best-evidence rule." Without going into technicalities, let us interpret this rule to mean that one is under obligation to bring the best evidence possible—not merely whatever happens to be easily accessible. For instance, secondary evidence is acceptable if primary evidence is not available, admissions against self-interest are usually valued, casual evidence is generally preferable to preappointed, negative evidence is free from contrivance, real evidence is stronger than a hearsay description, and factual statements often carry more weight than opinions. Suppose the controversial question before the house were "What should be done to prevent a catastrophe which a Red Chinese nuclear capability may bring about?" Of what comparative quality would a statement by President Chiang Kai-shek be if he argued ". . . that the only way to avoid a nuclear holocaust is the destruction of the Peiping regime through a Taiwan-based counteroffensive against the mainland . . . within one or two years"?[27]

Special tests of statistics apply to the procedures employed in obtaining and presenting them, not to the reasoning based upon them. A few leading questions will be raised here, but for fuller exposition the reader is referred to books and articles on statistics. Is the level of statistical significance given? If not, the result may be no better than a chance occurrence. Then too, a statistically significant figure may be

---

[27] *China Post*, Taipei, November 25, 1964, p. 2.

inconsequential in practical affairs. Is the correlation partial, simple, or multiple? The weakest is the partial, as in connecting housing conditions and crime. What does *average* mean, or what does *mean* mean, for that matter? Actually, median or mode would be more meaningful in some cases. Averages, if unspecified, are questionable at best. Have the influential variables been considered? This is where predictions of voting behavior have come to grief. Is it safe to predict the future in terms of a trend line established up to now? Pertinent factors may not stay in their present relationships. Can the phenomenon in question be quantified (expressed in numbers)? It is not meaningful to assert that beauty queens are fifty per cent prettier than they were in mother's day. Are the data relatively free from sampling error? This problem has plagued opinion pollsters, television-audience measurers, and market researchers who want to get a representative sample of the universe that interests them. Has the base of the percentage computation remained constant during the figuring? Suppose a registrar announces that the enrollment in 1962 was 5,000, that it rose four percent in 1963, and then it declined four percent in 1964. It is important to ask whether the 1964 figure was based upon 5,000 or 5,200. Are compared figures based upon the same definitions and unit values? When an old-timer tells how he once bought a new car for five hundred dollars, he may neglect to add that it was a much simpler machine and that five dollars was a good day's pay.

Of Sources

To say of an item of evidence that it came from a questionable source is not the same as saying it cannot have any value. A rascal, for instance, may tell the truth occasionally. This familiar test of source credibility is at times oversimplified and extreme; dishonesty or biasing interest considers only the intention of the source and ignores any intrinsic worth of his testimony. Actually, both the substance and the source are worth considering.[28] To disqualify some evidence because of its unpopular source may be the height of folly. Consider this evidence: "The scenic resources of the United States have been so ruthlessly

[28] C. H. Perelman and L. Olbrechts-Tyteca in Natanson and Johnstone, *Philosophy* . . . , Ch. 6.

exploited by . . . private interests that relatively few stretches of un-spoiled, high-quality, esthetic natural environments are left . . ." What if it came from *Pravda?* Or what if it came from the *New York Times,* which it did? It is hard to remember that an idea is not responsible for who believes in it.

Ordinary witnesses need to be tested as a group as well as indi-vidually, because the value of their testimony is primarily corroborative rather than designative or demonstrative. Thus we need to ask whether we have enough of them and whether they contradict each other. Testing may be worth the effort, because ordinary witnesses are often useful and occasionally necessary in general argumentation. An apt example of contradiction appeared in two letters to an editor on the same day: one lauded the admirable job of snow removal by the city crew, saying that even the side streets were something to be proud of after the heavy snowfall; the second writer charged that the city did not make a reasonable effort to clear the streets, adding that it "doesn't even remove the snow on the business streets which have parking meters."[29]

Integrity stands in a preeminent position among the tests of an individual, ordinary witness. Is he impartial in this matter, or does he have a stake in the outcome? Does he have a reputation for veracity, or has he been impeached by his own previous inconsistent testimony? Doubtful character, which sometimes is taken to include the lack of religious belief, is a basis for the impeachment of a witness. Sometimes the testing is done rigorously, especially when a witness behaves in a suspicious manner, that is to say, with hesitation or with assertiveness.

Opportunity to observe what he is commenting upon is a second, individual test. Credibility is bound to be undermined by the disclosure that the witness was not present when the event in question took place, or that he was there too little time, or that there was some obstacle to clear perception. If someone starts telling us what goes on in a meeting of the University Discipline Committee, let us ask him when he was there.

Mental qualifications, broadly defined, comprise a third test. Intel-ligence, education, memory, perceptiveness, verbal ability, and psycho-logical condition are the familiar components. Under psychological condition we should place "expectancy set," which refers to the readi-ness of the nervous system to respond to a given stimulus in a specific manner. Some persons expect to see certain things before they look;

others expect to hear things, such as ghostly sounds in an empty house. Some other mental qualifications, notably education and intelligence, are perhaps more familiar, as the following case will illustrate. During a controversy over the teaching of American history in a community high school, the local editor observed that ". . . . those who talk loudest and most violently will be those who have never read any of the history texts in question and who haven't any standards for judging them if they did."

Finally, physical qualifications, including vision, hearing, smell, taste, touch, and equilibrium, are subjected to testing when the senses of a witness are involved. This class of tests is typically less important in general argumentation than it is in judicial argumentation where observation rather than judgment is expected from the witness. But even there it is wrong to assume that witnesses can see, hear, and recall accurately.[30]

Expert witnesses have been facetiously characterized as persons who can make something we already know sound confusing. In a similar vein, our penchant for paying more attention to persons from distant places has prompted the cynical observation that an expert is an average person far from home. Despite these quips, expertness is recognizable and testable. The first question might well be, "Is opinion evidence the best kind to use here?" If the point concerns the volume of foreign steel coming into the United States annually, facts are preferable to opinions; but if quantitative data are too difficult to obtain, expert opinions are better than unsupported assertions. In general, we use experts for their judgments, not mere observations.

If it is the substance of testimony that really matters, why test the source? Perhaps the best reason is that many persons pay no attention to anonymous remarks. When a claim is made, those who know about such matters will ask, "Who says so?" Then the authority of the source comes into play. As Justice Brandeis said, "Your opinion is no better than your information."

Michael Polanyi, a British physical chemist turned philosopher, stated the need for an authoritative basis to investigation but distinguished between two kinds of authority, one that provides a *framework* of inquiry and another which *dictates conclusions*. The first lays down general presuppositions, while the second imposes conclusions. The

---

[30] For a critique of ordinary-witness evidence in court, see J. Marshall, *Law and Psychology in Conflict* (Indianapolis: The Bobbs-Merrill Co., 1966).

latter would, if generally applied, destroy science, while the former is indispensable to the existence of science, the law, and Protestant religions, he argued.[31]

Now for the general tests of expert witnesses. Does the source qualify as an expert in the field about which he speaks or writes? This is the essential, general test which includes many subsidiary questions, two of which are: (1) Has the field developed to the point that an expert therein can provide reliable knowledge on the point in issue? (2) Does this person have the credentials (trustworthiness, experience, etc.) of an authority in that field?[32] In court an opposing attorney will occasionally make disparaging insinuations to discredit an expert witness in the minds of the laymen in the jury. Remarks about race, religion, name, and reputations of relatives are made. Although factually irrelevant, such jibes are often persuasive and, in the view of this writer, unethical. They are in many textbooks classified as fallacies of "poisoning the well." Thus they have no legitimate place in general argumentation or in school debate.

While some attempts to discredit an expert witness obviously involve "crooked thinking," there is nothing improper about testing for conflict of interest or some other possible source of bias. After an editor of a college newspaper wrote with an air of authority about the wonders of a spring vacation at a certain resort hotel on Grand Bahama Island, a sharp-eyed critic noted in the classified advertisements that the young man who wrote the travel tip was selling reservations for that same hotel. Writers of biographies, especially of contemporary figures, can expect to face similar challenges. For instance, a reviewer of the biography of a political figure criticized the author's "preoccupation with images and smooth surfaces" and added that the writer had been the subject's main speechwriter and public relations aide much of the five years he was "inside the administration." A similar sort of bias may be found in some persons who expound supposedly expert advice but whose prominent identification with groups that have axes to grind casts doubt upon their impartiality.

One last thought to consider is that, even if the particular field of knowledge is reputable, and even if one has several acknowledged

---

[31] *Science, Faith, and Society* (London: Oxford University Press, 1946) p. 43.

[32] It is hard to disentangle the effects of trustworthiness and expertness as factors of credibility, according to C. I. Hovland *et al.*, *Communication and Persuasion* (New Haven: Yale University Press, 1953), p. 35.

experts from it, future developments may prove them wrong. However, there is some comfort in knowing that numerous factual statements have been proven as wrong as the statements of opinion.

Of Investigative Method

This test of evidence is rarely explained specifically, probably because of its complex interrelationships with the tests of sources, of reporting, and of documentation, to name a few. Perhaps many persons assume that faulty investigative methods inevitably yield results which fail to meet the other tests, hence the methodological test seems superfluous. This is sometimes true and sometimes not. Suppose a local newspaper editorial staff sought to ascertain community opinion on a new tax levy. Their published results of a survey might seem to satisfy the locally available tests of substance, source, reporting, and documentation, but a faster, more efficient test would consist in raising probing questions about their social science research methodology. Persons who have some acquaintance with academic research know about the principles of historical, descriptive, and experimental investigations. Much of what we have learned about analysis, investigation, and evidence comes to a focus on this point.

So far we have thought in terms of legitimate research which, if done poorly, was innocently faulty. However, there is a real problem with rigged research, especially in some consumer-products fields where the stakes are high and detection is difficult. The Food and Drug Administration has identified two types of research falsifiers who are causing increasing concern to that agency, to the medical profession, and to some of the general public. First, there is the professional research quack who set up so-called studies of products intended for direct sale to consumers. He tries out the product on a few patients and then permits the promoters and advertisers to claim that the product has been clinically tested. The second type of rigger might be a physician who has been retained for a fee to test clinically some new drugs, but he either does not test at all or he fakes the results to fit a predetermined conclusion. Millions of persons may be deceived when such false claims receive nationwide exposure through the mass media.[33]

[33] "Rigged Research," Wall Street Journal, June 30, 1965.

Of Reporting

Tests of reporting are not necessarily the same as tests of sources, because the media of transmission and the character of the reporting may be beyond the control or the responsibility of the human source of the evidence. Five questions, some of which partially overlap, are recommended as tests: Is the reporting clear? Is it accurate as far as it goes? Is an ample context provided? If there is interpretation, is it fair? Is the medium itself reputable?

In asking that the reporting be clear, one means that several persons who are presumably qualified to understand the content should derive essentially the same message from what was reported. The second question, namely, the one on accuracy as far as the report goes, involves asking whether the reporting was unfairly selective and whether the best questions were asked in the first place. Even if some selection is inevitable, a critical listener or reader may properly ask whether unfavorable information was omitted, whether important words or figures were left out, whether there was needless delay in giving some vital information, or whether the reporter was lying. But all of these checks are of little value if the reporter failed to ask the best questions initially. Suppose that a victim of a jewel robbery tells the police, some reporters, and an insurance investigator that $100,000 worth of gems were taken from her hotel room. Before reporting the value of the loot, the policeman and the reporter would do well to follow the example of the insurance adjuster, who is likely to ask skeptical questions about the possibly exaggerated claim, and he will be aware of the difference between the original retail price and the net (perhaps ten percent) which the thieves receive from a "fence" who buys their stolen goods. Adequacy of context includes the giving of attendant circumstances, dates, sources, and enough of the quotation in question to indicate its tone and intent. Quoting out of context is a familiar violation of this test. Fairness of interpretation becomes increasingly important as the nature of the report shifts from straight reporting to commenting. Some publications mix reports and commentary in a misleading fashion. This is still worse when irrelevant emotionalism is added to one side of the story for "slanting" effect. Finally, with respect to the reputation of the medium itself, it is thought that we are more likely to believe an otherwise doubtful story if we get the report through a reputable medium like the *Christian Science Monitor* rather than a sensational tabloid.

Two popular weekly news magazines, *Time* and *U.S. News and World Report*, which are often quoted by student speakers, have been challenged on the grounds of their ability and their willingness to tell the truth.[34]

Of Documentation

Listeners and readers have the right to know the date and the source of any evidence offered in support of a claim on their belief. Ideally, the documentation should be such as to enable an interested person to authenticate the evidence if he so desired. In the absence of any real risk of exposure, some advocates will cite nonexistent documents or will misrepresent the contents of existing materials. For instance, two atheists who were seeking an injunction against the issuance of postage stamps carrying the motto, "In God We Trust," quoted George Washington as having said, "The Government of the United States of America is not, in any sense, founded on the Christian religion." A "quote detective" traced the quotation to an old English translation of a treaty between the United States and Tripoli in 1797 and signed by President John Adams. The quotation was not part of the official text but apparently was written into the translation by Joel Barlow, the United States Consul General in Algiers at the time.[35]

In our own time the oft-repeated and apocryphal "government order on cabbage prices" has served many an editorialist or speaker who attacked "bureaucracy," "big government," "red tape," and kindred ills. It usually goes somewhat like this: "The Lord's Prayer has 65 words; Lincoln's Gettysburg Address has 266; the Ten Commandments, 297; the Declaration of Independence, 300; yet a recent government order on cabbage prices has 26,911 words." The proper response to this kind of alleged quotation is, "What was that order, and where can I find it in print?"

More notorious was the McCarthy charge that a Justice Department report dated July 28, 1952 showed there were Communists in the State Department. True, the report was dated in 1952, but it reported testimony on an *unsuccessful* plot during the Coolidge administration in 1928. The content of the so-called evidence was misrepresented, and the dating of the source was off the mark by twenty-four years. Senator Joseph McCarthy's sensational use of illusive evidence in the early

---

[34] R. P. Newman, "The Weekly Fiction Magazines," *Central States Speech Journal*, XVII (1966), 118–124.

[35] "Précis," *Presbyterian Life*, September 17, 1955, p. 29.

nineteen-fifties has been chronicled in the public press and stands as a case study in undocumented evidence.[36]

Under "How To Use It" we shall see whether, in the interest of persuasion, it is necessary, according to experimental studies and some surveys of actual practice, to document evidence as carefully as the preceding paragraphs advise.

Of Audience Acceptability

Under this topic we need not repeat all of the tests which may affect the acceptability of the evidence to an audience. Three of the most pertinent tests are these: Is the evidence consistent with their beliefs? Is the source acceptable? Can the audience understand it? Here we are concerned with the credibility of evidence as it is related to the attitudes and beliefs of readers or listeners toward points which the evidence is used to support. For instance, before a young Republican Club audience, one student gave an anti-New Deal speech without any evidence, while another gave a pro-New Deal speech with every point evidenced. At the end a vote by ballot was taken on this question: "Which speaker made the better use of evidence?" A majority voted for the speech with no evidence. A month later the same procedure was followed in a young Democrat Club meeting, and again evidence was "observed" where none existed.

An American student in a Dusseldorf high school experienced some difficulty in finding evidence to be acceptable to his German classmates. It seems that he attempted to dispel the myth that when the United States was constituted, the Congress voted by a majority of only one vote to make English instead of German the official language. First, he cited the minority status of German immigrants in the new country at that time, but this was not believed. Next he obtained from the United States Information Service a copy of a study prepared by the Library of Congress, but this was dismissed as American propaganda. Finally, he wrote to the West German Ambassador to Washington and received a reply which proved to be persuasive with his skeptical classmates.[37] Obviously the acceptability of these items of evidence was not dependent upon their intrinsic merit.

---

[36] R. H. Rovere, "The Most Gifted and Successful Demagogue This Country Has Ever Known," New York Times Magazine, April, 1967, Sec. 6, p. 23.

[37] "American Boy Dispels Nazi Myth for His Classmates in Germany," The New York Times, January 15, 1967.

This case is dwarfed in comparison with a current controversy concerning the effects of cigarette-smoking upon health. Positive, significant correlations have been found between smoking and lung cancer and some other dread diseases, but some persons do not believe the evidence. What quality and quantity of evidence do such persons require? The sources of incriminating evidence include the Surgeon General, American Cancer Society, Royal College of Physicians, American College of Chest Physicians, American Heart Association, National Cancer Institute, National Heart Institute, National Tuberculosis Association, World Health Organization, American Public Health Association, and many others.[38] Yet it would be possible to assemble audiences that would not react as if they accepted this evidence.

Apparently it is possible to measure some aspects of the audience acceptability of evidence. One reported study compared the credibility of biased, reluctant, and unbiased sources. It was found that reluctant and unbiased sources were more persuasive than the biased, that the reluctant were not dependably better than the unbiased, and that the unbiased may excel the biased, but the value of reluctant testimony is dependent upon the audience variable.[39]

The distressing implication is that we often see and hear what we want to rather than what is actually said. Perhaps this is why myths and symbols frequently outlast facts. It also reveals the folly of taking audience acceptability as the supreme test of evidence. It is supreme only in terms of the "results" criterion of popular persuasion; most of the other tests of evidence are superior in terms of critical standards which stress ethical and logical values. This point harks back to the distinctions between argumentation and persuasion and between proof and belief in Chapter 2.

HOW TO USE IT

In view of what has been said of proof in general and of evidence in particular, what should teachers and students of general argumentation conclude is the proper use of evidence? Whatever they conclude must be applicable to speaking, listening, writing, and reading. It should also

[38] "Book Reviews," *The New York Times*, January 22, 1967, pp. 20 and 22.
[39] W. E. Arnold and J. E. McCroskey, "The Credibility of Reluctant Testimony," *Central States Speech Journal*, XVIII, No. 2 (1967), pp. 97–103.

take into account the differences between the necessities of popular persuasion and the demands of rationality in terms of ethical and logical responsibilities. Whatever evidence is used fits under either "data" or "backing" in the Toulmin layout in Chapter 8. Finally, a decision on the proper use of evidence might be influenced by the results of descriptive studies, the data from experimental research, and the pre-scriptive advice from teachers.

According to Empirical Studies

Using the method of content analysis, several investigators have discovered what the actual practices of some advocates have been. These scholars described their categories such as "complete documentation" and "no documentation," and then they tabulated the occurrences of such phenomena in selected specimens of argumentative discourse. A graduate student in the author's seminar applied this method to the texts of two annual, final debates from the West Point tournament. In one of the debates the affirmative gave complete documentation (source, date, qualification) for fifty percent of its evidence, partial documentation for forty-four percent, and no documentation for only six percent. The negative in the same debate provided complete documentation for sixteen percent, partial documentation for twenty-nine percent and no documentation for fifty-five percent. In the second debate the scores were almost even: the two teams scored twenty-two and twenty-five percent on complete documentation, and twenty-three and thirty percent on no documentation. It is safe to say that the score of fifty percent on complete documentation is relatively high for school debates. This raises the question as to how one can judge whether the evidence is the best available if less than half of it can be verified.

Could a similar question be raised against real-life debates? A comparative analysis of four school debates and four real-life debates revealed that the latter used more cited evidence per one hundred words of discourse, but that the school debates had better documentation. These data are, of course, insufficient for a generalization. A more extensive survey of intercollegiate debates found that evidence of some sort was submitted for fifty-three percent of the contentions and that it generally met the tests of evidence.[40] In contrast to this, a study of four

[40] P. R. McKee, "An Analysis of the Use of Evidence in Ten Intercollegiate Debates" (Master's thesis, University of Kansas, 1959).

major speeches by Dean Acheson and Robert Taft turned up only five items of evidence in all.[41] A comparably low rating for real-life advocates was found in a comparative study of evidence used by high-ranking and low-ranking United States senators. Neither group used very much.[42]

On the basis of limited empirical data, we may tentatively conclude that current practice does not measure up to the standards expressed by teachers and textbooks. Possibly, as one writer suggests, it is not altogether the students' fault. The definitions of evidence may not be functional when students try to identify evidence in debates, and perhaps doctrine on the use of evidence is difficult for a listener to apply.[43]

According to Experimental Research

Instead of surveying what happens in actual advocacy, the experimenter contrives situations which will enable him to measure objectively the difference which a given variable such as evidence makes in the persuasive impact of a message. One experiment compared the persuasiveness of Speech 1 and Speech 2, both of which contained six quotations of expert opinion evidence; however, Speech 1 included names and credentials, while Speech 2 omitted the sources and qualifying phrases. No significant difference in effectiveness was found.[44] Four methods of handling evidence were compared in an experimental dissertation: no evidence, adequate evidence but no documentation, adequate evidence and documentation, and adequate evidence and documentation plus laudatory comments to add weight to the authority. The second and the fourth methods proved to be the most persuasive, showing that it paid to use evidence but that documentation did not help unless it included a buildup for the source.[45] In a somewhat

[41] C. S. Goetzinger, Jr., "An Analysis of the 'Validity' of Reasoning and Evidence in Four Major Foreign Policy Speeches, 1950–51" (Master's thesis, Purdue University, 1952).

[42] P. D. Brandes, "Evidence and Its Use by Selected United States Senators" (Doctoral dissertation, University of Wisconsin, 1953).

[43] W. R. Dresser, "The Use of Evidence in Ten Championship Debates," *Journal of the American Forensic Association*, I, No. 3 (1964), pp. 101–106.

[44] H. Gilkinson, S. F. Paulson, and D. E. Sikkink, "Effects of Order and Authority in an Argumentative Speech," *Quarterly Journal of Speech*, XL (1954), 183–192.

[45] R. S. Cathcart, "An Experimental Study of the Relative Effectiveness of Four Methods of Presenting Evidence," *Speech Monographs*, XXII (1955), 227–233.

similar study three ways of handling evidence were compared: no outside authority used, seven quotations used and authors' names given, and documented quotations plus a buildup for each source. There was no advantage for any of the three in respect to persuasiveness, but the third imparted information more successfully.[46] At least the familiar advice on the presentation of statistical evidence has been supported by an experiment. Three versions of a speech of advocacy were used: in one, statistics were compared with quantities which were familiar to the audience; in the second, only statistics appeared; in the third, generalized statements replaced the statistical evidence. The first form worked best.[47]

Possibly the most disturbing findings, at least to anyone who values critical thinking, are that unsound evidence proved to be as persuasive as the sound evidence, and that the college students who heard the speeches did not detect the flaws (internal inconsistencies) in the unsound evidence.[48] The four versions which were equally persuasive were distinguished as follows: one used evidence rated satisfactory by experts, the second used questionable sources; the third used irrelevant materials in lieu of evidence; the fourth used internally inconsistent evidence. A summary of the findings of experimental studies on the impact of evidence on decision-making is available. It questions the relation of the findings to common sense, and it does so because of the heretofore uncontrolled variables in the experimental designs.[49]

According to Prescriptive Advice

After consulting these findings, what shall we say about the use of evidence in advocatory discourse? One might counsel "realism," saying that a clever persuader can make a little material go a long way, or one might stand fast for the ideals of ethical and logical responsibility in all

[46] D. C. Anderson, "The Effect of Various Uses of Authoritative Testimony in Persuasive Speaking" (Master's thesis, Ohio State University, 1958).

[47] D. L. Costley, "An Experimental Study of the Effectiveness of Quantitative Evidence in Speeches of Advocacy" (Master's thesis, University of Oklahoma, 1958).

[48] W. R. Dresser, "Studies of the Effects of Evidence: Implications for Forensics," *Register* of American Forensic Association, X, No. 3 (1962), 14–19.

[49] "The Impact of Evidence on Decision Making," *Journal of the American Forensic Association*, III, No. 2 (1966), 43–47.

situations, or he might approve some compromises between these extremes in certain situations. On pragmatic grounds, evidence is more important in school debate and in law than it is in popular persuasion. The obvious reason is that those who do the judging in the forensic situations are more demanding. In the analytical and critical applications of argumentation, evidence is important indeed. In preparation for their frequent experiences as listeners and readers, students need to form the habit of demanding the best of the available evidence. When they do, future research will turn out differently, and so will human affairs in general—we hope.

There are, in addition to these broad principles, several specific recommendations relating to the use of evidence. They will be stated briefly in question-and-answer form.

1. Is the quoted source reporting a factual statement or expressing his personal opinion? The advocate should tell us which.

2. If it is opinion evidence, does the source give any factual basis for it? This could be done more often than it has been.

3. If it is opinion evidence, have the qualifications of the source been stated? Some indications of study, training, or other experience will improve both the logical adequacy and the audience acceptability of that evidence.

4. How much documentation is provided? For substantive adequacy as in making a critical judgment, the documentation should enable a listener or a reader to authenticate the reference if he desires. For purposes of persuasion, even if the criterion is what the advocate can "get away with," the attitudes in the audience will make a difference. In the face of hostility, an advocate will need to do all he can to bolster his credibility.

5. Is it ever proper to use secondary evidence, circumstantial evidence, or evidence from a prejudiced source? Here an approximation of the "best-evidence rule" applies. If any one of these three kinds of evidence happens to be the best that can reasonably be expected in the situation, it should not be disqualified summarily. Other tests should be applied.

6. Is it better to vary the kinds of evidence which one uses in arguments? Variety for its own sake is a stylistic matter, but it may appeal to audience interest. In terms of ethical and logical responsibilities, though, the kinds of evidence should be considered only for the purpose of choosing the *best* evidence.

7. Can the audience understand the evidence? In one sense, proof

can be made from evidence which most persons do not understand. However, when comprehension is desired, an advocate can facilitate it by explaining, repeating, or using a visual aid. One selection of evidence can be used to influence belief in two or more quite dissimilar conclusions. This is precisely why the teaching of critical thinking is so important.

8. Can the audience evaluate the evidence? A communicator can aid his listeners or readers by presenting his evidence specifically (verbatim) instead of paraphrasing, and by adding the qualifications of his sources. Giving to each piece of evidence its proper weight—no more and no less than it deserves—is a part of an advocate's ethical and logical responsibility, and it is a responsibility of readers and listeners as well. The difficulty of evaluation was epitomized in the case of a yearlong investigation of charges of cheating which were brought against a pair of bridge players in a world championship tournament. The charges were brought by the executive committee of the World Bridge Federation on the basis of testimony given by fellow players, including the captain and the coach of their own team. After a year of hearings the British Bridge League cleared the accused pair, but the World Bridge Federation rejected the decision. This situation parallels the 5–4 decisions of the United States Supreme Court.

9. Does general semantics offer some helpful advice on the use of evidence? Three principles seem pertinent here: The map should fit the territory. Remember the *et cetera*. Fact 1968 is not fact 1975. The first means that a report is not the fact it represents, the second means that a report is likely to be incomplete, and the third means that what we accept as true at one time may not be acceptable at another time.

10. How can evidence from someone else be made to fit smoothly into the advocate's speech or essay? No doubt this is one of the troublesome stylistic problems, but it is basically a thought problem. We do not think enough about the relationship between a piece of evidence and the inference it supports. Too often we state a point and then, without making any linkage, say, "And now permit me to quote. . . ." It is much better to weave evidence and one's own inference together into a consistent style so that each part complements the other without any jerkiness or abruptness. Some of the language of the quotation might be picked up in the interpretative statement before or after the citation. Evidence is important, but it is less so in educational exercises than is the expression of the advocate's own thinking about that evidence.

11. Finally, how much evidence is enough? A blanket answer cannot be given except in the most abstract terms. In academic exercises such as case outlining, the preparation of single speeches or essays of advocacy, or school debating, it is customary to advise that each unit of proof must rest either upon evidence or upon a premise that is admitted or assumed. The following is the most likely arrangement:

> I. Point in partition
>   A Principal sub-point
>   1. Evidence or premise.

QUESTIONS

1. Explain the differences between the definitions of evidence in law and its definition in general argumentation.

2. Compare the theoretical importance of evidence with the findings of empirical and experimental research with regard to the importance of evidence. In what circumstances might one be wise to give precedence to one or the other?

3. When might some of the legal classifications of evidence be useful in general argumentation?

4. Why test the source of evidence? Is not the substance of the evidence all that really should concern us?

5. When, if ever, should an advocate use second-best or third-best evidence in order to secure audience acceptance of his proof?

6. What research is still needed in the field of the persuasiveness of evidence?

7. At the 1929 peak, the Dow-Jones average was approximately 380, and for comparative purposes the dollar was worth 100 cents in buying power. Early in March of 1959, the D-J average reached 610 in terms of sixty-two-cent dollars. Which peak was really the higher?

8. Evaluate this comment in relation to the foregoing exposition of evidence:

> Entrance requirements at Notre Dame are equal to, or higher than those at any major university in the country. A higher percentage of Notre Dame football lettermen receive their degrees than at almost any other university. This was mentioned in a recent article in the *Daily News* . . .

Notre Dame spends no more hours practicing football than North-western, Stanford, or Princeton. Quantitatively, there is no more empha-sis upon football at Notre Dame than at any other major university. Qualitatively, there is more emphasis.

9. Classify and test this evidence:

Tales are still told of the time students were responsible for putting a shark in a private swimming pool. . . . a student, in a state of in-toxication, took a private cruiser and had to be retrieved from the Ever-glades. . . . In the spring the police force must be doubled. . . . Stu-dents who have been there say the increased force is needed to empty Atlantic Blvd. bars at 3:00 or 4:00 A.M.

10. Evaluate the evidence in this portion of a talk on the attractions of col-lege teaching as a career:

Many benefits that contribute substantially to the professional and personal well-being of the college teacher and his family are to be found in most colleges and universities. . . .

The sabbatical year is a well-known academic institution—nearly one-half of the colleges and universities make provision for sabbatical leaves for mature teachers, for educational travel and study. . . .

Among other provisions found in many institutions that contribute to the professional well-being of the individual teacher are other types of leave for advanced study, financial aid for individual research or publication, travel funds for attendance at professional meetings, and so on.

Other "fringe benefits" contribute. . . . Some institutions offer help to the new teacher with housing. . . . More commonly institu-tions provide protection in one form or another against the expenses of illness, accident, disability or death. . . .

Though the student who considers college teaching as a career may have only a remote interest in retirement provisions, it is a fact worthy of consideration that favorable retirement programs are avail-able in a great many institutions.

EXERCISES

1. Using a selected or an assigned essay, speech, or debate from the Ap-pendixes, list and count the points that are evidenced and those that are not. Which of the latter needed evidence, in your judgment? Which kinds of evidence were used? Evaluate the instances of evidence in terms of the appropriate tests of substance, of sources, and of docu-mentation.

2. Using the proposition which served for the oral and written exercise on analysis (Chapter 5) or investigation (Chapter 6), prepare a five-minute argumentative speech in which evidence appears as needed and is the best you can obtain in the available time. Quote the evidence and its documentation, and give qualifications of any experts you use. Follow the speeches with critiques, preferably oral if time permits, using some topics from "Tests" and "Prescriptive Advice." Specific topics might be assigned to individuals. This part is a lesson in critical listening.

3. Write an argumentative essay in the form of an editorial or a letter to the editor. Try to balance the sometimes conflicting demands of space, popular persuasion, and logical adequacy.

4. Describe and criticize the use of evidence in one of the Lincoln-Douglas debates in P. M. Angle, *Created Equal? The Complete Lincoln-Douglas Debates of 1858* (Chicago: University of Chicago Press, 1958).

5. After surveying the accounts of President Kennedy's assassination in newspapers and magazines beginning with November 22, 1963, compile the circumstantial evidence of Lee Harvey Oswald's guilt. What grounds might there be for any other hypothesis? Or do you believe the evidence of guilt, although it was not offered in court, was conclusive? Have any of the published critiques of the Warren Commission Report convinced you?

6. Report on matters of evidence in *The People vs. Hoffmann* in Q. Reynolds, *Courtroom* (New York: Farrar, Straus and Co., 1950.)

7. How did Louis Nizer attack the People's case against Mark Fein? See W. A. Reuben, *The Mark Fein Case* (New York: Dial Press, 1967).

8. What can one learn about evidence from reading A. Nevins, *Gateway To History* (Boston: D. C. Heath and Co., 1938), Ch. 7?

9. Compare footnote 34 with "The News Mags," *Wall Street Journal*, July 12, 1967, p. 1, and with "Ethics and the Press," *Wall Street Journal*, July 25, 1967, pp. 1 and 12.

CHAPTER 8

ARGUMENT: STRUCTURES,

KINDS & TESTS

ARGUMENT DEFINED

IN ITS SIMPLEST FORM, AN ARGUMENT (ENTHYMEME) IS A CONCLUSION
and a supporting reason, and these elements may appear in either order.
Thus one may say, "We must strike, because otherwise nobody will pay
us any notice," or, "Nobody will pay us any notice so long as we stay
on the job; therefore, we must strike." In the discussion of the structures
of arguments we shall see that arguments appear in many degrees of
complexity, but the general rule is that there be only one conclusion
per argument, regardless of how many reasons and subreasons are used
to support it.

When we say "regardless of how many reasons," is there no limit?
What if we have one conclusion supported by a complex structure of
main points, secondary points, and tertiary points? If there were no
limit on the complexity of an argument, the proposition could be the
conclusion, the entire case for one side could be the support for it, and
the total discourse would be the argument. However, on the assumption
that it is useful to distinguish between the case and an individual argument, let us impose some limits upon the meaning of *argument*. When
referring to the main topics (points in partition) in a case, a person is

[173]

likely to be understood clearly when he uses the expressions *need argument, cost argument,* and the like. But when doing a close analysis of argumentative discourse, he would be well advised to use the word *argument* to mean the smallest meaningful unit of conclusion and supporting reason or reasons. This microcosmic level of argument is called an enthymeme if it has only two parts (conclusion and reason) and achieves probability, whereas it is called a syllogism if it has a major and a minor premise followed by a conclusion which achieves formal certainty.

Obviously, once an argument has been expressed, the conclusion is fixed; in fact, the structure is static. The parts of the argument and their relationship to each other are no longer in process as they would be in the inquiry stage. This distinction will be made in the following discussion of nonargument.

It is advisable to distinguish arguments from nonarguments for two reasons: they are often mistaken for each other, yet they are basically dissimilar in terms of our purposes. Three varieties of nonarguments will be explained: conditional statements, causal explanations, and constructive reasoning processes.

Conditional statements, which typically include "if" or "if-then" clauses, often appear as the first part of hypothetical syllogisms. The complete syllogism is an argument, but anything less than a conclusion and a reason is not. "If you have cheated, then you will fail to pass" is a conditional statement, not an argument. The argument would go something like this: "If you have cheated, you will fail to pass. You have cheated. Therefore, you will fail to pass." Acceptance of this argument entails accepting *all* of its parts, but acceptance of just the conditional statement does not carry any obligation to accept the rest. The implied condition of the complete argument is that if the reason is accepted, then the conclusion should be. Confusion occurs when conditionals appear as reasons or conclusions, or when ambiguous language conceals the difference between a conditional statement and an argument.

Simple causal explanation as in "I didn't buy more life insurance because I don't think it would be the best investment for me" is not an argument. Neither is "I was absent yesterday on account of the railroad strike." The first explanation does not prove that the person did not buy the insurance, and the second does not prove that the person was absent. Words such as "because," "on account of," and "why" make some assertions *sound like* arguments. A reason in an argument is logically related to the conclusion and is presumably more acceptable than the conclusion. A reason in the sense of cause is something else. Giving a reason for an occurrence is not the same as presenting a reason for the acceptance of a belief or a causal principle.[1]

Constructive reasoning, which John Dewey expounded in *How We Think* and other works, is a mental activity which is used to reach a conclusion on the basis of reasons.[2] It is quite unlike argument, which starts with a conclusion or claim and supports it with reasons for its acceptance. For instance, to solve this puzzle one must think *toward*, not from, a solution:

> Three animals, named Alex, Bozo, and Cleo, occupy a row of three adjacent cages. One is a lion, one is a giraffe, and the third is a monkey. Alex occupies the cage to the immediate left of Bozo's. Since Cleo is the tallest, she is put in the left most cage. Since the giraffe is frightened by the lion, their cages are separated. What is the lion's name?

As we have seen in the earlier distinction between inquiry and advocacy, reasoning in the sense of a dialectical process properly precedes the arguments of advocacy.

Finally, in relation to the nature of argument, what is the relevance of logic? From 1905 to the present most textbooks on argumentation have asserted various degrees of relevance, although the extent and the usefulness of the exposition has varied enormously. Many writers have felt obligated to cite the categorical syllogism on the mortality of Socrates, to say a little about J. S. Mill's canons of induction, and to urge students to avoid an assortment of fallacies. Some have been more discerning in explaining how logic may serve in the analysis and criticism of argument. The most extreme position in this direction holds that debating is mainly an exercise in logic.[3] At the opposite extreme is the view that formal logic and probability have little to do with logical proof as we think of it, and that we are left with style and plausibility as our legitimate concerns. This chapter takes a position somewhere between these poles.

But before going into the theoretical issues, let us consider what *logic* means on the descriptive level. Generally speaking, logic is a formal, abstract science of structure. It sets out and analyzes those relations among symbols which permit valid inference. Two fundamental logical relations were illustrated in Chapter 2 under "Definition of

[1] See R. B. Angell, *Reasoning and Logic* (New York: Appleton-Century-Crofts, 1964), pp. 27–33; I. M. Copi, *Introduction to Logic* (New York: The Macmillan Co., 1953), p. 385.

[2] See M. C. Beardsley, *Thinking Straight* (Englewood Cliffs, N.J.: Prentice-Hall, Inc., 1956), xv–xvi; Angell, *op. cit.*, pp. 33–41, 447, 455; A. K. Bierman, *Logic: A Dialogue* (San Francisco: Holden-Day, Inc., 1964), p. 66.

[3] Kruger, *Modern Debate* . . . , p. 109.

Proof." From Aristotle to the present there have been several schools or movements, and each has added something to the discipline of logic. In the earliest works the logical relations of syllogisms, especially the categorical, were systematized. Argument connections and truth-arguments were critically examined, but value-arguments and the acceptability of reasons were of less concern. After Aristotle, the Stoics emphasized conditional statements and arguments using conditionals (either-or). For many centuries thereafter there were no major innovations, but in the nineteenth century logic came to include much more than it did in antiquity. Hegel, the Idealist, saw logic as a sort of cosmic dialectic, and his thought influenced the dialectical materialism of Karl Marx. Dewey's criticism of Aristotle and his broadening of logic to encompass both the process and the product of thought also show Hegel's influence. In modern times, symbolic or mathematical logic as epitomized by Russell and Whitehead in *Principia Mathematica* has gained much professional attention, but is less immediately useful to beginning students of argumentation. The purpose of this oversimplified history is to sketch the evolution of logics which will account for our dual concern with logical relations *and* with the acceptability of supporting reasons.

As for the previously mentioned view that formal logic and probability have little to do with logical proof as used here,[4] all that one can reply in limited space is that an ambiguity in Aristotle's definition of rhetoric together with a misunderstanding of value judgments in contemporary philosophy and the overlooking of modern inductive logic apparently account for this misconception.

STRUCTURES

Earlier remarks about the logic of argument have included references to structure. The use of the plural in the heading of this section indicates that there are two or more kinds, as indeed there are. Of more importance than their number is the question of their theoretical importance or their usefulness.

Three reasons for studying structures of argument are nearly self-evident: such a study helps one to identify reasons and conclusions, it aids in the classification of arguments, and it then enables one to apply

[4] D. W. Shepard, "Rhetoric and Formal Argument," *Western Speech*, XXX, No. 4 (1966), 241–247;

the appropriate tests. Only the first reason will be explained here. The remaining two will be covered in the following sections, "Kinds" and "Tests." If reasons[5] and conclusions are the essential elements of an argument, if they are sometimes confused, and if that confusion is of some consequence, we need some way to minimize the risk of confusion. Perhaps the first point to notice is that a reason or some evidence can be such only in context. Without the rest of the argument it is merely a non-argument. The second hint concerns the clues which argument connectives provide. Conclusions are typically preceded by *therefore, proves that, therefore, so, consequently, I conclude that, bears out our point that*, and others. Reasons are often preceded by *because, for, since, as shown by, for the reason that*, and others. Finally, there are arguments that have no connectives because of either the author's notion of subtlety or his poor composition.

Traditional Theories

In the study of logic, the traditional theories or principles of structure pertain to deduction, because formal validity relates to deduction only. The element of *connection* is essential in deductive structure. Note the absence of connection in "Warriors are brave, and tents are made of skins, so we should declare a holiday today." Now note the connection, actually a *necessary* one, in this argument: "Running Deer is a warrior, and all warriors are brave, so Running Deer is brave." (A is B; all B's are C; A is C). In this context there are observable patterns of connection: the valid, the invalid, and the invalid but sound. The utmost degree of rigor attaches to arguments that have necessary conclusions, according to the formal rules. On many subjects, however, there are likely to be sound and important arguments having conclusions not necessary or inevitable; they may be *amply supported* or *probably true*, for instance. But whether we use the premise-connective-conclusion type or the conditional (If X is Y and all W's are Y's, then X is W), the objectives are rigor and universality.

Textbooks for elementary courses in logic present a much more helpful exposition of the basic principles than this sketchy treatment can even introduce; however, a few points about deductive systems may assist the beginner who has not studied logic. Perhaps the most basic one is the principle of inclusion or exclusion, including partials or overlapping.

[5] "Premise" is substituted for "reason" in logic in order to maintain abstractness by avoiding any reference to subjective acceptability.

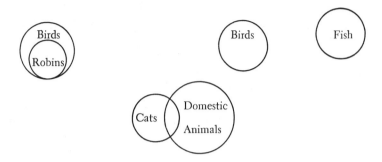

How this works with a categorical syllogism is shown next:

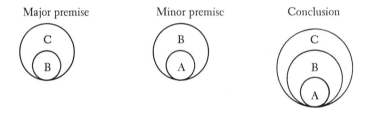

All warriors (B) are brave (C). Running Deer (A) is a warrior (B). Running Deer (A) is brave (C). It will be observed that there are five elements, which are called subject term (S), predicate term (P), copula (*is* or *are*), quantifier (*all* or *some*), and qualifier (*no* or *not* in negative [logical] propositions). Each logical proposition, in turn, is designated by one of four symbols: (A) Universal Affirmative (All S's are P's) has distributed ("all") subject term and an undistributed predicate term; (E) Universal Negative (No S's are P's) has both terms fully distributed; (I) Particular Affirmative (Some S's are P's) has both terms undistributed; (O) Particular Negative (Some S's are not P's) has an undistributed subject term and a distributed predicate term. Those who are unaccustomed to these abstract symbols will find this translation helpful: (A) All Arabs are Moslems; (E) No Arabs are Zionists; (I) Some Arabs are Coptics; (O) Some Arabs are not Moslems. Incidentally, there is no *theoretical* reason why these statements must be factually verifiable if one is merely explaining *form*.

A few suggestions concerning rules, forms, and the reduction of categorical syllogisms will enable a student to use this testing device. One rule states that at least one of the premises must be affirmative. No conclusion would follow from "No affluent societies are societies that turn Communist. No societies in Southeast Asia are affluent societies." A second rule states that if one premise is negative, the conclusion must be negative. Only an invalid syllogism results when one argues: "No acts of violence are ethically justified acts. Some punishments are ethically justified acts. Some punishments are acts of violence." A third rule states that the middle term must be distributed at least once. The middle term appears in both premises; it is a sort of hinge connecting the premises so that the combination can yield a conclusion. Each of the other two (end) terms appears only once in a premise and again in the conclusion. The fallacy of undistributed middle is a familiar result of this rule's being violated: "All Communist sympathizers are persons who urge the admission of Red China to the U.N. Some employees of the Department of State are persons who urge the admission of Red China to the U.N. Some employees of the Department of State are Communist sympathizers." Finally, a fourth rule states that an end term that is undistributed in a premise cannot be distributed in the conclusion. This is an example: "All friends of Bill are friends of mine. Jim is not a friend of Bill. Jim is not a friend of mine."

Six forms of Aristotle's "perfect syllogism" may be seen in some logic books.[6] These may serve in the process of reducing ordinary arguments to syllogistic form, whenever that is possible, in order to test their structure. Six steps are suggested[7]: (1) Isolate a single argument. (2) Label major, minor, and conclusion. (3) Locate the three classes and their general category, as in "proposed treaties," "agreements submitted to the Senate," "agreements the President thinks the Senate will approve," and "agreements with other nations." (4) State each part in syllogistic form. (5) Test by applying the rules above. (6) Possibly use diagrams which appear below. Suppose this were the essence of the argument: "There must be some proposed treaties that the President does not think the Senate would approve, because not all of them are submitted, but undoubtedly all treaties the President submits are the ones he thinks the Senate will approve." The reduction might look something like this:

Some proposed treaties are not agreements with other nations submitted to the Senate.

[6] Angell, *Reasoning and Logic*, p. 103.
[7] Beardsley, *Thinking Straight*, pp. 116–117.

All agreements with other nations submitted to the Senate are agreements the President thinks the Senate will approve.

Some proposed treaties are not agreements the President thinks the Senate will approve.

Two compound forms from traditional logic remain to be mentioned: sorites and epicheireme. The sorites (rhymes with "your nighties") is a shortened series of syllogisms in which the predicate of the first logical proposition is the subject of the second, and so on, and then the conclusion unites the first subject with the last predicate, as in

Protesters are idealists;

Idealists are sensitive persons;

Sensitive persons are disenchanted;

Disenchanted persons are unhappy; therefore,

Protesters are unhappy.

The epicheireme, which is the rhetorical equivalent of the sorites, can be defined as a series of enthymemes, as in

All living things are mortal;

All organisms are living things;

All persons are organisms; therefore,

All men are mortal.

Why the epicheireme was developed is said to be a mystery,[8] but it may have been an attempt to provide a descriptive layout centuries before Toulmin.

The efforts of Aristotle, the Stoics, Euclid, and others served to build deductive systems which subsequently have been improved upon, as we shall see below. The philosophy of formal science tries to solve the correct structure of any such system by specifying five criteria which all deductive sciences must follow.[9] Sometimes these are abbreviated to completeness, rigor, consistency, simplicity, and independence of axioms.

Later Theories

The first of these was an attack upon the "existential import," as several writers call it, which Aristotle gave to his universal propositions.

---

[8] J. D. Feezel, "The Mystery of Epicheireme," *Western Speech*, XXI, No. 2 (1967), 109–115.

[9] C. W. Churchman, *Elements of Logic and Formal Science* (New York: J. B. Lippincott Co., 1940), p. 134.

Thus, in Aristotelian logic, "All Zombies are disembodied" can be true if Zombies exist but is false if they do not. The mathematical logicians argued that "All Zombies are disembodied" meant "Whatever x may be, if it is a Zombie, then it is disembodied." A conditional does not require either the antecedent or the consequent to be true in order that the conditional be true. The truth of an A-proposition does not imply the existence of anything, they concluded.

Early in the history of logic the main concern was with terms or class-words, the structure of inclusion-exclusion, and consistency in categorical syllogisms. Later theories developed a logic of propositions, dealt with compound structures, and gave us the principles of hypothetical and alternative syllogisms. Time and space do not permit a treatment of rules and applications, but a specimen of each structure will be given. The first one is hypothetical:

If the first applicant lied about age, then only one applicant was a woman.

The first applicant lied about age.

Therefore, only one applicant was a woman.

The next specimen is an alternative syllogism:

Either that noise was thunder or it was a sonic boom.

(Because of clear sky) it was not thunder.

That noise was a sonic boom.

Symbolic logic is said to improve upon traditional logics in four respects: it can test many more kinds of arguments, it relates propositional logic to class logic, it has systematized old and new principles, and it has introduced greater rigor into analysis and proof. We cannot go into the complex truth-table tests here, but the simplest symbols will be applied to the hypothetical syllogism about the applicant who lied about her age: $p \supset q$, $p \therefore q$. One important reason for the greater range and rigor of symbolic logic is its use of quantification theory. The logic of propositions (hypothetical and alternative) does not provide for the analysis of the simplest components, so their internal structures may have unobserved logical connections. Consider this argument:

Everyone admires someone.

There are some whom no one admires.

Some persons admire persons who do not admire them.

The valid connections do not show up if one tries to reduce the argument to this AII categorical syllogism: All persons are beings who admire someone (All A's are B's). Some persons are persons whom no one admires (Some A's are C's). Some persons are people who admire people who do not admire them (Some A's are D's). This is invalid because it has four terms, one of which appears three times. The solution is to quantify two predicates with "all" and "some." These predicates in the present instance are ". . . is a person" and the relational ". . . admires . . . ," and they would be symbolized Px. Lxy to stand for "x is a person and x admires y." In our present setting this treatment of symbolic logic is meaningless except as a way of showing that there is much more in logic than an argumentation course can present.

Diagrams

There are, in addition to the logical symbols which have been used earlier in this chapter, several visual-aid types of diagrams or layouts which are intended to aid us in understanding structures of arguments. These structures are somewhat analogous to bridges and buildings in that they have foundations, superstructures, and connecting members, and their exterior design often conceals the inner structure. More will be said of this in the final chapter on evaluating argument, but for the present we may say that the use of these schematic devices can be helpful in calling attention to missing links (as in enthymemes and epicheiremes), revealing the complexities of fully stated arguments (as shown in logical outlines), and detecting circular arguments.

Four which are familiar to many persons will be demonstrated here: line diagram, logical outline, Venn diagram, and the Toulmin layout which has been presented earlier. The simplest argument, if one may so classify it, will be exhibited in the first two ways:

I. My boy friend doesn't like me anymore, because
    A. He didn't ask me to the prom.
    Conclusion (I)
    Reason (A)

One conclusion with several coordinate reasons may be shown in the same ways:

I. Our top debaters are top scholars.
    A. They are John, Mary, and Jim.
    B. John has a 3.9
    C. Mary has a 3.8
    D. Jim has a 3.7

Or one might have one conclusion supported by two or more pairs of coordinate reasons, but, as has been argued earlier, the structure is more likely to be a case than an argument. In a case on a value proposition, each pair of reasons would consist of a criterion and its application: Installment buying is harmful if it encourages people to live beyond their means, and it does so; it is harmful if it causes inflation, and it does so, etc.

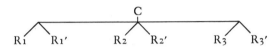

Outlines and line diagrams can easily handle arguments at three or more levels of complexity as in the case outline:

I. We ought to appoint Dr. X to a professorship.
    A. We ought to hire Dr. X.
        1. We ought to hire the best available.
        2. Dr. X is acknowledged to be the best available.
    B. If we hire Dr. X, we must give him the top rank, etc.

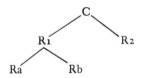

Suppose someone says, "Archaeologists must be absentminded; after all, they are professors." This can be reduced to a mood AAA, figure 1 categorical syllogism and made into a Venn diagram:

All professors are absent-minded.
All archaeologists are professors.
All archaeologists are absent-minded.

All M is P
All S is M
All S is P

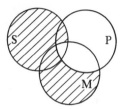

In case a conclusion is repeated with each reason, probably for emphasis, there is still only one argument:

We must vote because it is our duty.
We must vote to keep the rascals out.
    I. We must vote, because
        A. It is our duty, and
        B. It is the way to keep the rascals out.

Then there is the familiar telescoping of two arguments: "The time-and-room schedule is wrong, hence some officials must have been careless, and consequently many students will have trouble at registration." Using the traditional cause-effect analysis, one would get two arguments, one being effect to cause and the other cause to effect.

Careless (C) ← E
Schedule wrong
C → Registration trouble (E)

Finally, the Toulmin layout or something of that sort may serve to call attention to missing links in an argument. Referring back three paragraphs to the argument for appointing Dr. X, suppose someone had offered this enthymeme[10]: "Let's appoint Dr. X to a full professorship. We ought to hire the best available, you know." While it is possible to set up a logical outline which will leave blank spaces for the missing links, it is unlikely that many persons would take the trouble. Using the same points as before, we would get something like this:

[10] In logic books, *enthymeme* is invariably defined as an elided or truncated syllogism, meaning that one of the three statements is missing. Since the first publication of McBurney's research on this problem in 1935, several writers in speech have added to the logicians' definition the probability of the premises, the partial distribution of middle terms, the probability (instead of formal certainty) of conclusions, the derivation of premises from audience opinion, and so on.

I. We ought to appoint Dr. X to a full professorship, for
  (A)
      1. We ought to hire the best available
      (2)
  (B)

At least in this writer's experience there is some awkwardness involved when the Toulmin model is applied to the argument at hand. One attempt involves a double Data step, a compound claim, and two added steps placed in parentheses.

  (D) Dr. X is best available
      and only at the top rank, so (Q) probably (C)
                   we ought to appoint
                   him full prof.
          (R) (Unless we can't afford, etc.)
    (W) We ought to hire the best
        (B) (Assumed operating premise)

Or it may be that two layouts are needed to get at the two parts of the Claim (conclusion): hiring and rank.

Dr. X is best—so, probably—we ought to hire him
    (W) We want the best
He is available only
at top rank   —so, probably—we ought to give
                      him that rank
    (W) (We should do anything within reason to
        get the best.)

However, it seems more likely that an "if—then" conditional analysis would cope with this situation.[11]

KINDS

In Speech Textbooks

Textbooks on public speaking, discussion, argumentation and debate, and the criticism of public address typically contain some classifi-

[11] For a critique of the Toulmin model, see P. T. Manicas, "On Toulmin's Contribution to Logic and Argumentation," *Journal of the American Forensic Association*, III, No. 3 (1966), 83–94.

cations of arguments under captions such as "reasoning," "kinds of argument," "logic of argument," "substantive proof," "causal hypothesis," and "modes of reasoning." This is only the beginning of the confusion, as the following survey sample will suggest. Almost all of the twelve cited works have been referred to in preceding chapters. The formulations will appear in the order of length and increasing complexity. Following the descriptive report some questions will be posed for students and teachers to ponder.

Capp and Capp[12] present three types, two of which have two subtypes each: generalization, analogy (literal and figurative), and causal relations (cause-to-effect and effect-to-cause). Moulton[13] starts with induction and deduction. The former has three subtypes and some sub-subtypes: pictorial (sampling), causal (cause-to-effect, effect-to-cause, effect-to-effect), and analogous (argumentative or literal, and symbolic or figurative). By deduction he means structural matters of the syllogism. McBurney and Mills[14] explain four basic kinds: argument from sign, causal argument, argument by example, and analogy. Sign and cause are called deductive, while example and analogy are called inductive. A close reading of the text will show why it is a mistake to regard the four kinds as coordinates; actually, two bases of classification are expressly stated. Freeley[15] follows the same pattern and adds something of the Toulmin structure. Huber[16] offers four apparent coordinates which actually represent two classes and two subclasses: induction, deduction, causal reasoning (including sign), and analogy. Bryant and Wallace[17] have a similar problem with classification when they identify deduction, example (generalization), analogy, effect-to-cause, and cause-to-effect. Kruger[18] doubts the importance of the induction-deduction distinction to debaters, and he treats deduction as syllogistic structure. The kinds of argument appear to be analogy, hypothesis (descriptive and causal), and generalization (descriptive and causal). Classifying hypothesis-making as deduction is questionable;[19] the *testing* of an

[12] Capp and Capp, *Principles* . . . , Chap. 8.
[13] Moulton, *Dynamics* . . . , Chap. 3.
[14] McBurney and Mills, *Argumentation* . . . , Chap. 8. (This chapter is the first author's).
[15] Freeley, *Argumentation*, Chaps. 8–9.
[16] Huber, *Influencing* . . . , Chaps. 6–9.
[17] D. C. Bryant and K. R. Wallace, *Fundamentals of Public Speaking* (New York: Appleton-Century-Crofts, Inc., 1960), pp. 361–368.
[18] Kruger, *Modern Debate*, Chaps. 11-13.
[19] Compare Kruger, *op. cit.*, p. 150 and Beardsley, *Thinking Straight*, p. 44, to clarify the former.

hypothesis can be done by deduction. Abernathy[20] identifies induction and deduction, but the latter is treated as structure only. When defining the enthymeme he states that the "probability" part of the definition was once used by "certain older rhetoricians" but that this use "has been largely discontinued." His five general kinds of argument, all of which are classified as inductive, are generalization, analogy (literal and figurative), causal (C-E, E-C, E-E), hypothesis, and from criteria. Ehninger[21] writes of six kinds of mediate inference: sign, causal relation, generalization, parallel case (literal), analogy (figurative), and rhetorical syllogism. The last item introduces a third basis of classification, although the three bases are not named. Windes and Hastings[22] name at least nine kinds, each of which is diagrammed with a modified Toulmin layout: characteristics to description, characteristics to value judgment, example to descriptive generalization, example to causal generalization, effect to cause (calls it "sign" also), circumstantial evidence to hypothesis, cause-to-effect, comparison (literal), figurative analogy, and "others." Ray and Zavos[23] set out in one chapter a detailed explanation of the differences between induction and deduction. In their second they present what may be the longest classification of arguments in our literature. There are ten basic kinds and eighteen subtypes grouped under three general classes which are named "logical arguments," "rhetorical arguments with logical force," and "rhetorical arguments with psychological force."

Some Bases of Classification

After surveying these classifications of arguments from Abernathy to Zavos, one might wonder who is right. Whether a classifier comes up with three or eighteen kinds makes less difference, theoretically speaking, than his awareness of the *bases* upon which he makes distinctions. The number of kinds that might be identified on some basis or other is limited only by our imagination, but, if we practice the logic we preach, we will clearly state our bases of classification and categorize the specific kinds so as to make an internally consistent system. According to this view, the worst mistake is to mix and confuse the bases of classification,

---

20 Abernathy, *The Advocate*, Chaps. 4–5, esp. p. 102.
21 Ehninger in McBath (ed.), *Argumentation* . . . , Chap. 10.
22 Windes and Hastings, *Argumentation* . . . , Chap. 5.
23 J. Ray and H. Zavos in Miller and Nilsen, *Perspectives* . . . , Chaps. 3–4.

such as structural, material, psychological, intentional, and so on. Even though the consequences of this mistake are not earth-shaking, they do impair the construction and the criticism of arguments. Perhaps these cautions plus the following suggestions on bases of classification and some of their subcategories will encourage students to develop systems for their own use.

Six bases of classification will be named, but only four will be explained at some length. One of the lesser bases distinguishes between arguments which are main ones and those which are justificatory. In outlining a I-A-1 series, the I-A would be main, and the A-1 would be the proper place for the justificatory argument. The second lesser basis of classifying arguments is the intent of the communicator: to explain, to make a cogent argument, or to persuade, for instance. On this basis one could name his categories logical-rhetorical, proof-explanation, etc.

One recently suggested basis of classification is the kind of logic involved.[24] The kind we have been discussing is the more familiar to logicians. It consists of the traditional and the symbolic strains. The second kind, if it may be called logic, is place or topical, and it dates back to Aristotle's *topoi*.[25] In the next paragraph the familiar logic of induction and deduction will be discussed. Only the second part of the mainstream-topical dichotomy will be treated now, because the "lines of argument" (example, analogy, cause, sign, etc.) in argumentation theory are said to stem from topical logic. This space-saving outline (after McBurney) will indicate the nature of Aristotle's topical invention. The nature of the "formal" category of twenty-eight items may occasion some doubt that it belongs under the topical heading exclusively.

ARISTOTLE'S TOPICS

I. Material topics
   (Concerns the substance, not the form, of argument)
   A. Particular or special topics
      1. Essentially neither rhetoric nor logic
      2. Most arguments come from these
      3. Also called places or loci, such as branches of knowl-
         edge

---

[24] *Ibid.*, pp. 93–94 lists several bases of classification that have been used: induction-deduction, form or substance, type of logical propositions used, kinds of relationships, logical-rhetorical, and proof-explanation. The Ray-Zavos dichotomy of "mainstream" and "place" logics is specifically referred to here.

[25] L. Cooper, trans., *The Rhetoric of Aristotle* (New York: D. Appleton and Co., 1932), pp. 143–147, 155, 159–171.

B. Universal topics
(General principles of probability, or rhetoric's field)
1. More and less
2. Magnification and minification
3. Past and future
4. Possible and impossible
II. Formal topics
(Inferential "grounds" or "general propositions")
A. 28 lines of argument which can be put into enthymematic form
1. Opposites, 2. correlative terms, 3. *a fortiori*, 4. turn the tables, 5. definition, 6. part to whole, 7. cause to effect, 8. meaning of names, etc.

The second of the four major bases of classification is deduction and nondeduction (including induction),[26] as the introduction to topical logic indicated. Whether an argument is deductive or not is basic to all kinds, however they may be classified. This series of paired contrasts will point up the principal distinctions:

Deductive	*Nondeductive*
1. Often called general-to-particular.	Particular-to-general is inductive subtype of nondeduction.
2. From assumption to what follows as application.	From particulars to general principle, assuming uniformity of nature. In argumentation this is a *report* of prior induction or an argument from example.
3. Necessary relation between reason and conclusion.[28]	Probable relation; some say "probably" signifies an inductive argument.[27]
4. Avoidance of contradiction is crucial.	Denial of conclusion doesn't make inconsistency.
5. Moves from premises to conclusion.	Moves from evidence to conclusion.
6. Conclusion is contained in premises.	Sound argument supports conclusion not logically entailed by the evidence.

[26] This distinction and the truth-value dichotomy are expounded at length in Angell, *Reasoning and Logic*.
[27] Beardsley, *Thinking Straight*, p. 31.
[28] Some writers say that much of our deduction leads only to probable conclusions, because it starts with proportional generalizations like "Ninety percent of our teachers have Ph.D. degrees," "Most scholars use footnotes," etc.

7. Analyze the verbal structure to detect flaws.

Check the substance of the argument against the existential world. The acceptability of basal reasons and the closeness of the connections are outside traditional logic. The reason-conclusion construct is acceptable if each reason is relevant and confirms the conclusion, and if the reasons take cognizance of any contradictory information.

The third major basis for classifying arguments is the sense in which a conclusion is accepted or not. If the conclusion purports to describe the existential world, the argument is called a *truth* argument. If the conclusion expresses the wisdom or rightness of a proposed action or state of affairs, as some of our points do when we advocate propositions (resolutions) of value or of policy, it is a *value* argument, according to Angell.[29] Truth arguments about past, present, or future would be particularly important in a discourse on a proposition of fact, although they may be basal in relation to value and policy controversies. Most logics treat only truth statements, even though truth logic alone cannot get at the complexity of a value argument. What we need to deal with a subjunctive conditional ("What if one were to do thus-and-so?"), as in debating what *should* be done, is a nontruth-functional conditional. This must be provided for in our system because value arguments, too, have problems with ambiguity and inconsistency. "We should establish federal world government" is not true in the sense of reality, so it is not part of a truth argument; it is the conclusion of a value argument because it urges that reality ought to conform to that ideal. This kind of argument can be handled with modern logic so that the supports and the connections can be examined. Finally, the truth arguments and the value arguments should not be logically inconsistent.

Fourth and finally there are cause and sign which McBurney says are fundamental, but which Ray and Zavos "have ruled out . . . as distinct argument types."[30] Consider these two sentences: "John is a good student, *for* his grades are A's and B's, he is always on the Dean's List, etc.;" and "John is a good student *because* he studies hard, applies his high I.Q., meets his responsibilities, etc." Kruger[31] labels these

---

[29] See footnote 26.
[30] McBurney and Mills, *Argumentation* . . . , p. 116; Miller and Nilsen, *Perspectives* . . . , p. 96.
[31] Kruger, *Modern Debate* . . . , p. 47.

"descriptive hypothesis" and "causal hypothesis," but his reason for the distinction is *precisely* the same as McBurney's for the cause-sign distinction. Argument from sign (or descriptive hypothesis) indicates the truth of a proposition *without arguing why*, while causal argument (or hypothesis), as it is used here, *does argue why*. The point is that these two kinds of argument, whatever we choose to name them, are importantly dissimilar.

Perhaps causal argument is sometimes said to be nonargument because only the conclusion is stated, as in "Selfishness is a cause of divorce." An argument from example could as readily be disqualified if, as often happens, only the conclusion were expressed, as in "Most Irishmen are witty." It will be recalled that an argument, by definition, has a conclusion and at least one reason. A second reason for the disqualification of causal argument may stem from a failure to distinguish among four conceptions of causality: observational (observe A. and see B follow), manipulative (make A happen and see B follow), postulational (based upon our assumptions or expectations), and functional (as in ordinary discourse).

A Suggested Classification

What follows is an eclectic system of classifying arguments. It is based upon the deductive and nondeductive distinction and the truth-value distinction, together with some lesser bases which serve to identify the specific subtypes of arguments. In most instances the cause-sign distinction will also be made in order to facilitate "translation" into terms which are more familiar to some. This three-level outline indicates the bases of classification.

    I. Deductive Arguments
       A. Truth conclusions
          1. Class-inclusion, exclusion
          2. Category to traits
          3. Apply hypothesis to cases
          4. Apply causal principle to cases
       B. Value conclusions
          1. Characteristics to evaluation
          2. Principle to application

II. Nondeductive arguments
    A. Truth conclusions
        1. Circumstances to hypothesis
        2. Analogy
        3. Induction to generalization
        4. To causal explanation
    B. Value conclusions
        1. Evaluative prediction for one case
        2. Evaluative analogy
        3. Evaluative generalization
        4. Agreement and difference

I. *Deductive arguments*. *Deductive-truth arguments* (I) can usually be reduced to syllogistic form, and when that form is a categorical syllogism, the minor premise must be factual. This is a *class-inclusion argument* (IA1) of the "sign" type: "I expect that play to be a box-office hit because Shakespeare wrote it." The conclusion or claim predicts a factual situation, is non-evaluative, and can be represented by the innermost of three concentric circles labeled "box-office hits," "Shakespearean plays," and "this play." Next we have a class-inclusion argument of the "cause" (why) type: "The Union is by definition a contract, so the South is still part of the Union, even in the Civil War." *Category-to-traits argument* (IA2) goes like this: "The next President will make mistakes, because 'to err is human,' you know." This is "cause" if we take the essence of humanness to be the reason why one will err, but it is sign if one means only a correlative relation between humanness and making mistakes. An *argument to apply a hypothesis* (IA3) to a case at hand resembles in principle the general-to-particular relationship which obtains in applying a generalization to a particular case: "There must not be life on the Moon, because the accepted hypothesis is that the environment on cold planets cannot sustain life." This causal connection can be set out in either a categorical or a hypothetical syllogism. This one is categorical:

    "Environment on cold planets cannot . . .
    The Moon is a cold planet, therefore,
    The environment on the Moon cannot . . ."

Fourth among the deductive-truth arguments to be illustrated here is the *application of a causal principle* (IA4) to a case in point. The expressed portion might say, "This car will last a long time because it has a diesel engine." If the kind of engine is the reason why, the argument is causal. The causal principle, of course, is that diesel engines make cars last longer, and the application is to the car in question.

Deductive-value arguments (IB) can be reduced to syllogisms, too, but the difference is that the minor premise is factual while the major premise[32] and the conclusion are value statements. This argument moves from *characteristics to an evaluation* (IB1): "This magazine distorts facts, so it is an unreliable source." In syllogistic form the causal (reason why) argument is:

All magazines that distort facts are unreliable sources;
This magazine distorts facts; therefore,
This magazine is an unreliable source.

Principle-to-application (IB2) is the other deductive-value argument which will be given here. "A man ought to keep his word, so . . ." illustrates how one might begin with a principle. Suppose someone expressed an enthymeme with this unstated principle, "People ought to own common stocks in inflationary times." He might then say, "You ought to invest in common stocks, because we are in an inflationary period." A principle was also applied in this conclusion of a longer discourse (with minor premise missing):

> Believing that freedom of advocacy has little value in the absence of responsible advocates, we wish to express our disagreement with the idea that the meaningful problems of this university can be solved by rallying to the cry of "student power."

II. *Nondeductive arguments.* Be they of truth or of value, nondeductive arguments involve considerations of probability and perhaps statistics. Nondeductive arguments, especially the inductive variety, can achieve only probability, while the formally valid deductive arguments achieve a kind of certainty. Probability in this context is nonmathematical; it is Keynesian in the sense of degree of subjective certainty

---

[32] Three philosophical views of the evaluative major premise are pertinent here: (1) the emotive (Chas. Stevenson) holds that there is no real, justifiable, or valid way to convince someone of this; (2) the theory of the essence of man (H. Veach), which holds that man ought to do certain things in order to fulfill his essence; (3) the universal-prescriptive (R. M. Hare, *Language of Morals*), which holds that moral judgments must be universalized, so that "X is desirable" must entail "X is desirable for anyone" if it is to be a moral judgment. Then a syllogism can be formulated—
Y is undesirable;
A is also a Y; therefore,
A is undesirable.

attaching to a belief.[33] The logic of probability need not be quantified. It is sensible to argue, "Probably we shall not have a strike now, because the new union fears a test of strength, and the company wants to get the new model out." The important factor is the taking into account of all relevant data and assumptions which are available in the context. However, quantified data on statistical distribution can serve as support for an induction to a generalization about distribution of something, and from this one can deduce about the future.

Nondeductive truth arguments (IIA) say something about what was, is, or will be, but they do so without the formal or quasi-formal structure that characterizes deductive argument. The first subtype is called *circumstances to hypothesis* (IIA1). A distraught widow wrote this kind of argument to an "advice" column in a newspaper. She reported having married and made a business partner of a store employe after her husband's death, and subsequently narrowly escaping death because of a defective car exhaust pipe which appeared to have been tampered with, and being stung by a swarm of bees her new husband brought home in a shoe box. "I believe my husband is trying to murder me," she concluded. This sign-type of argument usually appears in a short form as in "The major dairies must have made a prior agreement; they all raised their prices at once." As Ray and Zavos put it, this kind of argument resembles a tabletop supported by legs, while a deduction resembles a chain which is no stronger than its weakest link.[34]

Analogy (IIA2) is the second subtype. It can be literal or figurative, single or cumulative. In its weak form it is sign argument, but in its strong form it is causal. Analogy involves induction to a general principle followed by deduction to particulars. Literal analogy, which is usually used with intent to prove, occurs in this argument: "Intervention saved South Korea, so it will save South Viet Nam." Figurative analogy, which is often illustrative or stylistic, may be seen in "Foreign aid is futile, because you can't buy friends." The preceding are single analogies, too. A cumulative analogy is often mistaken for a generalization because both start with two or more instances, but the cumulative analogy concludes with another single instance instead of a general statement about a whole class. An example of a cumulative analogy is: "The student judiciary idea works well at Bad Axe Normal, Wounded Knee

---

[33] J. M. Keynes, *A Treatise on Probability* (London: Macmillan Co., 1921), p. 3; Copi, *Introduction* . . . , p. 438 says that degree of probability can be in terms of more and less.

[34] Miller and Nilsen, *Perspectives* . . . , p. 101.

J. C., and Climax College; therefore, I think it would succeed here."
Each of the three other schools is compared with the one in question.
Of course, one could start with the three specifics, induce a principle,
and then deduce an application to another specific. But the fundamental
weakness of analogical argument is the rarity of acceptable assumptions
to make the reason relevant to the conclusion or claim. Comparison is
fundamental in thinking, but analogy seldom yields truly cogent arguments.

Induction to generalization (IIA3) can be either descriptive (sign)
or causal. A descriptive generalization was expressed in this argument:
"The faculty of the college is overwhelmingly in favor of open-occupancy legislation in Illinois. By unanimous voice vote of about 65 faculty
members who attended the May 24 meeting (out of 350 who might
have attended), the resolution was passed and sent to the State Government." The conclusion of a causal generalization is the only part we
normally hear. Such a statement is: "Whenever you crowd many thousands of refugees into concentration areas, disease is going to be
rampant." Perfect induction or complete enumeration is said by some
experts not to be induction at all, but this situation is so rare as to be no
problem. Generalizing to a conclusion from a sample is the usual case,
as we see in opinion polling and market surveys. The important consideration is to have a fair sample, yet novices or persons with axes to
grind often ignore relevant but unfavorable classes or items of data.

The fourth nondeductive truth argument is *to causal explanation*
(IIA4) "She quits the pill and has quads," proclaimed a headline on a
news item from Wales. Traditional cause-to-effect arguments follow this
pattern: "Passage of gun-control legislation would reduce the incidence
of murder." Effect-to-cause may be seen by implication in the quads
case above. In traditional causal argument, the connection is that C
accounts for E's happening. Since this variety of causal argument has
some inductive elements, as when supporting a causal principle, exceptions will weaken the soundness of the argument. Further, multiple
causes and multiple effects must be considered, as in the instance of
dealing with the causes of depressions and the effects of interest rates.
Finally, two senses of causal connection merit careful attention: "sufficient condition" (when C, then E, but there can be C_1, C_2, C_3, etc.)
and "necessary condition" (if no C, no E, but E doesn't inevitably
follow C). An inevitable connection requires both sufficient and necessary conditions. In the debate over cigarette smoking and health this
problem is exemplified.

Nondeductive value arguments (IIB) involve probability and have value conclusions. The *Port Royal Logic* of 1662 gave this advice on arguing for what we call a proposition of policy: weigh good and evil *and* their probabilities so as to consider practicality as opposed to impractical idealism. Probability here relates to incompleteness of data and recognition of unexamined factors, and not to a statistical treatment of distribution. Of the four subtypes of nondeductive value argument, the first to be discussed is the *evaluative prediction for one case* (IIB1). A professional football player argued this way in an attempt to avoid paying income tax on a sports car which a magazine awarded to him for his prowess. The plaintiff contended in the U.S. Tax Court that the Internal Revenue Service should evaluate his "Outstanding Player" performance as an educational, artistic, scientific, and civic achievement. Four evaluative arguments were offered in this unsuccessful plea: (1) The game is educational because it is taught in accredited colleges. (2) Outstanding performance is an artistic achievement because it demands a degree of artistry. (3) The skills must involve scientific principles because one practically has to be a mathematician to cope with the notebook of plays. (4) Appearing in the championship game was a civic achievement, because the President was interested in the player's obtaining an Army leave to play in that game. Commenting "with tongue in cheek" upon these four sign arguments, the Court noted the "shotgun formation" and opined that the petitioner should be "caught behind the line of scrimmage."[35] Evaluative predictions are not necessarily as flimsy as the four we have just seen. While arguing a serious proposition of policy, for instance, one might predict good or bad consequences. This would call for truth statements *and* value premises, because it would be risky to ignore potentially vital matters such as "new and greater evils," as the stock language has it.

Evaluative analogy (IIB2) is the second subtype of nondeductive value argument. It can achieve greater soundness than a truth argument by analogy, especially when several pairs of criteria and characteristics are offered as justification. Evaluative analogies about the federal budget and a business firm's budget or a family budget are weak on the score of too few common characteristics, to say nothing of the crucial dissimilarities. Take this analogical conclusion: "Joe was wise to join the club, so Jack would be." To justify this conclusion one would be obliged to marshal a series of relevant similarities of the two men.

[35] *Wall Street Journal*, January 30, 1967, p. 3.

Evaluative generalization (IIB3) is clearly an inductive type, and it is far less common than evaluative deduction. Our most familiar value arguments start from generalized value statements like "We ought to follow the Golden Rule," and they deduce a value judgment for a given case. But what we are now concerned with is where the generalized value statement came from. Most likely it came by acculturation or by some sort of induction from a series of experiences, real or imagined. The soundness of an induced ethical precept, such as "One ought to keep one's word," will depend upon the acceptability of the premises and the fairness with which one uses the available data.

Agreement and difference (IIB4) are better known as two of J. S. Mill's inductive tests of causation, although they do have application to nondeductive value arguments. Using something like the Method of Difference, Kant argued that the moral worth of a person depends upon his having good will. He maintained that intellectual and temperamental assets could work for good or evil, the difference being the guiding force of good will. Then, applying a form of the Method of Agreement, he argued that if all attributes save good will were removed, the person would still be judged good.[36]

TESTS

In Chapter 13, "Evaluating Argument," the major tests of the several kinds of arguments will be applied. For the present only a suggestive list of tests will be presented. In the instances of arguments based upon *class-inclusion and exclusion,* several questions are appropriate tests. Is one basis of division at a time being used? If not, a fallacy of cross-ranking is likely. Are the distinctions worth making in terms of some purpose? If not, the exercise is a waste of time. Is the argument properly built in terms of exclusion, inclusion, partial exclusion, or partial inclusion? If the argument is sign, in what respect is it fallible, as in the Shakespeare-box office success correlation? Are there likely exceptions to the basic generalization that all of the Bard's plays are "hits"?

In *category-to-traits* argument, as with all deductions, the factual adequacy of the premises and the correctness of the connections are points to watch. The "all" in a categorical argument may claim too

36 I. Kant, *The Fundamental Principles of the Metaphysic of Ethics,* trans. O. Manthey-Zorn (New York: Appleton-Century-Crofts, Inc., 1938), pp. 8–9.

much, the if-then relation may have exceptions, and the either-or may not be an accurate disjunction. How dependable is the substance-attribute relationship that is basic to the major premise? In other words, how prone is a human to error, as asserted in the specimen above? And what of differences in frequency and magnitude of errors on the "traits" end of the argument?

When *applying a hypothesis to a case*, the same general tests of deduction are used. Is the basic generalization sound? Are correct deductive steps taken thereafter? On the assumption that material accuracy is valued at least as much as formal validity, we should check on the informational dependability of the premises. In terms of the specimen, do we know the alleged fact about cold planets, and do we know that the Moon is such?

Application of a causal principle to a case calls for the same safe-guards as those in the three preceding paragraphs. To these one might add other causal factors and other effects, so that, in the case of the diesel-powered car, the sales argument could be weakened by associating the absence of rust inhibitors with an early rusting-out of the car's body. The two basic questions are: Is the causal principle soundly generalized? Does the given case fit it?

Characteristics-to-evaluation argument requires the same formal tests that apply to all deductions, except that the major premise and the conclusion must be value statements, and the minor premise must be factual. Because of this, the evaluative criterion requires a philosophical test, while the minor premise requires a factual test. In the specimen about magazines, is the criterion of unreliability acceptable, and is it a fact that the magazine distorts facts?

Principle-to-application is the last deductive argument. Again the usual tests of deduction apply. Specifically, one might ask, "Is the principle basically acceptable, or does it need qualifying in some respects?" In the specimen concerning common-stock ownership in inflationary times, does the principle mean everyone and in all financial circumstances? Are there no if's or but's? Is the time in question an inflationary one, and does it matter how much so it is? Are there no exceptions to the applicability of the principle?

Moving to nondeductive truth arguments, we take up first the *circumstances-to-hypothesis* variety. Here the tests become more concerned with the material and less concerned with the formal tests. To the former widow who suspected her new husband of murderous intent, one might ask several questions: Do you have enough events that your hypothesis can account for? Are they of the right sort for your hypothesis to cover them? Is there any evidence that can be explained by a rival hypothesis? Or have you even considered another explanation, such as coincidence or your own psychiatric condition? Is there a feasible way to test your hypothesis, either deductively or experimentally?

Analogy, as in the prediction that U.S. intervention in South Viet Nam would achieve certain goals as it did in South Korea, is an extremely vulnerable kind of argument. One way to test it is to force it into a form in which it rests upon a generalization which, in turn, can be tested. Thus one might make a syllogism, the major premise of which is this generalized principle based upon the Korean instance: "We should intervene militarily wherever in the world a Communist takeover threatens." Five criteria in question form will serve in most situations: (1) In how many respects are the compared cases similar? (2) In how many respects are they dissimilar? (3) Between how many items (single or cumulative) are the analogies said to hold? (4) How strong is the conclusion in relation to the premises? (5) Are the bases of comparison relevant to the point?

Induction to generalization is the old, familiar argument against which charges of "hasty generalization" or "over-generalizing" have so often been made. The case of the faculty vote for open-occupancy legislation poses certain questions, because the "overwhelming" vote of sixty-five who were present may not tell us much about the 285 who were absent and not voting. Some of these questions usually will suffice to test this kind of argument: (1) Is there any doubt that the sample is typical of the class covered by the generalization? (2) What instances are offered in evidence? (3) Precisely what is being claimed about the class in question? (4) To what class of phenomena does the generalization pertain? (5) How much of the class does the conclusion presume to cover?

To causal explanation is akin to induction; therefore, the testing of evidence is of central importance. Referring to the exposition on this kind of argument, one is reminded to ask whether the cause, if that is the controversial element, is sufficient, necessary, or inevitable. Could there have been other causes or other effects? Could something have intervened to alter the expected relationship? If someone argues that a certain gun-control bill would reduce the incidence of murder, riots, and so forth, what makes him think so? Or if one contends that some Supreme Court rulings have paved the way for massive civil disorders, what connections can he prove?

Perhaps the most notable set of inductive methods ever devised to test this sort of argument is John Stuart Mill's five canons. They are known as Method of Agreement, Method of Difference, Joint Method, Method of Residues, and Method of Concomitant Variations. According to the *Method of Agreement*, if two or more instances of the phenomenon under investigation have only one common circumstance, that point of agreement is either the cause or the effect. The finding that the cities with the lowest incidence of dental decay also had fluorine in their water supply is an example of Agreement. The *Method of Difference* can be used in cases similar to the preceding one. If an instance in which the phenomenon being investigated occurs and another in which it does not occur have every circumstance but one in common, and if that one occurs only in the former, the sole circumstance in which the cases differ must be the effect or the cause. By controlled experiment the connection between mosquito bite and malaria was shown. The difference between the men who contracted the disease and those who did not was the bite of the *Anopheles* mosquito. Combining the first two methods yields the *Joint Method of Agreement and Difference*. To test the connection between color-fading and exposure to sunlight, one could array the positive instances of fading among rugs, draperies, and paintings that had been exposed to sunlight; next, one could array the negative instances of fading among similar articles under various temperatures but without direct sunlight. *Method of Residues* works best with quantified phenomena. If the total retail price is determined by materials, labor, transportation, advertising, fixed overhead, and markup, and if the first five account for 20 percent, 25 percent, 8 percent, 2 percent, and 15 percent respectively, the mark-up must be 30 percent. Fifth and last is the *Method of Concomitant Variations*. It is used to check causal connection by charting parallel fluctuations, as in the cases of interest rates and real estate development, garbage collection and the rat population, tree growth and rainfall, and dating behavior and academic average. These methods are no longer taken to represent the whole range of scientific method.

Some tests of nondeductive value arguments will now be suggested. First, some for *evaluative prediction for one case* will be given. Any logical test should pertain to the interrelationships among relevant elements, not the truth of each item of prediction. Further, any test must consider the logical difference between *is* and *ought*, because a value conclusion involves the latter. In arguing for a municipal swimming pool, there would be truth predictions about keeping children busy, providing a focus for youth leadership, and teaching swimming and life-saving, but there would be a key premise, perhaps unstated, about the desirability of these outcomes. Testing should, therefore, encompass questions concerning the factual dependability of the predicted outcome together with one or more on the acceptability of the value premise. The case of the professional football player, it will be recalled, was tested (and found wanting) as an evaluative prediction of one case.

Evaluative analogy occurs in this charge: "Laymen shouldn't tell educators how to run the school, because laymen don't tell physicians how to practice medicine." Some of the familiar tests of analogical argument apply, but debating on the analogy itself would be futile. Anyone wishing to test this analogy would do better to look into the difference between what the educators are expert in and what they are not. Physicians, lawyers, architects, and sculptors, to name but a few kinds of experts, actually *do* receive advice from nonexperts, despite what the analogy assumes.

Evaluative generalization can be tested by asking, "Are the premises acceptable? Were ample relevant data taken into account? Were all relevant assumptions scrutinized? Were the used instances sufficiently different to cover the range of variations encompassed by the generalization?" So many evaluative generalizations are so abstract and vague that a conclusion like "Honesty is the best policy" requires definition if not semantic analysis.

Agreement and difference, not in the sense Mill used them but in the sense of the Kantian discourse on good will, can be tested, but probably not with "practical" questions. Perhaps the fundamental questions would have to deal with meanings, philosophical assumptions, and hierarchies of values. One might ask Kant in what contexts he would prefer an extremely stupid person of good will to a bright one with average good will, whatever that means. How we judge goodness or badness of acts, for instance, is worthy of analysis, but it can be difficult.[37]

---

[37] Angell, *Reasoning* . . . , pp. 346–347, especially the story of distributing food to the starving.

QUESTIONS

1. If the standards of rhetorical proof are less demanding than those of science or of logic, how should we interpret the claim that an advocate's main job is to discover truth?

2. Some writers define an argument (meaning the smallest unit of a sense-making argument) as a conclusion and a reason. This seems to resemble the Data and Conclusion of the Toulmin layout. If we extend this argument through all six steps of the layout, do we still have one argument, or do we have a series of interrelated arguments?

3. Which of the kinds of arguments are likely to be of central importance in developing a main point for a proposition of prediction or future fact?

4. Which, as in question 3, for a proposition of value?

5. If one of the major bases of classification of arguments is "truth" or "value," why don't we classify propositions (resolutions) the same way and forget about the "policy" class?

6. What does it mean to say that formal logic and probability have little to do with what we call proof in argumentation?

7. After noting the many classifications of arguments in a dozen textbooks, comment upon the question, "What does it matter?"

8. In what situation might each of the four diagrams of argument (line diagram, logical outline, Venn diagram, Toulmin layout) be the most suitable?

EXERCISES

1. Select from Appendixes some arguments for descriptive analysis. Some students might use line diagrams, others the Toulmin layout, and so on.

2. Again, after selecting some arguments, *classify* them according to some basis which can be found in this chapter.

3. Others might apply appropriate *tests* to selected arguments from the Appendixes.

4. Using the practice proposition you have been working with, write some short argumentative paragraphs containing an assigned number of the fourteen possible subclasses or kinds of argument as given in "A Suggested Classification."

5. Have a page or two of argumentative discourse read aloud to the class. During a brief pause at the end of each unit of argument, ask students to identify the kind or kinds of argument used.

CHAPTER 9

OTHER FORMS

OF SUPPORT

PERSONS HAVING AT LEAST A CASUAL ACQUAINTANCE WITH SPEECH COM-
position—or written composition, for that matter—are aware of several
forms of support. When a point, a topic sentence, or whatever else it
may be called, is to be developed for some communicative purpose,
there is need for materials to clarify, amplify, or prove it. Such materials
include exposition, description, illustration, evidence, logical argument,
motive appeals, suggestion, and related items.

In general speech composition one might with good reason treat all
of these forms of support with equal emphasis, but in argumentation
the setting is not analogous. Writing on "the available means of persuasion," Aristotle treated three modes furnished by the spoken word:
ethos, *pathos*, and *logos*. The "third depends on the proof, or
apparent proof, provided by the words of the speech itself."[1] Aristotle
wrote his *Rhetoric* to give logical proof its proper place, and while his
work deals with source credibility and emotional appeal, he "held to his
conviction that the most important ingredient of a speech is rational
demonstration through severe argumentation."[2] Thus if the present

[1] Aristotle, *Rhetoric*, I. 2, 1355b–1356a, in R. McKeon (ed.), *The Basic
Works of Aristotle* (N.Y.: Random House, Inc., 1941), p. 1329.
[2] L. Thonssen & A. C. Baird, *Speech Criticism* (N.Y.: Ronald Press and Co.,
1948), p. 331.

textbook were to treat all forms of support with equal emphasis, the title ought to contain *rhetoric, persuasion,* or *composition,* which it plainly does not.

EXPLANATION

A full explanation tends to be deductive in form, and when this is the case, the discourse resembles both explanation and argument. In this situation the distinguishing element between explanation and argument is the intent of the communicator, but this cannot always be known. One way to tell the difference is to ask what element is novel in a given specimen of discourse. If the conclusion is novel (controversial), the material is proof, but if the supporting reasons are novel (unknown or controversial), the material is explanation, say Ray and Zavos.[3]

When explanation is used as incidental material in argumentative discourse, it includes description, narration, and exposition. These supporting materials in various proportions are used to supplement the evidence and the inference in ways which will be explained in the next paragraph.

Of what importance is explanation as incidental material in an advocatory speech or essay? We know that explanation is of primary importance in a discourse to inform, but in advocacy it serves to improve understanding and interest. The reason is that listeners and readers tend to grow bored with prosaic, bare, or abstract ideas. They want details and particulars such as definitions, examples, figures, and sensory impressions which will clarify and enliven the ideas. Exposition, for instance, brings the unfamiliar into the understanding by associating it with the knowledge and experience of the listeners or readers. Description adds sensory imagery to the message, and narration lends action or a story line.

Applications of these principles may be seen in editorials, advertising, judicial opinions, philosophical arguments, school debates, and other forms of argumentative discourse. For example, the proposition of an editorial was that any decision on the nature of future space explorations should be based upon the criterion of efficient advancement of

[3] See Miller and Nilsen, *Perspectives* . . . , pp. 103–106.

knowledge rather than an emotional flush over successful competition with a rival country. The paragraphs which led to this conclusion were in part explanatory: they reported and sketched the backgrounds of the competing views on the comparative advantages of continuing the Mercury-Atlas flights as opposed to proceeding at once to the Gemini series. Explanation appeared as incidental material in a full-page advertisement for the Rolls-Royce automobile. In one paragraph we read that the automatic gear selector is bored to a tolerance of 1/4000 of an inch, that it is then blasted by particles of ground coconut shell, and that it is polished with ground oat-husks. When Walt Whitman wrote an editorial against slavery for the *Daily Eagle*, he included a vivid description of life aboard a slave ship, and when he wrote against capital punishment, he described the scene at the hanging of a woman. Judicial opinions, particularly those of Supreme Court justices, often contain cogently reasoned discourse, but there is usually an exposition of the grounds for the decision. In such discourse the traditional distinction between exposition and argumentation is difficult to maintain. And how about philosophical argumentation? In Chapter 3 the point was made that a philosophical approach involves more exposition than persuasion in the usual sense. In fact, exposition may in some cases be much more than incidental material; it may be the dominant material. Finally, if school debating is viewed as an exercise in primarily "logical" persuasion, and if the traditional debate format is retained, explanation will continue to serve mainly in the presentation of affirmative plans, negative counterpropositions, and, less obviously, the causal hypothesis in the "need" argument which explains *why* the staus quo is failing.

When explanation is the dominant material in persuasive discourse, the method is likely to be implicative rather than didactic. Instead of beginning with his proposition and supporting it with reasons and evidence, the implicative arguer starts with the background of the problem, narrates some relevant events, describes some conditions, explains the trend, and thereby builds up a pressure of facts and mental images which make the outcome seem inevitable. This is the method of implication, as Bosanquet named it, and it differs markedly from the method of linear inference such as we see in logical outlines.[4] Typically the implicative method delineates a problem, explains and disqualifies all solutions save one, and finally confronts the audience with a this-or-

[4] B. Bosanquet, *Implication and Linear Inference* (London: Macmillan and Company, 1920), pp. 1–30; also G. M. Graham, "The National Procedure in Argument," *Quarterly Journal of Speech Education*, XI, No. 4 (1925), 319–337.

nothing disjunction. In this manner Woodrow Wilson discussed three choices: armed neutrality, submission, and declaration of war against Germany. Then he showed why choices one and two were out of the question, thereby leaving a choice between declaration of war and nothing.

There are both advantages and risks in this method. Theoretically, implication reduces the probability of a contrarient idea in a doubtful or a hostile audience, and it reasons from the *whole* situation rather than from the biased points of one side. As in a jigsaw puzzle, when all parts but one have been assembled, the place for the last one becomes inevitable. However, the risk is that if the audience prefers to deny the whole thought rather than to accept the implied conclusion, the case fails. This is why the "nothing" choice should be made factually or psychologically unaccceptable to the audience.

A few illustrative applications of explanation as a persuasive method may serve to clarify the theory. Some years ago a student in a public speaking class met an informative speech assignment by explaining how frequency-modulation radio broadcasting works. After he finished, several members of the class charged that he had given a persuasive speech. They were convinced, they reported, that all radio transmission should be done in the way he had explained. Without intending to do so, the student had used a form of implication. Another student used this method intentionally in an attempt to convince his audience that the United Nations could succeed where the League of Nations had failed. First he listed the reasons given by historians for the failure of the League. This was reporting, not linear inference. Then, after merely stating that another organization was trying to do better, he explained the organization and functions of the U.N., including the police force, the provisions for the studying of social and economic problems, and the work of the Secretariat. At no time did he directly argue that the U.N. would succeed because of these provisions. Through reporting and explaining he built the implication that the U.N. would succeed because it did not start with the shortcomings which had doomed the League. Finally, if school debating were occasionally conducted as an exercise in popular persuasion but without demagoguery, and if its stylized form were on those occasions abandoned, we might find that explanation in the implicative form had become a much more familiar method than before.

So much for the theory of implication and the examples of its utilization. The hypothesis that this theory will be proved experimentally has not been sufficiently tested. The theory seems plausible, and some practical appplications have lent some confirmation to it, but a broad generalization concerning the persuasive impact of the implicative methods would not now be warranted. In the next chapter some instruction on the organization of persuasive explanation will be given.

ETHOS

This form of support has been briefly defined as the persuasive impact of a speaker's personality, but brevity may result in the oversimplification of a complex, suggestive phenomenon. More than twenty centuries ago Aristotle wrote in his *Rhetoric* that the character of a speaker is a source of persuasion when it makes him seem worthy of belief. He explained that in general we trust persons of probity more than others, and in relation to uncertain or debatable matters we trust them almost absolutely. If we cannot judge what is true and what is false, or what is wise and what is unwise, we must place our trust in worthy advisers. They merit our trust because of their intelligence, character, and good will. Even when one is behaving in the most rational fashion, he will have occasion to place his trust in some sources, particularly when he lacks the qualifications or the time to judge the evidence or the argument on its own merits. This is why the argument from authority, as some writers call it, is often effective.

In ancient times *ethos* meant the impressions which the listeners formed of the speaker while he spoke. Nowadays this concept includes the original meaning plus reputation, status, and the like. In fact, a man's prior reputation often accounts for the size of the audience which assembles to hear him. In contemporary social science research, ethos is known as credibility of the source of the message, and it includes speakers, writers, and the media in which they operate.

Ethos is a cultural variable; its constituent elements are not the same in all times and places. Persons differ in what they value in others. The implication for an advocate is that he should so analyze his public that he may ascertain what traits its members value in a person. For instance, the general voting public is thought usually to prefer a presidential candidate who has a solid American background, preferably humble; who looks moderately attractive on television and newsreels;

who appears healthy and vigorous; who has an attractive family; who is successful in a private career; who is identified with popular and safe issues; who acts as if he were drafted; and who makes himself conspicuous.

An advocate's ethos, aside from any matters of antecedent reputation, is ultimately determined by the choices he makes—by the proposition he chooses, by his evidence and reasoning, by his attitudes, by his emotional reactions, by his language and general demeanor—indeed by all the cues or signs which are available to the listener or the reader. For example, a speaker who is reasonably confident and well poised exerts a positive suggestion upon his audience. Likewise a person's grasp of his subject indicates intellectual competence and personal integrity. Other signs of general competence are enthusiasm, adaptability, sincerity, fairness, courage, directness, good taste, some trace of a sense of humor, and perhaps a modest reference to some experiences which qualify him to write or speak on the proposition.

Estimates of the importance of ethos or "image" can be based upon rhetorical theory, personal observation, and the findings of experimental studies. An importance such as Aristotle attributed to ethos stems in part from the advocate's personal identification with his subject. Any writer or speaker has some of this identification, but one who seeks to influence others is much more closely identified with his message in the minds of his public. When he supports an idea or an action, he stands as a sponsor of that cause. In many minds the spokesman and his cause are one. For this reason we may say that the use or nonuse of ethical persuasion is not a matter of choice. Ethos is inevitable; an advocate will surely be judged for something he does or fails to do. These are the generalizations from rhetorical theory and empirical observation.

More specific conclusions can be drawn from experimental studies because each investigation has focused upon a small part of what we call ethos. However, the concept is so broad and each study is so narrow that we still do not have enough results to permit definitive generalizing about the operation of ethos in real-life contexts. Instead of noting dozens of studies individually, let us refer to one report which summarizes the experimental research in ethos.[5] Both expert opinion and an announcement of what the majority opinion is will exert prestige suggestion. The prestige of the source affects the impact of the communication, but this wears off in time and loses its initial advantage.

[5] K. Andersen and T. Clevenger, Jr., "A Summary of Experimental Research in Ethos," *Speech Monographs*, XXX, No. 2 (1963), 59–78.

Some persons are more susceptible to prestige suggestion than others, but this correlates more highly with initial attitude than with education, age, intelligence, or sex. Both oral and printed propaganda can alter public images of persons, but direct attacks may backfire because of sympathy for the victim. Democratic strategists in the Kennedy-Nixon campaign were advised against attacking Nixon personally for fear they would lose more than they could hope to gain.[6] The highest character ratings were given to speakers whom their listeners perceived as belonging to their social class; in fact, the greater the social distance between speaker and rater the lower the rating of the speaker's character. Some laudatory remarks by an introducer may enhance a speaker's ethos, but the speaker's own expression of self-praise (direct ethos) usually does him no good. Attempts to appear broad-minded by presenting both sides of a controversy are better than one-sided presentations in few cases and under special conditions. As we noted in relation to evidence, documentation does not improve source credibility unless the qualifying comment becomes a buildup for the source. There is some effect which can be attributed to dress, voice, and manner, but this is indefinite. Finally, it appears that the typical listener is a poor judge of sincerity. Perhaps this is why some campaigners try to get away with calling each issue "vital," and opponent a "menace," a rival idea "Communist-inspired," and each election a "crisis."

MOTIVATION

When we refer to motivation in relation to persuasion, we mean the process of inducing or of modifying a response by supplying attractive reasons for the desired behavior. It involves the use of supporting materials which are intended to identify the listeners' or readers' goals, values, and so forth, with the acceptance of the advocate's message. Motivation is selective in that it lowers the threshold of stimulation for one appeal while raising it for competing appeals. It is said to be reinforcing or inhibiting because it adds to or subtracts from the intensity of stimuli which lead to one reaction, or it induces a set or a habit which aids or hinders a response. In motivation as well as in persuasion gener-

[6] *The Wall Street Journal*, February 1, 1960, p. 1.

ally, the objective is the modification of attitudes, and this modification may be as obvious as an overt act or as subtle as an internalized response which can be detected only by an attitude-measuring procedure.

This definition suggests that motivation has an affective core of feeling tones such as likes, dislikes, interests, and preferences. These elements are not drives nor are they universal; they vary among cultures, and their intensity varies among individuals in a culture. When situations matter to us, we experience feelings; and when because of our attitudes they matter very much, we have strong emotional reactions. Thus our affective (emotional) states sometimes outweigh our objective thinking in determining our behavior. Whether these affective states produce good or harm depends upon the adjustments we make. It is only when adjustments are immature that emotional behavior is deplorable.

Separate treatments of reasoning and motivation in this book do not imply mutual exclusiveness. No strict dichotomy of reason and emotion is intended. In other words, thoughtful and emotional reactions are interrelated and occur in varying proportions in different situations. It is a matter of emphasis or central tendency, not one of all this or all that. For example, if one urges that guns be handled in a certain way and supports the proposition by showing how persons may be hurt or killed, one is using an appeal which is both logically and psychologically sound. It is clear that all behavior has its motives; therefore, an advocate who relates certain desires or values to his proposition is *not necessarily* using illogical thinking, but he *may* be.

Anyone who wishes to test the probative force of an emotional appeal or an appeal from the credibility of the source can lay out the argument according to one of the schemes, insert the item of *ethos* or *pathos* as a premise, and trace out the consequences. Suppose someone says, "You'd better learn gun handling before going hunting; you don't want to kill someone, do you?" The first step, as explained in the preceding chapter, is to state the argument: (I) You should learn how to handle firearms before going hunting, because (A) Improper gun handling is responsible for many accidental deaths, and (A') Persons who have not been taught are likely to handle guns improperly. Or suppose someone says, "You should take lessons in gun handling, because the Editor of *Field and Stream* said so, and he ought to know." Here the missing major premise, "Whatever the Editor of *Field and Stream* advises on the use of sporting arms should be done," would be added to the basic layout before testing this "sign argument," "argument from authority," "deductive value argument," or whatever one names it.

There is no attempt here being made to deny that people have *feelings* about evidence, reasons, conclusions, and persons. The point is that, if anyone is interested in testing the kind of sense such as argument makes, there are ways to do it.

When motivation is the main form of support, as in popular persuasion, it is obviously important; but when it is ancillary, as in rational arguments to critical listeners or readers, it is less important. Questions concerning the importance of motivation in this lesser role will be answered with theories from the literature, some references to real-life applications thereof, and some findings of experimental research.

Not all speeches of advocacy require motivational support. There are instances in which the communicator's main concern is with material and logical validity, regardless of the desires of some listeners or readers. A less extreme case is one in which the communicator gives *some* consideration to his audience, but only to the extent of seeking a *thoughtful* response from the *critical* listeners or readers. Finally, it is possible, even when adapting to a popular audience, to base an argument on their attitudes or beliefs and to reason both cogently and persuasively in showing the consequences of those attitudes.

According to rhetorical theory, one of the significant functions of motivation as ancillary material is the gaining of attention. Introductory paragraphs are supposed to attract attention. Showing how the subject matters to us or by arousing our curiosity are only two of several ways to motivate attention and interest. This kind of supporting material which holds attention and facilitates the reception of ideas has the additional advantage of neutralizing the doubting, inhibiting, or objecting attitudes which lead to disagreement. The following introductory paragraphs were used in a speech on the Hoover Report which was delivered to an audience of businessmen in 1949. This introduction was designed to motivate attention:

Fellow Businessmen:
How long could you stay in business if your unit cost were 2½ times the selling price? The Post Office spends 2½ cents on each penny postcard, and its current annual deficit is five hundred million dollars.
Would any of you retain a purchasing agent who set up such complicated procedures that he spent ten dollars to order less than ten dollars worth of supplies? About half of the three million government purchase

orders issued each year are for ten dollars or less. The average cost of the paper work and other red tape far exceeds ten dollars per order. Thus, if you were an operating man in one of the government agencies and ordered a dollar's worth of pencils, it would cost the government eleven dollars to make delivery to you. You men would soon look for a new purchasing agent if you found anything like this going on in your business. Let us see how this problem affects us and what we can do about it.

A second function of motivational support as incidental or secondary material is to reinforce the logical argument with reassuring evidence of a favorable majority opinion. After arguing the reasons for our sooner or later joining the fight against the Axis powers in World War II, James B. Conant cited an opinion poll which showed nearly seventy-one percent of the American people to be in favor of naval belligerency rather than let the British lose.[7] Experimental studies have been done on facets of this phenomenon.[8] One finding is that the effect of majority opinion will vary with the degree of value one places on membership in the group. Another is that the influence of majority opinion is strongest when the majority is large. Of course, those who have a streak of nonconformity in their personalities are less influenced by disclosures of majority views. Some will, in fact, take the opposite side after they hear what the majority thinks.

Already cogent arguments can be psychologically supported by citing corroborating opinions from respected persons, as we noted in the discussion of ethos. In relation to evidence, we would speak of this as the addition of audience acceptability to logical adequacy. The effect of this added material is similar to that of the disclosure of favorable majority opinion as explained above. For example, after developing a logical case for his side of a proposition, a debater may quote a supporting opinion from a high-prestige source such as a popular president or a beloved benefactor of humanity. Beginners sometimes express it awkwardly: "We have proved that foreign aid must be continued and President Eisenhower agrees with us."

An advocate will often bolster his own ethos, credibility, or image before he introduces a cogent but unpopular argument. Minnick explains five methods of doing this: common-ground, yes-yes, yes-but, oblique, and implicative.[9] It is believed that an audience will react less

[7] "When Shall America Fight?" *Vital Speeches*, VII (1940–41), 518.

[8] C. I. Hovland, I. L. Janis, and H. H. Kelley, *Communication and Persuasion* (New Haven: Yale University Press, 1953), Chap. 5.

[9] W. C. Minnick, The Art of Persuasion (Boston: Houghton Mifflin Co., 1957), pp. 126–131.

unfavorably to an unpopular proposition if the introductory remarks serve to build up the advocate's acceptability. Certainly one of the striking instances of this occurred in the opening of Henry Ward Beecher's Liverpool Address: he reaffirmed the sincerity of his views; he explained that his opponents wished to silence him because their own case was weak; he said it mattered little to himself personally if he were not allowed to speak; he expressed courage and integrity ("You will not find a man—you will not find me to be a man who dared to speak about Great Britain 3,000 miles off, and then is afraid to speak to Great Britain when he stands on her shores"); and he closed his introduction with a request for fair play, for which Englishmen were renowned.

A fifth incidental use of motivational material occurs when one inserts into an otherwise rational argument some words chosen for their biasing effect. Words such as left-winger, fellow traveler, nigger-lover, radical, agitator, reactionary, and alien are all-too-familiar examples.

Or one might argue that the acceptance of a logically adequate argument happens also to be in the best interests of the listeners or readers. Identification of their desires and values with the acceptance of the proposition is the persuasive device involved here. For instance, after developing a logical argument against the prior censorship of motion pictures, Jerry Wald closed with the assertion that only by preserving the freedoms of the First Amendment can we preserve our nation and our way of life.[10]

Finally, one can arrange a case in an order that is easy to follow and to accept. More will be said of this in the next chapter on the organization of cases. For the present, though, we might consider the possibility of using in actual presentation an outline which is more interesting and perhaps more persuasive than the formal, logical, "because-because-because" outline.

Suggestion is a method by means of which a persuader tries to establish an idea more or less indirectly in another person's mind. While seemingly presenting one idea in the center of attention, the communicator subtly hints at another idea which may be perceived uncritically in the fringes of attention. This marginally perceived stimulus is intended to release habitual responses which require no intellectual effort. In this way Daniel Webster, as prosecutor in the Knapp-White murder trial, used what purported to be a narrative statement of the facts to dramatize the cunning and viciousness of the conspirators as contrasted with

[10] "Movie Censorship—The First Wedge," *Saturday Review*, April 8, 1961, p. 54.

the innocence and helplessness of their sleeping victim. Webster not only narrated the facts; he made the jury want to exact the supreme penalty even before he called for it.

Several factors influence the efficacy of suggestion. One is, as we have seen, the prestige of the source. This being true, a speaker should either quote recognized authorities or establish his own ethos on the subject. A second factor is the speaker's ability to make his listeners see and feel the idea. Vividness of imagery and forcefulness of presentation are essential devices. Thirdly, a positive approach combined with an implied reward for agreement is often persuasive. This may be accomplished by calling for the acceptance of the desired idea rather than the rejection of its opposite, and the act of acceptance should be associated with a pleasant outcome. Polarization or unification of the audience is a fourth factor. Undivided attention to a speaker plus a unified response to his remarks may be achieved by means of (a) compact seating, (b) unison activities such as applauding, singing, and raising hands, (c) the use of respected symbols such as banners, flags, pictures of respected persons, uniforms, and objects related to worship, (d) comfortable surroundings, and (e) the placing of the speaker in a dominant position on a raised platform. Repetition is a fifth factor in suggestion, but only if the style of composition produces a cumulative effect. Unskilled repetition is obvious, dull, and negatively suggestive. Sixth among the factors of suggestion is indirectness of approach. Through this approach a persuader may, by implication, induce his listeners to think the suggested idea was theirs. Finally, the avoidance of any suggestion of a rival idea is thought to be a significant principle in persuasion. For this reason we are advised not to repeat a rumor, even for the purpose of denying it.

Rationalization is a second method of motivation. This process of associating the persuadees' desires with the persuader's idea involves the use of an emotionally aroused conclusion which is made plausible on pseudological grounds. People prefer to believe that they are acting logically, even when they are influenced by emotional appeals. For instance, they often do what they desire to do, and then they invent plausible reasons for their impulsive behavior. Knowing this, some speakers and writers use emotional appeals coupled with pseudological "reasons" such as "Business is business," "You're young only once," or "If I don't get it, someone else will."

It is not suggested that students adopt the ethics of demagogues; they ought to feel more social responsibility than rabble-rousers do. But there are times when an audience, having been motivated by emotional appeals to accept an ethically sound proposition, still wants a seemingly rational justification for the action. Since some decisions are influenced more by desire than by evidence, an advocate can satisfy his audience and justify his own position by determining the motives in his public, associating those motives with his proposal, and finally presenting his logical support.

As listeners and readers, we need to understand the method of motivation by rationalization, even though we intend never to use it. Critical thinking is an important skill which involves the recognition of these characteristics of rationalization: it focuses attention on materials that merely *seem* relevant; its apparently clear ideas are actually vague; it disguises suggestion as deliberation; it treats plausible reasons as real ones; it masks subjective ideas as objective ones; it seemingly invites scrutiny while circumventing it; it capitalizes upon fallacies and stratagems which thwart critical thinking.

Open statement or direct suggestion associates desires or values with a proposition by means of an open, frank statement or a demonstration of the connection. Instead of being subtle or devious, the persuader directly establishes the desired connection; he may explain how the acceptance of his ideas will result in certain satisfactions, he may demonstrate or give a sample, or he may do both. This method utilizes that principle of learning which holds that the proffered motive should be logically relevant to the desired goal.

Speech techniques are not exactly coordinate with the three preceding methods of motivation, but they are sufficiently related to warrant treatment here. Speakers may use motivation positively or negatively, and it may be speaker-centered or audience-centered. A positive approach facilitates the desired response, while a negative approach inhibits some undesirable response. A speaker-centered (subjective) approach urges others to follow the speaker's appraisal of the listeners' needs, but a listener-centered (objective) approach is based upon the listeners' conceptions of their own needs. For instance, a speaker using the objective, positive approach would facilitate the desired response by encouraging the listeners to analyze their own needs or interests, by helping them to analyze their needs as an aid in designing solutions, or by associating their "need" stimuli with those leading to the speaker's desired response instead of pressing the audience to fit the speaker's notion of their needs.

Effective persuaders draw attention to some value and show how it can be realized or how it is threatened. Often the appeal is to the common values of patriotism, local loyalties, truth, sportsmanship, and the like. These values are brought vividly into play by suggestion, rationalization, or open statement; the claim is made that these values are in jeopardy; and the audience is moved to block the threat. Some of the popular, vivid narratives for this purpose are those involving the exploitation of the underdog, and other unjust acts. When the speaker thinks that the listeners at least temporarily favor his proposal as a remedy, he seeks to convert this impulse into a quick, overt action as in a vote, a show of hands, or the signing of a document. Such an overt expression of enthusiasm serves to prolong it and may lead to a more lasting expression.

These less rigorously rational forms of rhetorical support may serve to build what has been called "cognitive imagery in communication."[11] Some anarchists at the turn of this century spoke and wrote about their vision of an ideal social order, if that is the word for it, in which all would cooperate out of desire, no government would be necessary, and a good time would be had by all. Their indictment of the status quo was colorful and hyperbolic. According to their cognitive imagery, governmental actions taken under the pretext of the public good result in the ordinary citizen's being harassed, beaten up, garrotted, sold, betrayed, and dishonored. Nazi glorification of the master race, the absolute state, and war were of this same stripe. Those who stage public performances to glorify the alleged wonders of drug-induced hallucinations practice a kind of cognitive imagery, too, as do individuals and groups that promote generally accepted ideas and practices.

When we treat the persuasive components, particularly ethos and motivation, as secondary to the logical, does this imply that we think either that popular persuasion does not occur or that if it does occur it is evil? No such implication is intended, and this disclaimer should not be needed.

In practical terms, what *is* meant here? First, as Chapter 3 explained, a persuader has an ethical and a logical responsibility to make sense. He is likely to meet his responsibility if he practices the core principles of argumentation.

In addition to making sense, a persuasive communicator needs to analyze his audience and adapt thereto for purposes of interest, understanding, identification, and the like. There is nothing inherently un-

[11] R. B. Gregg, "A Phenomenologically Oriented Approach To Rhetorical Criticism," *Central States Speech Journal*, XVII, No. 2 (1966), 83–89.

ethical in taking account of the predisposing factors which may explain individual differences in persuadability. These may include attitudes toward the proposition itself, the appeals used, the logical merit of the case, the information presented, stylistic matters, delivery mannerisms, the personality of the speaker, the setting in which communication occurs, the medium of transmission, and, of course, the personality of the individual listener.

Then, in relation to the likely steps in the persuasive process, a speaker might properly ask: How can I get attention? How can I arouse interest? How can I induce understanding, assuming I am not a propagandist? How can I secure acceptance of my proposition? Finally, in terms of the philosophy of this book, a persuader must consider how to maintain an ethically defensible position throughout.

QUESTIONS

1. Why are explanation, ethos, and motivation treated as secondary forms of support? In what circumstances should they not be so classified?
2. Explain the differences between explanation as incidental material and as a persuasive method.
3. What is ethos? How important may it be in various situations?
4. Under what circumstances is it ethical to persuade others with motivation?
5. How can an emotional argument or one based upon source credibility be tested for logical adequacy?
6. What does published research tell us about the effectiveness of ethos? of motivation?
7. Does this chapter give the impression that the use of emotional appeal is evil? Explain your view.

EXERCISES

1. Identify the motive appeals in selected advertisements.
2. Cite and evaluate some instances of explanation as incidental material in the Appendixes.
3. Point out some ethos-building clues in assigned items from Appendixes.
4. Look for examples of some of the seven incidental uses of motivational material in the discourses which are reprinted in the Appendixes.
5. Locate and evaluate some specimens (in Appendixes or elsewhere) which illustrate some of the methods of motivation.
6. Outline and deliver a short speech of advocacy in which the three secondary forms of support are used in addition to the logical argument. Label them parenthetically in the outline.
7. Write an argumentative essay in which logical argument is supplemented by the three secondary forms of support. Use marginal notes or footnotes to identify these three materials.
8. Compare Chapter 7 of Beardsley's *Straight Thinking* on suggestion. (See "Notes" on Chapter 8.)

CHAPTER 10

CASE CONSTRUCTION

IN ARGUMENTATION, A CASE MAY BE DEFINED AS THE TOTAL REPRESENTA-
tion which one side makes on behalf of its stand on a proposition. A
total representation includes the evidence, logic, assumptions, narration,
exposition, description, motivation, and strategy upon which one side
elects to base its cause and upon which it will win or lose. The one side
which is referred to means either affirmative or negative, and it may consist of one person, an organization, or a school debate team.

When a case is expressed in full, it appears as a complete speech or
essay, or as a series of speeches or essays. An abridged case appears as a
case outline or a précis. Ideally, as has been shown in Chapter 3, a case
should be the best statement that a side can make in relation to its
logical and ethical responsibilities. This implies that a case may be
adapted to the opposition, the audience, and the occasion so long as the
substance of the proof remains consistent with the evidence, with a
reasonable interpretation of that evidence, and with the social responsibility of the advocate.

THE CONCEPT OF A PRIMA FACIE CASE

In Relation to Issues

A prima facie case is one which, on first view or on its face, is adequate to prove its side until it is refuted. Such a case has probative force for the reason that it is logically sufficient to establish a reasonably high degree of probability in its favor. An affirmative case is said to be logically adequate if it has evidence and reasoning to affirm all potential issues, as explained in Chapter 5, except those which the negative waived or admitted before the affirmative submitted its case. In practice, any affirmative must, except in the few special situations explained below, prepare as if every potential issue were to become actual. The negative, on the other hand, is expected to offer a case which will logically support a negative answer to *at least one* of the issues.

Even though issues are of crucial importance to a prima facie case, this does not mean that stock language such as "Is there a need for a change?" should be used. It is better to express an issue in a question such as this: "Are there important shortcomings in the present system of academic probation?" The principle is that an issue can be stated more meaningfully in terms of the subject matter of the proposition, the kind of proposition, and the type of argumentative situation (philosophical, legislative, or other).

While constructing a case to affirm or negate the issues, an advocate is concerned with talking points, otherwise known as points in partition. These are the main, declarative sentences which answer the issues. They appear as Roman-numeral topics in a case outline. Sometimes the issues and the points in partition differ only in that the former are interrogative while the latter are declarative. More often, however, the wording and the arrangement of points in partition differ from those of the issues. There need not be a one-to-one relationship between issues and points in partition. A difference in wording can be seen in these specimens: (issue) "Will compulsory arbitration prove to be an effective solution?"; (point) "Compulsory arbitration won't work."

When we think of argumentation as a critical apparatus, it is important to note that the requirements for a prima facie case serve to test an advocate's analysis as well as the completeness and the consistency of his case. Critical thinkers demand to know whether an advocate is developing all the essential ideas and doing so in a consistent fashion. In nonlegal situations "prima facie" need not apply to specific items of evidence in the same way that it does in court. In general argumentation we say that, if the evidence appears to support its point, it is prima facie. However, we usually apply the modifier "prima facie" to the whole case rather than to any small part such as an item of evidence.[1]

In Relation to Presumption and Burden of Proof

It will be recalled that a correctly worded proposition gives the presumption to the negative and places the burden of proof upon the affirmative. In consequence of this, the affirmative has to make a prima facie case before the negative is under obligation to reply. To put this idea differently, one might say that a presumption favors the negative at the outset of the debate, and this temporary advantage can be overcome only by the presentation of a prima facie affirmative case. After such a case is presented, the negative has an obligation which will be discussed under "burden of rebuttal." A fruitful debate cannot take place unless the affirmative sets out a prima facie case to meet its burden of proof, and the negative counters with a prima facie rejoinder.

Two situations, one involving a proposition of legal fact and the other a proposition of policy, will serve to illustrate the relationship between a prima facie case and the burden of proof. The government brought antitrust action against five drug manufacturers, charging criminal conspiracy to fix prices on polio vaccine. In dismissing the case, the judge opined that the government had not met its affirmative burden of proof because a prima facie case had not been made. It was not prima facie because the issue of intent had not been affirmed. Some facts had been established, but the inference that the actions were contrived was not proved. In school debates and orations on propositions of policy, many affirmative spokesmen fail to discharge their burden of proof. Their cases are not prima facie because in many instances they either fail to prove the causal connection in their "need" arguments, or they

[1] For a different view, see R. L. Scott, "On the Meaning of the Term 'Prima Facie' in Argumentation," *Central States Speech Journal*, XII, No. 1 (1960), 33–37.

neglect to show how their plans will remedy the ills which they lament. The reader may wish to review Chapter 3 on this point.

In academic debate circles in recent years there has been a controversy over the question, "On a proposition of policy, must the affirmative case show 'serious and inherent evils in the status quo', as the stock language goes, in order to establish the first stage of a prima facie case?" Kruger is most insistent upon this.[2] Ehninger and Brockriede say "serious" and "inherent."[3] Eubank essentially concurs.[4] Freeley implies "serious" and says "inherent," even though he explains the comparative-advantages case, which deviates from this so-called rule.[5] Windes and Hastings use neither adjective in their explanation-of-benefits case, only "serious" in their solving-a-problem case, and neither in comparative-advantages.[6] Newman argues why an "inherent and compelling need" should not be required.[7]

In view of the kind of logic that this book presents in Chapter 8, one should not be surprised to learn that the need-for-a-change arguments on propositions of policy will not be categorically required to use "inherent and compelling" in their statements. Specifics on this position will be given under "Types of Cases."

In Relation to the Burden of Rebuttal

In the light of what has been explained thus far, we may conclude that the negative does not have a burden of rebuttal or any obligation to go forward with the debate until the affirmative makes a prima facie case. In other words, the affirmative proofs must justify the acceptance of the proposition on rational grounds before the negative has any obligation to reply. When the affirmative does complete a prima facie case, the burden of rebuttal falls on the negative. Then, if the negative makes an adequate rejoinder, the burden of rebuttal is shifted to the affirmative side. Thus it is that the burden of rebuttal, but not the burden of

[2] A. N. Kruger, "The Inherent Need: Further Clarification," *Journal of the American Forensic Association*, II, No. 3 (1965), 109–119.

[3] Ehninger and Brockriede, *Decision* . . . , p. 241.

[4] W. Eubank in McBath (ed.), *Argumentation* . . . , pp. 107–108.

[5] Freeley, *Argumentation*, pp. 194–196.

[6] Windes and Hastings, *Argumentation* . . . , pp. 227–232.

[7] R. P. Newman, "The Inherent and Compelling Need," *Journal of the American Forensic Association*, II, No. 2 (1965), 66–71.

proof, may shift back and forth. In short, the presentation of a prima facie case by one side shifts the burden of rebuttal to the opponent. Thus if an affirmative spokesman who urges the cessation of financial aid to Slobovia shows that the money is not needed and that it is actually being used to aid the enemies of the donor, the defenders of aid for Slobovia have the burden of rebuttal. Methods of replying to cases which are prima facie as well as those which are not will be treated under "Attack and Defense."

When a Prima Facie Case Is Not Required

If an individual were to count the cases which are not prima facie, he might conclude that there are many situations in which a logically sound case is not required. He would probably be right if his criterion were audience acceptability in the context of popular persuasion. We know that many listeners and readers are gullible; countless unwarranted claims are accepted as if they were proved. But students of argumentation presumably hold higher standards. For them there should be fewer situations in which cases that are not prima facie are tolerable.

Three kinds of circumstances in which logically incomplete cases *might* be acceptable come to mind: when a time limit requires some abridgment of the content, when an audience is interested in fewer than all of the potential issues, and when the disputants waive some of the issues. The word "might" is intended to caution the lazy and the unprincipled advocates against the temptation to offer a shoddy case merely because some listeners or readers let it go unchallenged. The time element is familiar to classroom, radio, and television speakers. If a student has four minutes for an argumentative talk on the United Nations, he cannot do justice to all issues; he will be well advised to limit his scope to "Five Defects in the U.N.," for example. When school debaters have twenty-eight minutes of air time, they often agree in advance to limit the discussion to one issue such as "need." Limitations imposed by audience interest can be illustrated with the controversy over "Pay-TV." If the public is interested primarily in the comparative quality of programs under the subscription plan as compared with the commercial system, we should expect the rival advocates to speak to that issue almost exclusively. Finally, if the disputants are interested in only one issue, they are likely to waive all others. When many lawyers debated the proposed judicial amendment to the Illinois constitution in 1958, the popular issue concerned benefits versus disadvantages.

Frequently we receive incomplete cases when only one side is represented. Advocates tend to argue less cogently when they think it is safe to do so. Obviously the presence of a competent opponent motivates an advocate to make a case as best he can. Cases which are less than prima facie are frequently offered by campaigners, salesmen, propagandists, and writers of letters to editors, to list but a few of the sources. Those who would excuse this practice on the ground that the absence of opposition makes a prima facie case superfluous are giving an explanation but not a good excuse. Regardless of the presence or the absence of an opponent, an advocate has the ethical and the logical responsibilities which were expounded in Chapter 3. Defective proof as we often perceive it in popular persuasion is successful when critical thinking is wanting in the audience. That is why this book stresses rationality in preference to popular belief as the major test of proof.

In this sense, a prima facie case is the *only* kind of case that can prove a proposition. In actual practice, particularly in school debates and in argumentative conversations, we deviate from the rule that the affirmative must complete a prima facie case before the negative has any burden of rebuttal. Typically the give-and-take of conversation is informal, and attack and defense occur on each fragment of a case as soon as it is stated. In school debate the time limits, the order of speeches, and the division of labor between teammates result in the first affirmative speaker's giving little more than half of the case before the negative has an opportunity to attack it. Following the first negative speech, the second affirmative speaker has an opportunity to finish the affirmative constructive case.

STEPS IN DEVELOPING A CASE

General Hints

At this stage in his preparation an advocate knows what his proposition is and presumably understands his responsibilities for it, he has analyzed and investigated it, he has assembled his evidence, he has reasoned about his evidence and the secondary forms of support, and he is ready to build his case. If he has taken the steps listed above, he is now at the stage called "partitioning a case."

When a spokesman proceeds to build this "total representation of a position," as it was called at the beginning of this chapter, he will, it is hoped, be mindful of his logical and his ethical responsibilities to offer the strongest case the available materials warrant. In other words, cogency is the first, ideal goal, while persuasiveness in a popular sense may have to be the second, practical goal.

In the process of achieving either or both of these goals, several time-tested hints will be found helpful: (1) Determine the philosophical assumptions upon which the case must stand, such as laissez-faire economics or the notion that human rights should always take precedence over property rights.[8] (2) Select points that are necessary for a prima facie case, which means that they are *worth* proving. (3) Consider whether these points *can* be proved. (4) Use as few points as will fulfill your responsibilities. (5) Adapt to the demands of popular persuasion, if necessary, but without sacrificing sense or integrity. (6) Organize the *preparation* (case) outline rigorously. (7) Compose the final presentation attractively.

For Propositions of Fact

Following the pattern of Chapter 5 on analysis, this section will take up propositions of legal fact, of past fact, of present fact, and of prediction.

Since all four varieties of propositions of fact have in common two analytical steps, as explained in Chapter 5, it is feasible to illustrate the process of case construction with one real-life specimen. To locate the proposition in the following letter requires, first, a determination of the status quo at that time. The prevailing situation was that the Chicago Transit Authority had banned the sale of certain publications in newsstands located at CTA stations, and it had done so on the ground that it had the "right to say what can be sold on CTA properties." The letter writer, being the dissatisfied party who challenged the status quo, has the burden of proof for his proposition of legal fact: "The position taken by the CTA is unwarranted and illegal." Actually, in the light of

[8] This means imbedding the case in a theoretical framework of interconnected premises and their implications.

the case which follows, the word "unwarranted" should be deleted in the interest of limiting the proposition to a single idea.

Two issues are raised: Is the CTA a public, governmental agency? Has it failed to comply with the law concerning such bodies? In affirming the first issue, the writer first refutes the assumption that the CTA is a simple, private business which would have the right to control sales on its property. Then he argues that the CTA is a municipal governmental corporation created by state statute, and as a public agency it must respect certain constitutional guarantees. To affirm his second issue, the writer shows that the CTA resorted to an arbitrary, administrative fiat instead of seeking the enactment of an ordinance which would be subject to judicial scrutiny. Two lesser points were that the fiat contained no definition of "objectionable" literature, and it was enforced by threats to cancel leases to vendors. This case for a proposition of legal fact is much shorter than a lawyer would submit in court; it does not document evidence or cite statutes.[9]

Virgil E. Gunlock, chairman of the Chicago Transit Authority, in seeking to justify the CTA's ban on the sale of certain publications because of alleged lewdness and obscenity, has stated: "This is not censorship, but rather the exercise of our right to say what can be sold on CTA properties."

It would appear from Mr. Gunlock's statement that the CTA regards itself as a simple private business (which has indeed the right to control what may be sold on its property). The position taken by the CTA is unwarranted and illegal.

The CTA is a municipal governmental corporation created by state statute, and as such it is a public agency with the obligation to respect the guarantees of freedom of speech and press and due process of law contained in the Constitution of the United States.

The CTA has appointed itself as a public censor of the reading matter available to the public and has done so in the most arbitrary and capricious fashion—by administrative fiat—without the use of a standard or definition of what is objectionable material.

The issue here is not the literary value of a few unpleasant publications but rather the far more important issue of public governmental bodies abandoning their constitutional responsibilities and failing to act pursuant to statutory authority.

The CTA is granted by statute the right to pass ordinances regulating the use and operation of its property. By its refusal to adopt a valid ordinance the CTA has evidently sought to by-pass judicial scrutiny of the constitutionality of its actions.

The CTA's current policy is effectuated by the circulation of lists of banned publications and the utilization of the threat of cancellation of

---

[9] "Letters to the Editor," *Chicago Daily News*, April 13, 1960.

newsstand leases of dealers who do not comply with the CTA directives. These methods now being used by the CTA are clearly unconstitutional.

> John L. McKnight.
> Executive director,
> Illinois Division, American
> Civil Liberties Union.
> Chicago.

For Propositions of Value

These are often used in the philosophical kind of debate. In this application of argumentation we encounter a greater risk of ambiguity because there are fewer standard definitions of terms and common interpretations of concepts such as "desirable," "out of place," "detrimental," "better than," or "wrong in principle." As we saw in Chapter 5, the basic and frequently implicit human values which underlie these disputes cannot be proved in the objective way that facts can be demonstrated. It often happens that the dispute turns on what the evaluative term means or should be taken to mean. Frequently this involves weighing the rival value premises as in a *Consumer's Report* preference for a safe car over a stylish one.

Let us take the proposition that big-time football is out of place on a university campus. Assuming that an affirmative advocate were to start building his case by asking the three pairs of criteria-and-application questions, he could proceed in either of two ways: he could so define his proposition that the validity of the three criteria would be assumed, and then his constructive case would argue the application of those criteria to football; or he could argue in defense of both the criteria and their application. Taking the first option, the affirmative would include in his introduction a statement of this sort: "Before we can show that big-time football is out of place on a university campus, we must explain what 'out of place' means. In the light of what many prominent educators have said a university should be (quoting or paraphrasing some), we conclude that any activity is out of place if it is not academically relevant, if it becomes an end in itself, and if it exploits its participants. We shall proceed to show that big-time football is academically irrelevant, it has become an end in itself, and it exploits its participants." If the affirmative thought the criteria would be sharply contested, he probably would build a case in defense of them instead of briefly defining them and assuming their acceptability.

Taking the negative side for a moment, we can see that several positions are possible: challenge some of the criteria, show that other criteria have been overlooked, defend football against the unfavorable application of the affirmative's criteria, and show how football measures up favorably in terms of a revised set of criteria. Obviously two or more of these strategic options could be combined in one case.

For Propositions of Policy

In the next main section, "Types of Cases," there will be found more specific suggestions on the building of affirmative and negative cases. At this particular time we shall consider in general terms the relationship between analysis and case construction. Referring to "Analysis Illustrated" in Chapter 5, we see an arrangement of issues and subissues for a proposition which calls for a change from the quarterly calendar to the semester plan at some college. If the affirmative side were to choose to affirm all of those potential issues and subissues, the preliminary sketch of the body of its case would look something like this:

    I. A quarterly calendar has serious defects, for
        A. Shorter courses sacrifice some comprehensiveness in the students' grasp of the subjects, and
        B. Shorter courses allow too little time for independent study between meetings, and
        C. Short terms aggravate the problems of academic adjustment, and
        D. The frequent starts and stops break the continuity of learning.
    II. A change to the semester plan would remedy these defects, for
        A. Longer courses would provide more comprehensive treatment of each subject, and
        B. It would allow for more independent work, and
        C. It would provide more time for academic adjustment, and
        D. It would provide more continuity of study.
    III. The semester plan would be the best solution, for
        A. It would suit our purposes better than a trimester plan, and
        B. It would be better than some other scheme, and
        C. It could be adopted without serious inconvenience.

Three cautions need to be expressed concerning the tentative case plan sketched above: supporting materials must be supplied under the Roman-letter points; the affirmative might not elect to build such a traditional case; the arguments under Point III might be modified in response to the type of case the negative uses.

Referring back to inductive-deductive logic for a moment, we note that the overall pattern of most cases on propositions of policy is deductive. Consider the resolution that the United States should promote a common market for the Western Hemisphere. There probably would be an assumed major, evaluative premise: We should solve these (specified) economic problems. Then the main points would show the existence of such problems and argue that the common market is a means of solution (minor, factual). Finally, the conclusion of the overall pattern would be the resolution or proposition:

X is desirable;
A is an X;
A is desirable.

Applications to School Debate

Since almost all school debates are based upon propositions of policy, the following sketch of case development for school debate will be limited to that kind. Preceding chapters have treated the processes which a debater needs to work on before he constructs a case: analysis, investigation, the testing of evidence, reasoning about the evidence, and perhaps some lesser processes. Consequently, this brief exposition will deal only with the typical duties of each speaker in a traditional-style school debate. Other kinds of affirmative and negative cases will be described in the next section of this chapter.

The first affirmative constructive speaker usually has ten minutes for his part of the case. Since there is no preceding speech, he does not have to adapt or refute. His speech can and should be well prepared without being memorized. In approximately a minute and a half of introduction, the first speaker includes opening pleasantries, tries to arouse interest in the proposition, states the proposition, defines terms and the proposition as a whole, and sketches the affirmative approach. If the goal or the basic philosophy of the case were to be given as an assumption rather than an argument, it would be stated in the introduction. For instance, if the proposition called for a system of government scholarships to encourage young people to attend college, this assumption or goal might be stated in the introduction: "We want every youth in the United States to have the best education which his aptitude will permit." This *sounds* praiseworthy, but that may not suffice; someone may raise the troublesome *why* question, as an opponent did when a debater urged a common market in order to industrialize emerging nations and thus to raise their standard of living. The desirability of that high-sounding goal turned out to be debatable. If the negative attacks the assumption, the next affirmative speaker will have to defend it. When the affirmative doubts that the negative will accept the assumption, the idea is incorporated into the body of the case as a part of the first point. After the goal is handled one way or the other, the traditional "need" argument is advanced by means of points, subpoints, and evidence: "Our present methods of financing higher education leave many young persons educated below their potential level of achievement." This speaker should make two points: that there are many who could have gone higher in school, and that one important reason for their failure to do so was financial.

Some teachers of school debating say that the first affirmative constructive speech may end here. Others would include the plan, and there are some who instruct the first speaker to give the prima facie case *in toto*. In this last situation, the second affirmative "constructive" speech becomes a rebuttal, and the series of eight speeches sometimes degenerates into one constructive speech and seven rebuttals. This "cannot but make the judicious grieve," as Hamlet said of another excess. However, if the plan is stated amply in the proposition, the first speaker may have time to go on with the point that the proposal would remedy the alleged ills. A debate on the abolition of capital punishment would be a case in point. Regardless of how far this speech goes into the case, it should close with a brief recapitulation and a forecast of the colleague's line of argument.

Appearing in second position is the first negative constructive speaker. He and the following two constructive speakers have the same time limit as the opening speaker. His introduction is usually shorter than the first affirmative's. It includes opening pleasantries and a response to the affirmative definitions and assumptions. Depending on the kind of case the negative has chosen to use (see next section), this speech will take one of four actions with respect to the first affirmative speech: refute the cause for action and perhaps raise general objections to the affirmative plan, minimize the need for action and show how the present situation can be improved, defend the present situation, or admit the cause for action and offer a counterproposition. Close adaptation to the affirmative line of argument is required in any case. Finally, some first negatives pose a few questions for the second affirmative before closing with a recapitulation of the negative position and an estimate of the damage done to the affirmative case.

Third in the order of appearance is the second affirmative constructive speaker. He would do well to begin by countering the effect of the closing remarks of the preceding speaker. Sometimes this is called "taking one hot off the bat." Next he should rebuild the parts of the affirmative case which have been attacked (see Attack and Defense), stressing the language of the affirmative. Then he might show how some negative points do not pertain to the affirmative case, or how some affirmative points were missed by the negative. Before answering any questions posed by the first negative, he should request that their significance be shown, thereby nullifying any negative advantage from a time-wasting tactic. Next, if this has not been covered by his colleague, he will expain the plan and show how it will meet the needs expressed in the first speech. His last main point would very likely deal with the additional advantages of the affirmative plan or the contention that the plan is the best remedy. This speaker faces the danger of appearing to be on the defensive or of seeming to debate on the negative's terms instead of his own. In his closing recapitulation he should try to show that the affirmative case has thus far withstood assault.

The fourth and last constructive speech in the traditional format of school debating is that of the second negative. It comes immediately before the first negative rebuttal speech, and for this reason some coordination between them is essential. If the negative expects to get ahead, this is the time to do so. These two speakers have fifteen minutes in which to block the affirmative case. The duties of the second negative will vary in terms of the kind of case or approach that is used. If refutation were the negative approach, this speaker would attack the workability of the plan and perhaps argue that it would worsen the situation it was supposed to improve. If the negative chose to repair the status quo, this speaker might contrast the improved situation with the affirmative's plan, showing the former to be more efficacious, less expensive, etc. In case the negative were to defend the present situation, this speaker might either ignore the affirmative plan or contrast it with the present situation. Finally, if the negative were to offer a counterproposition, preferably in their first speech, the second negative would contrast the rival plans in order to show that the affirmative did not have the better solution. This would block the affirmative case.

TYPES OF CASES

In the immediately preceding section we have considered the traditional kinds of cases in terms of their general construction for use in school debates. Here we shall survey the varieties of affirmative cases and examine in greater detail the kinds of negative cases.

Affirmative Cases

A few general principles are basic to all kinds of affirmative cases. An affirmative case must affirm all issues if it is to be prima facie. In addition, it will be more difficult to defeat if it is based upon a sound interpretation of the proposition and is set forth in a clear and simple structure. In this connection it is wise to assume no more burden of proof than the proposition calls for and to limit the number of points and subpoints to be supported. Types of affirmative cases have been given various names: traditional (need-plan-advantages), principles (or moral issues, etc.), and comparative advantages. All of these are for propositions (resolutions) of policy (action).

Under "school debate" the traditional type of affirmative case on a proposition of policy was sketched. Topics of need for a change, plan, and advantages were briefly illustrated. However, in some propositions of policy there is no necessity to explain a plan; the statement of the resolution says all that we need to know about the proposed action. A proposition calling for the diplomatic recognition of Red China would be a case in point. Simple definition would be sufficient. Perhaps for this reason the affirmative would prefer to offer a "principles" case as explained below.

A "principles" case can be made for a proposition of value as well as for one of policy. In effect, this approach minimizes the difference between these kinds of propositions; there is no "plan" case for the implementation of the policy. This is the customary sense of the term, "principles" case. Five obvious applications of this approach come to mind: states' rights *vs.* federal authority in school desegregation cases, debates on lowering the voting age to 18, the moral issue in universal military training, voluntarism *vs.* compulsion in medical care plans, and admission of some unpopular government to the United Nations. On this last subject the principles could be these three: (1) International organization is preferable to anarchy, power blocs, etc. (2) Efficacy of the U.N. depends upon universality of membership. (3) Toleration of dissimilar governments and economies is essential to peace. One possible advantage in using this type of case is the reduced importance of card quoting and the encouragement of fundamental, philosophical debating. At the outset of the debate, any affirmative that intends to use the "principles" case on a proposition of policy ought to: (1) Make sure that it is suited to the situation. (2) Announce its intention. (3) State the principle or principles. (4) Define it or them. (5) Call upon the negative to respond to it or them.

Another deviation from the traditional affirmative case for a proposition of policy is the "comparative advantages" case. There is almost as much difference of opinion on how the case may be constructed as there is on its theoretical legitimacy. A few specimens will indicate the several conceptions of structure. When Musgrave offered the early version of this in 1945,[10] the need-plan-advantages topics were retained but in a new format:

I. Advantage of affirmative plan
  A. Need for action
  B. How new plan will effect advantage
II. Advantage No. 2
  A & B as above, etc.

If this were used on "Reduce United States foreign aid programs to nonmilitary assistance," it might look like this:

I. Resources could be better used to develop countries economically.
  A. Military aid does not help recipients economically.
  B. Nonmilitary aid will help recipients to develop viable economies.

Or if an affirmative advocate were to urge the change from a quarterly calendar to a trimester plan, he could employ this kind of case to ad-

[10] G. M. Musgrave, *Competitive Debate, Rules and Strategy* (N.Y.: H. W. Wilson Co., 1945), 55–60.

vantage. Topics of "need," "plan," and "advantages" could be covered either directly or indirectly in this kind of structure:

    I. A longer period for the study of a subject would be provided, for
        A. A quarter is only ten weeks, and
        B. A trimester would be fifteen weeks.
   II. There would be less frequent interruptions, for
        A. There are finals and registrations every three months or less under the quarter plan, and
        B. These breaks would be spaced much farther apart in trimesters.

There would be more points and evidence than these sketchy illustrations contain, but the principle is that the goals are stated in the main points while the subpoints compare the two plans in terms of their achievement of those goals.

Bauer explains[11] that the affirmative agrees with the negative that there are no drastic faults in the status quo (except that a counter-proposition negative may indict the status quo even more severely than a traditional affirmative does), but more advantages are claimed for the affirmative plan. If there are serious needs for action, they should not be circumvented, he adds. Some would say that the comparative-advantages approach is not as strong as the traditional case if serious needs for action can be shown. Be that as it may, the whole case, not just part of it, is predictive in the comparative-advantages format. Two patterns of arrangement are suggested in this source: (1) The absence of certain desired qualities is a cause for action. This means that some features of the present situation prevent the attainment of specific ends in the future. Next, the plan will solve future problems. (2) There is no cause-for-action step, but both the status quo and the affirmative plan are described so as to show differences and, thereby, the benefits of the new plan.

Brock[12] offers a more detailed affirmative outline, which will be abbreviated here:

    I. Affirmative accepts, perhaps implicitly, the goals and assumptions of status quo.

[11] Bauer, *Fundamentals* . . . , pp. 24–27.
[12] B. L. Brock, "The Comparative Advantages Case," *The Speech Teacher*, XVI, No. 2 (1967), 121.

II. Affirmative plan.
    A. State goals and assumptions to be stressed.
    B. How principles will be altered to reach goals.
    C. Explain needed administrative changes.
III. Resulting advantages, repeating 2 steps for each.
    A. Causal relationship between altered principles and desired goal.
    B. Show degree of gain toward goal.
IV. Affirmative plan the best solution (if negative offers an alternative plan).

The general idea of this approach is the comparison of the status quo with the affirmative plan on the basis of results for the purpose of predicting improvements. This comparative testing is intended to arrive at greater probability of desirability on the side of the proposed change. The standard of desirability is, of course, the goal which the affirmative should announce early in the proceedings. That goal might be greater justice, efficiency, economy, or some other ideal.

Is the comparative-advantages case theoretically legitimate? The position of this work is that it is, although there is some difference of opinion.[13] One writer in particular has on numerous occasions argued against this kind of case, principally because it does not consider the question of inherent, compelling need for a change. ". . . a well chosen, truly debatable proposition does not lend itself to comparative advantage analysis," he claims.[14] This may be true in academic debating on some recent propositions, but when college faculties debate changing their calendars from quarters to semesters or from semesters to trimesters, for instance, the comparative-advantages approach is often used. No "crying-shame" kind of need for a change can be shown in this context; the main question is whether one calendar is sufficiently advantageous to justify the effort to change. As Kruger points out, however, merely calling one's case "comparative advantages" does not make it so.[15]

Next we shall consider affirmative cases which have nothing to do with comparative advantages, because they are not on propositions of

[13] For a list of references, see L. D. Fadely, "The Validity of the Comparative Advantages Case," *Journal of the American Forensic Association*, IV, No. 1 (1967), 28–35.

[14] A. N. Kruger, "The 'Comparative Advantage' Case: A Disadvantage," *Journal of the American Forensic Association*, III, No. 3 (1966), 104–111.

[15] *Ibid.*, p. 111.

policy. For fact and value propositions which involve criteria and application or definition and classification, the affirmative does not always establish the standards before applying them. Sometimes the criteria or definitions are assumed to be valid, and the advocate proceeds at once to their application. For instance, a literary critic wrote on the proposition that the elements that make up the traditional novel are worn out. He discussed the demise of character and story without first establishing that these are the essential elements of the traditional novel, but his *Saturday Review* audience probably did not need the first point that he omitted. Similarly some political campaigners made an historical evaluation of the New Deal, alleging that it was bad for the country for seven reasons: it centralized power in the executive; it encroached upon states' rights; it developed a bureaucracy; it subverted the Constitution; it redistributed wealth; it leaned toward socialism; it retarded recovery. These affirmatives assumed that each of the above actions or characteristics was bad, and their case dealt only with showing that the New Deal did those acts.

Negative Cases

Any choice which a negative spokesman makes among the possible cases is judged by its ability to raise at least one vital objection to the acceptance of the affirmative's proposition. Such a case might contain many points, or it might have only one: "It won't work," or "No change is needed," for example. Five strategic options which pertain mostly to propositions of policy will now be explained.[16]

Pure refutation or denial involves attacking evidence and/or reasoning offered by the affirmative, and it may be used on one or more of the main arguments. The minimum requirement is the blocking of the affirmative on one issue. This strategy is risky when the affirmative is strong, because confrontation takes place on the affirmative's chosen ground. Furthermore, when an audience is present, the negative suffers a psychological disadvantage if it does not stand *for* something. It seems merely to bedevil the affirmative. Two tactical points in its favor, though, are its adaptability to all kinds of affirmative cases and propositions and its ease of preparation. No set case is ever prepared; one

---

[16] Freeley, *Argumentation* . . . , p. 207 lists eight, but several of them are subdivisions of "refutation."

readies several denials and selects appropriate items to suit the affirmative case as it develops. Although this is a theoretically legitimate negative approach, it is in general the least desirable choice. It gains in strength when it is combined with one of the other options. The president of an ethical pharmaceutical company used pure refutation against the "plan" case of the affirmative on the Kefauver-Celler bill in 1961: elaborate controls would hamper research; it would not reduce medical costs; it ignores the values of the patent system; it is based upon distorted facts. Pure refutation may be used against one or more of the main points or the connections between them. Against an affirmative case on a policy proposition, the negative might choose to refute "need," or "plan" or the connection between the two, or the entire case point by point.

Defense of the present situation, at least in principle, is a strong position if the status quo is defensible. This prepared case plus the refutation of the need-for-a-change point is theoretically sufficient to win for the negative. It has the advantages of a prepared position and of standing *for* something. Most propositions of policy and some of value offer opportunities for the use of this kind of negative case. "No serious problem exists" is the essence of this conservative position on a proposed change. In response to a demand for a change from school segregation to racial integration, the negative might say there is nothing seriously wrong with the present situation.

Adjustment or repair of the present situation is seemingly the most popular negative case on propositions of policy. Arguing that the status quo is basically sound, the negative minimizes the affirmative "need" argument with refutation and then explains how the present situation can be improved without going to the drastic extremes which the affirmative proposes. With this case the negative does not have to risk appearing ridiculous while denying any and all difficulties, even though some are glaringly apparent. When an opponent of the administration's medical insurance plan (in 1960) based upon Social Security proposed an alternative in the form of Title VI of the Mills Bill (H.R. 12580, 86th Congress), which provided "a locally administered health aid program designed to help those who need help," this was not a counterproposition; the essential features of the status quo remained inviolate.

Counterproposition or counterplan is that kind of negative case which concedes the essence of the cause-for-action issue but offers a rival solution in an attempt to defeat the affirmative plan. Plan A *vs.* Plan N is what the clash boils down to, and each side has the responsibility to prove its own case. The theory is that, if the negative makes its plan seem desirable enough to cast doubt upon the wisdom of adopting the affirmative plan, the negative should win insofar as the *logic* of the situation is concerned. But this does not mean that in a legislative situation the negative plan should be adopted forthwith. A motion to adopt the counterproposition would first have to be debated. When we say that the counterproposition needs only to cast doubt upon the wisdom of adopting the affirmative plan, the implication is that the negative plan appears to be as good as the affirmative plan. Thus the negative plan need not be shown to be superior to the affirmative plan; it is the affirmative plan which must be the better if that side is to discharge its burden of proof.

Three cautions are worth noting in connection with the use of this negative case: it should be submitted in the first presentation by the negative; the counterproposition should be stated with utmost clarity; it must be fundamentally inconsistent with the affirmative plan. For instance, if the affirmative calls for a six-nation common market in the Western Hemisphere and the negative counters with a two-nation scheme, the affirmative can easily win by taking over the negative plan as a stage in the development of their own, broader program. Let us suppose that a school debate team speaks in favor of revising the United Nations into a federal world government. If their negative opponents propose the dissolution of all international organizations, this is a counterproposition.

Outside of school debating the situation is sometimes different and sometimes not. In a parliamentary situation the nearest equivalents of a counterproposition are amendments and substitute motions. In either case the debate is on the *new* proposition; the original motion is no more. In 1850 the Northern Abolitionists and Free Soilers favored the Wilmot Proviso, and the Southerners wanted to extend the Missouri Compromise line to include California, but the actual debate was on the Clay Compromise. In a public debate growing out of a hearing conducted by the Congressional Joint Economic Committee in 1958, Senator Paul Douglas proposed a tax cut as the most effective counter-recession program, while Professor John Galbraith argued for public works.[17] In this situation both solutions were before the public at the same time. In another economic debate a Treasury official proposed to hire the Lone Ranger to sell savings stamps to children via television,

[17] *Chicago Daily News*, March 15, 1958.

but the negative countered with a program of fiscal reform to "rescue the dollar."[18]

Combined approaches are, as the name indicates, mixtures of some of the other four. Note in the following case outline[19] a combination of minimized need, adjustment and repairs, and a new-and-greater-evils attack upon the affirmative plan:

   I. The need for a new medical care plan for the aged is exaggerated, for
      A. Most oldsters are healthy, and
      B. Most oldsters are not needy, and
      C. Oldsters are individuals like the rest of us, for
         1. They differ only in the number of birthdays.
      D. Only a minority cannot be properly covered by existing means.
  II. Title VI of the Mills Bill is the best solution, for
      A. The House approved it, and
      B. The A.M.A. approves it, and
      C. It would help the really needy, and
      D. It would allow the non-needy to maintain their independence, and
      E. It provides local, expert, personal administration, for
         1. Medical care cannot be mass-produced or administered at long range.
 III. A compulsory scheme through Social Security threatens serious hazards, for
      A. The quality of medical care will decline from being the world's finest, for
         1. Government will tell doctors how to practice, and
         2. Government will tell nurses how to nurse, and
         3. Government will tell hospitals how to handle the sick.
      B. The cost would be staggering, for
         1. It would dent the pay envelopes of workers paying Social Security taxes.
      C. Magnificent, private, voluntary plans would be destroyed in time, and
      D. It would lead to complete regimentation in the health area, for
         1. This scheme is a beginning, and
         2. Eventually it would cover all ages, and
         3. More services would be added.

Against a comparative-advantages case the negative has somewhat different opportunities. Some of the standard procedures will not serve so well against the kind of comparative-advantage case which Brock

[18] *Wall Street Journal*, September 10, 1958.
[19] Based upon A.M.A. advertisement in *Chicago Daily News*, August 16, 1960.

outlined: straight refutation may be confusing or even inconsistent; defense of the status quo is pointless if it has not been indicted in a "need" argument; adjustment and repairs may make the affirmative's task easier; the counterproposition is appropriate, but, as in other contexts, it involves a negative burden. To meet this situation, two negative speakers on a school team might divide their responsibilities as suggested here.[20] The first speaker would state the negative philosophy (principles, goals, assumptions) on the proposition, attack the causal connection between the affirmative plan and advantages, and minimize the claimed advantages. Then the second speaker would, if necessary, emphasize the negative philosophy, attack the practicability of the plan, and allege new disadvantages ("new and greater evils").

OUTLINING CASES

After an individual or a team has decided upon the kind of case to be used and what it will contain, the next step is the outlining of that case. The general purposes of this step are three in number: to aid in the preparation of a case, to aid in the presentation of a case, and to aid in the understanding of a case. A knowledge of correct outlining helps a speaker's preparation in that it guides his placement of material and enables him to see where he needs more or less of it. A good outline enables an advocate to make a better presentation and allows more efficient listening or reading by his audience.

Divisions of a Case Outline

A case outline resembles other kinds of outlines in its three broad divisions—introduction, discussion, and conclusion. The introduction comes first, is generally noncontroversial, and is topically outlined as explained below. It prepares the audience for the arguments by gaining attention, arousing interest, providing a context, defining terms, stating the issues, partitioning the case, and making a smooth transition to the first argument. Sometimes no need exists for one or more of these

[20] After Brock, "The Comparative Advantage Case," 123.

functions, but advocates seem to err on the side of omitting some which would have been helpful.

In the discussion section, which is by far the longest, the advocate outlines the case proper. This is the array of points, subpoints, evidence, explanations, and any other materials in support of the position. The outline is logical and its topics are sentences unless an indirect or an implicative pattern, as described below, is used instead of the traditional format.

The last, relatively short portion of a case outline is called the conclusion, as most readers know. It contains no further development of any argument. Some of the possible purposes of the closing portion of a case are to emphasize main ideas, make an ethical appeal, call for action, and provide a note of finality.

Principles of Case Outlining

In the process of building the framework of a case, an advocate has occasion to use some sort of arrangement, and the one which has been especially developed for this purpose is called a case outline. It shares some of the characteristics of outlines generally, but it has some special adaptations which are required by its purpose. These adaptations will be explained in terms of eight principles of case outlining.

Simpleness is the principle which requires that each unit in the outline contain only one idea or statement. Note the difference between the "right" and "wrong" specimens below.

(WRONG)

1. Married women should not be allowed to work for pay because their husbands support them and many of them have inheritances; besides, unemployed men and unmarried women need these jobs, and married women let their outside work interfere with their duties at home.

(RIGHT)

1. Married women should not be allowed to work for pay, for
   A. They do not need to earn money, for
      1. Their husbands support them, and
      2. Many of them have inheritances.
   B. Their jobs are needed by others, for
      1. Some men are unemployed, and
      2. Many unmarried women have to support themselves.
   C. Outside work interferes with their home duties.

Coordination means that a series of topics has a generic relationship; in other words, the points have one or more important elements in common. The inclusion of a foreign or an unrelated idea in the otherwise homogeneous list is a violation of this principle. More will be said of coordination under the principle of symbolization. Observe the error in subpoint "C."

I. Chronic illnesses make great financial burdens, for
   A. This kind costs more, and
   B. The costs continue longer, and
   C. Untreated contagious diseases are a threat to public health.

Subordination has to do with the relationship of inferior points to their superiors. Whenever we express the simplest unit of argument, as in "This is true because that," the "this" becomes the superior point, while the "that" becomes the inferior point. The inferior supports its superior, and this relationship is indicated by symbols and indentation.

I. There is a need for civil service reform, for
   A. Abuses exist in the present method of appointing officials, for
      1. (Evidence here)

Discreteness requires each topic or point in an outline to be a separate and distinct idea. It is a mistake to allow points to overlap, merge, or otherwise become indistinct or confused. Subpoint "B" violates this principle.

I. Collective bargaining has failed, for
   A. Management and labor are deadlocked in the railway dispute, and
   B. Some important disputes have not been settled by this procedure.

Sequence is more of a convenience than a requirement. It means the arrangement of coordinate points in some order of progression such as problem-solution, cause-effect, motivated sequence, and the like. Subpoint "C" deviates from the chronological order.

I. Plans for international political organization have failed in the past, for
   A. This was true of the Cruce plan in 1623, and
   B. It was true of the League of Nations, and
   C. It was true of the Saint-Pierre plan in 1713.

Symbolization, as mentioned above, means that each topic in an outline requires a letter or a numeral which indicates its relative rank in terms of coordination and subordination. Points having similar symbols are expected to be of comparable importance in the hierarchy of speech materials. Common usage recommends Roman numerals for main points, capital letters for the principal subpoints, and Arabic numerals for lesser points, and so on. One symbol per item is the rule, and uniform indentation facilitates reading.

(WRONG)

I. A world government would solve the international peace problem, for
    1. A. It could succeed even if one country opposed it, for
        A. 1. The process of proposing it and the likely adoption of it would show up any recalcitrant as a potential aggressor.

(RIGHT)

I. A world government would solve the international peace problem, for
    A. It could succeed even if one country opposed it, for
        1. The process of proposing it and the likely adoption of it would show up any recalcitrant as a potential aggressor.

Logical relationships among ideas are indicated by the indentations, connectives, symbols, and other devices of case outlining. In logical outlining there is one relationship which is most important: each subpoint must support (assist in proving) the point to which it is immediately subordinated. Connectives *for* and *because* appear between main points and supporting points. Consecutive, coordinate points are connected by *and*. To test the logical adequacy of this type of outline, read it from top to bottom, stressing the connectives. Next, read the points in inverse order, substituting *therefore* for *because* (or *for*), but retaining *and's*. If both readings make sense, the outline is probably sound. Logical relationships apply to refutory as well as constructive arguments. These relationships may be seen in the following segment based upon a speech by Carl Schurz on civil service reform.

    I. There is a need for civil service reform, because
        A. Abuses exist in the present method of appointments to office, and
        B. The spoils system has an adverse effect upon the individual and the body politic.

Declarative sentences are required by the nature and purpose of logical case outlines. As the preceding specimens and those in Appendix A show, the chains of reasoning in case outlines are intended as confirmatory enthymemes. A series of words and phrases as in topical outlines would not serve so well as sentences in building a logically disciplined case outline.

Kinds of Outlines

One could list a dozen or more kinds of outlines if the several bases of definition and classification were considered as a unit. In the study of argumentation, however, three principal kinds are distinguishable on the basis of length, completeness, and complexity. They are the brief, the case outline, and the speaker's notes. Subtypes of the last two will be treated in appropriate places.

A *brief* is the longest, most nearly complete, and certainly the most complex of the three outlines. Years ago when many students were required to draw briefs up to twenty-five or thirty pages in length, they often asked what was brief about the document. They received slight comfort from the explanation that the speeches or essays which could be made from the brief would run much longer. Today there appears to be less emphasis upon the brief in nonlegal argumentation; several case outlines can be made in the same time, and they afford a wider experience in the basic processes.

Consequently no complete brief will be presented here, but the principles of briefing will be stated tersely. First is the matter of definition. Some books distinguish among brief, full brief, traditional brief, and flexible brief, but this one does not. The nonlegal brief is here defined as a detailed, logical outline which holds in readiness the usable materials on one side of a proposition. It differs from a case outline, which is another variety of preparatory instrument, in that it contains enough material for more than one case outline. In a sense the brief is a survey of the potential proof for one side.

Most of these general principles of briefing have been explained and illustrated in the preceding section on principles of case outlining: (1) State the proposition at the top. (2) Divide the matter into introduction, discussion, and conclusion. (3) Use sentences in the discussion. (4) Use symbols consistently to show relationships. (5) Indent to indicate coordination and subordination. (6) Limit each point to one idea. (7) If one point requires two or more lines, indent them the same. (8) Use impersonal language.

Rules governing the introduction of a brief have been partially covered earlier, but they will be expanded upon here. Include only those of the following eight items that may improve interest and understanding: statement of proposition, history of the problem, indications of present timeliness of subject, definitions, statement of excluded or admitted matter, list of issues, partitioning of the case. Use only non-controversial material, and state it in topical outline form.

Rules or principles pertaining to the discussion section have, in part, been mentioned above. They are listed here for emphasis: (1) Each point in partition is a Roman-numeral topic. (2) Each point should be supported with some kind of backing. (3) Logical outlining must be used. (4) Document the evidence and qualify the authorities. (5) Keep coordinate points free of overlapping. (6) Coordinate points should be all inclusive. (7) Objections to be refuted should be put in where they relate to the case. (8) State clearly any point to be refuted and outline the reply under it. ("The charge that this treaty will lead to war is unfounded because . . ."). (9) Any concession in connection with a point should be written in as a subordinate clause. ("While it is true that treaties have often been violated, we maintain that this one will be kept.")

The conclusion of a brief is almost always a short summary of the points in partition, followed by a statement of the proposition to be affirmed or negated. There are none of the rhetorical flourishes which have embellished some presentation outlines. It might be as bald as this: "Therefore, since no inherent defect has been found in the present ordinance, and since the proposed ordinance could not be enforced equitably, the negative urges the rejection of Ordinance X."

A *case outline* is shorter than a brief, because it is a preparation outline for a specific occasion. When a case outline is merely an abridgement of a brief, it is bound to be formal, rigorous, and not very interesting to most persons. If a case outline is the only outline a speaker makes, it is at once a preparation and a presentation outline. When this document is intended for public presentation, the considerations of interest and persuasiveness are added to those of completeness and logical rigor. Such concessions to audience psychology are rare in case outlines for school debates, possible because an audience is equally rare. There is some doubt as to which is the cause and which the effect here. Be that as if may, the case outline which resembles the brief in format may be called the enthymematic or the linear type. It will be demonstrated in Appendix A.

Indirect-order or so-called inductive case outlines have been recommended as having some advantage over the linear variety when used to persuade doubtful or hostile audiences. The hypothesis is that it is more effective to lead up to the conclusion than to begin with it. This is done with a series of examples followed by a proposition, or by an inverted enthymematic structure. Often the format is a mixture of logical and topical outlining. Note that in the partial outline below the inverted enthymematic structure is used. Note also that evidence, which has been omitted, should be used for each subpoint.

"DO WE NEED MORE REGULATION OF UNIONS?"
    (1) Evidence . . . , therefore
      a) There are serious problems in some union trusteeships, and
      b) There are serious problems in the handling of union funds, and
      c) Members can scarcely protest against ineffective or corrupt officials, and
      d) Compulsory membership presents problems, and
      e) Voting rights of union members are allegedly violated, therefore
    1. There are serious problems within unions.
      a) Big unions can affect the national economy, and
      b) Union-management collusion is a serious threat, and
      c) Some union leaders try to influence political matters, and
      d) Secondary boycotting is a menace, therefore
    2. There are serious problems which transcend internal union affairs, therefore
A. Serious problems stem from labor union activities
    1. National union leaders have been implicated in unlawful practices, and
    2. Local leaders in various places have been implicated in misdeeds, therefore
B. The problems related to labor unions are nationwide in scope.
    1. Increased state regulation cannot end these problems, and
    2. Union self-regulation cannot do any better than it has, and
    3. Moderately increased federal regulation will not remedy the problems, therefore
C. The problems in the internal and external affairs of unions are inherent in the present pattern of federal regulation, therefore
I. There is a need substantially to increase the regulation of labor unions by the federal government.

Implicative arrangements of material are, like the indirect order, intended for situations characterized by doubtful or disbelieving audiences. The merit of a questionable point or proposition is implied by the acceptability of the related points which are offered as a context. In the most familiar adaptation of the implicative outline, a problem is stated and two or more possible solutions are offered. When all but one have been disqualified, the procedure is called the method of residues, because the conclusion confronts the audience with a this-or-nothing disjunction.

"WHICH COURSE IN SOUTH VIET NAM?"
  I. There are four possible solutions:
     A. Continue to pour in aid to beat the Communists while keeping hands off the government, or
     B. Sponsor a coup d'etat, or
     C. Make continued military and economic aid contingent upon governmental reform, or
     D. Continue to aid the country while trying by gentle persuasion to effect some reforms in its government.
 II. It is folly to pour in aid with no strings attached, for
     A. It would cost us too much, and
     B. We can't defeat the enemy that way.
III. Any scheme to promote a coup d'etat is unwise, for
     A. There are no interested leaders, and
     B. This is out of character for the United States.
 IV. Tying aid to governmental reform is too risky, for
     A. It is a bluff, and
     B. When it is called, the United States will have to back down.
  V. Therefore, in the interest of winning the war without compromising our modern tradition, we should continue to aid South Viet Nam while using gentle persuasion on its government.

Attention-problem-solution-appeal patterns of various sorts appear in public speaking textbooks. Probably the most familiar scheme is the "motivated sequence," as Monroe calls it in *Principles and Types of Speech*: (1) attention, (2) need (for a solution), (3) satisfaction (plan), (4) visualization (dramatizes plan working), and (5) action (what to do now).

Speaker's notes constitute the shortest and least formal kind of outline. This kind is strictly a guide to presentation. Its function is to remind a speaker of points, quotations, and the like. Words and key phrases are often used in lieu of the sentences which may have appeared in the brief or the case outline. Thus topical outlining is most often used in speaker's notes. Any functional abbreviation of one of the kinds of outlines explained above will serve as speaker's notes. In informal controversy the disputants seldom prepare anything more elaborate than sketchy topics, and often they are not even written.

QUESTIONS

1. Select a case which was made for one side in one of the Appendix items. Is it prima facie? Explain your decision.
2. Choose (or invent) a case which you think is not prima facie. Explain why it is not prima facie and why this defect is or is not acceptable.
3. In discussing the steps in developing a case, why differentiate between policy and nonpolicy propositions? In what important respects do they differ?
4. State some propositions (and situations in which they might be used) as follows: one for which a traditional case would be appropriate, one for a "principles" case, and one for "comparative advantages."
5. Describe a situation in which the negative's best choice would be: (a) a case of pure refutation, (b) defense of status quo, (c) counterproposition, (d) adjustment or repair, (e) combination of approaches.
6. Identify the kinds of affirmative and negative cases used in one or more debates, either in an Appendix or elsewhere.

EXERCISES

1. With either two or four students on each proposition, resulting in one or two on each side, a series of cases could be assigned as written work for one week and oral for the next. For oral clashes they could be matched as follows:
   a) Affirmative on proposition of prediction *vs.* pure-refutation negative
   b) Affirmative on proposition of value *vs.* defense of status quo (prevailing evaluation)
   c) Affirmative on proposition of policy *vs.* either adjustment or counter-proposition.
2. After drawing up an affirmative or a negative case outline in the traditional pattern, write a second version in which the original is modified into an implicative or an indirect arrangement.

3. Using the appropriate doctrine in this chapter, report on the case which the Speech Association of America addressed to the Federal Communications Commission (*Quarterly Journal of Speech*, February, 1960, pp. 83–84).

4. Discuss the types and the logical adequacy of the cases in the controversy over debating both sides. See *The Speech Teacher* for January, September, and November, 1957, January, 1958, and September, 1963. This may be an oral and/or written report.

5. The equivalent of Exercise 4 may be based upon a controversy in an Appendix or elsewhere. These two exercises may be extended later to include the tactics of attack and defense as explained in the next chapter.

6. What case did the "New Left" offer? See L. M. Griffin, "The Rhetorical Structure of the 'New Left' Movement: Part I," *Quarterly Journal of Speech*, L, No. 2 (1964), 113–135.

7. Discuss a critique of the American businessmen's case as given by R. M. Fisher, "A Rhetoric of Over-Reaction," *Central States Speech Journal*, XVII, No. 4 (1966), 251–256.

CHAPTER II

ATTACK

AND DEFENSE

INTRODUCTORY CONCEPTS

THREE TOPICS WILL BE TAKEN UP IN THIS CONNECTION: DEFINITIONS OF attack and defense, opportunities for and importance of these activities, and the requisite knowledge and attitudes. Attack is traditionally defined as an attempt to destroy the opposing proof, but in some situations it might better be viewed as critical analysis for the purpose of revealing the matter in a different light. Such scrutiny of an argument or a case might point to other interpretations, different premises, alternative hypotheses, and so on. Several methods of attack or of critical analysis will be explained, but for the moment we may say that when this process is viewed in its destructive sense, it involves the refutation of premises, evidence, reasoning, or other essential elements for the purpose of preventing an opponent from making good on one or more of the issues. Defense is defined as the attempted rebuilding of any proof which has been attacked. Its purpose is to reestablish a position on one or more issues. Sometimes this process is named rebuttal, but this intended synonym is potentially ambiguous in that it may also mean a second round of speeches in school debates. Attack and defense are explained separately for convenience, but in practice they are interdependent and complementary. Obviously the rebuilding of an argument implies an attack upon the objections which necessitated the defense. To put it differently, we know that one can justify personal preference for one case over its rival either because of its own merits or because of the defects in the alternative. Sometimes it is much more effective to integrate these two. This is the essence of genuine debate in anyone's language.

Opportunities and Importance

When opportunities or openings for attack and defense are considered, the detection of faulty analysis and interpretation, of flaws in evidence, and of fallacious reasoning is implied. Faulty analysis appears as the lack of a prima facie case, the use of vulnerable assumptions, the use of questionable definitions, the giving of undue prominence to a minor point, and other defects in proof which will be explained. Flaws in evidence, fallacies in the structure of argument, and miscellaneous fallacies will also be defined and illustrated in this chapter.

Six typical instances of opportunities for rejoinder will be cited from real-life controversies. The first two are claims based upon poor evidence. A workman sued his employer for substantial cash damages for a cancer allegedly caused by an injury incurred on the job. "I got hurt, and so I got a cancer," he claimed. The plaintiff did not have the support of experts on forensic pathology and medicine because, at that time, they did not believe that a blow could produce cancer. Experimentally, a single trauma had not been able to initiate a malignancy. At most there was merely a possible causal connection in six cases per one hundred thousand. Lack of supporting evidence and the existence of contradictory evidence offered an opportunity for attack. The second instance of weak or missing evidence as an opening for attack may be seen in some campaigns to promote anti-obscenity laws or to ban erotic literature. The affirmative side often assumes, or asserts without evidence, that exposure to pornography provokes antisocial behavior. "It stands to reason" or "We all know. . . ," they confidently state. In arguments before higher courts, defense attorneys have successfully identified the assumption, challenged the prosecution to show evidence, and have introduced contradictory evidence to challenge the alleged causal connection.

Detection of faulty analysis was used as the opening for attack in the next two cases. The first involves an affirmative charge, a negative attack, and an affirmative defense. The opening for this affirmative defense was the allegedly partial reply by the negative. For the affirmative side a Democrat argued that the design and the size of the Eisenhower defense plan was inadequate to meet the possible events. Some Republicans answered that our nuclear striking power, mainly in manned bombers, was an effective deterrent because it was the world's strongest. While conceding that the bomber force was the strongest in the world, the affirmative countered with the idea that the negative had failed to consider the fact that a first-strike nuclear attack against us could destroy our bomber force before it could react. In the second specimen we have questionable causal analysis which we seized upon by the other side. A teen-age boy suspected his girl friend of dating someone else, so he stole a car, drove it without an operator's license, violated some traffic ordinances, and was arrested. His mother charged that it was the girl's fault, but the defense made short work of that analysis.

Finally, let us look at possible inconsistency or contradiction in a case as an opportunity for an attack. When the Republican strategists opened their 1958 campaign to regain control of Congress, "President Eisenhower took the high road" on the politics-in-defense issue, "Sherman Adams took the low road," and Vice President Nixon "trod" the middle road, as the *Wall Street Journal* reported (Jan. 24, 1958). While the leader seemingly was speaking of national defense as being outside of politics, his assistant was blaming Democrats for a missile lag, Pearl Harbor, and the Korean War. Whatever the tactical considerations may have been, the fact remains that the Republican case, taken as a whole, was vulnerable to the charge of inconsistency. In the second example a lawyer attacked some decisions of the National Labor Relations Board on the ground that the Board seems to regard the average worker as both a fool and a genius. When an employe listens to management's case, he cannot separate truth from falsehood, but when he listens to his union representative, he is crafty and knowledgeable, the rulings seem to imply.

Most reasons for the importance of the principles of attack and defense are obvious, but some advantages and limitations of these procedures are less well known. One significant but little-known value of training in attack and defense of ideas has come from psychological research on "brainwashing." A shielded mind has been found easiest to change by propaganda, but one that has been exposed to the give-and-take of arguments is much more resistant. The resistant ones first heard arguments against their beliefs, then heard these refuted, and finally were given strong propaganda against their beliefs. William McGuire's experiment at the University of Illinois suggests that many persons hold to their beliefs simply by avoiding exposure to contrary views. However, it should be noted that the techniques of attack and defense are not designed to persuade rival advocates; they are intended to make one case appear the better in the judgment of those who are to decide. When Senators Fulbright and Russell spoke for opposite sides on the nuclear test ban treaty, each one was hoping to influence some undecided opinions, not his opponent. If one were to try to persuade his equal by means of a conversation, a Rogerian approach might be more fruitful: assure your opponent that he has been heard and understood, state the valid elements that you see in his position, and invite him to do likewise for yours.[1]

Attitudes and Knowledge

There is something to be said for the foregoing advice when applied to public situations, too. For instance, if a person finds himself in a situation which offers occasions for attack or defense, he will do well to read or listen carefully in order to understand what is said and why. Some tolerance of others' views is an asset; at least it seems advisable to avoid equating differences and error or villainy. The analogy of the stopped clock that is correct twice a day may be instructive. Another suggestion is that the focus of an attack be upon ideas, not persons. Of course a complete separation is too much to expect when there is ego involvement in the arguments, as there often is. However, a clearcut violation of this ideal is both a personal affront and a fallacy. Finally, the attitudes of honesty, fairness, and courtesy in attack and defense are taken to be inherently related to any ethical conception of advocacy. This implies stating opposing points fairly, making requests or charges courteously, and being truthful.

Knowledge of many kinds and in ample amount is patently useful in preparation for attack and defense. Much of what was said of analysis and investigation (Chapters 5 and 6) applies here. In addition to those procedures a well planned rebuttal file is useful. It typically contains preconceived tactics and related notes on evidence. A rebuttal card differs from an evidence card or a bibliography card. For ready use in attack and defense, a rebuttal card should state the side that will use

---

[1] Anatol Rapoport, *Fights, Games and Debates* (Ann Arbor: University of Michigan Press, 1960).

it, the opposing point to be met, the relevance of the item to an issue, the replies that are possible through two or more exchanges on the point, and possibly some cross-references to evidence cards. The importance of knowing what both sides can do with each point cannot easily be exaggerated. One-sided preparation is a poor protection against surprise attacks. Finally, in oral controversy, a command of the extemporaneous method is practically essential.

ORGANIZATION

Where to Place Refutation

Any advocatory speech or essay after the opening affirmative presentation, assuming that the one in question is in opposition to the one it follows, has opportunities for attack or defense. The problem at the moment concerns where to place that part. Some adaptations to the requirements of real-life confrontations as well as those of rebuttals in school debates will be suggested. In some circumstances there are conventions or rules which place constructive points, replies, and questions in specific locations.

When is it appropriate to start with refutation? If the other side makes a point which logically requires an answer before the following speaker or writer can safely continue with his own case, the situation clearly calls for refutation at the beginning of the rejoinder. Lodge did this in reply to Boothby when he retorted that the United Nations is "not the only point of contact" between the United States and Red China. In school debates on propositions of policy, the second affirmative constructive speaker typically begins with a defense against some attack which the first negative brought against the first affirmative.

When is it wise to follow up refutation with positive proof? "Generally but not always" is the best short answer. The reason is that most often an advocate tries to discredit one item and gain acceptance for its opposite. In this situation refutation is insufficient. Even though pure refutation proves to be sufficient throughout most of a negative speech, for example, it is better to end on a constructive note. The theory is that positive proof deserves the most emphatic place.

This leads to the question, "What are the emphatic positions in a message?" As with constructive proof, the strongest positions are the beginning and the end. Thus, if the answer is important and needs to be made as persuasive as possible, the beginning or the end of the speech would be the place for it. Lesser arguments, which are often shorter, can be placed between the major ones, which tend to run longer.

Finally, is it better to make the reply a separate point or to weave it into one of the constructive points? Its importance to an issue should be the controlling factor. If the reply is moderately important but not closely related to a point in one's own case, it should be made separately and prior to the continuation of the case. If it is moderately important and closely related to a constructive point, the two can be developed together. Howeve, if the reply to an opponent's attack is of such importance that an issue is at stake, there need be no hesitation in making that reply a main point in the case and placing it where it fits best. Whichever choice one makes among these four, he should plan to conclude with a statement of his own position.

Steps in Attack and Defense

Even a sleepy reader (for reasons other than any soporific effect of this book, it is hoped) will notice parallels between the suggested steps in attack and those in defense. The reason is the close relationship which makes them almost indistinguishable at times. "A good offense is the best defense" applies to more than football. These are the recommended steps in attack: (1) Select an item *worth* attacking, and show why it is so. (2) State it clearly and fairly. (3) Show how it will be attacked (methods below). (4) Evaluate the result in terms of issues. The affirmative tries to keep the clash on its own case, while the negative tries to lure the affirmative into a discussion of the negative case. In defense of a point these steps are to be taken: (1) Review your point which was attacked. (2) Sketch the essentials of the attack. (3) Show how that attack will be answered. (4) Launch a counterattack or rebuild the point in the language of your case (methods below). (5) Evaluate the result in terms of issues. In the following condensation of segments from an extended written controversy, we can observe some instances of both good and poor tactics of attack and defense. Our readers are invited to examine the dialogue in its entirety.[2]

[2] John Fischer, "A 'Scientific' Formula for Disarmament?" *Harper's*, January 1963, 12–19; also "Bertrand Russell on the Sinful Americans . . . ," *Harper's*, June, 1963, 20–30.

While commenting in generally favorable terms upon an English scientist's disarmament proposal, John Fischer remarks that Dr. Blackett's idea is based upon a questionable assumption. It is clear that Fischer is selecting a point which he deems worthy of attacking. Then he states it clearly and fairly, pointing out that Blackett assumes that Russia and the United States are essentially alike in their motivations. Fischer's third step consists in attacking this assumption on the ground that Russia is aggressive while the United States is defensive. The effect of this attack is to show that negotiations such as those which take place between men of good will should not be expected to occur when we deal with the Russian government.

Later in this exchange of letters we observe the steps in defense as used by Lord Russell in replying to Mr. Fischer. But before the significance of this defense can be appreciated, it is necessary to trace the give-and-take on the issue in question. In his June *Harper's* article, Dr. Blackett questions the wisdom of the American missile buildup. In the "Easy Chair" essay in the same issue, Editor Fischer replies that the defense must be superior when facing an aggressor that is willing to launch the first blow. Entering the fray with a letter on March 4, Bertrand Russell contends that mankind is in danger of annihilation by an "apparatus of global butchery" which depends upon radar that cannot tell the difference between a missile and a meteorite. Fischer's letter of March 10 attacks Russell's point by stating that it is factually demonstrable that our nuclear weapons do not rest upon short-warning systems and do not depend upon the kind of radar that Russell describes. The defensive tactic with which we are concerned may be seen in the Russell letter dated March 15. He does not specifically review his own point which has been attacked, but he quotes the language of that attack, thereby reminding us of its essentials. He says he will examine the facts and expose Fischer's ignorance of them. Then he goes about counterattacking and thereby rebuilding his point about annihilation by radar error. If warning time is not crucial, did President Kennedy lie when he charged that Russian missiles in Cuba reduced the warning time? And why does the United States have the Distant Early Warning radar network and the North American Air Defense Command? These are designed to provide a fifteen-minute response. Experts are quoted indirectly as saying that radar cannot distinguish between natural phenomena and missiles. Further, there have been accidents due to radar failure, he claims. In this connection he alleges that the safeguards are inadequate. Russell does not specifically evaluate the effect of his defense upon the issue at hand.

While the tactics on the previous issue are moderately good, the same cannot be said for the exchange on the question of each other's expertness or ethos. Fischer starts the personal abuse (*ad personam*) with a gratuitous insult to the effect that Bertrand Russell "has been pathetically susceptible nearly all his life to neat but harebrained schemes for reforming everything from education to matrimony to international affairs." Replying in kind in his first letter, Russell refers to "an article by a Mr. J. Fischer" and characterizes it as being unworthy of examination. Nevertheless, he disavows the views which the Fischer article attributed to him. He will explain his views in language sufficiently simple for his opponent to understand, he promises. Fischer's retort is that Russell's reply clearly illustrates the man's incompetence outside his own field. Russell next reminds Fischer that an *ad hominem* argument is illogical, but he goes on to decry his adversary's "invincible ignorance." Finally, Fischer accuses Russell of spreading misinformation. Apparently tiring of this unsophisticated technique of controversy, both men reduce it sharply in the last exchange of letters.

EXPOSING DEFECTS IN PROOF

Why Fallacies Occur

How often does one admit that he has done some crooked thinking? The infrequency of such candid self-criticism might tempt us to define a fallacy as an error in reasoning committed by someone else. If we will avoid self-deception for a moment, we can see in ourselves some tendency to commit fallacies when the conditions are propitious. Perhaps an amateurish psychological explanation of this behavior will help us to cope with it in a constructive way. It is useful to know that rationalizing and straight thinking are similar except for the self-critical characteristic of cogent reasoning. Then comes the question, "How can I make my thinking self-critical?" Intelligence and education as commonly defined are not the complete answer, although stupidity and lack of information do account for much fallacious thinking. Barring the psychiatric problems for which this book has no answers, we may say that a functional grasp of the principles of argumentation plus an application of some psychological insights into the phenomenon of prejudice can be of significant value.

Those who are expert in such matters tell us that a closed mind has set notions about what is and what ought to be. It rejects and resents dissonant information and reasoning. In other words, selective perception is practiced. A bigot selects only the items which fit his preconceived framework, and he excludes any perceptions which fail to fit his preferred stereotype. He can be insensitive to some stimuli while being hypersensitive to others. A large-scale example of closed-mindedness occurred in the fall of 1957, when two young ladies returned from a trip to Russia with accounts of progress in housing, higher education, jet aircraft, and other developments. They found to their dismay that scarcely anyone would believe the Russians could do anything worthwhile. Some Americans took to calling the girls pink and pro-Communist, while others scoffed at the possibility of fearing an atomic bomb attack from a country that couldn't even make a decent automobile. Needless to say, the young tourists soon quit talking about their trip. Maybe it is easy to dismiss the testimony of two young women as being inexpert, but what about the report of Charles Lindbergh on the apparent power of the Nazi air force prior to 1940? He knew what he had seen, and subsequent events proved him right, but his countrymen refused to take his report seriously when he made it. According to the old saying, "What you don't know can't hurt you," there seems to be an abiding faith in ignorance as a form of protection.

In controversy a bigot uses supporting material (if any) from authority (persons of like views), faith, intuition, and special insight which seems not to be available to others. When pressed, he responds angrily, and this induces reckless reasoning. Perhaps he knows that an argument cannot be beaten without meeting it, but when his pet prejudice is questioned he responds irrationally with a stratagem like namecalling, imputing bad motives, or some equally irrelevant diversion. "The one thet fust gits mad's most ollers wrong," said Lowell in *The Bigelow Papers*. There are those who blame labor unions for almost everything but the weather, and there are others who label every legitimate criticism of union excesses as "labor baiting."

Perhaps what has been called our national vice for overdoing things accounts for numerous fallacies of exaggeration. In a temperate community the critics of the government say their leaders made a mistake, but in the United States the critics of the President blame him for the war in Viet Nam, poverty in Harlem, civil disorders, and "denounce him for everything from . . . not having read Schopenhauer to having had the gall to be born in Texas."[3] Our abuse of public personalities is a kind of popular sport, but it can become a menace if it generates a climate in which acts of violence, including assassinations, are fomented.

Questionable Analysis and Interpretation

First among the four general classes of defective proof is questionable analysis and interpretation of the proposition. It is placed first because it concerns the most fundamental process, and that process logically comes first in the order of events. One could say that any proof which violates the appropriate principles in Chapter 5 is defective and consequently vulnerable to attack, but a discussion of some specific attacks and ways to meet them will be more instructive. Definitions of key terms are so vital to the controversy that any questionable one should be attacked on the ground that it is not recognized by experts in that field, that it has been applied in the wrong context, or that it is only partly true, for instance. In defense one might cite authoritative sources in the appropriate field instead of relying upon a general dictionary for definitions of highly specialized terms. If the negative attack on a proposition of policy tries to interpret "should" to mean "will," the affirmative should defend on the ground that these two verbs are not synonymous.

Analysis is often attacked for not producing a prima facie case, although this terminology is not often used outside of judicial and school debates. More likely the charge will be the omission of some vital point or the assumption of a questionable premise. During a debate on national Republican strategy in 1959, one side said the party must find out what the people want and promise to give it to them. The idea was to select a popular image and then find skilled politicians who could put over the program. The other side replied that salvation for the party must grow out of its men rather than being foisted upon them. "Let someone raise high a standard, and men will repair to it," editorialized the *Wall Street Journal* (Jan. 15, 1959). From an editorial in a North Carolina college paper comes an interesting specimen of analysis which offers an enticing opening for refutation. The gist of the argument is that the decision of the student-health officers not to provide birth-

---

[3] R. Baker, "America's Ten Least Sacred Cows," *The New York Times*, February 12, 1967, p. E12.

control materials to unwed coeds "is condoning one of the greatest tragedies in our society: illegitimacy."

Possible defenses against attacks upon analysis are implied by the theory of analysis in Chapter 5. In reply to an attack upon a premise or an assumption, the soundest alternative is to explain and defend the philosophy of the case. Closely related to this would be the affirmative use of a "Principles" case when the proposition of policy apparently called for a program. If the proposition said California should change the district boundaries for election purposes, an affirmative advocate might discourse only upon the theory of redistricting, but the negative attack would probably demand a workable scheme for doing it. Then the affirmative would have some explaining to do. Finally, there is that affirmative defense which does not deny what the negative attack says, but it replies with a wholly different standard of judgment which it says is preferable. When the Wilderness Bill was before Congress, an opponent argued on materialistic grounds that the preservation of a wilderness would create a wasteland. The affirmative defense retorted that trees are not just for lumbering, that vegetation is not merely livestock feed, that mountains are not valuable solely for ores, and that money is not the only value worth serving.

Three general defenses against attacks which allege defects in proof will be indicated briefly. They apply to allegations of faulty analysis, deficient evidence, fallacious reasoning, and, indeed to all the kinds of defective proof. First, one might defend his proof against the charge that it is defective, either by showing that it was misinterpreted or by explaining its validity. Second, he might be able to show that the deficiency was overstated and that his proof still holds up. Finally, he might counterattack by showing defects in the opponent's argument which alleged the deficiency. The defense could score by pointing to a fallacy in the attacker's argument, for instance.

Flaws in Evidence

Unsupported assertion or a total lack of evidence is an inviting opening for attack. In the example referred to here, the lack of evidence is compounded with question begging. An editorial writer asked *why* President Roosevelt "gave away whole nations" (Poland, Czechoslovakia, Hungary, etc.) . . . to do a politeness to Stalin." The attack asked for factual support: "Where is the evidence that F.D.R. gave those nations away?" If the giveaway were proved, then the *why* question would have been proper.

Insufficient evidence is generally a little less vulnerable to attack, but in this case it was a serious defect. Justice William O. Douglas, of all people, asserted in this 1954 book, *An Almanac of Liberty*, that in 1952 in New York City there were at least 58,000 orders issued for wiretapping. Asked by a Congressional committee to give his source, Justice Douglas named a Mr. Davis, who was then called to testify. His testimony indicated that he had conversed with some unidentified policemen and lawyers and that his investigation took "about a day or two." The district attorney of Kings County subsequently testified before the same committee, reporting on a careful investigation which turned up 480 cases—not 58,000—in New York City in 1952.[4]

Biased or unqualified evidence presents many opportunities for attack, but sometimes an arguer makes it easy for his opponent by undermining his own source. Such was the misadventure of Professor Bestor in his article, "We Are Less Educated Than 50 Years Ago."[5] His major sources of evidence were some publications of the U. S. Office of Education, which he branded as a propaganda outlet for professors of education who cling to the nonsense about education as life-adjustment.

Inaccurate and possibly careless reporting has occasionally led to embarrassment. One habitual writer of letters to editors complained that a newspaper story on transit fares neglected to explain why Chicago fares were forty per cent higher than New York fares. He went on to say that no newspaper had ever answered the question, although several of them had been asked repeatedly. The editor replied that the New York system was subsidized by taxes and that the explanation had been printed many times.

Using something less than the best evidence, or the habit of rushing to the attack without the latest and the best, gives the defense an easy opening. It seems that a magazine science editor wrote a feature on brain research in relation to President Eisenhower's stroke.[6] A physician challenged a statement which the editor had attributed to a researcher, Dr. Penfield. The attacker charged that no documentation had been given, but that a Penfield paper in 1954 had given different information from that used by the editor. In defense the editor advised his critic to "do his own research more carefully before criticizing

---

[4] *Chicago Daily News*, June 15, 1963, p. 12.
[5] *U. S. News and World Report*, November 30, 1956, pp. 68–82.
[6] *Saturday Review*, December 14, 1957.

others." The editor *had* cited his source, which was a Penfield paper given in 1957—three years more recent than the one used in the attack.

Irrelevant evidence is as serious a weakness as too little if the persons who might reply are sufficiently alert to detect the defect. "So what?" is the blunt introduction to an attack upon this flaw in proof. An affirmative speaker on complete medical care for all citizens at public expense used three factual statements in support of his charge that our present system of medical care fails in preventive medicine: there is much preventable cancer, most cases are diagnosable, and most people do not have examinations. The negative attack was, in effect, "So what? There is no correlation shown between these facts and the number of visits to doctors." Attacks based upon failure to give relevant information occurred an estimated total of sixteen times in two final debates of West Point tournaments.

Boners in statistical methods make up a substantial group of flaws in evidence, just as misinterpretations of statistical data account for many fallacies in reasoning. Actually, it is often difficult to determine whether a given instance is one of method or of interpretation; an inference based upon an inadequate sample involves too little evidence and a hasty generalization. Be that as it may, here are a few flaws that provided openings for attack. President Kennedy told a business audience that the average age of equipment in U. S. factories was roughly nine years, while in West Germany the proportion of equipment under five years of age grew from one-sixth of the total in 1948 to two-fifths in 1957. The obvious criticism is that the figures are not comparable; one is an average figure, while the other is a percentage of a total. In Chicago the police statistics for 1955 showed an increase of 6.7 per cent in juvenile arrests over 1954. This was used to prove a worsening situation, but the defense pointed out that increasing police attention to this problem and a larger population, not a per capita rise in juvenile delinquency, comprised the factual situation. A trade paper crowed that Kuwait's purchase of some 10,000 air-conditioners had given that state the world lead in units per capita (one per 16 inhabitants *vs.* one per 23 in the U.S.A.). The attack pointed out a ratio of 7,000,000 units to 10,000 in favor of this country and called the per capita figure meaningless. To a brokerage house announcement that 9,000,000 American families own shares of stock, a critic replied that eighty per cent of our families must therefore own none.

Defenses in response to attacks such as those above may be varied to fit the nature of the attacks. To the charge of too little evidence one might explain that in a matter of common knowledge that is no defect, or he should produce more evidence if the matter is not one of common knowledge. If a source is attacked, the defense might point out that this need not discredit the content, or he might defend his source, or he might add evidence. When evidence is attacked by overmatching rather than by impeaching it, the defense might add better evidence, but it may be wiser to reason more cogently from the evidence than the opponent did. There is little profit in a card-quoting contest. Finally, in case the validity of the evidence itself is attacked, the defense might add substantiating evidence or defend the content of the first evidence. He may be able to show that his opponent has taken a fact for an inference, or vice versa.

Material Fallacies

An acquaintance with the ways in which crooked thinking weakens arguments not only alerts us to the openings for attack or refutation in the cases of others but also serves to make us aware of potential weaknesses in our own. Fallacies have been named and classified in many ways, but more important than rigorous classification, at least for our present purpose, is a representative listing with brief descriptions. Material fallacies will comprise the first and longer list, while formal fallacies will make up the second.

Each of the major kinds of argument has characteristic, potential weaknesses, but there are a few that need special attention. They are associated with the generalizing process, the comparing process, and the causation phenomena. In the class of generalized arguments we have hasty generalization, accident, and weak hypothesizing. *Hasty generalizing* occurs in the argument "Candidates for office don't tell what they really think; X didn't, Y didn't, and Z didn't." The fallacy of *accident* occurs when one accepts a generalization as true without exception, as in "Democracy means freedom of the press, so wartime censorship of news should not be allowed." *Weak hypothesizing* may be seen in "Students must be working harder nowadays, because there are more cases of fatigue in the infirmary." In the arguments based upon comparison, *imperfect analogy* is rather common. The notion of social Darwinism as espoused by Herbert Spencer is a familiar example. This is another: "This administration is convinced that we can achieve social security only by surrendering a little bit of freedom for every little bit of security.

That is exactly what our enemies thought. So their people first lost their freedom and then their security." *False cause* and the *confusion of cause and sign* also occur frequently. This is one form of the fallacy: "World War II would have happened even without Hitler, because the economic situation in Western Europe had been worsening for years." Another variation may be seen in the argument that education surely produces higher earning power because education and income levels correlate so closely.

Other flaws in thinking include equivocation, bifurcation, composition, division, inconsistence, non sequitur, and speculative argument. *Equivocation,* or linguistic ambiguity, can also be classified as a formal fallacy of four terms. It arises from the two senses of "right" in this argument: "Whatever is right should be legally enforced. Voting is a right, so it should be legally enforced." *Bifurcation,* or the improper use of polar words, occurs in "The government has to be concerned only with the rich and the poor; the rich because of the power they will try to exert, and the poor because they depend upon welfare." Fallacies of *composition* result when one assumes that what is true of each class member holds true for the class collectively, as in "High tariff on watches benefits skilled labor, and on meat products it helps farmers, so let's raise tariffs on everything and help all of us." *Division* goes the opposite way, assuming that a generality applies equally well to the constituent particulars, as in saying, "Each department in this factory will have to reduce its work force by ten percent, because our total production is to be cut ten percent."

Inconsistency is here taken to mean either the appearance of irreconcilable statements in one message or the use of a conclusion which does not follow from its premise. Some persons quote Shakespeare in praise of consistency: "Consistency, thou art a jewel." Others prefer Emerson's dissent: "A foolish consistency is the hobgoblin of little minds, adored by little statesmen and philosophers and divines." An inconsistency in the traditional sense was found in a Beveridge speech on child labor. At one point he said new immigrants should be guaranteed job opportunities equal to those of older American groups because they are equal as citizens. A bit later he argued that child labor degraded the Anglo-Saxon race to a level which ought to be forced upon only the children of "foreigners."

The simple *non sequitur* (does not follow) occurs when someone uses an argument in which the conclusion does not follow. "There are some impoverished old persons, therefore the nation needs a system of compulsory, complete medical care at public expense." "Decent housing is a basic need of every citizen; therefore the proposed national housing bill should be enacted." "The federal income tax deprives states and localities of some revenue; therefore it should be repealed." Some apparent non sequiturs would become acceptable if missing links such as assumptions and implied premises were supplied.

Speculative argument shifts from "ought" to "is," and, as is the case with most fallacies, the mistake can be innocent of any devious intent. This is a specimen: "Man is comforted by the belief in immortality; and since all creation is in the main friendly to man's aspirations, we may assume that we are immortal."

Diversions can be attacked by showing their irrelevancy and the possibility of their being stratagems to change the subject or to stop debate on a losing proposition. In order to disprove the point that fraternities stereotype their members, it would be necessary to show that at least some do not do so, but the user of *irrelevant conclusion* argued instead that stereotyping is unfortunate. Another speaker tried to show that athletes on his campus had taken tribes, but his arugment was that bribery must not be permitted. Diversions to other ideas *beside the point* occur when speakers ignore intellectual argument and resort to appeals to interests, motives, and prejudices. Student speakers have been known to urge the rejection of an innovation on one campus on the ground that it is in use on the campus of a disliked, rival institution. The merit of the idea is ignored. Attacks upon persons instead of ideas can be classified here.

Diversions may be made to other ideas, as above, or *to stop argument on a losing point*, as in the cases which follow. The use of abstruse statement, technical jargon, and other incomprehensible remarks is a means of escape for some bluffers. Improper use of expert opinion occurs when one lists allegedly favorable authorities without quoting them or reasoning about their supposed testimony. While speaking for an honor code a student said, "The administration, student leaders, and prominent alumni all favor this idea." Another version of this can be seen in a speaker's use of his own *prestige or status* in lieu of logical support. Or a speaker may appeal to *tradition or custom* in advising against a course of action because it has not been done that way before. In times of hysteria associated with wars, depressions, and witch hunts, demagogues play up nonrational and *irrational appeals* to fear, ignorance, anxiety, prejudice, and the like.

Substitution of nonrational matter or manner for a sensible treatment of a controversial point is a familiar sophism of the diversionary type. Intimidation, or *appeal to force*, ranges from threatening someone's job to international rocket rattling. Lesser bullies, having less power, must content themselves with *ridicule*, irony, bombast, and *anger*. They raise their voices instead of reinforcing their arguments.

A few of the diversionary stratagems that have Latin names will be mentioned here, in some cases for the second time: (1) Personal abuse (*ad hominem*)—"What does my opponent know about the problems of agriculture? The only time he ever set foot on a farm was to foreclose the mortgage." (2) Playing to the gallery (*ad populum*), as in Bryan's peroration of his "Cross of Gold" speech. (3) Appeal to pity, or tear-jerking (*ad misericordiam*), as in Darrow's appeals for the underdog. (4) Appeal to prestigious sources (*ad verecundiam*), as in citing Washington's "Farewell Address" for guidance in current affairs. (5) Appeal to ignorance (*argumentum ad ignorantiam*), as in "We must believe in the hereafter, because nobody can disprove it."

Manipulations to confuse are in the fourth subclass of material fallacies. They do not necessarily leave the point entirely, but they do distort it. An *unfair extension* of someone's argument to the point of absurdity is one form of manipulation. Some years ago the arguments for prison reform and the eight-hour day for labor were extended by the negative to mean "giving convicts and workers everything on a silver platter." Whenever we have a controversy which arouses strong feelings, we can expect *both* extremes to practice unfair extensions of arguments.

Special pleading is a manipulative tactic which involves using in one situation an argument which the same person would reject in another. The person who demands a police crackdown on traffic violators—until *he* gets a ticket—is a familiar instance. Omission of relevant but unfavorable evidence is akin to special pleading. We have observed it in spokesmen for certain states that boast of their low taxes but neglect to mention their low standard of public education.

A *genetic fallacy* occurs when an idea that is before us is judged solely on its source: "That ordinance must be a bad one for us tenants, because it was proposed by the real estate interests." Related to this is "poisoning the well," which involves discrediting a source even before the testimony has been received: "My opponent will no doubt quote from Mr. X, whom you can't believe even under oath."

Forcing ideas into arbitrary classes, as in saying that one must be a radical if he is not a reactionary, is a manipulation which some polemicists use. Those who habitually seek a middle-of-the-road position on any controversial subject on which they are asked for an opinion apparently think an idea is right if it lies halfway between the extremes.

Trick questions are intended to confuse ideas and persons by means of an apparently meaningless sequence of questions, a distortion of the respondent's answers, ambiguous questions, pseudo (unanswerable) questions, and complex questions ("Have you quit cheating in examinations?").

Misuse of language appeared in some of the speeches above, but in the following instances it seems to be a category of fallacies in its own right. Three variants will be cited here: ambiguity, loaded language, and tautology. *Ambiguity* formerly meant the use of words having two meanings, but now the usage seems to include vagueness. In this broader sense, ambiguity can be found in many places; in fact, it is frequently used intentionally. This is what the man in the street means when he complains about the "doubletalk" of his employer, some politicians, and diplomats. A study of the Kennedy-Nixon television series of 1960[7] indicated some ambiguous passages in the speeches of both men. Their remarks on farm policy in the first program were among those designated as ambiguous.[8]

Loaded language is highly subjective in that expressions which presumably are meant to describe actually convey the attitude and feeling of the user toward the subject. Figurative language, often hyperbole, is the typical locution. Slanted expressions are familiar in political discourse, particularly at campaign time. In fact, it is easy to identify the party preference of many newspapers by noticing which way the language is loaded. This specimen left no doubt: "Millions of dollars were spent by New Deal propaganda mills to create and spread the myth that F.D.R. was an all-seeing, all-knowing, and all-honorable commander, philosopher, and philanthropist."

Tautology may be taken to include circular reasoning, question-begging words and definitions, and nonevident premise. This is a simple case of reasoning in a circle: "The story must be true, because I read it in a book, and it wouldn't have been published if it weren't true." Question-begging was explained in relation to propositions, but here is another specimen: "Un-American activities should be declared unpatriotic." An oversimplified instance of nonevident premise appears in this

---

[7] L. A. Samovar, "Ambiguity and Unequivocation in the Kennedy-Nixon Television Debates," *Quarterly Journal of Speech*, XLVIII, No. 3 (1962), 279.

[8] S. Kraus (ed.), *The Great Debates* (Bloomington: Indiana University Press, 1962), pp. 355–356.

sentence: "Since the system of free enterprise has made this country what it is, we should preserve the system as it is."

Formal Fallacies

If we "don't go around talking syllogisms," as some say, then we do not hear many formal fallacies in their complete form. What we do say are enthymemes, and some of their defects can be shown analytically by means of syllogistic structures. These formal fallacies can be more easily applied to the deductive truth and value arguments which were explained earlier. *Two negative* premises will invalidate a syllogism, as in "None of Beethoven's symphonies is easy to play, and no symphonies that are easy to play are good ones; therefore, all of Beethoven's symphonies are good." It will be recalled that one's belief or disbelief in the conclusion is irrelevant to formal analysis. *Shifting (or four) terms* invalidates this syllogism: "All candidates with good records are endorsed by the unions, and all candidates endorsed by the A.M.A. have good records; therefore, all candidates endorsed by the A.M.A. are endorsed by the unions." *Undistributed middle term* invalidates this syllogism: "All weapons ought to be outlawed, and all psychological warfare ought also to be outlawed; therefore it is clear that psychological warfare is a weapon." *Illicit terms*, major or minor, occur in violation of the rule (Number 3) that no term may be distributed in the conclusion if it is undistributed in the premise. This is an illicit major: "All actors have creative intelligence, and no actors are good science students; therefore, no good science students have creative intelligence." *Denying the antecedent* is an invalid conditional argument: "If man can travel faster than light, he can go to the moon eventually, but man cannot exceed the speed of light, so he can never travel to the moon." *Affirming the consequent* is the other invalid form of the conditional argument: "If man travels faster than light, he can reach the moon eventually, and he will reach the moon eventually, so he will travel faster than light."

TACTICAL PROCEDURES

There are several tactical procedures, sometimes referred to as special methods, which have been used in attack and defense for centuries. They may be used in addition to the tests of analysis, of evidence, and of argument which have been explained. Some are so crude and patently fallacious that they will be named but not explained here. In a Russian rhetorical manual, for example, four tactics of retort are given: (1) scorn and disrespect, (2) reproach and denunciation, (3) voluminous discourse against a telling argument, and (4) charges of untruth and bad judgment.[9]

Turn the Tables

Once in a while a debater will have an opportunity to turn an opponent's proof to his own advantage. In reply to the argument that parents who send children to private elementary and high schools bear a double burden (taxes plus tuition), Walter Lippmann wrote: "Whether it is fair to describe as 'discrimination' such double payments for education can best be tested by asking what would be the situation if private schools were supported by the taxpayer. In that case the parent whose child goes to the public school will be paying twice over—once to support the public schools which his child attends and once to support the private school which his child does not attend."[10] In a thoroughgoing refutation of the previously cited Bestor argument (footnote 5), Professor Hand[11] turned the tables by using Bestor's own source to disprove the affirmative claim. After showing the statistical comparison between 1900 and 1950 to be fallacious because of an invalid base, Hand went on to cite other pamphlets from Bestor's favorite source which proved that the high schools offering no geometry, physics, or chemistry enroll only two per cent of American high school students.

Sometimes there is no good reply to the table-turning tactic, but the possibilities to consider include attacking the opponent's frame of reference or his interpretation of the point, showing that he admits the point, or pointing out that he has shifted ground.

Reduce to Absurdity

As in table-turning, one uses the opponent's proof, but in this tactic he extends it to the absurd. It is simple, direct, and vastly entertaining

---

[9] J. H. Butler, "Russian Rhetoric: A Discipline Manipulated by Communism," *Quarterly Journal of Speech*, L, No. 3 (1964), 234.

[10] "Opinion: Federal Aid to Education," *Presbyterian Life*, May 15, 1961, p. 23.

[11] H. C. Hand, "Black Horses Eat More Than White Horses," A. A. U. P. *Bulletin*, XLIII (1957), 266–279.

to the "groundlings," as Shakespeare called them. An apocryphal story tells of a lawyer who contended that a corporation could make no oral contract because it had no tongue.The judge replied that it could not, by the same token, make a written contract because it had no hand. Combining irony, ridicule, and reducing to absurdity, a student wrote a letter to the campus paper to attack the proposal to delete questions on race and religious preference from the admission application forms. He argued that all these admissions questions and procedures could lead to discrimination: applicant's name, home address, name of high school, grade transcript, father's occupation, education of parents, age, sex, serial numbers, etc. On this last point he wrote: "If serial numbers are assigned, they must not be given in sequence as this would allow discrimination against applying later than others. Ridiculous, isn't it?"[12]

Some debaters have replied to such tactics by reaffirming the original point, attacking the analogy (if any), showing an irrelevancy, charging an unfair extension of the point, or pointing out that no substantive flaw was found in the argument which was ridiculed. An exchange in *Harper's* illustrates a *reductio ad absurdum* and two modes of reply. The first event was an "Easy Chair" (February, 1960) item which was critical of billboard advertising. The April reply said the critic's argument, if carried to its logical conclusion, would do away with store window displays, theater marquees, and all business signs. "Billboards are an integral part of the great system of free enterprise . . . ," it concluded. The editors replied that window displays are on the advertiser's own property, that abolition is the only constructive answer to billboards, and that such action has no more relevance to free enterprise than the abolition of slums. It should be noted that a charge of absurdity may either amuse or alienate an audience, and it can boomerang in the form of table-turning by the intended victim.

Match the Proof

Instead of discrediting the proof or its application, the person replying may choose to match or overmatch his opponent's proof. He can do so by using evidence and/or reasoning of the same or of a different kind. Two cautions need to be observed: quality is more important than quantity, and the user must make clear the fact that he is employing the tactic of outweighing proof. In a written controversy over the proper

12 *Daily Northwestern*, February 15, 1956, p. 2.

balance between police powers and civil liberties, the negative did not attempt to attack the affirmative's evidence directly; instead, he marshaled his evidence to show the opposite conclusion.[13]

One defense against the matching tactic is the argument that mere quotation counting is not enough. Another is the possibility of pointing out that the matcher has shifted ground. A third kind of reply was made in the 1961 final debate of the West Point tournament. The second negative constructive speaker proposed to match evidence on the distribution of medical facilities in the United States, but the affirmative replied that *interpretation* of evidence was more significant than quantity.

Pose a Dilemma

Two or more untenable consequences of a position are alleged to exist. Seeing a person drown, a nonswimming bystander may jump in and become a dead hero or stay out and be a live coward. The principle of the dilemma is that the choices (horns) cover the possibilities, and each one is damaging. Without foot soldiers we would either lose on the installment plan or resort to a suicidal nuclear holocaust, it is argued. In opposition to wage increases for steelworkers, an editorial[14] posed this dilemma: if the wage increase were to come out of profits, the firms would have difficulty in finding capital for expansion and replacement, and the resultant retarded growth would harm the nation and the workers themselves; but if the wage hike were passed on in higher prices, the workers would find their raises nullified by a price spiral.

In reply one might take an option which was not covered (tie the wage rate to productivity or to the value of the dollar), break down one of the given options (different effect from the cause), or reduce the argument to an absurdity (permanent wage freeze apparently implied).

Apply Residues

Both sides can use this procedure. It consists of the division of a point into parts, as in a dilemma, but here one part is left intact after

[13] Inbau *vs.* Kamisar, *Journal of Criminal Law, Criminology and Police Science*, LIII, No. 1 (1962), 85–89, and No. 2 (1962), 171–193.
[14] *Wall Street Journal*, March 17, 1959.

the others have been disqualified. The result is constructive proof for the refuter's side. Exhaustive division plus ample proof of the residue will make it work. In his renowned speech on conciliation with the American colonies, Edmund Burke treated three ways of proceeding: remove the causes of the stubborn spirit, prosecute it as criminal, or comply with it as necessary. After disqualifying the first two, he concluded by saying the only reasonable choice was to submit to the situation as a necessary evil.

Not all residues are as formidable as Burke's. The division may not be exhaustive, or the residue may be refuted, or one of the disqualifying arguments may be refuted. Sometimes two of these can be combined, as in denying the residue and supporting one of the disqualified choices. Defenses against the dilemma have some parallels here.

Force the Defense

Keeping the opponent on the defensive is the favorite sport of the negative side. This is accomplished by means of all the tactics discussed in this chapter. In general the idea is to get the affirmative to use the language of the negative case. There is no doubt that the negative side is the easier one for persons who wish merely to bedevil the opposition. One method which has not been discussed is the use of questions as exploratory refutation. It is called setting up a point for refutation, and it is accomplished by asking, for instance, how the affirmative plan would be financed, assuming that the negative has a devastating rejoinder to the likely affirmative answer.

In the management of his defense, an affirmative will find several hints most useful. When confronted by questions and objections, he can press the negative to explain each objection, to show the significance of each question, and to support every dire prediction. He will follow each answer to a negative attack with a reaffirmation of his own point. He will answer legitimate questions, but he will not react gullibly to "scatter gun" and "straw man" attacks. He will not allow the negative to concentrate on one or two objections; instead, he will call attention to any negative failures to deal with some matters. Finally, he will keep the affirmative case in its own language before the audience, not by mere repetition but by adding support in each exchange on a point.

Argue a Fortiori

This tactic uses the idea of "all the more probable." If a conclusion is true in a less favorable case, so the argument goes, think how nearly inevitable it must be in a more favorable one. "If the head of an institution devoted to the training of engineers was thus misled . . . (by Bestor's statistics) the likelihood is very great that most of the readers . . . came to the same grossly erroneous conclusion . . ."[15] "An argument from the stronger," as it may also be translated, falls under the rules of relational syllogisms. Whether it is used constructively or destructively, it follows this form: The truth of A is admitted, and the support for B is stronger than the support for A; therefore, B must be admitted.

DIALECTIC AND CROSS-EXAMINATION

In Chapter 2 dialectic was briefly defined and shown to be a forerunner of argumentation. Now, both in its original form and in the modern form of cross-examination, it will be discussed as an important procedure in attack and defense.

A Neglected Method of Argument

In 1921 Professor Hunt wrote on dialectic under this title.[16] He urged that interest in it be revived because of these values to be gained through practice in cross-examination: (1) It accustoms one to study both sides of a question. (2) In problem solving, the differing opinions serve as constant checks on each other by constantly clashing and adapting to each other. (3) It is more of a thinking together process than are long speeches by one individual. (4) It is a stimulating mental exercise. (5) It is excellent preparation for formal debate. (6) An audience listens more closely and with more interest to cross-examina-

[15] See footnote 11.
[16] E. L. Hunt, "Dialectic: A Neglected Method of Argument," *Quarterly Journal of Speech Education*, VII (1921), 221–232.

tion than to one speech or even debate. (7) It has a wider range than debate. It may be used for stimulation and discussion as well as problem solving.

Socrates asked the disturbing question, "What do you mean?" In Plato's *Dialogues* we see the old master, as Plato would have us remember him, deflating humbug by testing ideas to see if they could stand honest, logical examination. In ancient times and again in the twelfth century there were periods of great interest in Aristotle's works on dialectic, the *Topics* and *On Sophistical Refutations*.[17]

In its original sense, dialectic could serve as a teaching-learning discipline to reduce the tendency toward dogmatism. The disputants were encouraged to achieve understanding, if not agreement, by placing their opposition within a common universe of discourse. Sophistication in the sense of poise, courtesy, and controlled temper was essential. These were some of the occasions in which this version of dialectic was used: 1. differing interpretations of the meaning of a statement, 2. differing assumptions, 3. differing consequences of assumptions, 4. a desire to reduce disagreement by focusing upon agreement first, 5. a desire to clarify the basis of disagreement, and 6. a desire to explore a point of agreement.

But not all evidence in support of the dialectical methods is ancient. Some is modern and scientific. Prediction and verification, as well as the method of multiple working hypotheses, involve some dialectical procedure. We say "some" because dialectic alone is inconclusive. Talk cannot determine what is a fact, but it can examine the meanings of facts. Another value has been discovered through psychological experimentation; it is that questioning, as in the Socratic method, increases the consistency of beliefs.[18]

At this point a discussion of how dialectical thinking functions may be helpful. In Aristotle's *Topics* (100ª 18) demonstrative reasoning, as in most advocacy, starts from premises which are true and primary, or are such that we know about them through primary, true premises. Dialectical reasoning, which is our present concern, starts from opinions that are generally believed on the strength of themselves alone. Hegel distinguished dialectic from induction and deduction within one mind and showed that its essence was opposition, conflict, and duality,

[17] J. J. Murphy, "Two Medieval Textbooks in Debate," *Journal of the American Forensic Association*, I, No 1 (1964), 3.
[18] C. I. Hovland and M. J. Rosenberg, eds., *Attitude Organization and Change* (New Haven: Yale University Press, 1960), p. 204.

whether within one mind or between two. Adler[19] says dialectic is the way in which opinions are placed in opposition and attacked, defended, combined, and so forth. It is intended to aid us in answering the question, "What does it mean to say thus-and-so?" The three stages in the process are definition, analysis, and synthesis. In the first two the opposition is clarified by setting out its systematic consequences. Originally and in an educational sense, the question-and-answer procedure was used for speculative inquiry, but when it is used in cross-examination, the purpose is to build a progression of dialectical syllogisms. How this is done in court, in school debate, in philosophical dialogue, and in hearings will be explained and illustrated.

Cross-Examination in Court

In the courtroom there are four possible aims of cross-examination: (1) to discredit the testimony of the witness, (2) to use this testimony to discredit unfavorable testimony of other witnesses, (3) to use this testimony to corroborate the favorable testimony of others, and (4) to use it to contribute independently to the favorable development of the questioner's case.[20]

What makes a good witness in this trying situation? The author of *The Art of Advocacy*[21] characterizes five difficult types in terms of responses to the psychological pressures: nervous, "wise-guy," suspicious, fawning, and lying. His ideal witness has five traits: (1) He is conscientious about telling the truth. (2) He is well prepared, knows his facts, and can narrate them clearly. (3) He has courage, strong character, and toughness. (4) His vision, hearing, and memory are good. (5) In appearance he is healthy and wholesome.[22]

Application to School Debating

Purposes of questions in cross-examination school debating are not quite same as they are in judicial debating. In educational forensics

---

[19] M. J. Adler, *Dialectic* (N.Y.: Harcourt, Brace and Co., 1927).

[20] L. W. Lake, *How To Cross-Examine Witnesses Successfully* (Englewood Cliffs, N. J.: Prentice-Hall, Inc., 1957), p. 6.

[21] L. P. Stryker, "What Makes a Good Witness," *New York Times Magazine*, May 16, 1954, p. 13.

[22] See also A. Steuer, *Max D. Steuer, Trial Lawyer* (N. Y.: Random House, Inc., 1950).

there is typically less emphasis upon trapping witnesses in lies and badgering them to make damaging admissions. Instead, the stress is supposed to be on getting information, testing inferences, verifying sources, clarifying meanings of statements, and sharpening the contrasts in their cases. Instead of pressing for conclusions, the skillful practioners ask questions, the answers to which may provide premises for further argument. This is what was meant by the earlier assertion that the purpose of cross-examination is to build a progression of dialectical syllogisms.

Preparation is the key to better cross-examining and answering. It includes attitude as well as knowledge. Both parties are expected to be reasonable, even-tempered, courteous, and interested in getting at the essentials. They are supposed to regard this period as a vital part of the debate. These attitudes should lead to thoughtful preparation of questions and answers. This means anticipating and adapting to the possible twists and turns that the dialectic may take.

Suggestions for questioners are not rules, but they are common-sense advice based upon considerable experience.[23] The interrogator should use the time for questions only. Instead of making interpretative or evaluative asides, he should bring out such inferences by asking follow-up questions. The questioner has control of the time; he may probe whatever matters he wishes, but he may prevent the respondent from wasting time in rambling or evasive replies. This does not mean that he may insist upon yes-or-no answers except on simple questions of fact. His questions, in turn, should be brief and to some point. He may very properly be aggressive in his interrogation, but obnoxious behavior as in personal abuse is out of bounds. Instead of trying to get an admission of defeat from a witness, he should start on common ground and probe deeper and deeper, looking for weak spots in assumptions, evidence, reasoning, and omissions. A planned but flexible order of questions is best for this purpose. Beginners err in slavishly running through a written list of questions regardless of the case they meet or the answers they get. The idea is to follow through to some point or basis for a premise and then to stress the unit by repeating the opening question. Audience interest can be improved by clear presentation of questions and efforts to make the proceedings intelligible. Events become exceedingly complex at times. Questioners are advised to know the answers to

---

[23] See R. P. Newman, *The Pittsburgh Code for Academic Debate* (Pittsburgh: University of Pittsburgh Press, 1962).

most of their questions. There is to be no conferring between colleagues during the examination. Finally, it is poor technique to use "Isn't it a fact that . . ." and question-begging questions.

Suggestions for witnesses have been foreshadowed by the advice given on purposes of questions, preparation for dialectic, and questioning. An individual or a team should, through analysis, determine what positions must be maintained, how they may be attacked, and how to reply. Anticipation of traps is essential, because no conferring is permitted during the examination. It is equally important for this side to remember and use later the results of the questioning. Replies are to be brief and pointed, but the respondent should feel free to request clarification of ambiguous questions. Mere stalling for time is improper, but a witness need not let the examiner rush him unduly. This implies answering directly and fairly but with reasonable qualifications. One may, of course, decline to answer question-begging or unclear questions if the examiner refuses to amend them. In case a witness does not know an answer, he is advised to admit it. With respect to behavior, he should maintain good humor, speak so as to include the audience, and stay in his role as the witness. In some school tournaments there are rules governing appeals to the chair.

Standard formats of school debating which include some dialectical procedures may be seen in several textbooks[24] designed to serve contest debaters. The familiar formats are designated by names such as Oregon Style, Montana Style, Heckling Debate, Mock Trial, and others. For classroom exercises this short form will serve the purpose:

First affirmative constructive	5 minutes
Second negative questions first affirmative	3 minutes
First negative constructive	5 minutes
Second affirmative questions first negative	3 minutes
Second negative rebuttal	3 minutes
Second affirmative rebuttal	3 minutes

In his comparison of dialectic, cross-examination in court, and their influences upon school debate, Beard[25] reports this format:

---

[24] J. H. McBurney and G. E. Mills, *Argumentation and Debate*, rev. ed. (N.Y.: The Macmillan Co., 1964), pp. 340–356; A. J. Freeley, *Argumentation and Debate* (San Francisco: Wadsworth Publishing Co., 1961), pp. 306–312; J. H. McBath, ed., *Argumentation and Debate*, rev. ed. (N.Y.: Holt, Rinehart and Winston, Inc., 1963), pp. 285–298; D. Ehninger and W. Brockriede, *Decision by Debate* (N.Y.: Dodd, Mead and Co., 1963), pp. 320–328.

[25] R. S. Beard, "A Comparison of Classical Dialectic, Legal Cross-Examination, and Cross-Question Debate, *Journal of the American Forensic Association*, III, No. 2 (1966), 53–58.

(1) Constructive case by the affirmative
(2) Constructive case by the negative
(3) Cross-examination of the affirmative by the negative
(4) Cross-examination of the negative by the affirmative
(5) Summary by the negative
(6) Summary by the affirmative

Specimens

Printed records of dialectical jousts, including cross-examinations, vary in length from three terse remarks to dozens of pages. One attributed to Lincoln qualifies as possibly the shortest. He said to a campaign opponent,

"Suppose I call the tail of a mule a leg, how many legs would the mule then have?"

"Five," said his witness.

"No," replied Lincoln, "he would still have four. Calling a tail a leg doesn't make it one."

The audience probably thought that Abe had made a fool of his rival, even though the dialectical situation would have permitted any of three answers: five legs, four legs, or one leg. The question actually implied, "What is meant by calling a mule's tail a leg?" Toward the other extreme in length we might place Senator Thurmond's questioning of Secretary of Defense McNamara, not because of its total length but because of its low yield in information per 100 words.[26]

Two interesting little exchanges took place when the Young Republican Club of Evanston, Illinois, met to hear spokesmen for and against the city manager form of government. After one antimanager debater finished his prepared statement, a lawyer in the audience asked him the name of his home town. It happened to be Highland Park. Pressed further, the witness admitted that his home town had the manager form of government. The clincher came in this question: "Isn't it a fact that Highland Park last year was selected as an "All-American City, best governed in its class?"

The second antimanager debater admitted under questioning his conviction that an alderman under the manager system might become too powerful in his ward. Asked why he thought so, he exclaimed, "My

26 *The New Yorker*, June 15, 1963, p. 82.

alderman wants more power. My alderman demands more power. My alderman needs more power to be effective." Asked if he really believed this, he answered emphatically in the affirmative. Asked if he were certain of his alderman's appearance and feelings, he again answered firmly in the affirmative. Then the questioner gave the coup de grace: "It hurts me and embarrasses me . . . but I must break the news to you that you live in the eighth ward and I am your alderman and I don't look and don't feel that way."[27]

Next is a short extract from the cross-examination of the plaintiff in a civil suit for damages. Notice how quickly his story comes apart:

Q. After this occurrence, were you ever employed by them again?
A. No.
Q. Did you go back to your job with them?
A. No, I didn't.
Q. Did you seek to go back to your job with them?
A. I knew that I couldn't stand on the floor no [sic] length of time so it was useless.
Q. So the answer to my question is you didn't, is that correct?
A. No, I didn't.
. . .
Q. When you worked at a lathe, that was at a bench, was it?
A. Yes.
Q. Did you work standing up or sitting down?
A. Sitting down mostly.

The final specimen of dialectic in this collection is reported to have taken place at Oxford Uniersity. It is a philosophical-theological dialogue between logical positivists and Catholics.

Logical positivism (a close relative of American philosopher John Dewey's pragmatism) erects its system of thought on the premise that no statement (except in logic and mathematics) may be considered meaningful if it is not potentially verifiable by evidence of the senses. The idea of God is one of the first things that logical positivists throw overboard. Last week philosopher Tony Quinton of All Souls' College undertook to dispose of God in the heart of the enemy camp, the Roman Catholic undergraduate Aquinas Society.

Notice the Boop. To hear the assertion that God exists, declared handsome Tony Quinton, is like visiting a friend and having him ask: "Did you notice our boop when you came through the garden?"

"No, what is it—an animal of some sort?"

"Yes, it's a sort of dog; it guards the house."

"I didn't see anything like a dog."

[27] *Evanston* (Illinois) *Review,* March 19, 1959.

"Oh, you wouldn't see it. It's invisible."

"Well, can you smell it, touch it, hear it?"

"Not exactly . . ."

"Anyway, I thought you'd been burgled recently; it can't be a very good guard."

"Ah, you wouldn't talk like that if you knew what it was to have a boop. Of course, it hasn't dealt with the burglars yet, but it knows who they are and is going to punish them."

God, said Quinton, is just about as evident as a boop. Then he went on to draw a prestidigitator's "proof" of God's nonexistence from Christian dogma: "God created the world." "World" in this sense, said Philosopher Quinton, means not "earth" but "everything."

"God," he went on, "obviously didn't create Himself. The only thing outside of everything is nothing. Therefore, if God created everything except what is outside of everything, namely nothing, and if God is the only thing outside everything, then God is nothing."

I Believe. After 55 minutes of such fast-stepping talk, the Rev. Thomas Corbishley, chubby Jesuit Master of Oxford's Catholic Campion Hall, got to his feet. "Mr. Quinton," he began, "do you believe the statement that no statement is true unless it is verifiable?"

"Certainly," replied Quinton.

"How," asked Corbishley, "can you verify that statement?" Quinton admitted that this cornerstone of positivism is unverifiable.

"Then why do you believe it to be true?" asked the priest.

"I believe it to be true because it is true," Quinton answered.

"There!" shouted Father Corbishley triumphantly. "So I believe that God exists because He does exist. Now where are we?"[28]

REBUTTALS IN SCHOOL DEBATE

Extensive treatments of this subject can be found in textbooks and journal articles which are intended for school debaters and their directors.[29] The brief discussion in this place is intended to show in a general way how the procedures of attack and defense apply here. This will be done by sketching some familiar flaws in rebuttal speeches, indicating some possible improvements, and outlining the work of each rebuttal speaker in the traditional format.

[28] *Time*, June 3, 1950, p. 82. Courtesy of *Time*, copyright *Time, Inc.*, 1950.

[29] J. M. Mazza and J. B. Polisky, "A Macroscopic View of Rebuttal, *The A. F. A. Register*, XI, No. 1 (1963), 16–19.

Familiar Flaws in Rebuttal

Poor organization and stereotyped style can be observed all too often in contest debates. A critical reading of some published debates which have not been edited will reveal occasional rebuttal speeches which seem to be composed of disconnected remarks. Failure to carry the main ideas beyond the point reached in constructive speeches accounts for the widespread complaint that nothing much happens in rebuttals. Perhaps some students do not know what a rebuttal period is for, or at least they fail to do what is needed. For instance, in a final debate for the "national championship," the first affirmative rebuttalist defended at length the "need" point which had not been hit very hard, but he almost neglected the negative "objections" point which had been pressed vigorously. These and other shortcomings stem from several causes, one of which is the trend toward moving the rebuttal type of activity closer to the beginning of the debate. Some adaptation is essential, but, as has been stated earlier, there is little sense in having one constructive speech followed by seven rebuttal-type speeches. Negative cases of pure refutation, at least in the way they are often handled, tend to aggravate this problem.

Suggested Remedies

Memorable rebuttal speeches have not been characterized by the attempt to attack or defend practically everything which was said previously. The skillful debaters selected important items in terms of positions and issues. Some were selected to be clarified, others to be attacked or defended. Attention was certain to be called to the points which the opponent had not attacked. Rebuilding of points which had been hit was done with new evidence and variations in the original strategy; it was no mere repetition. Effective summaries have given emphasis to arguments handled, significance of each, and how crucial ones were resolved in the speaker's favor.

Duties of Each Speaker

What each of the four speakers should do in a school debate depends upon the type of proposition, the side, the kinds of cases, and the tactical stiuation at the moment. However, several general principles can be stated: (1) Try always to be honest, fair, and courteous in attacking and defending ideas. (2) Never bring up a new constructive point in the rebuttal series. (3) Tie all attack and defense to the crucial parts of each case as a whole. (4) Remember the previous advice to keep the other side on the defensive so far as possible.

Within the limits expressed above, each speaker's duties can be suggested. The first negative rebuttal speaker has five minutes immediately following the second negative constructive speaker's ten-minute period. This awkward situation results from the custom of having the affirmative side both open and close the debate. But since this convention is likely to persist, the best course for the negative teams is so to divide the responsibilities that each speaker knows what to do and can thereby avoid duplicating his colleague's efforts. The first rebuttal speaker should take up where the preceding constructive speaker stopped, and he should focus on a few topics, or at most the "need" issue. However, if the negative uses a counterproposition, there is no clash on "need." In any event this speaker concentrates on the affirmative's duties and tries to keep that side on the defensive.

Following fifteen minutes of negative speaking, the first affirmative rebuttal speaker takes the floor. If the opponents have spent their time advantageously, this speaker faces a critical period. He must make every second count, not by speaking at a frantic rate, but by focusing upon a few matters and composing his remarks clearly and briefly. The "need" issue may or may not require attention, but the "plan" and "advantages" most likely will. Even while defending against negative objections, this speaker should keep the affirmative case in terms of its own language before the audience.

The last rebuttalist for the negative should try to make the main attacks on the affirmative case prevail; and if his side has a constructive case, he should try to make the negative points stand out in preference to those of the affirmative. This is the last opportunity to focus upon ("boil down to") major clashes. In anticipation of the final affirmative speech, the last negative speaker usually points out what the affirmative side has failed to do and why that is serious.

In closing the debate, the final affirmative rebuttal speaker tries to reestablish the main thrust of the affirmative case. A three-stage treatment of each vital element includes setting up an affirmative point, refuting the negative attack on it, and reaffirming the original point.

QUESTIONS

1. Why are attack and defense called the essence of genuine debate? Describe an imaginary or a real joint appearance of announced affirmative and negative spokesmen in which attack and defense did not occur.

2. Suppose someone were to say that attack is the negative's business while defense is the affirmative's. What would you reply?

3. Point out the opportunities for attack against one speech or essay in Appendix B or elsewhere.

4. Select an exchange in which one affirmative message has been followed by one negative. Point out the opportunities and obligations that would apply to any affirmative spokesman who might appear next. This does not assume a school debate.

5. Again using a debate as a specimen for analysis, point out where refutation was placed and explain how the steps in attack and defense were used. Use Appendix C.

6. Using Section III (Exposing Defects in Proof) as a frame of reference, explain how each side in Appendix C used these items in attack and defense.

7. Cite as many as possible of these tactics in Appendix C: a) turn the tables, b) reduce to absurdity, c) match the proof, d) pose a dilemma, e) apply residues, f) force the defense, and g) argue a fortiori.

EXERCISES

1. For at least a week, conduct a "fallacy hunt" in editorials, letters, speeches, advertising, conversations, etc. In reporting the findings, classify the items according to Section III (Exposing Defects in Proof).

2. After hearing or reading a school debate or an approved substitute, write a critique of the attack and defense.

3. Conduct a direct-clash exercise, using one clash point for each exchange. If four persons were in each exchange, the order might be as follows:

a) five minutes to set up a point (either affirmative or negative) from a previously announced proposition; b) four minutes for an attack upon that point; c) four minutes for defense; d) four minutes for attack. Suppose the announced proposition were "The sale of cigarettes to minors should be prohibited by law." This is one of several clash points on which the affirmative side could begin: "Cigarette smoking is a menace to health." Or a clash could begin with a negative point such as, "This prohibition would be less successful than the Volstead Act."

4. Conduct one or more cross-examination debates with four students in each. Use propositions that have served in earlier exercises. The 22-minute format near the end of Section V (Dialectic and Cross-Examination) is suggested.

5. Pairs of students might be assigned to edit and reenact some noteworthy dialogues and debates such as Lincoln-Douglas (*The Rivalry*), Bryan-Darrow (*Inherit the Wind*), the trial of Socrates (*Barefoot in Athens*), the limited test-ban treaty (*Congressional Record*, Sept. 9–20, 1963).

6. Oral or written critiques based upon observations of the work of classmates on Exercises 3, 4, and 5 might be assigned to vary the experiences and to get at different aspects of the principles of attack and defense.

7. Report on the tactics in Allan R. Bosworth's *America's Concentration Camps*.

CHAPTER 12

PRESENTATION OF

ARGUMENT

WHEN A SPEAKER PRESENTS HIS CASE TO LISTENERS, THERE ARE COMPLEX interactions which are only partly understood. Even though the ancients identified constituents such as invention, arrangement, style, and delivery, there have been rhetoricians who have chosen to emphasize only one or two of the elements. Some have stressed invention, others have concerned themselves mostly with style, while still others were elocutionists, as they were known before the turn of the century.

In this book the heavy emphasis is upon the analytical-critical dimension; consequently, treatment of style and delivery is brief. This is not to say that presentation is either irrelevant or of little significance. The point is that books in which presentation is a major concern have done a better job than this brief treatment can presume to offer.

More will become known about the functioning of presentation as new research is reported. One study will be cited as indicative of a possible trend. In this experiment the idea was to measure the effect of feedback from the audience upon a speaker's attitudes toward his subject, himself as a speaker, and his audience. Audience approval was given on a percentile scale, and a linear trend was shown.[1] Questions

[1] D. W. Huenergardt, "An Experimental Study of the Effects of Increasing Percentages of Simultaneous Non-Contingent Audience Approval on Speaker At-

concerning the kinds of speaker behavior that will induce specific kinds of feedback are in need of dependable answers. Meanwhile, we mix a modicum of description with a generous proportion of prescription while discussing composition and delivery.

COMPOSITION

Significance of Style

Liberty is infusive. Civilization stops not with the seas. Commerce is the ally of civilization. The Almighty puzzles man with the barriers of mountains and the billows of the sea, just to find out who is worthy of permanent footholds in the world. There was a moral fitness in the war with Spain. Why should barbarism blight the world when civilization occupies the ocean's wide expanse or block the course of commerce which is the servant of civilization? The sea is treacherous to ignorance, to enlightenment it is kind. . . . The sea said to Dewey, "Come this way," and in the gray dawn of the morning he carried the Stars and Stripes—the emblem of civilization—by the cannon to Cavite . . . and when the smoke had cleared away, the tax-burdened slaves of the Philippines beheld the banner of the stars triumphant in Manila Bay. The sea said to Sampson and Schley, to Clark and Wainwright, to "Fighting Bob" and "Praying Philip," "Catch Cevera and I'll give your country rich possessions near to Nevis of the Lesser Antilles, the birthplace of Alexander Hamilton," and in less than an hour the sea-gulls looked in vain for a Spanish flag.[2]

"Hot air," you say? It would be wiser to ask whether it was so evaluated by the audience in 1898. At least the above quotation helps to make the point that style *does* matter.

As a constituent of rhetoric, style means choice of words, sentence structure and movement, paragraph development, literal and figurative expression, and like matters. "Proper words in proper places" was Jonathan Swift's oversimplified definition. Wilhelm Wackernagel, in an equally general remark, said the concern of style is the surface of linguistic expression, not its substance. Both definitions are acceptable as

---

titudes" (Unpublished dissertation, Northwestern University, 1967). Ways in which audiences can influence speakers is the concern of research in verbal conditioning and reinforcement.

[2] Rep. R. G. Cousins of Iowa, "Causes and Issues of the Spanish War," Hamilton Club of Chicago, November 5, 1898.

far as they go; their weakness is their lack of specificity. In the following paragraphs we shall see that style is more than a kind of mechanical knack or a lifeless mask placed upon the body of ideas. It is the manner of linguistic expression which has been conditioned by the speaker's background, the subject, the purpose, the audience, the occasion, and possibly other factors.

Oral and written discourses do not always differ in style, although they should have distinctive characteristics more often than they do. The general reason is that listening and reading involve perceptual processes which are somewhat dissimilar. We know that listeners have the greater need for instantaneous intelligibility of the material; they cannot go back over it as readers can and do. Then too, the oral situation is more intimate or personal, hence it calls for patterns of language that are more like those of conversation. In fact, this is precisely what directness in style means.

The observations of many teachers and the findings of a few empirical studies support several generalizations concerning the differences between oral and written styles. These are estimates of central tendencies; consequently, exceptions are to be expected. Oral style tends to use fewer complex sentences, fewer interrogative and imperative sentences, fewer uncommon words, and less formal English. But oral style has simpler sentences, shorter and more loosely structured sentences, more repetition and restatement, simpler words and contractions, more idioms, and vastly more devices of direct discourse. For these reasons someone has declared that a speech is not just an essay standing on its hind legs!

If we turn from the viewpoint of the listener to that of the speaker, we can understand another dimension of the differences between oral and written styles. The writer has more interest in permanence and artistry, while the speaker must be more concerned with immediate effect, as Wichelns has explained.[3] Thus the speaker cannot be as leisurely in his composition; he must quickly adapt to changing moods in his listeners if he would increase their involvement in what he is saying. Note the directness of real talk in this extract from a student's prepared speech:

"How do you explain the fact that you own an album of Paul Robeson records? Didn't you join a liberal club in college? Do you deny having de-

[3] H. A. Wichelns, "The Literary Criticism of Oratory," *Studies in Rhetoric and Public Speaking* (N.Y.: Century Co., 1925).

bated in favor of United Nations membership for Communist China when you were in school? Your answers to questions such as these can cost you plenty some day."

Most of us could, with slight effort, cite passages from speeches or quote testimonials to indicate the importance of style. Daniel Webster said on this point, "For, depend upon it, it is with our thoughts as with our persons—their intrinsic value is mostly undervalued, unless outwardly expressed in an attractive garb." This does not imply one style for all persons and times. There must be adaptations to speakers, subjects, occasions, and audiences. A style which seems tactless, crude, dull, stilted, mechanical, humorless, or otherwise ill-suited will damage the ethos of the speaker. Students who give argumentative speeches in class or in contest debates need to stress the communication of ideas, attitudes, and feelings—not merely the jargon of the practice exercise or the game, however they view it. These and other expressions are frequently used to excess: *colleague, post hoc, ergo, propter hoc, burden of proof, so we see, need, plan, inconsistency,* and *proved beyond a doubt.*

Perhaps we would not use such poor oral composition if we took more time to plan our remarks and practiced extemporizing in the presence of critics who cared. This is not to say that the hazards of extemporaneous speaking can be eliminated. Spontaneity occasionally exacts a price: a sentence that goes nowhere, a grammatical error, a barbarism, and even an embarrassing double-entendre. The following are specimens of "The White House Syntax Problem"[4] with ad libbing in press conferences:

Eisenhower, April 9, 1958: "I have not had an official or exhaustive poll made of this thing, but my mail shows that; except for a number of people come in and they have a particular excise tax, but it is always applying to the particular business in which they are engaged. That seems to be a favorite point in the correspondence that comes to me, but I notice this: it's that *particular* tax, and they want to show how we can keep all the others off the books."

Kennedy, January 15, 1962: "We're talking about $2 billion a year which we are now, I think that we—I'm hopeful that we can use our productive power well in this field. But I think the question of the balance and I think that [the Presidential Assistant] and [the Secretary of Agriculture] in my judgment will be in balance by the time they go before the Congress."

In commenting upon this "sprawling syntax," *Time* said it was "a little hard to guess which President said what." The writer must not

4 *Time,* January 26, 1962, p. 18.

have noticed that *hopeful* and *judgment* were two of Kennedy's favorite words.

Desirable Qualities

Emphasis, force, and *vigor* can be grouped into one desirable quality of oral style. The opposite quality is styled as weak, tame, drab, colorless, lifeless, or dull. Animated, colorful style suggests an active mind and responsive emotions behind it. It permits the listeners to hear, see, and feel what the speaker thinks and how he feels about it. In order to achieve emphasis through word choice, speakers use short and specific words, active voice, affective language, and short groupings of words. To get emphasis by the selection of supporting details, they use figures of speech, vivid experiences, quotations from highly regarded sources, dramatized ideas, striking facts, and emotive allusions, to literature, for instance. Achieving emphasis by means of sentence arrangement involves choices among these devices: suspense-order or climax-order of key ideas, antithesis and balance in some sentences, varied sentence structures, placing strong words at beginnings and ends, and giving more space to important materials. It is well known that the principal emphatic devices are intensives (*profoundly, deeply,* etc.), repetition, position, and pause (in delivery).

Accuracy means grammatical correctness, precision of denotation and connotation, fidelity of sentence to idea, specificity of words, and the ability to express desired nuances of meaning. When this quality is lacking we get verbal atrocities: *enormity* misused to mean *enormousness, disinterested* for *uninterested, imply* for *infer, lion's share* for *larger part, American way* for *my way of doing things,* and *un-American* or *socialistic* or *communistic* referring to *people, ideas, and practices I dislike intensely.* Some writers on semantics call these "blah" words.

How can accuracy in oral style be improved? One suggestion is to select simple, familiar, specific words which have relatively precise referents. An abridged dictionary, by the way, is of little value when words like *discrimination* and *reasonable* are at issue. Extremists on both sides avidly seize upon whichever one of several listed meanings suits their purposes, and in the case of *discrimination,* the choices could be *ability to make nice distinctions* (virtue word) or *unfair* or *injurious distinction* (bad word). A second suggestion is the use of apt illustration, called by Beecher "a window in an argument." Other means include the use of vivid description, the citation of specifics that constitute a generalization, and, best of all, a systematic program of personal vocabulary improvement.

Suggestiveness is the quality which enables a speaker's language to say more than the words explicitly state. For one thing, it says something about the speaker. As Buffon put it, "Style is the man himself." One implication of this is the individuality of style, which should warn us against imitating the styles of others. The charge of affectation is the imitator's reward. In some of the writings and speeches in the appendixes there are interesting specimens of suggestive style. Here are a few of the connotations a reader might notice concerning certain persons or ideas: that someone was naive, that someone felt his adversary to be inferior to himself, that a situation was intolerably bad, that there was a shameful motive behind an act, and that of course we want the United States to be ahead of all other countries in whatever one is discussing.

Directness in the mental sense is a function of style. The goal is a conversational quality but only in the best sense of the word. The sloppiness of much conversation is not being held up as a standard. What we do want is the spontaneity, genuineness, and intellectual crackle of the most stimulating conversation. Assuming that a speaker has something worth hearing, he can improve his directness by means of certain adaptive techniques. He can adapt his expressions to the experiences of his listeners, the purpose of his speech, and the occasion, for instance. A direct speaker senses what his listeners think and feel, and he adjusts to them, even though he does not intend to agree with their conclusions. He uses their experiences and talks their language. Devices of direct discourse—questions, answers, imaginary dialogue, personal pronouns—are specifically intended to increase directness. Observe the directness of Newton Minow's "Vast Wasteland" speech.

Unobtrusiveness or ease characterizes an oral style that does not call attention to itself, either because of its polish or because of its roughness. If there be ornament, it should be used without a suggestion of display or pomposity. The style should not "smell of the lamp," an ancient way of saying that one's style should not sound as if he had worked on it far into the night. Nor should it sound as if the total preparation had taken place in the few minutes between classes. Appropriate language cannot be precisely prescribed for all occasions, but at least one can avoid any superfluous "big" words, immoderate language, boners, and the like. Some speakers have achieved unobtrusiveness with figurative and rhythmic prose, others with rather plain styles. The test is the listeners' subjective appraisal; if they think a speaker is more concerned with his language than his ideas and his listeners, they will consider his style obtrusive.

Clearness is, from many points of view, the most important quality of oral and written discourse. Although we cannot literally convey our ideas to others, we can use audible and visible symbols which our audiences interpret in their own terms. Thus the clarity of our symbolization is of great importance. There must be a community of reference between a speaker and his audience if clearness is to be achieved. This implies the importance of audience analysis beforehand and some feedback during and after the speech. Two test questions are suggested: Will the typical listener understand the arguments? Will the best-informed listeners find the arguments impossible to misunderstand?

If we may assume that a given speaker's thinking is clear, which is assuming a great deal, there are steps he can take to clarify his verbal expression. The use of specific and concrete language to clarify general and abstract concepts is one such step. Those who follow each abstraction with a "for instance" are using this procedure. Generalities have their place, but it is not to disguise shallow ideas. Specificity in language means closeness to reality, as in saying "a tall, slender, sharp-featured man" instead of just "a man." Concreteness refers to physical substance as in "Honest Joe," while the abstraction would be "honesty." Other aids to clearness are the minimal use of involved sentences, a serious attempt to use the language of the audience, the development of a smooth progression of ideas which make the drift of the speech clear, and the use of definition where needed for instantaneous intelligibility.

Variety or freshness implies originality and imagination as opposed to monotony and banality. Attention and interest are often captured and held by this quality of style. Two intercollegiate speech events have provided some negative instances of variety. A winning oration in 1961 opened with this trite sentence: "Picture, if you will, a jury room in one of our large Midwestern cities." Each speaker in the West Point final debate of 1962 seemed to have some favorite words which were used to excess. The unedited tape reveals the frequent use of these sentence openers: *and then, this then, but then, and then, then what, now, well, what about,* and *one, two, three.* There is a figure of speech called anaphora, which involves the use of the same beginning in a series of clauses or sentences, but the repetition of *then* in the example above grew tiresome. However, it was no worse than "stranger than fiction," "better late than never," "it's a small world," "teeming millions," and "usually reliable sources."

Figures of Speech

Any scholarly effort to distinguish between the characteristic figures of speech in oral discourse and those in written discourse would have to be based upon an extensive survey using the technique of content analysis. This would mean defining the figures, finding and counting them in a large number of speeches and essays, and determining in which mode of discourse each figure was more likely to appear. This has not been done here. Instead, the familiar figures of speech will be discussed under "Oral Composition," even though they appear in written discourse as well.

Simile is a somewhat exact form of comparison, and it is identified by the presence of *like* or *as*. It seems to come to mind more readily than the subtler metaphor, and for that reason it is typically an oral device. When a likeness is developed at greater length and is used as a form of reasoning, we call it either an argument from comparison or an analogy, depending upon whether the parallel is literal or figurative. This simile appeared in a student's speech on a constitutional controversy: "Two of the basic principles of democracy are like two pillars which support the arch: one the principle that all men are equally entitled to life, liberty, and the pursuit of happiness, and the other the belief that such opportunity will best advance our civilization."

Contrast or antithesis means the juxtaposition of opposites in order to highlight differences. Advocates often use it to show the differences between the present situation and a proposed change, or between affirmative and negative plans. A student speaker said, ". . . first in war, last in peace; talk big, but act little." Another student contrasted the sudden type of war we knew in 1917 and 1941 with the long, uncertain, smoldering kind of conflicts we have to cope with nowadays.

Direct discourse, which has been alluded to earlier, takes several forms, four of which are popular in speechmaking. They are pronouns of the first and second person, quotation or dialogue, rhetorical question, and questions and answers. The personal pronouns are *I, my, mine, me, we, our, ours, us, you, your,* and *yours.* They can increase the personal touch in a speech, but the first four can, if not used judiciously, suggest a speaker who is self-centered. Real or imaginary conversation can improve directness through creating the illusion of real talk, as in

"I'd rather be found in the beam of an enemy searchlight than in the awful glare of an understanding woman." In the strict sense, a rhetorical question is interrogative in form but not intent. The speaker expects listeners to infer the desired response, as in this example: "Shall our mineral wealth sleep undeveloped in the soil? Shall our waterpower run idle, and the bustle of our factories cease? Shall our laborers go unemployed?" Sometimes a speaker leaves nothing to chance; he answers his own question. In that event the question is not rhetorical. Here is a combination of dialogue and question: "Joe, the Italian boy who worked next to me, wants to ask a question: 'What is more important—the tin can or the man?' To whom shall he go for the answer? To the foreman? . . ."

Exaggeration for emphasis rather than for deceit is called hyperbole. It is popular in political controversy. According to many campaigners, disaster looms just before each election, and it can be averted only by voting as the speaker requests. Rufus Choate's use of hyperbole in this specimen is less heavy-handed and much more fanciful than the average:

> I would as soon think of bounding a sovereign state on the north by a dandelion, on the east by a bluejay, on the south by a hive of bees in swarming time, and on the west by three hundred foxes with firebrands tied to their tails, as of relying upon the loose and indefinite bounds of commissioners a century ago.

Sarcasm and ridicule should be marked "handle with care." Even if a speaker does not hesitate to hurt the feelings of his personal target, he should ponder the probability that his listeners will think less favorably of him for his unkind remark. Any unsportsmanlike, ill-mannered, or intemperate remark may undermine a speaker's ethos. In sarcasm the distinguishing feature is its harshness; it has none of the playfulness of some satire and irony: "If your plan is so good, why don't you call up the President and tell him about it?" In the heat of a high school debate, one boy said with reference to his opponent's Western footwear: "He has to wear cowboy boots so he can wade away from the lectern after his speech." With reference to ridicule, a professor of philosophy once said, "If it's ridiculous, why not ridicule it?" The answer is that ridiculing a foolish idea is not so bad if one can resist the temptation to ridicule the person. True, the two are not easy to separate, but many of us do not even make an attempt to separate them.

Metaphor is a short, compact, and implied comparison. It serves to arouse images, gain attention, and enable persons to see significant resemblances. "Our present mode of making appointments is a blind-fold game," said Carl Schurz. A student orator used this metaphor: "Without freedom of thought . . . we can blow out the light and fight it out in the dark . . ."

Metaphors are risky in extemporaneous speaking because of the probability of mixing them and producing boners: "We must bring this deadly viper (liquor traffic) to its knees." "The administration has knifed the male students in the back once again. Maybe this time they've hit the straw that will break the camel's back."

Irony and satire are related but not identical. When a writer or a speaker implies something quite different from what he says, either to amuse or to hold up to disapproval, he is using irony. Thus a writer who intensely disliked the late publisher of the *Chicago Tribune* referred to him as "that eminent historian, learned military strategist, political philosopher, savior of America, and expert on revised spelling." Satire may include irony or sarcasm used for serious, playful, or malicious purposes. For example, when the English customs officers imposed a duty on some crates of snow which were imported from Norway for a ski-jumping contest, a satirist wrote, "Ready, men? Watch out for French air in the bicycle tires, Swiss mud on the ski boots, Italian sunburn, Continental élan."

Lesser figures include alliteration, pun, onomatopoeia, interjection, and some others the names of which either amuse or astound. Alliteration means the use of the same letter or sound at the beginning of a series of words, as in "cunningly concocted," "only the bunting but not the blood," and "haughty, hating Tories." Imitative words suggest natural sounds, as in *buzz, whirr,* and *splash.* This interjection was written in a prepared speech: "The continued security of our country demands that we aid the enslaved millions of Europe—yes, even of Germany—to win back their liberty and independence." Amplification by climax order was used by Debs: "I said then, I say now, that while there is a lower class, I am in it; while there is a criminal element, I am of it; while there is a soul in prison, I am not free." Style like this is rarely an impromptu phenomenon; it takes practice and time.

Some Compositional Steps

After having done the preparatory steps up to and including the outlining of a case, the advocate is ready to compose sentences and paragraphs either orally or in writing. The typical logical outline does not make interesting listening or reading; it requires some modification or dressing-up in terms of attention factors, audience receptiveness, and what Kenneth Burke calls symbolic strategies. It is assumed here that we are discussing argumentative discourse of serious purpose rather than that communication which is mere ritual, magic, or catharsis.

It may be, for example, that the overall deductive structure of the preparation outline is not psychologically the most acceptable to the audience. In that case one could invert the rank-order of subpoints, use the implicative order, or open with a master example or a series of illustrations. For an unfavorable audience one might begin with accepted facts, beliefs, and values in order to gain a hearing. Here we are concerned with the psychology of acceptance, not in any sense meaning that adaptation requires the sacrifice of ethical and logical responsibilities.

Sentence construction would presumably follow the adaptation of the outline to suit the task at hand. The principles of construction will be taken to apply to either oral or written composition, even though in the finer points there are dissimilarities. It is, incidentally, recommended that extempore speakers practice writing to improve their style. The following sentence in a student's argumentative editorial was also a paragraph. Its construction exemplifies some of the problems we face in writing and in criticizing the writing of others:

> To sneer on the small jobs that are being done toward this end and to suggest that there is no starting point is an advocation of an inert attitude that would hope for prejudice and discrimination to be eradicated by their own momentum.

One may say that a sentence is defective if it fails to represent the writer's purpose or his view of the subject matter; also, if it does not improve the reader's grasp of the subject, or if it actually confuses him. A systematic study, including writing of sentence elements, the ordering of the elements, and the relationships among those elements is the best way to effect the desired improvement.

Paragraph development is the second major step in the composing process. In argumentative writing one is concerned with logical paragraphs as distinguished from the chronological and the impressionistic. A logical paragraph begins with a topic sentence which was a point or a subpoint in the case outline. The rest of the paragraph supports the topic sentence with reasons, evidence, and kindred materials. Suppose a writer has a case outline in which the first point in partition is set up like this:

I. —
  A. —
    1. —
    2. —
  B. —
    1. —
    2. —

How many paragraphs should he write? For a short essay he might write only one or two paragraphs, but for a longer case he might easily write four. Much of what has been written in this book pertains to the process of building such paragraphs.

Revision of the resulting manuscript can be accomplished by adding, deleting, and changing. Content, arrangement, and style—especially style at this stage—are possible candidates for revision. One writer should have done a bit of editing on this sentence: "My feelings in the matter are not alone, as I have many upright citizens who are friends of mine and of yours who agree with me that the present action of the city and Northwestern is uncalled for." The following paragraph was in the first draft of a written speech:

The second organization that I would consider this afternoon is the Rio Pact, the pact of defensive nature that exists between the nations of the Western Hemisphere. One major defect of this organization is its limited membership, that is, it only concerns the Western Hemisphere. And aside from that, again, it does not provide for the economic bolstering of Europe. It does not provide a coordinated propaganda attack or approach to the Russian people.

Below is the revised draft of the above paragraph from a student's speech manuscript:

Thus it appears that the largest international organization, the United Nations, has some serious defects. "But," you may ask, "is there no other scheme that will help?" Perhaps there is. Let us consider a second attempt, the Rio Pact. As you probably know, this is a defense pact among the nations of this hemisphere. That is of some value, to be sure. But this regional defense pact has three weaknesses which may concern us seriously. It includes *only* the nations in *our* part of the world. It does not do anything about the economic bolstering of Europe. It provides no way to influence the captive peoples behind the "iron curtain."

Hints From Semantics[5]

Language is much more than choice of words for stylistic grace or for "rightness" according to a dictionary. It is part of our thought

[5] J. C. Condon, Jr., *Semantics and Communication* (New York: The Macmillan Co., 1966), pp. 1–112 and reading list 112–115.

process and, indeed, of our total behavior. There is more to it than this brief sketch can suggest, but a few practical hints may be of some help until a student reads specialized books on style and the psychology of language.

Of the several functions that words serve in our language, three are especially relevant here: to label or describe in a neutral manner, to evaluate or to reveal an attitude, and to evaluate under the guise of labelling. Difficulties stem from intentional and innocent confusion among these kinds of usage, as in assuming that all or most language usage is neutral.[6] *Man, law, order, fascist, peace, freedom,* and many other words *can* be used neutrally, but often they are not. The surrounding context of verbal language, vocal inflection, and gesture make the difference. One can utter the word *man* so as to suggest a he-man, an effeminate male, or the dictionary meaning. If their intent is understood, words that evaluate are not as troublesome as they might otherwise be. Herein lies the risk in metaphorical language. It may be intended to communicate, but it can also be a substitute for thought. It is, generally speaking, risky to analyze and elaborate upon metaphors in argument. The first two kinds of language are much less troublesome in argumentation than the evaluative when it masquerades as labelling, denoting, or reporting. When a speaker orates for law and order, is he objectively describing a societal condition, or is he actually in favor of a police state, or is he merely complaining about some excesses? It is easy to have order in a police state, and it is possible to have laws and law enforcement to maintain that kind of order, but is that what is meant? Listeners and readers owe it to themselves to ask, and speakers and writers have an ethical-logical responsibility to divulge their meanings, even without being challenged to do so.

From the study of semantics one can get many more helpful suggestions, a few of which will be briefly noted here. One is that our words for realities are not the realities themselves, and this is why naming something does not entail understanding. One can pin the "fascist" or "communist" or "conservative" label on a person without understanding either the person or the philosophy. Another precept is that perception and inference are not identical, even though they are often taken to be so. The difference between what a witness saw and what he reported seeing was mentioned under the tests of evidence. Our penchant for abstractions, as in making generalizations, is a mixed blessing; it enables us to make order out of chaos, but it can draw us far

6 J. W. Bowers in Miller and Nilsen, (eds.) *Perspectives* . . . , Chap. 7.

from reality, too. Perhaps this suggests an explanation for the increased interest in existentialism: a rebellion against the tyranny of abstractions. When speaking of persons, things, and ideas, we classify, apply adjectives, and recall associations in ways that create bias for or against. Two-valued orientation, polar terms, or "good guys and bad guys" are the familiar names for this phenomenon. Finally, the dating of an item is an important qualifier. *When* did the quoted authority say we should increase the rediscount rate? Conditions may have changed so much since he made that statement that he would now say something quite different. "Economic conditions, 1970" is not the same statement as "economic conditions, 1965."

DELIVERY

As the introduction to composition pointed out, a brief treatment in this book does not imply a lack of importance in the total process of communication. Quite the contrary, this work concurs in Bryant's view[7] that style and utterance merit serious attention both in teaching and in criticism. As McBath and Cripe explain, published studies exist that tell us something about the importance of presentation, and the interrelationships between style and delivery are too important to be overlooked, and yet numerous teachers defensively avoid any identification with what some refer to pejoratively as "mere skills."[8]

Expressive Voice

Vocal aspects of delivery add meaning to what is said. Listeners judge how a speaker means his remarks, and they derive impressions of his personality through the suggestive impact of his presentation. A voice that is to communicate and thereby influence others must be heard, be pleasant (or not unpleasant) to listen to, and not be so unusual as to distract attention from the message.

---

[7] D. C. Bryant, "Critical Responsibilities of the Speech-English Program," *The Speech Teacher*, X, (1961), 277.

[8] J. H. McBath and N. M. Cripe, "Delivery: Rhetoric's Rusty Canon," *Journal of the American Forensic Association*, II, No. 1 (1965), 1–6.

Melody, which is expressive modulation in pitch, is absent in monotonous voices. Dull, flat voices inadequately express ideas that require sincerity, animation, and intensity. Exercises for drill in vocal variety include questions and answers, dialogue between characters, and assertions which are to be given several meanings by changing the vocal melody.

Time or rate can be too fast or too slow. Tournament debaters as a class belong in the first category. However, a halting, *and-uh, well-er* rate can be even more annoying. Variety in pause, rhythm, and rate prevents the monorate form of indirectness and facilitates the communication of nuances of meaning.

Force or emphasis enables one to be heard without electronic augmentation. A speaker must make himself heard, and he should vary his loudness or his intensity to indicate the stress he wishes to place on each word or phrase. Vocal force in speech serves the same function as underlining and exclamation marks do in writing. While using force in this way, a speaker should maintain a reserve for use in moments of maximum emphasis.

Quality is suggestively related to the sincerity and intensity of a speaker's emotional reactions. Listeners are influenced by the clarity, purity, resonance, and general timbre of vocal sounds. A responsive vocal instrument can convey the emotional color that stems from genuine feeling. Voices that squeak, whine, whisper, wheeze, or rasp do not make oral argument sound impressive. We prefer a voice that suggests integrity, self-assurance, warmth, and other positive attributes.

Articulation is the process of shaping the consonants with the action of tongue, lips, jaw, and soft palate. Intelligibility and even social acceptability are impaired by slurred articulation, strange accents, mispronunciation, and some dialects or regional peculiarities. Some of the common faults are lisping, infantilism, tight jaw, and talking with a foreign substance in the mouth. Clinical attention is suggested for cases that do not respond to simple drills.

Visible Aspects

The visible code includes posture, movement, gesture (including facial expression), eye contact, and external visual aids. It is important because audiences look as well as listen, and because the *whole* person speaks. The visible part of delivery suggests something of the personality, aids in conveying meaning, provides emphasis, adds variety, helps to hold attention, serves as an outlet for nervous energy, and stirs up emphatic responses in the audience.

Mechanical directions on stance and movement are elocutionary and passé. This is not to disparage the use of general hints. First, effective movement is coordinated, meaning that all of the body must work as a unit. Second, the whole body should be animated and respond to what the voice and the language say. Third, all action is better when integrated with the ideas, inwardly motivated, and somewhat uninhibited. Fourth, there should be some reserve in a speaker's action, that is, action should be spontaneous yet controlled. But the reading of these general hints will not serve to modify the physical behavior of many student speakers. They need also to be observed and criticized by qualified teachers. These seemingly slight behavioral changes are not ends in themselves; they contribute to that abstract but priceless quality, stage presence.

Meaning of Extempore

In the literature of public speaking, *extempore* does not mean offhand or without preparation, as some dictionaries have it. When speech people speak of completely unprepared or ad lib speaking, they call it *impromptu*. Extempore, extemporaneous, or "extemp." speaking is the kind of public address in which the speaker knows in advance what, in general, he is going to say, but in which the final composition takes place during the act of speaking. The speaking advocate knows his proposition; he has analyzed and investigated it; he has assembled his proof; he has outlined his case. It may be that he has also modified the outline into speaking notes and has learned his opening and closing paragraphs. There remains only the task of composing oral sentences and paragraphs while he speaks. *Only* is deceptively simple. The best extemporaneous speech has the desirable qualities of good conversation plus appropriate modifications in rate, sentence structure, and vocabulary. It is prepared yet flexible. It is not read, done from memory, or given without preparation; it is composed from notes by the speaker while he is speaking. Anyone who cannot learn from this exposition the nature of extemporaneous speaking can be assured that participation in the direct-clash assignment will remedy the deficiency.

Directness is the quality most to be cultivated in speaking. It is a complex function of attitude, eye contact, physical control, ideas, style, arrangement, and perhaps other elements. It comes across even by radio when the speaker is invisible to his hearers. However, it does not require courtesy, open-mindedness, or other virtues unless the audience expects and respects them. One can cite amazingly effective speakers, as judged by immediate results, who shouted and snarled, incited their hearers to burn and kill, and treated their opposition with scorn. But, as has been said so often in this book, what about the ethical-logical responsibilities?

QUESTIONS

1. In terms of your own observation, what would be a fair statement of the role of presentation in oral argument?
2. Comment upon the style of the obviously written messages in Appendix E.
3. Evaluate the oral styles in Appendixes B and C.
4. Identify and evaluate the figures of speech in designated speeches or essays.
5. Comment upon the potential usefulness of these words in speechmaking (they appear in W. F. Buckley's *The Unmaking of a Mayor*): appoggiaturas, eschaton, epicene, triptych, paralogist, diaspora, succubi, salvific, pastiche, chiliastic, usufruct and saprophytic.

EXERCISES

1. Recast an essay (Appendix D or E or another) into a speech as you would care to give it. Explain the differences you have seen fit to make.
2. Prepare a manuscript of a short argumentative speech. After someone else has read it and made comments, prepare a revision.
3. Compile critical notes on a round of extemporaneous argumentative speeches or a series of debate exercises. Note the matters of style which

were treated in this chapter. A played-back tape would aid in the corrective procedure.

4. Discuss the kind and the qualities of style in a piece which is satirical or ironical. Might it have the effect of argument? One specimen is Harry Golden's "My P-T Plan" in *Saturday Review*, January 17, 1959.

5. Report on an amusing discussion of metaphors by L. Rogers in the *New York Times Book Review*, July 9, 1967, Section 7, p. 2.

CHAPTER 13

EVALUATING

ARGUMENT

ONE WHO HAS STUDIED THE PRINCIPLES OF ARGUMENTATION FOR SOME weeks can be presumed to have some interest and competence in evaluating, criticizing, or judging advocatory discourse. What will be sketched here in brief compass is a sort of critical apparatus to be used for that purpose. However, it is not intended as a judge's ballot for use in tournament debating. It is more nearly a review of some of the main topics which have been treated in earlier chapters.

First, whether we have a unilateral presentation or a debate, what is the basis of the controversy? What kind of proposition or resolution is that statement? What kind of debate would be involved if both sides were heard from? Who is on which side? Who, therefore, has the burden of proof? What are the other responsibilities and opportunities of the parties?

Second, in relation to the crux of analysis, how is the proposition interpreted? In terms of the kind of proposition involved, were the proper issues found? What concessions were made to the exigencies of popular persuasion? Was the intended partitioning of cases made clear in the opening statements? Were any basic assumptions left unstated? If so, what effect might this have upon the candor of a case?

Third, was the case clearly and cogently organized? Did it meet the responsibilities as mentioned in the first criterion above? Which type of case was it? Did it meet the criteria for that type of case plan? If affirmative, was it prima facie? If negative, did it make an adequate reply? Did the logic of the points above the level of evidence measure up?

Fourth, in supporting the case structure, did the advocate or advocates know enough about the subject and effectively bring evidence to bear? Here the tests of evidence apply, but the problem of what to accept as the basis for each unit of argument is so involved that a review of the traditional tests of evidence will not suffice. For instance, without getting down to the finer points on the principles of acceptability, we can distinguish five bases or grounds of acceptance of material offered as evidence: direct experience, inherited belief, authoritative source, self-evidence ("We hold these truths to be self-evident . . ."), and intellectual scrutiny, which *could* go so far as to lead to infinite regress.[1]

Historically there have been, and there continue to be, four major barriers to the rigorous testing of evidence. One is the unsettled question of truth: what it is, where it comes from, and what it has to do with advocacy anyway. In ancient logic and in philosophy prior to this century, argument was conceived of as a search for truth. Plato is often cited on this point. But there are two limitations of that notion: one cannot be certain when one has the truth, and the value premises we deal with are not true or false. We also know that works of the imagination can be accepted as such, and that imperative ("should") statements as in propositions of policy can be deliberated on. Some current theories of knowledge have broadened our definition of truth beyond the empirical, which is experiential, to include the analytic, which is in language.

A second barrier, which has been discussed in relation to definitions of proof and as a part of the classification of fallacies, may be called emotional irrelevancy. Erroneous acceptance—or rejection, for that matter—can often be attributed to the psychology of persuasion. The crucial question is this: Are the emotional considerations relevant or not? When Beard, the historian, hypothesized that the economic bias of certain "Founding Fathers" may have accounted for parts of our Constitution, his explanation was widely and vehemently denounced solely on emotional grounds.

---

[1] See Angell, *Reasoning and Logic,* pp. 395–413; Beardsley, *Thinking Straight,* pp. 41–42; H. S. Leonard, *Principles of Right Reason* (N. Y.: Henry Holt and Co., 1957), pp. 57–73.

The third barrier, which some call semantic, relates to the ambiguity of our all-purpose language. The same words may be used in science, logic, literature, and humor, to list but four, and this omnibus language is potentially deceptive. As we have seen, fallacies of language and confusion of fact and value often occur.

Finally, the acceptability or unacceptability of the setting in which an argument appears may interfere with intellectual testing. It is not at all uncommon to read or hear about allegedly inconsistent behavior in which persons accept an argument or a premise of an argument in one context while rejecting it in another. For instance, "Honesty is the best policy," except when one thinks "a little white lie" would help.

Fifth, after the testing of evidence, was the logic of argument sound? Here we mean rational acceptability, not the psychology of reward and punishment in relation to reasons and conclusions. Intelligence in discourse consists mainly in grasping the implications of one's beliefs, points, or arguments. Here the main concepts of Chapter 8 are relevant. The kinds, tests, and fallacies of argument are of central importance in this kind of critical analysis. Laying out each argument to determine where it begins, where it concludes, and how it got there is the first step. Thereafter the steps of classifying each argument and applying the appropriate tests may be undertaken.

Sixth, if this question was not raised in connection with the fourth or the fifth, what forms of support other than evidence and logic were used, and what impact did they have upon the intellectual acceptability of the arguments? If they contribute mainly to emotional acceptability, and if the questioner knows this and does not delude himself concerning the grounds of his acceptance, who should cavil?

Seventh, if two sides were presented in debate, and after the affirmative case has been evaluated as in question three, how good was the negative attack upon it? What arguments were attacked, how were they attacked, and with what effect upon the case as a whole? If there was an affirmative rejoinder, what procedures were used, on what points, and to what effect?

Eighth, at least in educational settings, what was the quality of the presentation, whether in a single presentation or a debate, or in an oral or a written medium? On strictly intellectual grounds this question is irrelevant except for the minimal requirement that an advocate's case must be understood before it can be evaluated fairly. But beyond the matter of minimal communication, how shall we deal with differences between advocates in popularity, reputation, and presentational skills?

In practical affairs one cannot, realistically speaking, rule out personal appeal, emotional appeal, and delivery skills. Instead, as the discussion of the fourth criterion-question explained, the solution is to recognize what is going on, decide upon a standard of judgment, and let the chips fall where they may.

EXERCISES

1. Evaluate the argumentation in a one-sided presentation, such as Appendix B.
2. Evaluate a short exchange, such as Appendix E.
3. Evaluate, or give a critic's decision on, the debate in Appendix C. (A critic judges on the merits of the debating, a legislator judges on his preference for an outcome, and a juror judges on the convincingness of evidence.)

APPENDIX A

CASE OUTLINES

AFFIRMATIVE AND NEGATIVE ON A PROPOSITION FOR SCHOOL DEBATING[1] (Resolved, that the federal government should provide complete medical care for all citizens at public expense).

AFFIRMATIVE

Introduction

Affirmative philosophy rests upon three assumptions: complete medical care is the right of all citizens; it is the responsibility of government to provide essential care which individuals cannot provide for themselves; all citizens should have equal health care opportunities.

Discussion

I. Significant harms result from failure to have complete medical care for all citizens, for

[1] Adapted from materials prepared by students in the National High School Institute in Speech at Northwestern University, August, 1963.

A. Much loss could be prevented with adequate medical care if disease is detected early, because
   1. Many deaths and illnesses could be prevented with prompt and early treatment, for
      a) "At least 90,000 lives are lost needlessly each year because of chronic illness. If these diseases were caught in time, at least these 90,000 could have been saved." (E. E. Witte, *Social Security Perspectives*, 1963.)
   2. Many days of work and school are lost due to illness that could be prevented, for
      a) "A total of 250.3 million days were lost by workers during 1960. On an average day during that year, there were 1,050,000 employees absent from work." (Health Insurance Institute, *Source Book of Health Insurance Data*, 1962, p. 8.

B. Many unnecessary deaths and illnesses occur because people are unable to pay for adequate medical care, for
   1. Income is the overwhelming determining factor of the ability to get needed medical care. (University of Michigan Study Appearing in the Report to the Senate Finance Committee, June, 1960.)

C. There is a great national injury suffered because of unnecessary death and illness, because
   1. National efficiency is hurt because of work days lost, for
      a) "Employed Americans lose millions of days of work each year because of acute illness, the U.S. National Health Survey reports. A total of 250.3 million days were lost by workers in 1960. On an average day during the year, there were 1,051,000 employees absent from work." (Department of Health, Education, and Welfare, U.S. Health Survey, 1962.)
   2. Contagious diseases are a threat to national health, for
      a) "Eight hundred thousand Americans with serious contagious diseases need medical supervision to protect the health of the general public, but four hundred thousand of these—that's one half—are receiving no supervision of any kind." (*Public Health Reports*, 1960.)

D. Certain groups of the population have particularly poor health, for

 1. The aged have poor health, for
    a) "While the aged constitute about 9 per cent of the population, they make up more than 55 per cent of all persons with limitations due to chronic illness." (*Basic Facts on the Health and Economic Status of Older Americans*, June, 1961.)
 2. The indigent have poor health, for
    a) "Most forms of cancer, arthritis, asthma, respiratory infection, disorders of the genital organs, and skin diseases are more prevalent among the poor. Even heart disease, commonly regarded as the affliction of bankers and executives, occurs at higher rates among people of lower income." (A Committee of Physicians, *Monthly Review*, September, 1960.)

E. General health levels of the U.S. are not as high as needed or desirable, for
 1. Infant death rates are lower in other countries, for
    a) "Our infant mortality rate per 1,000 live births in 1958, was 26.9 which compares with 23.9 in the United Kingdom, 22.2 in Switzerland, and 15.8 in Sweden." (Marion B. Folsom, "Goals of a National Health Program for Meeting Needs," *Annals of the American Academy*, September, 1961.)
 2. Life expectancy is higher in other countries, for
    a) "Dr. O. L. Peterson, Assistant Director of the Rockefeller Foundation, reported that a dozen countries in the world have lower mortality rates than the United States, that Americans see a doctor more often (5.3 visits a year) than Britons (4.7) or Swedes (2.5) and that the citizens of the United States have the shortest life span of the three countries." (*New York Times*, August 30, 1962.)

II. The economic flaws in the present system are serious and inherent, for
 A. The cost of medical care is high and rising, because
  1. The cost of medical care is high and growing faster than the average consumer price index, for
     a) ". . . we find that the cost of medical care has been increasing at a faster rate than any other part of the cost-of-living index. The overall increase in consumer prices

from 1947 to December 1960 has been 27.5 per cent. The cost of medical care during that same period has increased 58 per cent or more than twice . . ." (M. B. Folsom, *Annals of the American Academy*, September, 1961.)

2. This trend will continue, and
3. The cost of medical care is rising faster than the per capita income, and
4. Hospital, doctor, and drug costs have risen greatly, for
   a) "The biggest increase has been in hospital rates, which have risen since 1947–9, 123 per cent. Other health costs have risen in this fashion: physician's fees, 45 per cent; dental care, 37 per cent, eye care, 21 per cent, drugs, 23 per cent. Health Insurance premiums are up, too—for instance, hospitalization policies cost 74 per cent more now than in 1952." (*Changing Times*, "Budgeting for Medical Bills," June, 1961.)
5. People are spending a greater portion of their income on medicine, for
   a) "They put out close to $20 billion a year now—about 6 per cent of their disposable income. In 1950, it took about 4½ per cent of disposable income." (*Business Week*, "Health Insurance: Why Spending Is Soaring," June 24, 1961, p. 148.)

B. The causes of the cost increase are inherent in our medical system, for
   1. In general, this cost increase is the result of medicine's being a private business, and
   2. Some hospital cost increases are due to essential specialization and research for better equipment, and
   3. Doctors' fees increase for inherent reasons, for
      a) Attempts to provide comprehensive medical care under a fee-for-service system have always resulted in progressive pyramiding of costs. (Dr. George Baehr, *Doctors, Patients and Government*, 1953.)
   4. High drug costs are caused by tremendous mark-ups necessary to make a profit, support publicity campaigns, engage in research, and provide a profit for the several middlemen involved, for
      a) ". . . some prescription drugs have been marked up

7,000 per cent by the time they reach the sickroom table."
(William Michelfelder, *It's Cheaper to Die*, 1960, p. 15.)
5. Cost increases result from the wasteful duplication of our
medical facilities, for
    a) ". . . another general problem needing urgent attention
is the lack of proper coordination of health activities.
There is far too much duplication of effort and far too
little overall planning at local, state and national levels.
Our resources of men and money could be employed more
profitably if more wisely administered and more closely
coordinated." (Marion B. Folsom, *Journal of Public
Health*, June, 1963.)
C. Many groups cannot afford complete medical care, because
  1. The aged cannot finance their medical care, for
    a) Aged insurance policies are inadequate, for
      (1) "Private health insurance doesn't meet the problem.
Most insurance companies simply will not insure persons sixty-five or over, those that do charge premiums
of seven dollars to ten dollars monthly which most
older persons cannot afford. So more than half of the
aged have no private insurance coverage at all, and
those who do have limited protection." (*Nation*,
"Which Bill Is Best," May 28, 1960.)
    b) The aged need an excessive quantity of medical care, for
      (1) ". . . more than half of these old people have yearly
incomes of less than $1,000. One government study
in 1958 showed that nearly half of them had less
than $500 in liquid assets to their name, and nearly
a third had no assets at all. And only 40 per cent
have some kind of private medical insurance. On a
per capita basis, people 65 or over spend twice as
much time in hospitals, and pay out nearly twice as
much in medical bills as those under 65." (*Newsweek*, August 29, 1960.)
    c) The aged have higher health costs, for
      (1) "People 65 and over have two to three times as
much chronic illness as the rest of the population.
. . . Their expenditure for health services is 90 per
cent greater than expenditures on health by the rest
of the public; for hospitals, it is 120 per cent higher

and for drugs it is also 120 per cent higher." (Senator Wayne Morse, *Congressional Record*, October 26, 1961.)

2. The indigent are not provided medical care, because

    a) Indigent persons can afford very little of anything and must budget first more necessary items, and

    b) Welfare programs do not adequately provide care for the indigent for

        (1) "Seven million persons on public relief, and other low income families, have more than their share of illness and receive by ordinary standards inadequate health care." (Dr. James Dixon, stated in Congress, July, 1959.)

3. Youth cannot afford care because incomes are inadequate below the age of twenty-four, and

4. Middle-income groups cannot afford complete medical care, because

    a) They cannot withstand severe and prolonged major bills, and

    b) Constant drug treatment is too costly.

5. Rural groups cannot afford adequate medical care, for

    a) Generally, they have low incomes, for

        (1) "While private health insurance is inadequate for most city folk, farmers have even less; it is of poorer quality; it costs more; it pays less of the bill." (Senator Pat McNamara, *Congressional Record*, May 17, 1962.)

    b) Most health insurance is associated with industrial salary plans.

        (1) "It is a sad fact that the individual commercial policies which give such a poor return in benefits are more prevalent among low income families, particularly rural ones, who tend to fall less obviously into some insurable groups. (*The Economist*, August 29, 1959.)

D. Private health insurance is an inadequate means of financing medical care, for

    1. Insurance rates are too high and are increasing, for

        a) "The charges made to subscribers and policy holders for hospital, medical, and surgical costs have been increasing sharply during recent years . . . they are justified and further increases might be expected." (National Association of Insurance Commissioners, 93rd Annual Meeting, 1962 proceedings, Volume II, Conclusions of Blue Cross–Blue Shield Studies, p. 497.)

2. The aged cannot purchase insurance, for
   a) "Private health insurance programs are not meeting the special needs of aging, because such programs discriminate against the elderly through higher premiums and reduced benefits." (Senator McNamara, United States Senate Committee on Aging, July 11, 1961.)

3. National enrollment in insurance programs is insufficient, for
   a) "Allowing for duplication it appears that 44 per cent of the population at most were covered, altogether less than one half of the population had any insurance against non-surgical doctor bills." (Herman M. Somers, *Doctors, Patients and Health Insurance,* 1961, p. 230.)

4. Much of the cost of private insurance policies goes into a profit margin for the company and middlemen, for
   a) "On some individually purchased policies, the broker gets 25 per cent, the general agent another 10, and the company itself charges more for its overhead." (Sidney Margolius, *A Consumers Guide to Health Insurance Plans,* p. 18.)

5. Low-income groups cannot afford insurance, for
   a) "Although they are the most in need of hospital insurance the poor have the least, since they can't afford the premiums: only 40 per cent of poor families have it, as against 63 per cent of all families." (Dwight MacDonald, *New Yorker,* January 19, 1963.)

6. Insurance policies are limited by maximum levels of benefits where no more will be paid to the insured, for
   a) "Because even in group policies there is frequently a maximum money limit leading to cancellation, the protection for many employees may prove at least partially illusory." (H. Somers, *Labor Law Journal,* July, 1958, p. 470.)

7. An unemployed person, who needs insurance most, cannot pay for it, for
   a) "A major problem with respect to group insurance cov-

erage is its general dependence on the employment status. Those who lose coverage at retirement or on being disabled or unemployed are in a poor position to obtain any other health insurance." (Herman and Ann Somers, *Doctors, Patients and Health Insurance*, The Brookings Institution, 1961.)

8. An ill person cannot get insurance, for

a) "Generally speaking, experience has indicated that serious inequities may arise if the insurance undertakes to pay benefits for conditions that existed at the time the policy was purchased. Hence, individual policies almost always exclude such pre-existing conditions from coverage." (Charles A. Siegfried, "Medical Expense Insure Group and Individual," *Life and Health Insurance Handbook*, 1959, p. 551.)

9. Health insurance is the first budget item to be dropped in an economic depression although it is needed most, and

10. Insurance companies often enforce deductible clauses on the benefits they pay to the insured, for

a) "Since most medical cost losses are small, a deductible provision eliminates the substantial claim payments and settlements associated with a great number of small losses. (O. D. Dickerson, *Health Insurance*, 1959, p. 96.)

E. Public aid is not adequate, for

1. State welfare programs are inadequate, because

a) Many indigent do not know what facilities are available, and

b) The ability of states to support welfare programs is often inverse to the population's need for public welfare assistance, for

(1) "Such thinking that all states are capable of adopting Kerr-Mills completely ignores the fact that many states are unable even with substantial help from the Federal Government to adequately finance the health needs or even the basic living requirements of the most indigent aged." (Special Committee on Aging, June 15, 1962.)

c) Often no doctor choice is allowed the welfare recipient, for

(1) "Even those relatively few aged persons who are declared eligible for some help under MAA frequently find that they can't get care from doctor of their own choice." (Staff Report to Special Senate Committee on Aging, "Performance of the States," June 15, 1962.)

d) Federal-state fund programs, such as Kerr-Mills, are inadequate, for

(1) "As a result of 25 states not adopting the Kerr-Mills bill coverage and quality vary from state to state. Surely it would be far better and favorable to provide a universal approach instead of a needs test program which doesn't prevent indigency; but operates only after indigency is created." (Address by John F. Kennedy, January 21, 1963.)

2. Workmen's Compensation care is inadequate, for

a) "Of the total premiums paid by insuring employers under workmen's compensation, it has been estimated by various authorities that only about 60 to 65 per cent reach the beneficiaries in the form of compensation payments or medical care . . . in contrast to between 95 to 98 per cent in such insurance as O.S.S.D.I. or Unemployment Insurance where the program is financed by governmentally collected taxes." (Dr. Burns, "Unemployment Insurance and the Workmen's Compensation," *Public Welfare*, January, 1962.)

3. The means test discourages the use of welfare, for

a) "A major objection to the Kerr-Mills law . . . is that the patient must prove to a welfare interviewer that he can't pay his own medical bills. Many oldsters, the argument goes, are too proud to take the "means test." (*Newsweek*, April 12, 1962.)

4. Local control of welfare programs is often arbitrary and discriminatory, for

a) "Arbitrary predetermined cutoffs, while simplifying somewhat the task of determining eligibility, do not take into account existing debts for medical care or anticipated medical costs. Thus, in a state with an income limit of $1200, an aged individual with an income of $1300 a year who has a heart condition which necessitates medical and nursing home care costing $3000 or $4000 a year is ineligible for medical assistance under the AMA program." (A Staff Report to the Special Senate Committee on Aging, "Performance of the States," June 15, 1962, p. 18.)

F. Private charity as a method for providing medical care is inadequate, for

   1. Charity pays only a small portion of medical bills, for

      a) "The charity load in all communities is rising, and the county and state pay only a portion of the cost of indigent care. The balance of this cost must be put on the private patient, the local charity, and the members of the prepayment program." (J. R. L. Johnson, Jr., "The Competitive Position of Blue Shield in Today's Market," *New York State Journal of Medicine*, Dec. 1, 1961.)

   2. Many needy persons avoid charity, for

      a) "The indigent often do without the care they need to avoid receiving medical charity." (Edward Chase, *Reporter*, May, 1961).

III. The present system fails to provide adequate nationwide health care, for

A. There are serious shortages of medical personnel and facilities in the United States, because

   1. There is a shortage of doctors, for

      a) There is a shortage of medical students, for

         (1) "Decisive federal action is necessary to stimulate and assist in the establishment and expansion of medical and dental schools and to help more talented but needy students to enter the health professions (while bolstering the quality of their training.)" (John F. Kennedy, Special Health Message to Congress, February 7, 1963.)

      b) The working conditions and income in general practice are unattractive, for

         (1) "Many GPs are disenchanted with long hours, night calls, etc. and leaving the field to specialize. As a result, medical students are reluctant to enter a "family doctor" career. This is supported by the fact

that 70 per cent of physicians were GPs in 1930; five
per cent are now." (*Science Digest*, May, 1963.)
2. There is a lack of hospital facilities, for
   a) "Complete medical care cannot be obtained today, because there is a lack of hospital accommodations. There is
   a shortage of beds. Over 40 per cent of the counties have
   no general hospitals to serve their 29,000,000 people."
   (*Nation's Health*, August 7, 1962, p. 34.)
3. There is a lack of nursing homes, for
   a) "The Senate Subcommittee on Problems of the Aged and
   Aging reported that nearly one half of the 308,000 nursing homes were found nonacceptable because they failed
   to meet the fire and health standards. Even so, no beds
   at all were available for another 30,000 persons who need
   nursing home care."
B. There is a maldistribution of doctors and hospitals, because
   1. Most facilities are located in urban areas, for
      a) "The doctor has become preponderantly a city man.
      Today slightly more than one half of our people live in
      metropolitan areas but 70 per cent of the physicians are
      found here. Conversely, only 4 per cent of the physicians
      live in counties that have no larger than 2500 population
      whereas 8 per cent of the people live in such counties."
      (*Saturday Review*, February 26, 1955.)
   2. Facilities tend to concentrate around the greater wealth
   found in urban areas, for
      a) "The distribution of hospitals is far from equitable.
      Wealthy communities are better provided than those less
      endowed; and urban areas have many more hospital beds
      than the rural." (Avedis Donabedian, "Organizing Medi-
      care Programs to Meet Health Needs," *Annals of Amer-
      ican Academy*, September, 1961, p. 51.)
   3. Some areas suffer from a harmful shortage of medical facilities, for
      a) "There are urban centers with one physician per 600
      population, while some towns have 1 per 2000–3000 . . .
      and some communities with 5000 have no physician at
      all." (*New York Times*, April 10, 1960.)

C. There is a harmful lack of preventive medicine in the U.S. today, for
  1. A large portion of the population doesn't see a doctor even once a year, for
     a) "28 to 27 per cent of the population do *not* see a doctor even once a year." (*Doctors, Patients and Health Insurance*, 1961, p. 156.)
  2. Economic factors deter persons from getting checkups, for
     a) "Under fee-for-service, consumers will tend to economize by seeking attention only when they are very ill. This discourages early diagnosis and treatment and extends cost and illness in the long run." (Jerome Rothenberg, "Welfare Implications of Alternate Methods of Financing Medical Care," *American Economic Review*, May, 1951.)
  3. Preventive and early treatment drugs are prohibitively expensive, for
     a) "Studies by economists, insurance carriers, and responsible cost analysts go as high as 200, 300, and 400 per cent increases since 1947 in the price of ethical (prescription) drugs." (William Michelfelder, *It's Cheaper to Die*, 1960, p. 10.)
  4. Because people wait until they are seriously ill before using medical facilities, our hospitals are overcrowded with people who would not have to be there if their illness were detected early.
D. There is a harmful lack of coordination in our medical care system, for
  1. There is little planning for the system as a whole, and
  2. Wasteful duplication results, for
     a) "There is far too much duplication of effort and far too little overall planning at local, state, and national levels. Our resources of men and money could be employed far more profitably if more wisely administered and more closely coordinated." (Marion B. Folsom, *American Journal of Public Health*, June, 1963.)
IV. There is a program to provide complete medical care to all citizens at public expense, for
  A. Administrative control will be under the Department of Health, Education, and Welfare, and

      B. Doctors and medical agencies will submit bills to local boards, and

      C. A federal board will be established to control abuses and set fee rates, and

      D. Financing can be done through one of several methods: income tax, employee tax, employer tax, or a combination of these, and

      E. Enforcement can take the form of suspension from the program or lesser fines.

V. Such a program is workable and will meet the affirmative need, because

      A. By paying the medical bill, the plan will eliminate the financial factor which bars the public from medical care, for

           1. "It is through some nationwide insurance program applicable to our entire population that the economic burden of illness can be met and a desirable degree of utilization attained of what medical science has to offer for the promotion and preservation of a healthy nation." (Subcommittee on the Aging, 86th Congress, April, 1960.)

      B. The plan will eliminate the financial factor to the individual, because it will strike at the cause of rising medical prices, the profit motive.

           1. "Although attention has been drawn to its manifest defects, the National Health Service has served the nation well. Year by year the chief medical officer of the Ministry of Health is able to report striking progress in the treatment of diseases. Medical and hospital facilities are more evenly distributed over the population and, with some exceptions, have shown notable improvements in quantity and quality. Over a wide range of care there is no barrier to anybody, whatever his position in society, obtaining treatment of the highest standard." (*New Statesman*, "Health Service Under Scrutiny," April 30, 1960, p. 632.)

      C. The plan will increase our supply of doctors by offering a greater financial opportunity to prospective doctors, and

      D. Doctors would distribute themselves more evenly because the paying abilities of the public would be more evenly distributed, for

           1. "In 1948, with private practice pulling doctors into more prosperous areas, 60 per cent of the people of Britain were living in . . . underdoctored areas. Today, only 18 per cent

of the people now live in underdoctored areas. . . . The total number of doctors in the United Kingdom has increased from 36,500 to over 49,000." (Don Cook, *Harper's*, May, 1959.)

E. The plan will encourage preventive medicine by paying the first costs of medical care and early treatment, for

1. "It is surprising how much illness that used to remain undisclosed and unchecked, particularly among women, has come to light in the last six months. The period the doctor is speaking about was the total time in which the Health Service had been in effect. One can conclude that the Health Service encourages preventive medicine, since actually only the aged and the dependents of workers were ones not covered by the Health Service before 1948." (Dr. J. Leslie MacCallum, *New York Times Magazine*, June 9, 1949, p. 14.)

F. Because of its record abroad, a national health program would probably be successful here, for

1. "Following countries have governmental health care programs: Argentina, Belgium, Brazil, France, West Germany, Great Britain, India, Italy, Japan, Mexico, Sweden." (House Interstate and Foreign Commerce Commission, *Congressional Digest*, March, 1955, p. 79.)

VI. The affirmative plan will not cause serious disadvantages, for

A. The cost of the program will not pose a serious problem, for

1. It will not create a financial strain on the individual because

a) The tax would not be an added burden, for

(1) "Do not treat the taxes which support such a system as if they would be additional burdens on each American; most such taxes would merely replace what is now spent on medical care." (William DeMougeot, *Congressional Record*, February 15, 1962.)

b) People would be relieved of the expense of paying medical or insurance costs out of pocket.

2. The cost will not harm the national financial position, for

a) It would relieve the tax program of the medical expense deduction, and

b) Taxes would be adjusted upward to meet these new costs, and

c) The cost of the program is not likely to be great, for

(1) "The cost of administering a single nation-wide plan

would be less than the administrative costs under many competing private insurance plans. The savings in administrative costs would make it possible to pay the same benefits as private insurance at less cost, or more adequate benefits at the same cost." (W. J. Cohen, *American Journal of Nursing*, April, 1960.)

3. The setting of fees will reduce the cost of health care, for
   a) "The basic answer to controlling unnecessary usage of services is not the imposition of fiscal controls upon the medically indigent. . . . The answer lies in the use of medical controls whereby the person's physician and the physicians who comprise medical review boards are responsible for the decisions as to the necessity, appropriateness, and duration of medical care." (Special Committee on Aging, June 15, 1962.)

B. The quality of medical care would not deteriorate, because
   1. Facilities and services would not be overused, for
      a) ". . . it has been proved that the administrative overhead may be surprisingly low. The very limited number of surveys of the general practice in Europe does not offer evidence that the quality of medical care is lower in countries with prepaid medical systems." (Karl Evang, M.D., *American Journal of Public Health and the Nations Health*, April, 1958, Vol. 48, No. 4.)
   2. Removing financial barriers would improve the doctor-patient relationship, for
      a) "The absence of any financial barrier between doctor and patient must make the doctor-patient relationship easier and more satisfactory." (Dr. Guy H. Dain, *Harper's*, May, 1959, p. 33.)

C. There will be no shortage of doctors, because
   1. Doctors have no place to flee to; all other industrialized countries have similar systems, and
   2. Doctors in all other countries have eventually supported national health programs after they have been instituted, for
      a) "British doctors have their choice to join the National Health Service or not. Ninety-eight per cent have chosen to join." ("British Doctors and National Health Service," *Time*, January 26, 1962.)
   3. The British experience reveals that the number of persons

studying for the profession has not decreased because of
government health activity, for

a) "There has always been a certain flow of young English-
trained doctors to America as there is a traditional flow
in the opposite direction of doctors seeking postgraduate
experience in Britain. No evidence can be found of any
change in this pattern attributable to the Health Service."
(Kenneth Robinson, "Case for England's Health Service," *New York Times Magazine*, November 18, 1962.)

Conclusion

Therefore, since significant harms result from failure to have complete medical care for all citizens, since the economic flaws in the present
system are serious and inherent, since the present system fails to provide
nationwide health care, since there is a program to provide complete
medical care to all citizens at public expense, since such a program is
workable and will meet the affirmative need, and since the affirmative
plan will not cause serious disadvantages, we conclude that the federal
government should provide complete medical care for all citizens at
public expense.

NEGATIVE

Introduction

The philosophy of the negative is that the federal government should
not be responsible for the medical care of all citizens, because it is not
a federal obligation to provide medical care to *all* citizens, and a defi-
nite need should be shown before any person should expect to get free
medical care from *any* source.

Discussion

I. The present situation in medical economics does not warrant drastic action, for

A. Factors other than money deter many persons from using medical facilities, for
1. Lack of education is a factor, for
   a) "Educational attainment of the head of the family is directly related to the rate of physician visits among family members. The rates for the two-year period ending July, 1959, varied from a low of 4.3 visits per year for members of families whose head of family had had less than 5 years of education to a high of 6.0 visits for those whose head of family had attended college." (*Health Statistics*, from U.S. National Health Survey, U.S. Dept. of Health, Education, and Welfare, June, 1957–June, 1959.)
2. Fear is a factor, for
   a) "A survey of health needs and income revealed that in both low and high income groups unmet medical needs could be traced back to fear of treatment rather than to the amount of income." (E. G. Jaco, *Patients, Physicians and Illness*, 1958, p. 161.)
3. Religion is a factor, for
   a) "There are approximately forty religious denominations in the United States whose members number in the millions, believe in divine healing and who do not use medicine or medical treatment." (Dominico Gagliardo, *American Social Insurance*, Harper and Brothers, 1955, p. 513.)
4. No ill person will be denied care for financial reasons, for
   a) "The AMA, which represents 90 per cent of the practicing physicians in the country, has repeatedly affirmed its position that no one in America will be denied medical care solely because he cannot pay for it." (George M. Fister, *Saturday Evening Post*, February 23, 1963) and
   b) "We have an understanding among our members whereby anyone unable to pay or anyone without means of paying the regular fee is attended to without charge or at a fee based on inability to pay." (*Today's Health*, July, 1962.)
B. The financial barrier has been exaggerated, for
1. Today we work fewer hours to pay for more medical care, for

a) "The real cost of medical care in terms of hours of work to purchase it, is less today than it was 20 years ago. To pay for doctor's services required only 55 per cent as much working time in 1959 as in 1939. Surgeons—49 per cent; Dentists—56 per cent; Drugs—43 per cent; all care —61 per cent." (U.S. Bureau of Labor Statistics, *Today's Health*, April, 1961.)

2. Persons nowadays receive more for their health dollar, for
   a) "From 1950 to 1960 medical science has made enormous strides. Lifesaving techniques and operations unheard of 10 years ago are widely available today. New diagnostic skills bring far earlier discovery and thus better chances for curing of disease. Drugs and equipment are available now to beat diseases and defects that only a decade ago were almost always fatal." (*Business Week*, June 24, 1961) and
   b) "Eighty per cent of the drugs commonly prescribed today were unknown just 10 years ago. The United States has made more important drug discoveries in the last two decades than all the rest of the world combined, or seven times as many as the next leading country." (George Fister, *Today's Health*, February, 1963, p. 6.)

3. Private health insurance can meet most needs, for
   a) Enrollment is high, for
      (1) "Between 1960 and 1962 the number of private health insurance companies increased by 59.2 per cent from 1,147 to 1,739. Not only did the number increase but the benefits grew by 63 per cent. It is estimated that by 1972, 95 per cent of the nation's medical bills will be paid by private insurance companies." (*American Journal of Public Health*, March, 1963.)
   b) Plans cover medical needs, for
      (1) "In 1925, only 10 per cent of the cost of hospitalization was paid by insurance of one form or the other. The remainder was met by the individual from his own resources. Ten years ago, insurance paid 25 per cent of the hospital costs. Today it is 60 per cent. The prediction is that by 1970, 90 per cent of all private expenditures for hospital care will be paid for by some form of prepayment insurance." (Harry

S. Salzstein, M.D., Detroit, Mich., *Journal of the Michigan Medical Association*, 1960.)

c) Rates are not prohibitive, for

    (1) During 1961 Blue Cross paid out $2,058,317,080 to hospitals for care of 11,621,550 members for 65,-108,910 days of care. This amount represents 92.36 per cent of total income, the remainder being devoted to total operating expenses, 4.98 per cent of total income and added 2.66 per cent to reserves. (1963 *World Almanac & Book of Facts*, p. 306.)

d) Limits on coverage are reasonable, for

    (1) "For total discharged patients, some 56 per cent of the male patients and 49 per cent of the female patients had ¾ or more of their hospital bills paid by health insurance. Of patients for whom health insurance paid some portion of their hospital bills, 79 per cent of the males and 73 per cent of the females had ¾ or more of the hospital bill paid (in 1961)." (Health Insurance Institute, "Source Book of Health Insurance Data," 1962, p. 65) and

    (2) "Even a $25 deductible would constitute a tremendous saving to insurance carriers through the elimination of a very considerable administrative cost, and through its effect in stimulating more efficient methods of care." (Walter Kidde, *Journal of the Medical Society of New Jersey*, March, 1960.)

e) The aged are covered, for

    (1) "3,500,000 over 65 now have Blue Cross–Blue Shield programs. The new programs will pay full cost of medical and surgical services for persons whose annual income is $2500 or less and couples whose income is below $4000. Surgery in office or hospital, 30–70 visits, anesthesia, radiation treatment, x-ray, and laboratory tests. Cost: $3.00 per month." (*New York Times*, January 19, 1962, p. 1.)

4. Public assistance can cover the remainder, for

  a) Workmen's Compensation applies to many employed laborers, for

    (1) "In 1961 more than 43 million wage earners were protected by insurance or other formal arrangements

against loss of income incurred during disability periods." (Health Insurance Council, 1963.)

b) Veterans have Veterans Administration benefits, and

c) There are provisions for the indigent, for

  (1) "The Federal Government makes grants to the states to help them provide financial assistance, medical care, and other social services to the needy aged, blind or disabled, or to children dependent because of the death, disability, absence, or unemployment of a parent; and medical care for those aged persons who can provide for their maintenance, but are unable to pay for their medical care. In addition, in all the states some help is provided from state and/or local funds only to some other needy persons." (*Information Please Almanac*, 1963, p. 295.)

d) The aged are being increasingly covered, for

  (1) "Probably close to 30 per cent of total public expenditures for patient care in hospitals goes for treatment of the aged who comprise only 9 per cent of the population." (*Health Care of the Aged*, U.S. Dept. of Health, Education, and Welfare, 1962.)

e) Unemployed persons are included, for

  (1) "It long has been the position of the members of the medical profession that no one needing medical attention should go without it because of inability to pay. This policy has been given greater publicity in recent years through special programs designed to inform the public of the medical profession's determination to see that no legitimate need for medical care goes begging." (*Today's Health*, March, 1962.)

5. Title VI of the Mills Bill (or its equivalent) would remedy any minor flaws, for

  a) It would cover the gaps in existing programs for the needy, and

  b) It would exempt those who do not need help, and

  c) It would be locally administered

C. The place of medical bills in the family financial situation is often distorted, for

  1. Only a minority have great costs, for

    a) "A survey prepared for the Federal Reserve Board showed

that 80 per cent—43 out of 53 million—of American families reported no medical debts whatsoever. Only 1.2 million families, a mere 3 per cent, reported debts of over $200.00." (Walter B. Martin, House Committee on Interstate and Foreign Commerce, January 28, 1954.)

2. Tax deductions may be taken for medical bills, and
3. It is unreasonable to exempt health costs from inclusion in consumer credit, and
4. We spend as much on nonessentials as we do on medical care, for
   a) "Many so-called low-income families have cars, radios, TV's, and other once considered luxury goods. The concept of the bare American grubbing for a bare existence is becoming obsolete. (E. G. Jaco, *Patients, Physicians and Illness*, 1958, p. 69.)
5. Loans for paying bills are available.

D. The health situation in the U.S. is good, for
   1. Mortality rate is constantly declining, for
      a) "The general death rate has gone down steadily since the turn of the century. In 1900 there were 17.2 deaths per 1,000 people; in 1958 there were 9.5 deaths per thousand. This marked the tenth consecutive year in which the death rate was below 10 per thousand of population." (U.S. Dept. of Health, Education, and Welfare, 1959.)
   2. Survival rates of mothers and infants has been increasing, for
      a) "The safety of mothers at childbirth has increased drastically from a mortality rate of 63.3 per 1000 live births in 1933–34 to a low of 4.5 in the 4 years ending in 1958. In the same period, the mortality of infants after their first week of life dropped from 33.9 per 100 live births to 9.6." (Dr. Austin Smith, "The Health of a Nation," *Vital Speeches*, January 15, 1960.)
   3. Life expectancy continues to improve, for
      a) "The life span of Americans has lengthened 20 years since 1900. In 1920, only 4.7 per cent of the population were 65 years of age or over. Today, this figure has risen to 9.2 per cent. This year there are almost 17 million Americans who are 65 or over." (*America*, June 9, 1962, p. 383.)
   4. The shortage of physicians is exaggerated, for

      a) "According to official estimates there are approximately 261,000 licensed physicians in the U.S. today. That works out to one physician for every 760 people, the lowest ratio in the world except for Israel." (*U.S. News & World Report, May* 28, 1962) and

      b) "Many diseases that once required prolonged medical treatment now can be cured quickly through the use of new drugs and antibiotics. In a pneumonia case a doctor once made about 36 visits. Now he makes about 5." (*U.S. News & World Report*, May 9, 1958.)

  5. Hospital building is provided for under Hill-Burton Act.

  6. Nursing homes are increasing rapidly, for

      a) "The number of nursing homes in the U.S. has increased from 7000 to 9700 from 1954 to 1961 . . . but the bed capacity rose from 180,000 to 338,700." (*Chicago Daily News*, April 11, 1963) and

      b) "Nursing homes have now mushroomed to provide nearly as many beds in the nation as do general hospitals." ("The Health Care of the Aged," U.S. Social Security Administration, 1962.)

II. The proposed plan would not solve the alleged problems, for

  A. Comparisons with other countries are invalid, for

    1. "America cannot be strengthened by copying medical systems under which one country after another has lost leadership in the science and art of medicine. The strength of this nation does not lie in the direction of substituting medical failure for medical success." ("Case against Socialized Medicine," *Journal of the American Medical Association*, March, 1962.)

  B. It would not get at the important noneconomic factors, for

    1. The Los Angeles County Medical Association regularly advertises in local newspapers that free medical care is available to anyone who (A) needs it, and (B) phones in to numbers listed in the ad. The most recent ads ran within the last month. Not one person has phoned. (Emil E. Brill, "Why a 'Must' Now?" *Missouri Medicine*, October, 1960) and

    2. Healing is an integral part of some religions.

  C. It would not increase the number of physicians, for

    1. "Students by a margin of more than 5 to 1 say they would

be less enthusiastic about entering the medical profession
if health services were eventually nationalized as they are in
Great Britain. A majority of the students favor private rather
than federal funds for assistance in financing medical education. Half of those who say they would accept federal
help insist it would have to come without strings attached."
("Future Doctors Oppose Federal Medicine," *Nation's
Business*, June, 1962, p. 34.)

D. Preventive medicine would not be improved, for

    1. "Compulsory health programs, wherever they operate, always
result in overcrowded waiting rooms and long waiting lists
for admission to hospitals. Both conditions reduce the chance
of early diagnosis of truly serious ailments—often billed as
the most important aspect of government program." (Dr.
Helmut Schoeck, "Why Socialized Health Schemes Fail,"
Nation's Business, March, 1963.)

III. Serious disadvantages would follow the adoption of the federalized
health plan, for

A. It would prove to be costly, for

    1. "Expenditures under Sweden's compulsory health insurance
plan have exceeded by far all expectations. The cost of the
subsidy for prescriptions alone more than tripled in the first
6 years. Overall expenses for the NHS reached $545 million
in 1960. A further increase to at least $900 million by 1970
now is anticipated." ("How Europe Deals with Medical
Care," *U.S. News & World Report*, July 30, 1962) and

    2. "The British budget soared from 12 billion dollars in 1950 to
an all time high of 18 billion in April, 1961. Two-fifths of
this greatly increased sum now goes to the welfare state. And
this is over and above local taxes for such social services as
education, subsidized housing." (Graham Hutton, "America
—Beware of the Welfare State," *Reader's Digest*, October,
1961.)

B. It would be inefficient, for

    1. "Under compulsory insurance, the government would be-
come practically the sole buyer of the private practitioner's
services. It could establish the rate of pay as surely as any
monopoly can establish the price of a commodity. It has
been estimated that about ¼ of our people don't adhere to

or depend upon the services of medical institutions. The poor doctor would make about as much as the best. More patients, more annual medical visits, innumerable forms to be filled out, with no immediate increase in the number of doctors must . . . result in a rationed and degraded quality of medical care." (Haven Emerson, "Why Compulsory Medical Care Fails," *Christian Science Monitor*, March 8, 1963, p. 3) and

2. "The cost of medical care would presumably increase because of administrative expenses and the tendency of insured persons to make unnecessary and often unreasonable demands upon the medical care service." (*Business Week*, September 27, 1960.)

C. The shortage of doctors would be aggravated, for

1. Increasingly, England is relying on the general hospital staffing from doctors from overseas, particularly from the underdeveloped countries, from India and Pakistan. By 1960 they already had 41 per cent of all residents and interns born and trained outside England. (*U.S. News & World Report*, May 28, 1962, p. 72.)

D. The quality of medical care would deteriorate, for

1. "Concerning patient treatment, if the doctor must see as many patients as doctors under the British system do, the U.S. doctors will never have enough time. Doctors see 60 to 80 patients per day in England—can't spend a sufficient amount of time with any." (*New York Times Magazine*, February 18, 1962, p. 76.)

Conclusion

Therefore, since the present situation in medical economics does not warrant drastic action, since the proposed plan would not solve the alleged problems, and since serious disadvantages would follow the adoption of the federalized health plan, we conclude that the federal government should not provide complete medical care for all citizens at public expense.

APPENDIX B

RESPONSIBILITY
AND RHETORIC

DAVID ZAREFSKY
NORTHWESTERN UNIVERSITY

THE SHIPS SAILED SOUTH AS THE SUN ROSE OVER THE PACIFIC. IT WAS the dawn of May first, 1898, the twilight of the nineteenth century. Under orders from President McKinley, Admiral Dewey was out to expel the Spanish fleet from the Philippine Islands. The order was given with little thought to its import and less to its consequences. But the flag planted on the Philippines began seven decades of involvement in Asia.

If we were derelict in debating our initial involvement, we've more than made up in arguing about ending it. Scarcely a day passes without a new genre of opposition—yesterday the teach-in, today the fast, tomorrow who knows what. Scarcely a day passes without a call to rally in support of our fighting men. The clash of issues has been joined; the debate has begun.

But if this is debate, then I want none of it. For what are debate's virtues? It rejects absolutes, the tenacity of dogma, the cant of authority, the truism, the irrelevancy, the hullaballoo of sophistry. In short, it

* Awarded first place at the Northern Oratorical League contest, Western Reserve University, Cleveland, Ohio, March 6, 1967. Used by permission of the author and the N.O.L.

strives for confrontation of opposing ideas, so that from the struggle the best will emerge.

But the would-be debaters of 1967 don't want confrontation; they try to avoid it. Their strategies proclaim the firmness of beliefs they already hold. They talk past each other in endless repetition, and the debate isn't getting anyplace. More important, this facade of controversy actually preempts the kind of reasoned, sustained debate that this important a question demands.

If the only effect were to frustrate our definitions and values, there'd be little harm done. One could argue that there's plenty to debate about already, and the volume of verbiage would certainly bear him out. The problem is that a kind of Gresham's Law operates in the marketplace of ideas. The less rational drives out the more rational; the less responsible drives out the more responsible. We are left with an unrealistic dialogue about policy options, and no real alternatives. Absence of debate over sending Dewey to the Philippines made of the Spanish-American War not a struggle for well-defined rights but a fight for manifest destiny. Refusal to discuss real options in the last presidential race produced a campaign in which one candidate could ask, "What kind of country do you want to have?" and the other could reply, "We believe in lovin' people, not hatin' 'em."

Forgive me if I am stating the obvious. We know from political research that the public is not well-informed, that politicians must appeal to the lowest common denominator to stay in office. We know that even a meaningful choice among television programs is preempted by concern for Nielsen ratings and network rankings. These things we accept. But what of us? We examine questions critically. Certainly we're not responsible for the absence of debate.

Oh yes we are. There are the passionate militarists among us who claim we must defeat the enemy at any cost. There are the passionate pacifists who say we must withdraw at any cost. And though surfeited with passion and involvement, we are pathetically short on reason.

Look around you.

You'll see first the militarists, who make of a practical cause a great crusade. We must demonstrate that communism can't triumph in Asia; that the people of South Viet Nam can choose their own destiny; that we fight for freedom. Nary a word is said about what would be wrong with a communist Viet Nam, or why self-determination is good there because it is here, or what business it is of ours to make such guarantees anyway. Neither the State Department nor the lady from Dubuque is willing to debate.

Oh, sure; there are the facades of justification. We must aid Viet Nam because of the SEATO alliance—neglecting to note that we are committeed only to discuss, and that South Viet Nam as a protocol state never asked for help from SEATO anyway. Congress approved involvement in the Tonkin Gulf crisis—in a measure which itself was adopted without deliberation, amidst manufactured urgency and shallow consensus.

But mostly the merchants of militarism trade in historical analogies. Last fall on my campus a group of students met every Wednesday noon to protest American involvement. The first week went without incident. The second, the group met signs painted "Remember Munich! Stop the Reds!" As if Neville Chamberlain's world could ever exist again, the militarists have decided that conciliation, like crime, never pays. Whatever happened to the words of the President who said, "Let us never negotiate out of fear. But let us never fear to negotiate"? They are gone, unlearned, to be set down in the histories and read by other men in another time.

The militarists don't meet the arguments; they shadowbox them. But the hawks aren't all you'll find. See also the doves, the rhetoricians of withdrawal. We know them by their nicknames—the queers, the beards, the Vietniks.

What of their arguments? They too shun critical discussion. They claim, for instance, that our intervention was "illegal" and should never have begun. Not that such discussion is unimportant—frankly, I think the advocates of withdrawal are right on the point. If only they had been so vocal in 1954! For to say we were wrong in getting in then is not to say we are right in getting out now. Times and conditions change, and the goals of conflict inevitably change as the conflict wears on. Arguing the wisdom of past decisions says little about the wisdom of future actions. No confrontation of ideas takes place.

Then, too, the patrons of peace argue that war is costly. We are flooded with reminders of civilian damage, the evils of napalm, the atrocities committed by both sides. But what is this if not the old truism that war is hell? And who can argue with it? Though entirely correct, it sheds little light on the question of withdrawing from this particular war at this particular time.

And the pacifists aren't without their analogies either. I remember the philosophy professor who told a class of undergraduates, "Remember back to World War I. We fought the war to make the world safe for democracy, and we won it, so now the world is safe for democracy. Then, if that weren't enough, we had World War II to end all war. We won it as well, so now there's no more war. The only thing man learns from history is that man learns nothing from history; let's get out of Viet Nam."

Don't you see? This kind of argument—from whatever quarters it may come—serves not to determine rational policy but to silence the men of reason. Who is to argue for escalation when he is likened to the general who wanted to defoliate North Viet Nam and make it a parking strip? Who is to argue that we should pull back when he is ridiculed as a Nervous Nellie, disloyal to our boys in uniform?

Thus what Walter Lippmann described as the "chaff of silliness, baseness, and deception." How can we escape it?

We must learn to quit making policy in terms of moral absolutes. We must renounce what Adlai Stevenson called simple solutions and endless elocution. We must get rid of the obsession for policymaking by analogy.

A Columbia sociologist named Daniel Bell wrote five years ago, claiming that the end of ideology would hasten the end of rhetoric. Perhaps he was right. Perhaps the best guarantee for responsible policymaking is just to let individuals form opinions as they will, without trying to influence or change them. Perhaps—but I don't think so. There are certainly issues about which men can think and discuss and argue. There is room for the interaction of advocates, the opposition of ideas.

Let the advocate come forth who will argue whether the constituent assembly improves prospects for self-determination, whether reunification will spur the development of Southeast Asia, whether the American presence helps or hinders the maneuverability of others. Let these questions be decided as they will, but let them be decided after debate rather than the continual chant of nonsense.

If politics is to be the art of the possible, then rhetoric must become the art of the responsible. Decisions about what we can do must be buttressed with arguments justifying them. Responsible rhetoric can never be enforced by legislation. That only closes off some avenues of expression without improving those that stay open. It can come only by the free-will action of each buyer in this marketplace of ideas.

Let's decide to hasten peace negotiations if that is in our best interests—and I think it is. Let's escalate the war if that will serve us best. But let's decide by debate, not by noisemaking. The whirligig of time and the pressure of events lead us down paths we can neither foresee nor retrace. So let's do the best we can in deciding. Let's confront the arguments, engage in full debate, and decide wisely, responsibly.

APPENDIX C

CHAMPIONSHIP DEBATE

TWENTIETH WEST POINT NATIONAL DEBATE TOURNAMENT*

23 April, 1966

Resolved:

That Law Enforcement Agencies in the United States Should be Given Greater Freedom In the Investigation and Prosecution of Crime.

FIRST AFFIRMATIVE CONSTRUCTIVE SPEECH

Mr. Michael Denger
Northwestern University

In their statement before the House Appropriations Committee on March 1, 1965, officials in the Justice Department acknowledged that, despite the gains made since 1961, organized criminal activity continues to be a major social, political, and economic problem. To better combat

---

* This transcript was compiled from the tape recording of the Championship Round. Reprinted from *Debate Sourcebook*, University of Arkansas (1967), with permission of editors and United States Military Academy.

syndicated crime, Bill and I are resolved that law enforcement agencies in the United States should have greater freedom in the investigation and prosecution of crime. Specifically, we are concerned with organized crime as defined by the President's message on crime of March 8, 1965. Organized criminal activities embrace gambling, narcotics and prostitution, usurious loans, racketeering, stock and bankruptcy fraud, and the infiltration of labor unions and legitimate businesses. Further by way of definition, I'd like to outline the proposal Bill and I would advance to better attack organized crime. It has two parts: First, all forms of organized crime would be made felonies under both state and federal law, with penalties up to twenty years in prison. Secondly, special agencies under each State Attorney General and in the United States Department of Justice will be given the authority and the responsibility of investigating and prosecuting local violations committed by organized crime when local agencies are either unable or unwilling to do so; special agencies under each State Attorney General and in the United States Department of Justice will be given the authority and the responsibility of investigating and prosecuting local violations committed by organized crime when local agencies are either unable or unwilling to do so.

Now, Bill and I do not claim that this proposal will eliminate the entire problem of organized crime, but we do feel, however, that by eliminating three substantial barriers to effective law enforcement, our proposal will have three distinct advantages.

First, it will remove jurisdictional barriers to effective law enforcement. As Earl Johnson, Special Attorney for the Department of Justice, wrote in the *Journal of Criminal Law*, December 1962, "Most of the activities of organized crime are not now illegal under federal law. Thus, jurisdiction over most of the crime committed by the criminal organization is entrusted to a patchwork of local and state law enforcement agencies each segment of which is hemmed in by limited powers, artificial boundaries, and restricted responsibilities. Thus, primary responsibility to attack organized crime is given to local officials and the result is twofold. First, organized criminals can locate in jurisdictions with weak units of law enforcement." As Special Attorney Johnson wrote further on in that article, "By concentrating its illegal enterprises in those self-governing hamlets within a metropolitan area which have small, largely untrained police forces and no investigators, a criminal organization is often able to protect its operations from effective prosecution. For example, Detroit Police Commissioner Edwards reported in his 1963 testimony before the Senate Committee on Government Operations that, "Organized criminal operations have left Detroit proper and have sought easier soil to till in suburban areas with weak units of law enforcement."

Now, the second problem created by giving primary responsibility to attack organized crime to local officials is that the syndicate leaders can escape prosecution by living outside the jurisdictions where their illegal operations exist. William G. Hundley, Chief of the Justice Department Organized Crime and Racketeering Section, wrote in the 1963 *Notre Dame Lawyer* that, "Artificial jurisdictional boundaries that divide state from state, county from county, and city from city, prevent local law enforcement officials from pursuing a criminal whose operations are conducted within his jurisdiction, but who remains outside of it." Thus Milton Russell, the Assistant Attorney General wrote in 1961, "By committing crimes within only local jurisdiction, prosecution can be splintered into a large number of local districts, and the syndicate leaders thereby effectively insulate themselves from vigorous law enforcement." Tampa Police Chief Neil Brown indicated this problem of splintered jurisdiction in his 1963 testimony before the Senate Committee on Government Operations. He reported that, "The Tampa Police Department has been unable to do anything about the activities of Santo Troficanti, a major Florida racketeer, because it has no jurisdiction over his affairs elsewhere in central Florida." Now, clearly, by making all organized criminal offenses violations of state and federal laws as well as local law, our proposal will remove these jurisdictional barriers to effective law enforcement. Now, since the syndicate must face nationwide jurisdiction and uniform law enforcement, it no longer will be able to capitalize on jurisdictions with weak units of law enforcement, nor will it be able to operate in one area and reside safely in another. As Professor B. Swartz of the Pennsylvania Law School stated, "You can count on more effective law enforcement through federal agencies than through local agencies which may be immobilized by jurisdictional restraints."

The first advantage of our proposal then; it will remove jurisdictional barriers to effective law enforcement.

Our second advantage is that it will remove political barriers to effective law enforcement. As the American Bar Association concluded, "The largest single factor in the breakdown in law enforcement agencies in dealing with organized crime in the corruption and connivance of many public officials which exists in most American cities." This collusion is so widespread that Virgil Peterson, Director of the Chicago Crime

Commission, estimated in 1963 that fully half of the syndicate's nine billion dollar income from gambling is earmarked for protection money paid to police and politicians. Now, the result is simply that local police, prosecutors, and judges will not vigorously investigate and prosecute organized crime. Special Justice Department Attorney Johnson wrote in the December 1962 *Journal of Criminal Law*, "Through corruption, the criminal organizations has been able to purchase virtual immunity, not only for its management level members, but also for its lower echelon members and its vulnerable enterprises." For example, Charles Adrian, Professor of Political Science at Michigan State University, wrote in his 1961 book, *Governing Urban America*, that "The city council of Camden, New Jersey, stripped the mayor of control over the Police Department after he tried to eradicate organized gambling in the city."

Corruption, then, we might say, is a normal condition of American local governent. Our proposal will better attack corruption in two ways. First, if the local law enforcement is corrupt, the state, and if need be the federal government, can quickly move in and eliminate the organized criminal operations themselves without having to wait months or years to eliminate the corruption.

Secondly, our proposal will make it more difficult for the syndicate to corrupt law enforcement since the organized criminal now will not only have to buy off local officials, but state and federal authorities as well, if it's to make its local operations safe from prosecutions. Both Mr. Hundley and Mr. Johnson of the Department of Justice say that cost to organized crime in having to corrupt all three levels of law enforcement would be much more difficult than it is under the present system when only one authority of law enforcement has responsibility. Our proposal, then, will remove political barriers to effective law enforcement.

Third and finally, it will remove penal barriers to effective law enforcement. As Morris Ploscowe, Professor of Law at New York University, notes, "Every prosecutor must be selective in choosing the cases in which he will set the machinery of the Criminal Law in motion. He does not have the time and the resources to punish all law violations. Thus, if the expense to the government in carrying out a prosecution far outweighs the advantages to be gained by obtaining a conviction, it is the prosecutor's statutory duty to exercise his discretion not to prosecute." Now, since most organized criminal offenses on the local level are only misdemeanors carrying the penalty of a small fine or a short prison sentence, the prosecutor often legitimately exercises the statutory discretion not to prosecute. Chicago's own Superintendent of Police, Orlando W. Wilson, testified before the Senate Committee on Government Operations in 1963 that, "A long drawn-out investigation to implicate the higher-ups in a large-scale gambling enterprise would simply not be worth the time and effort, as they would only be convicted of a misdemeanor." Now, our proposal will remove these penal barriers by making all organized criminal offenses felonies, carrying penalties up to 20 years in prison. These penalties will, number one, make it worth the time and the effort the prosecutor has to spend to gain a conviction; and, number two, will at the same time provide a more meaningful deterrent to the criminal activity itself. The third advantage of our proposal—it will remove penal barriers to effective law enforcement.

Finally, I'd like to cite a precedent for the affirmative proposal. The Federal Bureau of Narcotics has authority similar to the provisions of the affirmative plan. Both statewide and federal law enforcement agencies are available with complete jurisdiction in this area, and the penalties are severe, ranging up to twenty years in prison. As the only type of organized crime which has these unique provisions, narcotics has been particularly susceptible to the attack by the Bureau of Narcotics and the state law enforcement agencies. We would simply remind you that in 1951 the American Bar Association's report on organized crime and law enforcement and the Kefauver Committee both concluded that narcotics was the most serious problem of organized crime. Today the Bureau of Narcotics can report, however, that since 1956 we've had 206 important gangsters who have been convicted of narcotic law violations, eliminating 19 percent of the Genovese, 40 percent of the Luchese and 20 percent of the Gamino criminal organizations.

Secondly, this pressure of law enforcement was so intense, that high-ranking Mafia leaders prohibited their members from dealing in the narcotics trade. Third, those few members who defied the Mafia's prohibition, have been arrested, indicted, and convicted in such impressively large numbers that Professors Block and Geis of Brooklyn College can conclude in their 1962 book, *Man, Crime and Society*, that narcotics no longer represents a serious law enforcement problem.

Bill and I would like to see the day when we could say that about all forms of organized crime, and we suggest the best way to achieve that goal is to tailor our efforts after those used by the Bureau of Narcotics in approaching the narcotics problem. We propose to do so by giving complete federal and state jurisdiction and by making organized criminal offenses felonies, carrying up to twenty years in prison. While not claiming to eliminate the entire problem, we feel such a proposal can be of comparative advantage in combating the syndicate.

FIRST NEGATIVE CONSTRUCTIVE SPEECH

Miss Kathleen McDonald
Wayne State University

As many of you probably know, the case that Northwestern has is very similar to the case that Doug and I have been using all year. And now that the debate season is just about over, let me tell you what's wrong with the affirmative case. Doug and I are going to be contending in today's debate that, number one, the police have all the weapons necessary in order to effectively combat organized crime. And number two, that if we gave the police greater freedom in the areas the gentlemen suggest, it would not only be seriously disadvantageous, but it wouldn't be of any greater help to the police in combating organized crime.

Now, before I go to that first contention, I'd like to take note of the fact that the gentlemen have presented us with a comparative advantage case, and we'd like to be very clear as to what the goal of this affirmative team is—because we don't want a double standard to develop. In other words, we don't want the gentlemen to tell us that on the one hand the present system hasn't eliminated organized crime, but on the other hand they just want to do a little bit better than the present system. We want some reasons why the present system can't do a little bit better. I don't think we've been given those reasons.

Let's turn to that affirmative case. They said, first of all, that they would remove the jurisdictional barriers that cause law enforcement to be ineffective. And they began by telling us that the activities of organized crime don't violate any federal laws. Well, the piece of evidence that Doug just handed me is crucial here, because we're going to contend that the activities of organized crime do violate federal laws. We're going to turn to an article by Mr. Earl Johnson who is Special Attorney for the Organized Crime Section of the Department of Justice. He says, "Various phases of organized crime's enterprises have been made federal crimes through legislation based upon one or sometimes more of these constitutional provisions. Of the six chief sources of organization profits, four are susceptible to federal jurisdiction, at least in some circumstances, whenever they violate a federal law." I don't think the gentlemen ever indicated that these activities don't violate these specific federal laws. The federal government can move in. Has the federal government been doing a very effective job? That's our second position. The federal government has been doing an effective job against the activities of organized crime.

Ever since those anti-racketeering laws were passed in 1961, the federal government has been very effective in the area of gambling. Robert Kennedy, the former Attorney General, tells us, "Because of these new laws, the hoodlums who control gambling have curtailed or shut down their activities. Some are even making plans to dispose of their homes and move to other countries." In 1963, the Attorney General's Report stated, "Internal Revenue Service figures further indicate the decline in illegal gambling." Gamblers across the country report accepting bets of 53 million dollars, and this represented a 20 percent drop from fiscal year 1962. We're going to suggest that if the federal government can get a 20 percent drop in gambling activities in only one year, they've got jurisdiction, and they're doing a pretty effective job with that jurisdiction.

Well, that's gambling. What about the second major area of the activities of organized crime—narcotics? Again we're going to turn to the Attorney General's Report for 1963. They tell us, "Although it may be expected that some racketeers will continue to engage in illicit narcotics trafficking, informants have reported that many racketeers will not now handle illicit drugs as a result of effective enforcement of these laws." We're going to suggest the federal government has jurisdiction, and has been very effective. So even if we accepted everything the gentlemen had to say about corruption on the state level, about the jurisdictional problems on the state level, we're going to suggest we can solve the problem.

And secondly, they told us that organized crime can avoid prosecution merely by concentrating in those areas in the state where they don't have very effective law enforcement. Now, the position that Doug and I are going to take here is, that the localities can cooperate with the state government, and the localities can cooperate with the federal government, and they can get at these organized criminal activities. Because, you know, it really doesn't make very much difference whether the locality has a very effective law enforcement agency, because if the federal government will come in and use all of its weapons and then turn the information over to the locality, then any locality in the country can do a pretty effective job against organized crime. And that's exactly what's happening. J. Edgar Hoover in *U.S. News and World Report*, April 18, 1966, reported, "The FBI develops from its sources within the underworld, and from its investigations, considerable information which does not relate to violations within its own jurisdiction. This is promptly passed on to the proper law enforcement agency either federal, state or local." We're going to suggest, then, that the federal government can use the weapons in any of these localities where their law enforcement is weak. If the federal government doesn't want to do it, the state governments can do it. You know, the gentlemen told us that there are no laws that allow the state to go in, but the gentlemen never told us the state couldn't go in if they were asked to come in. The gentlemen never said you couldn't have cooperation between the states and localities, and I don't think there could be any reason why there wouldn't be any cooperation—unless, of course, there was corruption—and I'm going to deal with that when I get down to the second point. So we'd like to know why with cooperation all these localities cannot fight any organized criminal activity.

Well then, the gentlemen suggested to us that leaders escape prosecution, either by living in another state in which the crime was being committed or by living in another locality within the state. We're going to suggest jurisdictional barriers are not a problem in getting at the leaders of organized crime either, and for exactly the same two reasons. Number one, if the leader lives in a different state than the organized criminal activities engaged in, you can have cooperation between those states as a result of the extradition law of 1955. William G. Hundley, the Chief of the Organized Crime Section of the Department of Justice points out, "This provision of the Uniform Extradition Act illustrates that states can work together in coping with the interstate aspect of organized crime insofar as no person will be able to secure immunity from prosecution solely because he never enters the state where his illegal activities are being carried on." Then through this extradition law we can eliminate the problem if it's between the states.

Again, if it's between localities I think I've already indicated there are no inherent barriers to the localities cooperating with each other, so there is no reason why any leader needs to escape prosecution merely because of jurisdictional barriers. What have we seen on this first contention then? We've seen, number one, that the activities do violate federal laws. As a result of this, the federal government has been very effective against organized crime. We've seen, number two, that jurisdictional barriers are not a problem in getting at the activities of organized crime. We've seen, number three, jurisdictional barriers are not a problem in getting at the leaders of organized crime. I think we're going to have to reject that first contention.

Let's turn to that second contention, where the gentlemen told us they're going to remove the political barriers to effective law enforcement. Let me preface my arguments on this point by saying even if we accepted this entire contention, we could still conclude that the present system can be effective against organized criminal activities, because all the gentlemen have told us is that we have corruption on the state and on the local level. And if that's true, then the federal government, through its jurisdiction, can clean up the activities of organized crime, and it really doesn't make much difference whether or not this corruption exists. That's my first position.

My second position is that this corruption, while it may be widespread, is not protecting the activities of organized crime. And the reason it isn't protecting the activities is because apparently there are enough honest officers left so that they're doing a pretty effective job against organized crime. I'm going to turn to signed evidence in order to indicate this. The *Detroit News* of January 13, 1966, pointed out that it was because of the cooperation we've been receiving from the courts and prosecutors, both at the state and the federal level, that traffic in narcotics is no longer the lucrative business it used to be. They had to get cooperation on the state level—apparently that corruption isn't so widespread—they were able to get that cooperation, and we're going to contend if corruption is a serious problem it can be eliminated under the present system. The gentlemen never really talked about the possibilities of eliminating corruption. I'd like to suggest to you five mechanisms that can be used in order to eliminate the problem of corruption, so that we don't have to turn to this affirmative plan. Number one, we have special prosecutors. Earl Johnson pointed out that as a technique for circumventing a corrupt local prosecutor, substitution of a Special Prosecutor has much to recommend for it. In other words, if a locality has a corrupt prosecutor, then the state Attorney General merely appoints another prosecutor, who isn't corrupt, as substitution for the local prosecutor.

Secondly, we have the grand jury, which is particularly effective against organized crime, because you know the purpose of all of our country grand juries is in order to seek out that corruption on the local level. Robert G. Scigliano tells us, "The special inquisitorial powers are vested in the grand jury. It may subpoena witnesses and compel testimony. It may grant immunity in exchange for possible incriminating testimony." We're going to suggest that's a second mechanism.

A third mechanism is our self-check units. Local police have units within themselves to see that there is no corruption in that particular unit. The *Saturday Evening Post* of July 31, 1965, reports, "It's the job of the Bureau of Internal Affairs to make sure that we have no corrupt police. And they do their job very well in Los Angeles." There's no reason why it can't work in other areas.

Finally, we have Crime Commissions. *Newsweek* reports that in Massachusetts the Crime Commission has been very successful as of October 19, 1964.

And finally, the federal government has jurisdiction over corruption. Because the reason the federal government has jurisdiction over corruption is that the individual getting a bribe obviously cannot report it on his income tax as illegal funds. Therefore they have to violate federal laws, and therefore the federal government has jurisdiction over all of this corruption.

So I think we've indicated that we can eliminate the problem of corruption.

Finally, as far as those advantages were concerned, the gentlemen said it would be faster. I think we've indicated the present system is pretty fast. The gentlemen indicated it would be harder to pay off four levels. I think Doug's going to be able to indicate to you, if it means they won't be corrupted, they're going to pay off all four levels. And what about those penalties? The gentlemen said they weren't stiff enough. You know, that's not unique to the affirmative plan. If we want stiffer penalties, then we can legislate stiffer penalties. But that's not any greater freedom. We're going to suggest that we reject this affirmative case.

SECOND AFFIRMATIVE CONSTRUCTIVE SPEECH

Mr. William Snyder
Northwestern University

I'd like to discuss my three advantages that we believe freedom for law enforcement agencies can provide in the attack against organized crime. I don't believe the young lady's analysis really denied that the plan would be advantageous in three respects.

Before doing that let me respond to the introductory comment. She wanted to know what is the goal of the affirmative proposal. We certainly mustn't impose a double standard upon the negative team or the present system. We don't intend to impose a double standard. Our goal is to substantially reduce the organized criminal activities. We don't intend that we're going to entirely eliminate them. We don't expect the present system to do that either. But we think there's a great deal of room for improvement, and we think our proposals can substantially fill the void. President Johnson, in his message to Congress in March, 1966, said that "Despite the fact that we've reached record levels of indictments, these programs are only initial steps on a long road. And the plainest fact we can see is that piecemeal improvements will not be enough." Now when the President of the United States calls the present system piecemeal improvements, Mike and I think that there's pretty good grounds for believing that the present system leaves a great deal to be desired. We think our proposal can substantially fill the void in three ways.

Now let me take these out of order. I'd like to begin with our third advantage because I don't believe the lady of the affirmative team said very much about it. I believe that that advantage stands at the present time. What did we argue? We argued, number three, penal barriers can be removed by the affirmative proposal. We pointed out, first of all, the penalties employed in most forms of organized crime are extremely weak, usually small fines. The lady doesn't deny that. We pointed out, number two, that the result of this is that if we had vigorous law enforcement, it wouldn't produce any really valuable result to society—they'd only escape with a fine, and go right back to their activities. Well what was her argument? She said after all, we could legislate these penalties and that does not constitute greater freedom for law enforcement agencies. Now if the negative team disagrees that it constitutes greater freedom, we hope they'll respond to the reasoning of the affirmative team for believing that it does. Our reasoning goes as follows.

The legal duty of the law enforcement agencies requires them to invest society's resources only when they know that it will produce some tangible result to society. If they know that the penalties are so weak that a vigorous law enforcement campaign would not produce a valuable result to society, they don't have the freedom to invest their resources as is necessary. All right—first of all, let's get to the legal duty. Newman F. Baker, Professor of Law at Northwestern, writes in *The Journal of Criminal Law,* "To decide whether or not to prosecute, district attornies' legal duty requires them to determine if it will serve any good purpose to society or if it will be too expensive or a waste of time." The Michigan State Court in *Goen vs. Smith* held that the Police Commissioner is bound to use his discretion with which he is clothed. He must use sound discretion as to how the resources of the community will be applied for the good of the community. Now, are penalties so weak as to render this freedom absent to commit themselves to a strong law enforcement campaign? Yes indeed the penalties are too weak. Orlando Wilson, Police Chief in Chicago, "A long investigation to implicate the higher-ups would simply not be worth the cost and effort. They would only be convicted of a misdemeanor." The result is cited by Morris Ploscowe, Professor of Law at New York University, "One of the most common reasons for failure to prosecute is that the expense may far outweigh the advantages of obtaining a conviction." We'd like to give law enforcement agencies the freedom to invest society's resources in a vigorous attack against organized crime, and the only way we can do that is to make meaningful penalties. We believe we can claim a third advantage. I don't believe the lady of the negative refuted it.

Now, let's go back to the top of the case. We said, first of all, we can remove jurisdictional barriers to effective law enforcement. My colleague pointed out that at the present time while most forms of organized crimes violate only local law, it results in concentration of organized criminal operations in units with weak law enforcement and splintering the operations across jurisdictional boundaries. The negative speaker didn't deny that these things take place, nor did she deny the conclusion of Mr. Brown in Tampa, Florida, Mr. Edwards in Detroit, and Mr. Schwartz, speaking in general terms—that these boundaries in fact impair the attack on organized crime.

All right, what did she say? She said first of all we have many federal laws which can be used against organized crime, according to Earl Johnson of the Department of Justice. Now, Mr. Johnson said four out of the six major forms of crime, in some circumstances, violate federal law. But his quotation in the first constructive speech said that by and large, the organized criminal operations violate only the local law. The lady recommended, for example, that we turn to the area of interstate gambling. And indeed, in 1961, we passed some laws to regulate interstate gambling. But the problem with those was cited by J. Edgar Hoover in the *De Pauw Law Review*, Spring 1964. He says, "The first arrests made by the FBI for violation of the new 1961 laws had the profound effect of causing the underworld to tailor their operations so that they exist on the intra- rather than the interstate level, therefore avoiding violations of federal laws." Mr. Nicholas Alga, formerly of the FBI, wrote in the *Nation*, December 20, 1965, that "The primary problem with the federal government in enforcing the laws against organized crime is establishing a violation of the federal criminal law." All right, then, what were the two examples? She said first of all that we'd been very effective in gambling—that's right. What did we do? We caused them to go to the intrastate level, and Mr. John Scarney, Consultant to the Department of Justice on Organized Crime, stated in the *Wall Street Journal* of January 29, 1964, that this has not produced any decrease in the total revenue of organized gambling.

Well then, the second example was in the area of narcotics. We're glad she read that example. That was our precedent for the affirmative proposal. The Bureau of Narcotics is the only law enforcement agency that really has nationwide jurisdiction to enforce its laws. We think that kind of freedom should be given to all law enforcement agencies. Well, then the lady suggested that at the state and local level we can have cooperation. She said after all, the federal government can come in and cooperate and solve this particular problem. Now we're not denying that the federal government sometimes can come in and participate in a raid, particularly if they think there is a violation of interstate commerce. That possibility doesn't deny the fact that when you don't have a strong patrolling force in the community, and when the operation is splintered across jurisdictional lines, the result inevitably has been weak law enforcement. We gave you examples in Tampa, Florida, in Detroit, Michigan, and the lady really didn't discuss them. The conclusion, for example of Milton Wessall was that by committing crimes within local jurisdiction, prosecution is splintered and effectively insulated from vigorous law enforcement. Then the negative speaker said, well, the state government can come in if asked. Now, of course the total government won't come in. Which agency did she have in mind? She didn't tell us. Perhaps she was thinking of the State Police, but Frank D. Day, Professor of Police Administration at Michigan State, wrote in the *Book of the States*, 1965, that State Police exercise statewide jurisdiction, but it is subject to prescribed restrictions like limitations on police in urban and semi-urban areas. We don't think the state has any agency at the present time so designed. Our plan creates that kind of agency. We believe we have a very substantial advantage over the present system.

Well, finally she suggested that we can always cooperate between states by means of extradition. That would be fine, if the jurisdictional problem we were talking about were the state boundaries, but the trouble is they tailor their organization so they don't cross the state lines. They stay within the state, but splinter them over jurisdictional barriers within the state. We suggest then, that extradition isn't going to help the problem. We suggest then that we have jurisdictional barriers, now. We suggest that creating an agency at the federal and at the state level can substantially remove those jurisdictional barriers, we think, substantially enhancing the attack on organized crime. And we believe secondly, that we can remove penal barriers to effective law enforcement. Now we pointed out first of all, that corruption has been the most significant barrier against organized crime, to the tune of four and a half billion dollars per year. The lady didn't really deny that that takes place. What she did say, first of all, is that the federal government can come in and clean them up within its own jurisdiction. And her only example was in narcotics. That's right. The Bureau of Narcotics is the one federal agency that has that jurisdiction. The other agencies rely on interstate commerce, which the organization has tried to tailor its operations to avoid.

Well, then, she suggested that corruption in fact does not protect the organized criminal operation. Mike and I find that very difficult to believe on two counts. First of all, the authorities seem to have found that it does. Attorney General Katzenback in an interview in *Look* magazine said that one of the primary reasons why the federal government or all law enforcement is ineffective is because the organization has been able to corrupt many local officials. Well, she went on to point out, after all, we can always have a local policeman within the area to check up on these particular people. She said if it takes place we have five mechanisms which can be effective. She suggested first of all special prosecutors. Now, the article she was quoting by Mr. Johnson said that we have special prosecutors, but, he says, it's in a limited number of states. By and large this is not available. R. S. Babcock, Professor of Political Science at Vermont, says that in almost every state the District Attorney is completely autonomous from any state official, and the Attorney General of the state has no real authority over the District Attorney. Then she suggested we could use grand juries. That might be good, except that J. C. Phillips wrote in *Municipal Government and Administration*, that the grand jury is usually at the mercy of the local prosecutor. He is the one who must call it into session. If he's corrupted, obviously the organized criminal operation will remain impregnable. Then the lady suggested we could always have a unit within the police force which is going to solve the problem. Once again we'll admit that this might be a possibility once in a while, but it doesn't deny the fact that we could have greater advantage or the fact that you can corrupt a few policemen and render the effect virtually unimpregnable of the organized criminal. J. C. Phillips, Professor of Political Science, says, "While a few police departments are under indirect control or have their own efficiency units, in most cases they have not been able to prevent the corruption of state and local officials." We suggest that we continue to have the problem.

Well finally, she suggested crime commissions. We would like to hear some evidence that says not only that they exist, but they have any law enforcement ability whatsoever. I don't believe her evidence said that they could get at corruption. Finally, she said that the federal government could establish jurisdiction by means of taxes. But Earl Johnson of the Department of Justice wrote in the *Journal of Criminal Law* that, "Most organized criminals and the people they've corrupted are able to conceal their financial interest in such a way that a tax violation is very difficult to establish." We're not denying that once in a while the federal or the state can come in, but by and large we do claim a substantial advantage by creating agencies at the state and federal level, and by giving meaningful penalties. We think we can substantially enhance the attack on organized crime.

SECOND NEGATIVE CONSTRUCTIVE SPEECH

Mr. Douglas Frost
Wayne State University

Mr. Chairman, ladies and gentlemen, before the debate started I asked Captain Murphy if he had some matches for me. He handed me a book of matches and said, "Wonderful for nervous stomach." They light my cigarettes well, but that's about all they do.

I'm going to be discussing this affirmative case primarily by analyzing the plan that they presented. Before I go and examine that plan, however, I want to go back and make two observations on the negative's contentions. First of all, Kathy said, "Making the penalties greater is not giving greater freedom." Now Mr. Denger came back with some rather interesting reasoning that said well, the law states that the prosecutors can only prosecute if they're spending their money wisely and if they're going to get convictions. And he said when they spend it in gambling, you see, they're not spending it wisely. Well, you know, the *Uniform Crime Report* said that we had one million convictions in gambling last year. I suggest every one of those convictions, then, and investigations were illegal according to the reasoning of the affirmative team. The point I'm making here is that giving greater penalties is not giving greater freedom. We can do that under the present system.

The second comment I'd like to make on this particular affirmative case is where Kathy told you the federal government has jurisdiction. You know they came back and said no, they really don't—only if they violate federal laws. Yet, Kathy read Mr. Johnson's evidence to you that said the four major sources of funds came under federal jurisdictions. Let me read you the footnote at the bottom of the page. He tells us that, "Organization profits appear to be derived primarily from the following: gambling, shylocking, racketeering, narcotics, and prostitution." He said these all come under federal jurisdiction if any facility of interstate commerce is used. What I want Mike to do in his rebuttal is tell me that these organized criminals, number one, never use the mail, never use the telephone, and number two, never travel interstate. I think the federal government has clear jurisdiction. The fact that they do is pointed out by the Attorney General Katzenbach in 1965. He said the FBI, for example, has done excellent work. The new racketeering laws gave the FBI clear statutory weapons to deal with organized crime. How effectively the FBI has used those weapons is readily evident in the fact that they have already undertaken 18,355 investigations. Of course Mr. Denger is going to come back and tell us that those were illegal investigations because, you see, they're using the taxpayer's funds unwisely because the penalties are so low.

I'm going to go back now and examine those affirmative plans in two areas. Number one, I want to discuss with you some reasons why there is no assurance of a significant advantage from that affirmative proposal, and secondly, discuss some disadvantages with you.

My first position is going to be that the gentlemen's analogy is inaccurate. You know, they told us that the narcotics prosecution has proved that federal jurisdiction will solve the problem. Well, they got that little gem of an idea from Mr. Johnson's article. I have a photostat of it here. Mr. Johnson goes on to explain that this is not a fair analogy in all areas because, number one, narcotics are a physical commodity. Number two, narcotics must be transported intrastate and into the country. Number three, that the narcotics leave a corpus delicti in the form of an addict. Number four, that the narcotics necessarily have to be sold, and this results in continual contact. He tells us in the footnote at the bottom of the page. He says that, "The narcotics traffic, in turn, however, requires a high degree of cooperation between persons located at different geographical locations in order to accomplish the many steps involved in producing, processing, importing, reprocessing and distributing this particular product." The analogy is very weak. I'm going to have more to say about it when I get back to those disadvantages. I don't think they can talk about the narcotics law and say that this is going to solve all areas of organized crime by extending federal jurisdiction.

Secondly, I'm going to suggest to you that they cannot prove corruption any more effectively than can the present system. Robert F. Kennedy, in the hearings before the Senate Judiciary Committee said, "We have information now where major political leaders and figures in those communities are being corrupted and are on the payroll of some of our big time gangsters and racketeers." The first point, of course, is that that means the federal government has the jurisdiction to investigate that corruption. He goes on to say, however, now that, "We cannot move in on these areas. Now, if legislation such as this proposed wiretapping legislation is passed, we could then prosecute." I suggest the problem of course is the federal government may well be able to investigate, but they can't prove that corruption Mr. Kennedy said they needed by wiretapping.

The third objection I'm going to raise to this plan is the fact that corruption and the protection of illegal activities depends on not merely a political bribe, but many other factors that the gentlemen cannot solve. Number one, political influence. Morris Ploscowe, formerly director of the ABA's Commission on Organized Crime, in 1963 said, "Mob money is used not only for direct payments to police and law enforcement officials who will be sympathetic to its aims." I suggest then that this political influence is not going to be able to be prosecuted by that affirmative team. Secondly, I'm going to suggest that organized crime is protected if they have incapable prosecutors. Earle Johnson in that same article tells us, "Consequently, if they can be blessed with a less than capable chief prosecutor, the members of the criminal organization are usually satisfied." I want the gentlemen to tell us how they're going to assure that all prosecutors are capable.

Moving on, I'm going to suggest that another reason that organized crime exists is not because of corruption, but because of lack of funds. [Of] gambling and organized crime, the *Report of the Senate Committee on Government Operations*, in 1963, said, "It must be conceded that for various reasons, mostly justifiable and understandable, local law enforcement agencies cannot adequately cope with the grave national threat posed by organized crime. Lack of sufficient funds to provide adequate manpower or modern equipment are among the most frequently cited obstacles to the attainment of these objectives." Another factor then that the affirmative team is doing nothing about—inadequate funds.

Another problem is lenient judges. This was pointed out to us by *The New York Times* when they said, "A Senate Committee was told today that gambling was flourishing as a multimillion dollar industry, partly because of the leniency among judges, sheriffs, and policemen." Not necessarily that they were corrupt, but that they were just lenient. I want the gentlemen to explain to me how they're going to do away with lenient judges.

Finally, organized crime protects itself not by bribery but by blackmail. William G. Hundley, in *The Notre Dame Lawyer*—he's the Chief of the Organized Crime Section of the Department of Justice—said, "The organized criminal does not hesitate to use blackmail if he cannot buy off an official." I suggest, then, that what I am telling you here are a number of reasons why that affirmative team can't guarantee to you and I that they're going to be a great deal more effective than the present system is. Problems such as blackmail, lenient judges, lack of adequate funds, incapable prosecutors, political influence, all reduce the assurance of a significant advantage. The fact that Mr. Kennedy said the federal government had jurisdiction but couldn't prove the corruption, because they didn't have wiretapping, casts further doubt upon the efficacy of this plan, and their analogy by their own source, Mr. Johnson, is unfair and inaccurate, and I ask you to reject it.

Now I'm going to discuss with you some disadvantages. Number one, it really was interesting to hear that the significant advantage of this proposal is that now the organized criminals are going to have to corrupt all levels of the government. My first disadvantage is going to be that they will corrupt all levels of government. What about their wonderful analogy, narcotics? *Time, Inc.* in their book, *"The Drug Takers,"* tells us last April, Miami Federal Narcotics Bureau Chief Eugene Marshall shocked his colleagues when he was arrested for accepting a bribe from a narcotics peddler. That's my first disadvantage. If the gentlemen think it's only applying to the Narcotics Bureau, I'm going to turn to the Committee Report to Investigate Organized Crime in Interstate Commerce, when they said the committee found evidence of corruption and connivance at all levels of government—federal, state, and local. My first disadvantage is the federal government will be corrupt.

My second disadvantage is going to be that it reduces the financial support of our local law enforcement, because they're telling us that we're going to set up all these agencies in every state and let them handle the problem. You know what Elliot H. Lumbard tells us in the *American Academies*? He says that, "A properly compensated, trained, equipped, and supervised police force with community stature and support is not likely to be receptive to improper measures or corrupting influences." I think it would be better then to give them the money that they need—not rely on the federal government to come in to every state and observe these individuals, to try to prove that they're corrupt, and take the responsibilities for enforcing the laws away from them.

My third disadvantage to this affirmative proposal is what the gentlemen are really telling us is let's admit defeat to the corruption on the local level. Now they're telling us that the local levels can't be expected to clean up their own corruption. I think Kathy cast significant doubt upon that—that the local levels can and are cleaning up their corruption. Yet Northwestern would say, "No, let's give up and call in the federal government." Kathy and I just don't think that's desirable. We suggest that's a rather serious disadvantage.

My fourth disadvantage to this affirmative proposal was voiced by Mr. J. Edgar Hoover. He told us that such a proposal as a national police force was undesirable. And I ask you if you now have the federal government in every state, enforcing all of these laws, trying to prove corruption—it's tantamount to a national police force. Mr. Hoover said, "I vigorously oppose such a system in the United States, including any clearing house established by the federal government." That's my fifth disadvantage.

Finally, I'm going to suggest that such an invention on the part of the federal government will sap the morale of our local police force. *Newsweek*—last week of this month—Last week?—I hope it's this—said that police officials counter that any outside watchdog unit saps police morale and panders to troublemakers who are trying to undermine respect for authority. I suggest then, it saps the morale of our local police.

And finally, I'm going to suggest that it's been indicated that the local police forces are the most effective in dealing with this problem of organized crime because they're more familiar with the activities at the local level, they can more adequately cope with it, it would be better to let the local police handle it. A federal watchdog unit saps morale. A national police force is undesirable. It admits defeat to corruption on the local level and calls in the federal government immediately. It reduces the financial support of our law enforcement agencies. I suggest greater financial support would be more effective, and it will force the corruption of not only the narcotics bureau now, but all the federal agencies. Moreover, I told you a number of reasons why they cannot assure significant advantages accruing from that program. I turn to Mr. Johnson who said the analogy is really unfair, and we've still got that curious reasoning that says every time you prosecute a gambling law now it's really a violation of law because it's misuse of our finances. I don't think that's greater freedom. If all we need are greater penalties, let's repair the present system and have greater penalties. Kathy and I reject this analysis.

FIRST NEGATIVE REBUTTAL SPEECH

Miss Kathleen McDonald
Wayne State University

I'd like to go back and reexamine those areas of advantages and suggest to you why the present system can obtain all of those advantages without the affirmative plan. Number one, you remember, I began by asking the gentlemen what their goal was. They told us their goal was a more effective prosecution of organized criminal activities, and they said our present laws had just been a beginning. Well, of course, the laws that we have at the present time haven't totally eliminated the problem. Of course, they're only initial steps to eliminating the problem. They were only passed in 1961. I don't think that denies the fact where they've been used, they've been very effective. If we continue to use them, they can continue to be very effective. What's the prospect for their success within the future? George Edwards, who is former Police Commissioner of Detroit, told us in May of 1965, "I think that a ten-year period could beat the Mafia. I don't mean that we could put them all in jail, necessarily, but we could drive them out of the rackets." I'm going to suggest present laws can be pretty effective against organized criminal activities. Let's see why.

Number one, they said that they were going to remove the jurisdictional barriers. They said that most of the activities of organized crime didn't violate any federal laws. I suggested to you that all of them violate federal laws whenever they cross any state lines, and the gentlemen came back and said they're attempting to conduct their activities on a totally local basis. Well, perhaps they're attempting to operate their activities on a totally local basis, but it is impossible; because, you know, the gentlemen are talking about organized crime. Organized crime is a national crime syndicate, run by a national hierarchy, as any of you know who have heard our affirmative case. The report of the Committee on Government Operations tells us the Attorney General testified that federal investigative agencies are now certain, because of intelligence gathered from Joseph Valachi and other informants, that the national crime syndicate is operated by commission of top-ranking criminals. It's a national syndicate. Whenever they come into contact with those national leaders, whenever money crosses state lines, whenever there's any runners between the activities and the leaders of organized crime, then they violate that travel law that says you can't use any facilities or cross any state lines in furtherance of organized criminal activities. We think the federal government can be effective. When the gentlemen tell us that according to Mr. Scarney the federal government hasn't been very effective, I don't think that's very impressive evidence compared with the three Attorney General's reports, 1962, 1963, and 1964 that tell us that organized crime in the area of gambling has been declining. I think the federal government's been very effective.

All right—secondly, the gentlemen told us that organized crime avoids locating in those jurisdictions in which they don't have very strong law enforcement. And I suggested that wasn't a very serious problem because if they locate in these areas, then that weak jurisdiction merely needs to cooperate with either the state government or with the federal government. The federal government uses its law enforcement agencies and then gives the information to the local governments. Now, I don't think the gentlemen ever answered that argument. They said, number one, that there are restrictions in the State Police going in when they're not asked. Well, number one, we're going to suggest that that's simply not the case. We're going to turn to the academic lectures on lie detection, 1956. I don't know why this piece of evidence was on lie detection. It said, "Most states have law enforcement divisions directly under the government's supervision. They offer services and facilities to any authorized law enforcement agency in the state, and they have jurisdiction throughout the state." We're going to suggest that they can go in, but that only says that even if they're not asked they can go in, and my whole point was that if they are asked, they can always go in, and I don't think the gentlemen ever denied that. As far as the federal government was concerned, the gentlemen just said he didn't think it would be very effective. I gave you examples of where it had been very effective. I don't think there is any reason why you can't have cooperation. I don't think these activities are being protected. What about the leaders of organized crime? I said the same two arguments apply. You can have cooperation between the states. The gentlemen merely suggested that they didn't think it would work very effectively. That was the whole purpose of the Extradition Law passed in 1955, so if a criminal living in one state violates a law in another state—then they can cooperate with each other. I don't think the gentlemen have given us any reason why it can't be effective. We can have cooperation and jurisdictions don't have to be a very significant barrier.

All right then, let's go on to that second contention when the gentlemen talked about corruption. I said it wasn't a very widespread problem and the gentlemen said, "You were just talking about narcotics." But the point of the piece of evidence I read was they had cooperation on the state and local level, and that's the reason they were effective. Apparently that corruption wasn't a very significant problem. But what about those ways of eliminating corruption? I don't think Mr. Snyder answered them. The Special Prosecutor—the gentlemen merely said, "We don't have them in all states." Well, we do have them in some states, so it can be effective. In the other states we use the other means. What about the grand jury? The gentlemen suggested to us that this wasn't very effective because they rely on the local prosecutor. No evidence that it was the local prosecutors that were corrupt. It wasn't a problem in New York where they now have three grand juries in Manhattan working on the problem of organized crime. Self-checks? The gentlemen didn't think it would be very effective. I read you evidence saying it was effective in Los Angeles. I don't think the gentlemen gave us any reason why it couldn't. Crime commissions—do they have any law enforcement power? The same piece of evidence I read you in my first speech—since its creation in 1962, the Massachusetts Crime Commission has trudged through the jungles of Bay State politics, bagging Democrats and Republicans with equal vigor. Apparently they do have law enforcement power. We're going to suggest it's a very effective way. The gentlemen never denied the fact that the federal government always has jurisdiction. We're going to ask you to reject this affirmative case.

FIRST AFFIRMATIVE REBUTTAL SPEECH

Mr. Michael Denger
Northwestern University

Ladies and gentlemen, let's first turn to the precedent of the affirmative proposal. He suggested it was not analogous because it's a physical commodity. It has to be smuggled into the country and there's an addict left over. I don't think that denies the central points of the analogy. Number one, we have federal jurisdiction and stiff penalties both commencing in 1956, and it brought a decline in the narcotics problem. Let's turn to Henry Elcourt Giordano, Director of the Bureau of Narcotics: "Strict enforcement and severe penalties have curtailed narcotics traffic. Many of the principal underworld traffickers will no longer risk dealing in narcotics." I don't think he showed how those particular descriptive points denied the analogy.

All right, his second point was that we can't prove corruption now. The federal government could have jurisdiction if it could use wiretapping. There're two points we're going to make here. The key point is effective jurisdiction. Having jurisdiction involving phones, and interstate commerce over those phones is no good unless you can convict those individuals. You need broad jurisdictions so you can go in and circumvent the corruption. I suggest that's not a very useful tool unless they advocate wiretapping.

Then he suggested there's going to be a problem of political influence, incapable prosecutors, and lacking local funds. I'm going to suggest these cause us to turn to the affirmative proposal. If political influence hinders them on the local level, I'm suggesting it's advantageous to have the state and federal come in to get the organized criminal operations. Our advantage was as much to circumvent corruption as it was to eliminate it. I suggest we can do that. If we have incapable prosecutors on the local level, that's simply cause for giving it to the state and federal authorities. They've told us themselves the federal government are capable prosecutors. Again that's merely cause for going to the federal level. What about lacking local funds? That's simply cause for going to the state and the federal government to come in. I don't think it denies the workability of the affirmative proposal.

And as to the leniency of judges and sheriffs, I'm going to suggest we can go to the federal and state courts here. I don't think it denies the advantage of the affirmative proposal, circumventing those areas. Remember, our proposal had two advantages in the area of corruption. The first one was, it would be harder to corrupt the federal government. His analogy here was to turn to the area of narcotics to suggest there were a few corruptions of the federal officials. Three points to make. Number one, Earl Johnson notes that the Mafia has been impressed by the relative incorruptibility of federal law enforcement officials. Number two, we said it's harder to corrupt all three levels of government. You heard the documentation way back in the first speech. I don't think he denied the point. Number three, we're going to suggest a deterrence in this area. Charles Adrian, Professor of Political Science at Michigan State, tells us that "As far as narcotics are concerned, local officials will not make an alliance with the purveyors of narcotics since it would be futile, as state and federal law enforcement officers are particularly alert and active in seeking out the narcotics rings." Three points; I don't think they denied the problem.

All right, then we suggested they should give the money to the local level. I'm going to suggest, indeed, this is quite inefficient for the following reason: we're going to suggest the reason it's inefficient is because you're going to give the money to one little local hamlet, they're simply going to move to another. The American Bar Association says, "A statewide effort to fight organized crime is necessary because no single community alone can effectively deal with organized crime. Efficient policing in one community simply drives the gangster and racketeer to other areas where law enforcement is more lax." The point we're making here is very simple. You don't throw tons of resources into one little municipality so they can move to another one. I suggest it's more advantageous to have the state and the federal government come in. I don't think they denied the advantage. As far as the national police force goes, we're not taking away original local power. They still have their initial responsibility. I want to know the harm of the affirmative proposal. Simply labeling them a national police force doesn't mean it's disadvantageous.

Then he suggested we're going to sap morale at the local level. Here's the very important point. If the local officials are doing an effective job right now, we're not going to come in. It's only when they're lax, when they're corrupt or they lack jurisdiction, and here it doesn't sap the morale. Orlando W. Wilson testified in 1963, "We not only accept, but welcome federal agents as in the enforcement of the narcotic laws. Federal participation in the organized crime drive does not undermine local law enforcement agencies. It's been helpful."

What was his disadvantage? It's better to let the local police handle it, because they're more familiar with the problem. If they lack jurisdiction in areas, if they're corrupt, if the penalties aren't significant, it doesn't do any good to let the local police handle it. I suggest the federal government can be just as effective by coming right in.

All right, let's go to that affirmative need analysis. Number one, I don't think the federal government has jurisdiction in a good many areas. They suggest it's easy to establish federal jurisdiction, but they didn't adapt to the evidence. *The Wall Street Journal*, January 29, 1964: "The more knowledgeable gamblers," says the Justice Department, "have tailored their operations so they don't become part of interstate commerce." William Hundley tells us, "We're looking for possible violations of federal law. If we find any, we will prosecute. But we haven't in Hot Springs, Arkansas, and a good many other localities." I don't think we have those federal jurisdictions in many areas. I suggest they're going intrastate.

What about that cooperation? They can cooperate all they want, but that doesn't let the federal and the state governments investigate and prosecute. They can cooperate but that still doesn't overcome those investigative and prosecutive barriers.

What about those areas in corruption? We suggest you're not solving the problem. We suggested many states don't have grand juries. They suggested we could use the other techniques. This is very interesting. They suggested prosecutors may not be the problem in calling grand juries, yet before they're going to appoint people to replace the prosecutors who may be corrupt, I don't think they've shown us that we haven't solved the problem of organized crime. I think there's a serious problem of corruption.

SECOND NEGATIVE REBUTTAL SPEECH

Mr. Douglas Frost
Wayne State University

Mr. Chairman, ladies and gentlemen: Let me begin with my plain objections. First of all, you remember I told you there was no assurance of a significant advantage resulting from this affirmative proposal, because Mr. Johnson himself admitted that the analogy could not be extended to all forms of organized crime, because it was the nature of the narcotics industry which resulted in the success of the federal prosecution. Now the gentlemen came back with another piece of evidence that said strict enforcement and severe penalties caused this decrease in narcotics. But nothing about federal jurisdiction, nothing about what the gentlemen really are proposing in this plan. I suggest Mr. Johnson denied his own analogy, and the gentlemen could never come back and deny that fact.

Secondly, I said you can't prove corruption and Mr. Kennedy said we have the jurisdiction to investigate it; but, because we didn't have wiretapping, we couldn't prove it. I don't think Mike really answered that one.

Then, I indicated that there were a number of other factors which resulted in the protection of organized crime. I thought Mike's answers were interesting. First of all, I said, well, you know political influence is used to protect gamblers. He said well, let's circumvent the corruption. Let's give up to it, in other words, and have the federal government's attempts to get at organized crime. Yet they're not doing anything about that political influence.

Secondly, I said incapable prosecutors. The gentlemen said well, let's do it on the federal level. I suggest now the gentlemen are going to have all crimes prosecuted on the federal level, still having incapable prosecutors on the local level, by which these other prosecutions will be ineffective. They didn't do anything about that.

I said we have lack of funds, and the gentlemen said let's call on the federal government if there's lack of funds. But remember what my evidence said to you? It said we can beat corruption if we properly compensate, train, and equip our law enforcement officers. I think in a comparative advantage case it would be better to give them the money and train them properly, not give up and go to the federal government. Then I said lenient judges are going to be a problem. Again, Mike came back with what seemed to be the same answer for all of my objections. Let's go to the federal courts. I suggest those lenient judges, number one, are a serious problem—and the gentlemen really aren't doing anything about it. And then I said, you know, blackmail protects organized crime, and Mike didn't even want to talk with you about that. What about my disadvantages?

First of all, I said it's going to force them to corrupt the federal government. He came back with a rather curious piece of evidence that said the organized criminals were impressed with the relative incorrupti-bility. Number one, they got the narcotics chief in Miami. Number two, the evidence said that there was corruption at all levels of the govern-ment, and I suggest to you that if those organized criminals have to corrupt the federal government, they'll get over their impressed state of mind and they'll corrupt them. I want that disadvantage answered in that last speech.

Finally, I said it reduces the support of this organized crime. We pointed out to you, I think, that the money will result in incorrupt and honest police forces if we give it to the local level. But no, Mike just wants to have the federal government come in and do everything. Then I said a national police force admits defeat to local corruption, and I think Mike admitted that earlier when he said, "Well, we'll circumvent this corruption—that's only one part of our case." I suggest using the present system and get at that corruption. A national police force is bad. What's the harm? I pointed out to you that the harm was that it saps the morale. Now O. W. Wilson doesn't mind the federal govern-ment participating, according to Mr. Denger, but I'll bet you O. W. Wilson would mind plenty much if the federal government were in there supervising all of the activities and looking for corruption under every rug. I think it does sap the morale, and I don't think Mike answered it.

Finally, I said the local efforts are most effective because organized criminal activities primarily are there on the local level operating even though in violation of federal laws. We can't expect Washington to know where the local bookie is in New York, but the New York Police Department will know. There are five serious disadvantages to this affirmative proposal. In a comparative advantage analysis, I think they better be answered very satisfactorily in that last rebuttal. I don't think they can be.

Now, let's go back to those need contentions. Number one, they told us we'll remove the jurisdictional barriers. All Kathy is telling you here is, first of all, the federal government has jurisdiction in this area—specifically in terms of gambling. Now Mike came back with a *Wall Street Journal* article that said, "The more knowledgeable gamblers have tailored their operations so they don't become a part of interstate commerce." Mr. Denger, in his eagerness, forgot to read two words in that quotation. "The more knowledgeable gamblers have attempted to tailor their operations so they stay out of interstate commerce." I want proof that they have. I want proof that they don't use the telephone, that they don't use the mails, and that they don't use that interstate commerce in any way whatsoever. As proof that the federal government does have jurisdiction, Mr. Kennedy said they had investigations. He goes on to say, "We have investigations of this nature now going on in twenty-two states." That was in the report to the President from the Attorney General January 10, 1963. I think the federal government has jurisdiction. What about cooperation? We're telling you that if the localities may not be able to go in, but if they need cooperation because a gangster lives outside their jurisdictions, there's no reason why they can't cooperate. They came back and said, "Well, they won't cooperate because they're corrupt." These are the investigative and prosecutive barriers they're talking about. Yet, Kathy said, number one, the federal government has jurisdiction to deal with this corruption. Number two, we have special prosecutors, we have grand juries, we have the Internal Revenue Service, we have these self-check units that have been effective in Chicago and Los Angeles. And all that Northwestern has done is committed what I consider the fallacy of division by telling us, "Well, each one of these is either in all the states or each one of these can't solve the problem." But I want to know why all of these in conjunction can't solve the problem. I think they can be pretty effective. I want some legitimate indictments to these mechanisms.

And finally, they're going to remove the penal barriers. You know, Mike never did explain how those 100,000 prosecutions were illegal because, see, our prosecutors are legally bound to prosecute only in that area where the money is spent most judiciously. Yet they're getting 100,000 convictions in gambling every year. We reject that analysis.

SECOND AFFIRMATIVE REBUTTAL SPEECH

Mr. William Snyder
Northwestern University

Let's begin with the objections to the affirmative proposal. Number one, the narcotics analogy is not an accurate one. Mr. Earl Johnson says after all, you always have the corpus delicti, you have the smuggling operation, you have the interstate level. Now that was Mr. Johnson's description. We never heard an exact quotation that said the Narcotics

Bureau's effective law enforcement had nothing to do with effective fight on organized crime. My colleague in his rebuttal speech pointed out to you from Mr. Siragusa in 1963, "A major reason for the decline in narcotics addiction and traffic in recent years has been the tougher legislation adopted in 1956 aimed at ending the narcotics." What did that legislation provide? Complete jurisdiction and strong penalties. We think it's a rather remarkable coincidence that in 1956 we gave that freedom to the Narcotics Bureau. They had extremely great success. We think all those characteristics of narcotics operations applied before 1956, just as much as they did afterwards. We think we've identified the reason for success.

Number two, the gentlemen said we're not going to be able to get the corruption. You can't prove it unless you have the right to wiretap. Now, perhaps once in a while there's been a case of corruption in which we needed wiretapping to prove it. The gentlemen themselves told you we had gotten corruption in some cases without the right to wiretap. What did we come back to say? We pointed out the success of the Bureau of Narcotics was what? Mr. Charles Adrian, Professor of Political Science at Michigan State, "While quite a few public officials will cooperate with underworld vice operations, few will make an alliance with the purveyors of narcotics, since it would be futile, because state and federal law enforcement is particularly alert here." They don't have the right to wiretap. We don't think there is going to be a severe problem with regard to corruption if we can give jurisdiction to state agencies and to the federal government.

Third, the gentlemen suggested we're not going to solve the problem of protection. Sometimes it's not in the form of the bribe. Let me make two remarks. Number one, often it is in the form of a bribe—4½ billion dollars worth. We suggest they don't deny the advantage there. Number two, when it isn't in the form of the bribe, such as a lenient judge, the possibility of little money, an incapable prosecutor, political influence; doesn't it have more of an advantage to rely not on one local agency, but to create an agency also at the state and federal authority, so that we can go in and get this, even if it's leniency, even if it's a lack of money, even if it's an inept prosecutor at the local level? I don't believe they've denied the advantage there.

All right, then, finally they suggested some disadvantages. Number one, there's always the danger of corrupting the federal government. We pointed out, number one, if they had to corrupt all three levels of government, it would be prohibitive. That's in the first constructive speech. The negative haven't replied. Number two, we pointed out, it's been extremely difficult to corrupt at the federal level. They think one example disproves that. We pointed out that when we have had corruption, we've been able to get them in the Bureau of Narcotics. Number three, we suggested if we can have three levels, it makes much more sense to have a check on three levels of government rather than relying on one level of government. I don't believe we're going to have complete corruption throughout the United States.

Then the gentlemen suggested that we would reduce financial support for the local law enforcement agencies. They told us that a national police force would sap morale, and they said it would be a mission of defeat. These were three separate disadvantages, but we think they're all virtually the same thing. My colleagues comment, we only send in these agencies when jurisdictional barriers prevent, or corruption prevents an ability or a willingness to attack organized crime. We didn't say they would be looking over Orlando Wilson's shoulder supervising all of his operations. Mr. Wilson indicated that they welcome that kind of jurisdiction. We don't think we're going to sap the morale. We don't think there's an admission of defeat. We think we can do better against organized crime. How? In three ways.

Number one, we can remove jurisdictional barriers to effective law enforcement. The lady of the negative team and her colleague have told us we can always get federal jurisdiction. In four out of six cases, in a few instances, but the conclusion was in most cases the federal law is not violated. They don't have jurisdiction. They suggested we can have cooperation. We pointed out we don't have any agency at the state or federal level to provide that cooperation. It only takes place in one or two cases. We're trying to argue comparative advantage. We're not saying that it's absolutely impossible ever to have that kind of cooperation. But, when we review the conclusion of *The New York Times*, "Most states lack any centralized control over law enforcement," and Mr. Hundley tells us that, "Without centralized authority to enforce the criminal laws the state is unable to move in on local enclaves of organized crime," we think we can substantially reduce those jurisdictional barriers which in Detroit, Tampa, and throughout the nation, continue to impair the attack upon organized crime. And, I don't believe the negative team has ever denied the fact that they impair that attack.

Number two, we suggest we can remove political barriers to effective law enforcement. The lady of the negative team read five specific mechanisms. I pointed out most of them aren't available in most of the states. I pointed out the crime commission isn't a law enforcement body. All she did was re-read her evidence which said that it exposed a few things—not that it was able to enforce the law. What did we argue? Here, isn't it more advantageous to have an agency at the federal and state level that can move in when these particular mechanisms are unavailable or when they break down? I don't believe she denied the conclusion of the American Bar Association that it would be far superior to have federal and state agency jurisdiction to go in and attack corruption when they're unable to do it on the local level. We claim an advantage there.

Third, and finally, we can remove penal barriers. We're not saying it's illegal to attack this particular organized crime if you have raids and a few convictions. We talked about the major conspiracy case in which a great deal of time and effort is necessary. That cannot be done at the present time because the penalties are too weak to justify it. Mr. Ploscowe said that was the major reason for nonenforcement of the law. We can remove the penal barrier. We think we can emulate the success of the Bureau of Narcotics and have a far more effective attack on organized crime.

APPENDIX D

TV AND

THE ELECTIONS

THE GREAT DEBATE: GOOD POLITICS?

*James A. Robinson**

To evaluate the role of television debates in political campaigns, I should like to adopt a standard for the evaluation of many aspects of the electoral process. The one I employ in this paper has been used in the evaluation of presidential primaries and national nominating conventions. This standard asks the following question: "Do the electoral procedures focus attention on factors, characteristics, and issues relevant to the conduct of the office *after* the election?" Such a question provides the criterion for evaluating the "rationality" of electoral procedures according to whether the requirements for getting elected are similar to or relevant to the requirements for filling the office if elected. For example, if an electoral system excluded bald men from the presidency, it would be regarded as nonrational, unless we had good reason for believing that baldness correlates highly with being a poor

* Originally presented in Central States Speech Association Conference, Chicago, 1961. Dr. Robinson is Mershon Professor of Political Science at Ohio State University. Paper used by permission of the author.

president. That such a standard for the evaluation of various aspects of electoral procedures is not an uncommon one may be seen in an exchange of views between Senator Mike Monroney and Adlai Stevenson in hearings before a subcommittee of the Committee on Interstate and Foreign Commerce of the United States Senate in 1960.[1] The subcommittee held hearings on a bill to exempt television stations from the equal time requirement for the 1960 elections in order that they might provide some form of joint appearances between the two presidential candidates. Senator Monroney developed a line of argument with Governor Stevenson that can be summarized in the rhetorical question: "If major networks will give the president virtually any time he asks in order to explain his policy, why shouldn't the major networks give the leading candidates for the presidency sufficient opportunity to explain themselves before one of them is chosen for the presidency?" In short, Senator Monroney advanced the proposition that the requirements for choosing a president ought to be related as nearly as possible to the requirements for filling the office after elected.

There seem to me to be two ways, at least, to answer the question whether joint appearances by the two major candidates for the presidency are a rational part of an election campaign. One way is to list the requirements of the presidency and then determine whether joint appearances are relevant to determining which candidate better measures up to these. Such a procedure presupposes some consensus on the requirements of the presidency; but as I will show in a moment, we presently lack such a consensus. A second way to answer the question is to list certain salient features of the joint appearances—as we witnessed them in the 1960 campaign—and to inquire whether an analogy exists between these features and the presidential role.

Let me try to show briefly why I think the first way of answering the question about the rationality of joint appearances is not a fruitful one. The major reason is that we have great difficulty in agreeing on the qualities, characteristics or requirements of great presidents. Let me cite a number of different qualities that students of the presidency believe are important to an adequate or a great president. Professor Clinton Rossiter lists seven qualities that he believes a man must cultivate, if he is to be an effective modern president. He adds that these are qualities

---

[1] "Presidential Campaign Broadcasting Act," hearings before the Communications Subcommittee of the Committee on Interstate and Foreign Commerce, United States Senate, Eighty-Sixth Congress, Second Session, on 5.3171. Washington Government Printing Office, 1960, pp. 9–10, 206.

necessary only for success and do not necessarily insure greatness. These seven qualities are bounce, affability, political skill, cunning, sense of history, newspaper habit, and a sense of humor.[2] Professor Henry Steele Commager has a somewhat different list. He suggests that the conduct of the presidential office requires patience, prudence, humility, sagacity, judiciousness, and magnanimity.[3] Arthur Schlesinger, Jr. believes that the essential quality of strong presidential leadership is "capacity for creative innovation," which "comes most of all . . . from the president's personal vision of the future."[4] Senator Margaret Chase Smith holds that courage and initiative are the chief qualities that a president needs.[5] Walter Lippmann, in a widely publicized television interview, listed four qualities of leadership. The first is the capacity to see what is permanent and enduring in the situation, a quality he summarized as "second sight." The second is a judicial mind, meaning the quality of hearing contending factions and then deciding between them. The third is articulateness and the fourth is sympathy.[6] Professor James Burns believes that moral leadership in the presidency requires conviction, capacity to inspire, grasp of events, commitment, and capacity for growth. Least of all, Professor Burns believes that administrative experience is a requirement.[7]

If the men and women who write about the presidency disagree among themselves about the requirements of a good or an outstanding president, one will not be surprised that college students of administrative processes also list a wide number of qualities which they think might be relevant for the president. In 1960, a class of students told me that intelligence is the quality most needed in a president, followed by leadership abilities, integrity, experience, courage, effective speaking, decisiveness, and several other qualities that drew a smattering of votes each, including organizational ability, diplomatic skill, physical strength, emotional stability, attentive listening, and a sense of humor. To be sure, these illustrations, both from commentators on the presidency and

<hr/>

[2] *The American Presidency.* New York: Harcourt, Brace & Co. 1956, pp. 135–137.
[3] "Washington Would Have Lost a TV Debate," *The New York Times Magazine,* October 30, 1960, pp. 13 ff.
[4] "The Right Man for the Big Job," *The New York Times Magazine,* April 3, 1960, p. 120.
[5] *Ibid.,* p. 27.
[6] CBS-TV, July 7 and August 11, 1960.
[7] "The One Test for the Presidency," *The New York Times Magazine,* May 1, 1960, pp. 9 ff.

a college classroom, are hardly authoritative or adequate samples of views on the nature of the presidency, but they illustrate a rather wide range of qualifications believed to be relevant to the office. Unless we can have greater consensus than I think we presently have on the qualifications for the presidency, we will despair of trying to determine whether joint appearances of presidential candidates is relevant to the conduct of the office.

I am, therefore, inclined to the view that the second way of answering the question of the relevancy of joint appearances to the presidency is the more useful. This is to inquire whether joint appearances and the presidential role are analagous. If one excelled in the debates, would such excellence be relevant if he were elected? Or asked another way, would the winner have opportunities to use the same forensic skills again?

Let us first list the major speaking occasions for any president, after which we will see whether the joint appearances are related to these major occasions. One of the president's most frequent and highly publicized occasions for a major address is to Congress. In such speeches he does not debate, but rather presents formal addresses, written in advance and from which few departures are made during delivery. Not since President Washington's famous rebuff, when he visited the Senate for advice and consent on a treaty, has a president personally put in an appearance at the Senate on the matters on which the Senate is constitutionally entitled to a voice, except to make a formal address. A second opportunity for a president to engage in public address is at international conferences. On such occasions, *e.g.*, at the United Nations, he does not debate. In both the General Assembly and Security Council, participation of American representatives in debates is confined largely to the ambassador and to other delegates. Even in these cases, however, debates differ in several ways from television appearances with one's opponent for the presidency. When heads of states or heads of governments convene, their speaking is not debating. Indeed, such meetings are often decision-ratifying rather than decision-making. Although it is sometimes said that debating reveals the capacity for quick thinking, this is a proposition for which I have not seen reliable evidence. Furthermore, international conferences rarely require an immediate or impromptu response. For example, translation time allows for deliberation; and even in the Security Council where there is simultaneous translation, time for sequential translation may delay response. Other oral presentations by the president include addresses to the country by television and radio and special addresses to particular groups. None of these in any way resemble a debate. The oral presentation most analogous to the joint appearances seems to me to be the presidential news conference. President Kennedy, like President Eisenhower, changed the presidential conference as it was known under Presidents Truman and Roosevelt. But even the modern press conference differs in two important ways from the joint appearance. First, its format is one that the president can more effectively control than the candidates can control the joint appearance. This is so because the president can call on some questioners rather than others, something that the candidates could not do in their joint appearances in 1960; and it is also probably easier for a president not to answer a question than it is for one candidate to say "no comment" as the other stands by. A second way in which the news conference differs dramatically from the joint appearance is in the size of the audience. There is a considerably smaller audience for a news conference than for a joint appearance, probably because the former is more frequent. Therefore, any one performance is less crucial. Approximately nine million people are said to have watched the first presidential press conference of Mr. Kennedy, while between forty and eighty million people watched one or more of the joint appearances. As more and more presidential press conferences are televised, one would expect the number of viewers to decline.

Accordingly, I conclude that there is very little in the speaking occasions of the presidency for which joint television appearances of the kind we saw in 1960, or for any debating format that I have heard discussed, are preparation for or an index of the competency of a man in the presidency.

The position just taken argues that the debates are irrelevant to the presidency, or rather they are irrelevant to a judgment about the adequacy of a candidate to the presidency; but they do not in principle make an argument that the debates are unconstructive. I should now like to state a line of argument, or really a line for research and thought, that holds that further joint appearances of the kind we witnessed in 1960 might in fact be harmful to the presidency. This line of argument is based upon the assumption that a continuation of the joint appearances will lead politicians to add television debating skills to the requirements necessary for nominating candidates. Many people believe that television debating made the difference for Senator Kennedy; although as several observers have pointed out in an election as close as the 1960 contest, many factors can justifiably claim to have made the difference. Whatever the objective facts, however, candidates and commentators hold the view that the joint appearances were decisive. President

Kennedy says he will debate again, which will likely establish the precedent more securely. I think it natural to expect, therefore, that party leaders will add television debating skill to the other characteristics which candidates should have. Already we have adopted many non-constitutional requirements in addition to the constitutional ones. Mr. Sidney Hyman has compiled fifteen rules for exclusion, as he calls them, which are employed in the selection of presidential nominees. Region, race, religion, occupation, social strata, these and other factors already limit the number of people who meet the simple constitutional requirements of age and national origin. Mr. Hyman believes that ". . . the minority that can pass all these tests at any one time is probably in the neighborhood of one hundred men."[8] If we add to this television debating skills, we may expect to further reduce the pool of eligible people for the presidency. Professor Commager has said that neither General Washington nor Mr. Jefferson nor Mr. Lincoln nor Mr. Wilson, statesmen ordinarily regarded as great presidents, could have performed adequately under the circumstances of the joint television appearances of 1960. I think it is a safe prediction that if television debating becomes a requirement for the presidency, and I predict it will if continued, we shall further reduce the number of eligible men on whom we may draw to fill the highest office in the land.

It is tempting, I think, to believe that somehow television debates give people better information on which to make their voting decisions. It is also tempting to believe that excellent performance in such a situation is an index of something important to the presidency. On both these points, I think we need more and better research than we presently have. As for what people see or think they see in the debates, and whether the debates are from some point of view a "constructive" influence on voters, we cannot know until we have studies on the relationship between the debates and the voter. I think it unfortunate that neither the American Political Science Association nor the Speech Association of America nor any individual or other collectivity of political scientists and rhetoricians engaged in a theoretical and empirical study of the 1960 debates. They were a classic example of a natural experiment.[9]

As for the second tempting thought, namely, that forensic skill is

8 *The American President*. New York: Harper and Bros., 1954, pp. 183–236, with the quotation at p. 232.

9 For a collection of essays and isolated studies, see Sidney Kraus, *The Great Debates*. Bloomington: Indiana University Press, 1962.

an index of qualities necessary or helpful to the presidency, I think we are also in need of more research and of a codification of some findings that might indirectly bear upon this point.

Therefore, in the absence of better knowledge of these two points that one frequently hears made in defense of the debates, I prefer to rest on the other propositions outlined earlier. They are two: first, that nothing in the joint appearances *per se* resembles the forensic occasions for a president; and second, that the imposition of television debating skill as a requirement for the presidency will further reduce the number of people eligible for that high office. These two factors have led me to the conclusion that television debating among presidential candidates is not an element of rational electoral procedures.

EDITORIAL FOLLOWED

BY LETTER TO EDITOR

THE DREARY CYCLE[1]

WAR AND POLITICS BEING WHAT THEY ARE, THE CONGRESSIONAL JOINT Economic Committee is probably correct in figuring that the Administration is again underestimating the cost of the Vietnam war. If so, it is up to Congress to take the appropriate action.

Last year, it may be recalled, Government officials put the cost about $10 billion below the actuality—a calculation the cynics considered not unrelated to the then prospective November elections. The upshot, as the committee says, was havoc in the economy. Congress was unable to examine the advisability of a tax increase in its true light; combating inflation was left almost entirely to monetary policy and a near-crisis developed in the money markets.

Now, "the same dreary cycle of events threatens again in 1967," the Congressional group warns. More specifically, Vietnam spending in calendar 1967 may run $4 billion to $6 billion over the original estimates. The possibility adds weight to the predictions that the budget deficit in the current 1968 fiscal year may be $30 billion or more.

1 *Wall Street Journal*, July 11, 1967, p. 16. Reprinted by permission of the *Wall Street Journal*.

Granting the difficulty of reckoning expenditures in any war, the committee members nonetheless suggest that the Administration could do a considerably better job. They urge "timely conveyance to Congress of the latest estimates," and the Administration has promised to try to bring its figures up to date later this month.

But there is much more to it than merely improving the reliability of the fiscal outlook. The prospect of ever-increasing Vietnam costs makes it imperative to reduce Federal nondefense spending. Since the Administration has no stomach for the task, it goes to Congress by default.

It's often alleged that it is all but impossible to effect significant savings; so many costs are fixed or uncontrollable. Some are, to be sure, but the budget is ripe for pruning, as President Johnson himself unintentionally underscored in a recent speech.

Pointing with unjustified pride to how much the Government is spending domestically while fighting a war in Vietnam, the President mentioned the following: The poverty program has been increased every year and is going up 25% this year. Education is $12 billion this year, three times the level three years ago. Health, a little over $12 billion, also triple what it was three years ago. A new "far-reaching" model cities program.

To call that kind of binge irresponsible is putting it mildly. Projects like the so-called war on poverty are an administrative mess as even federal officials occasionally concede. Not only that; if all the poverty spending has made any sizable dent in the problem, it must be news to the poor.

In the light of such wild and wasteful outlays, it is an insult to the taxpayer for the Administration to keep insisting on higher taxes later in the year. Plainly the budget is in terrible shape; the right way to deal with it is not to aggravate the onerous tax burden on the people but to restrain the outpourings of the executive branch.

The Republicans in Congress and some of the more level-headed Democrats are talking bravely of finding substantial savings amid the budgetary chaos, but the obstacles are formidable and the hopes appear dim.

Congress, after all, is still dominated by liberals. In addition, any politician hesitates to pare or eliminate projects in being, on the venerable if not necessarily valid theory that the more dollars go out the more votes will come in. And Congress' own piecemeal, horse-and-buggy mode of tackling the budget makes it hard to weigh one program against another, establishing reasonable priorities.

Despite all the hurdles, a condition of rapidly mounting war and non-war costs, building a towering deficit, can fairly be called critical; Congress must be importuned to rise above its frailties. For if our profligate Governmental planners are not held in check, they will set in motion a cycle of events that will be not only dreary but desperate.

GOVERNMENT AND DEBT[2]

EDITOR, *The Wall Street Journal*:

The "Review and Outlook" column of the July 11 edition of your paper is another dreary exhortation that the federal budget be balanced. This seems to be a regular feature of your paper and undoubtedly has wide appeal in the business community where there is strong propensity to make a grossly inaccurate analogy between business and government budgets. The government is not like the department store in Phoenix, nor any other business, for that matter, for a number of reasons. First, it is not a profit-seeking institution. And it is not the case that it just turned out that way; it was never intended to be. Unlike any business, its debt is not externally held. In addition it has money-creating powers.

If there is room for analogy with business, it is in the area of the need for and the capacity to carry debt. Do you know of any prudently managed business that does not need debt? And as far as capacity to carry debt is concerned, the record is clear—it is increasing much faster than debt. I would suggest that any business with the same level and stability of earnings would be foolish not to carry far more debt than what the government presently carries.

There is a rule of thumb in personal financial management that an individual can safely carry a total debt of two and one-half times his annual income. And built into this safe limit is amortization of the principal. With continuous refunding an absolute certainty, a national debt that is less than half of national income should be no cause for concern for anyone, least of all the business sector where markets for government debt issues are strong and trading is always brisk.

[2] *Ibid.*, July 26, 1967, p. 14, as excerpted. Original letter used by permission of Mr. DeFelice.

But there is a far worse error that such pap about a balanced budget commits. And that is the complete disregard for one of the most elementary points of modern economic theory.

In modern economic theory the level of spending is the key determinant of output, employment, and prices. Though federal spending has been *decreasing* as a percent of total spending in the economy, it remains as the only sector over which much control can be exercised. Business and consumer-spending, which constitute all the nongovernment spending, sky-rocketed last year in spite of the Fed's attempt to curtail them with tight money and the highest interest rates ever. This should serve as sufficient evidence that monetary policy alone cannot curb inflationary spending—particularly the unsustainable level of investment spending done by the business sector because buoyant optimism about profitability far outweighs the increase in interest rates and large internal sources make market shortage of funds irrelevant. In such a situation as prevailed last year the government should decrease spending or increase taxes, or do some of both to hold down the level of aggregate spending. But please note: under any of these alternative recommended policies, the budget would *not* be balanced; there would be a surplus, not a balance.

At other times—like now—the total level of spending in the economy will not be enough to keep all our resources fully employed. In this situation the government should increase its spending, decrease taxes, or some of both to raise the level of total spending. Under any of these alternative recommended policies the budget would *not* balance; there would be a deficit. So unless the level of total spending in the economy were "perfect" there should always be either a surplus or a deficit. And it would be highly unlikely that the surpluses and deficits would be equal and offsetting.

Furthermore, requiring a balanced budget would *not* be neutral in its economic effect. In a business downturn—like the present one—tax revenues automatically decline. To require a cutback in government spending at such a time would only aggravate an already bad situation. The converse holds when the economy is in an inflationary boom.

The federal budget therefore is an important tool to be used for the important economic goals of growth, full employment, and price stability. And this is not a distortion of government's rightful duties. To the contrary, such action is required by the Employment Act of 1946. It is only of secondary importance that the budget balance. This is not some economic heresy; it is the currently accepted doctrine of the science of economics. Most economists, like myself, who *last year* did advocate a tax increase did so to reduce an inflationary level of spending—not to balance the budget. Currently the correct fiscal policy is to reduce taxes and/or increase government spending to reduce unemployment and increase output—the budget be damned.

Sincerely yours,
FRANK DeFELICE, Ph. D.
University of North Carolina

INDEX OF TOPICS

Adjustment or repair, see Case, 239
Adversary system, 59
Advocacy, 29
Affirmative:
    burden, 53
    cases, 234
A fortori argument, 276
Analogy, see Argument, 194
Analysis:
    defined, 89
    flaws in, 262
    importance of, 89
    issues, 94, 222
    of propositions, 99, 101, 102
    special cases, 106
    steps in, 91
Argument,
    defined, 173
    kinds of, 185
    structures of, 176
    tests of, 197
Argumentation, defined, 13
Assumptions of argumentation, 7
Attack and defense:
    cross-examination, 276
    defined, 253
    fallacies, 260
    organization of, 257
    rebuttal, 283
    tactics of, 271
Attitudes toward argumentation, 9
Audience, 27, 40, 109
Authority, evidence, 148

Backing, 110
Belief, 40
Body, of outline, 242
Brainstorming, 134
Brief, see Cases, 246
Burden, of proceeding, of rebuttal, or of
        going forward, 57, 224
Burden of proof, 53, 223

Card catalogue, see Investigation, 124
Case:
    building of, 226
    defined, 221
    outlining, 242, 311
    prima facie, 222
    types of, 234
Causal, see Argument, 186
Certain, 48
Civil liberty, 4
Claim, 111
Comparative-advantages, see Case, 235
Comparison, see Argument, 194
Competition, 34
Composition, 290
Conclusion of argument, 110
Conclusion of outline, 243
Constructive reasoning, 175
Controversy, defined, 1
Cooperation, 34
Counterproposition, see Case, 108
Critical apparatus, 15
Cross-examination, 276
Current affairs, 118

Data, 110
Debate:
    defined, 26
    kinds, 60, 339, 371, 379
    specimens, 339, 379
Deduction, 193
Defense, see Attack, 253
Defense of status quo, see Case, 239
Definition to characteristics, see Argument,
        191
Delivery, 302
Democracy, 2
Description, 14
Dialectic, 24, 276
Dilemma, 274
Discipline, academic, 22
Discourse, forms of, 13

Discussion, see Investigation, 133
Dissent, 6
Diversions, 268
Documentation, 162

Effect to cause, see Argument, 186
Enthymeme, 23, 173, 184
Epicheireme, 180
Ethics, 8, 47, 58, 65
Ethos, 23, 209
Evaluating or judging, 307
Evidence:
    Classification, 144
    defined, 139
    flaws in, 263
    forms of, 141
    importance of, 139
    legal types of, 146
    tests of, 152
    uses of, 164
Example, see Argument, 186
Existentialism, 2
Explanation, see Exposition, 206
Exposition:
    as argument, 208
    incidental use, 206
    form of discourse, 13
    persuasive uses, 207
Extempore, 304

Fact:
    proposition of, 78
    as evidence, 141
Fallacy, see Attack and Defense, 260, 266
Figures of speech, 296
Forcing the defense, 275
Freedom of speech, 4

Generalization, see Argument, 185

Humanism, 7

Implication, 207, 248
Inconsistency, 267
Inquiry, 29, 115
Interviews, 125

Introduction of outline, 242
Investigation:
    defined, 115
    discussion, 133
    importance of, 116
    interview, 125
    kinds of, 116
    library work, 120
    steps in, 117
Issues:
    analysis, 89
    defined, 95
    finding, 94
    in special cases, 107
    kinds of, 96

Judging, 307
Judicial debate, 63
Judicial notice, 142

Kennedy-Nixon debates, 6

Language, 290
Legislative debate, 61
Library, see Investigation, 120
Limits of controversy, 10
Logos, 23, 41, 175, 177

Matching proof, 273
Motivation, 211

Narration, 14
Negative, see Cases, 238
Nonsequitur, 267
Note-taking, see Investigation, 129

Oration, 335
Outlining:
    kinds, 246
    principles of, 243
    specimen of, 311

Partition, 109
Pathos, 23

Persuasion:
  ethos, 209
  motivation, 211
  related to argument, 18
  related to debate, 26
Philosophical debate, 62
Plausibility, 48
Policy proposition, 80
Political debate, 61
Possibility, 48
Prediction, 192
Presentation, 289
Presumption, 50, 223
Prima facie, see Case, 54, 222
Principles case, see Case, 234
Probability, 47
Proof, 38
Propaganda, 26
Propositions: 69
  defined, 71
  forms of, 70
  functions of, 74
  kinds of, 75
  selection of, 82
  sources of, 81
  wording of, 84
Pure refutation, see Cases, 238

Qualifier, 110

Rationality, 2, 8
Rationalizing, 2, 216
Reading, see Investigation, 118
Reasoning, see Argument, 173
Rebuttal, see Attack & Defense, 283
Recording, see Investigation, 129, 144
Reducing to absurdity, 272
Reference works, 120
Reflective thinking, 31

Refutation, see Attack & Defense, 257
Research, see Investigation, 115
Responsibilities of advocates, 47, 58
Responsible speech, ethical & logical, 5
Rhetoric, 22

School debate, 231, 339
Semantics, 300
Sign argument, 190
Social context:
  democracy, 2
  education, 2
Statistics, 155
Status or stasis, 102
Stock issues, 105
Stratagems, 268
Style, 290
Suggestion, 215, 217
Support, forms of, 205
Symbolic logic, 181

Televised debate, 371
Testimony, 142, 148
Topoi, 188
Toulmin layout, 110, 184–5
Turn tables, 272

Value proposition, 80
Voice, 302

Warrant, 110
Warren Commission, 172
Witness, 142
Writing, 298

INDEX OF NAMES

Abernathy, E., 141, 187
Adler, M. J., 278
Andersen, K. E., 25, 210
Anderson, D. C., 167
Angell, R. B., 174, 175, 179, 189, 201, 308
Aristotle, 16, 23, 176, 188, 205

Arnold, W. E., 164
Auer, J. J., 36

Bailey, G. M., 120
Baird, A. C., 27, 36, 37, 76, 205

Baker, G. P., 22, 76
Baker, R., 262
Barnlund, D., 28
Bauer, O., 52, 66, 76, 236
Beard, R. S., 280
Beardsley, M. C., 175, 179, 186, 189, 220,
    308
Beecher, H. W., 215
Bergamini, D., 48
Bettinghaus, E. P., 40, 138, 144
Bierman, A. K., 175
Bormann, E. G., 40, 139
Bosanquet, B., 207
Bosworth, A. R., 287
Bowers, J. W., 64, 301
Brandes, P. D., 141, 166
Brock, B. L., 93, 236, 242
Brockriede, W., 17, 19, 22, 27, 28, 34, 36,
    40, 44, 52, 56, 58, 76, 90, 109,
    138, 144, 224, 280
Bryan-Darrow, 287
Bryant, D. C., 19, 186, 302
Buckley, W. F., 305
Burke, E., 104
Burke, K., 16, 299
Butler, J. H., 272

Cain, E., 62
Capp, G. R., 36, 76, 141, 186
Carmack, P. A., 62
Cathcart, R. S., 166
Churchman, C. W., 180
Clevenger, T., 19, 210
Conant, J. B., 100, 214
Condon, J. C., 300
Copi, I. M., 174, 194
Corax, 49
Costley, D. L., 167
Cousins, R. G., 290
Craig, G., 145
Cripe, N. M., 302
Cronkhite, G. L., 19, 53, 75

Denger, M., 339
De Felice, F., 383
Dewey, J., 175, 176
Douglas, W. O., 264
Dovre, P. J., 25
Downs, R. B., 120
Dresser, W. R., 154, 166, 167

Edwards, P., 39
Ehninger, D., 10, 17, 19, 22, 27, 28, 33,
    34, 36, 40, 44, 52, 56, 58, 76,
    90, 109, 138, 144, 187, 224,
    280
Eisenhower, D., 292
Esfandiary, F. M., 117
Eubank, W., 224

Fadely, L. D., 237
Feezel, J. D., 180
Fischer, J., 258
Fisher, R. M., 251
Fisher, W. R., 19, 52
Foster, W. T., 76
Freeley, A., 18, 22, 30, 32, 36, 37, 43, 52,
    56, 66, 76, 134, 141, 186, 224,
    238, 280
Frost, D., 353

Gardner, E. S., 7
Giffin, K., 65, 107
Gilkinson, H., 166
Goetzinger, C. S., 166
Golden, H., 306
Graham, G. M., 207
Gregg, R. B., 16, 218
Griffin, L. M., 251
Grisez, G. G., 9

Haberman, F. W., 153
Haiman, F. S., 28, 34
Hance, K. G., 31, 133
Hand, H. C., 272
Hand, L., 3
Hare, R. M., 193
Harlan, R. E., 65
Hart, H., 154
Hastings, A., 18, 32, 36, 37, 39, 44, 52, 56
    72, 76, 89, 138, 145, 187, 224
Hegel, G. W. F., 176
Hovland, C. I., 159, 214, 277
Huber, R., 18, 36, 76, 138, 141, 186
Hudson, H., 9
Huenergardt, D. W., 289
Hultzén, L. S., 102
Humble, H. W., 108
Hunt, E. L., 22, 276
Huntington, H. B., 76
Hutchins, R. M., 3

Inbau, F. E., 274

Johnstone, W. W., 15, 24

Kamisar, Y., 274
Kant, I., 197
Kennedy-Nixon debate, 6, 30, 61, 96
Kensington Stone, 118
Kerr, H. P., 109
Keynes, J. M., 194
Klopf, D., 66
Knepprath, E., 19, 62
Kraus, S., 270, 376
Kruger, A. N., 27, 33, 36, 37, 43, 52, 76,
    175, 186, 190, 224, 237

Lake, L. W., 278
Larson, C. E., 65
Lashley, W., 88
Laycock, C., 76
Leonard, H. S., 45, 308
Lincoln-Douglas, 61, 68, 172, 287
Lippmann, W., 5

Mader, T. F., 103
Magill, K., 107
Manicas, P. T., 185
Marshall, J., 158
Martin, H., 40
Marx, K., 176
Mazza, J. M., 283
McBath, J., 21, 22, 27, 30, 32, 34, 36, 37,
    43, 52, 56, 66, 76, 138, 280,
    302
McBurney, J. H., 21, 31, 36, 37, 43, 52,
    66, 76, 77, 133, 186, 188, 190,
    280
McCroskey, J. E., 66, 164
McDonald, K., 344
McKee, P. R., 165
McKnight, J. L., 227-9
Meiklejohn, A., 3
Mill, J. S., 11, 200
Miller, G. R., 6, 22, 27, 39, 44, 52, 76,
    138, 140, 144, 194, 206
Milton, J., 11
Minnick, W., 214
Monroe, A., 249

Monroe, R., 6
Moulton, E. R., 27, 36, 76, 134, 186
Mudd, C. S., 109
Mueller, G. O. W., 50
Murphy, J. J., 277
Murphy, R., 134
Musgrave, G. M., 235

Nadeau, R., 97
Natanson, M., 15, 24, 63
Nevins, A., 172
Newman, R. P., 66, 97, 162, 224, 279
Nilsen, T. R., 22, 27, 39, 44, 46, 52, 59,
    76, 138, 140, 144, 194, 206

O'Brien, J. F., 62
Olbrechts-Tyteca, L., 156
O'Neill, J. M., 21, 76, 77

Paulson, S. F., 166
Perelman, C. H., 156
Polanyi, M., 158
Polisky, J. B., 283

Rapoport, A., 28, 256
Ray, J., 48, 187-8, 190
Rickover, H., 6
Rives, S., 9
Roberts, H. M., 62
Robinson, J. A., 371
Robinson, J. L., 64
Rogers, L., 306
Rovere, R. H., 163
Rowan, C. T., 100
Russell, B., 41, 176, 258

Samovar, L. A., 270
Sanders, K. R., 66
Sayles, E. M., 19, 52
Scales, R. L., 76
Scott, R., 2, 45, 223
Shaw, W. C., 36, 65, 76, 104
Shepard, D. W., 72, 176
Sikkink, D. E., 166
Sillars, M. O., 109
Smith, B., 49

Synder, W., 348
Socrates, 277, 287
Sorensen, T. C., 11
Steuer, A., 278
Stevenson, A., 27
Stevenson, C., 193
Stoics, 176
Strother, D. B., 149
Stryker, L. P., 278
Sturgis, A. F., 62
Swift, J., 290

Terris, W. F., 77
Thompson, W., 55
Thonssen, L., 205
Toulmin, S., 16, 42, 110, 184

Veach, H., 193

Wackernagel, W., 290
Wagner, R. H., 36, 37, 43, 76
Wallace, K. R., 186
Webster, D., 215
Welch, J. N., 59
Whately, R., 16, 22, 31, 50, 52, 72
White, M., 24
Whitehead, A. N., 176
Wichelns, H. A., 291
Windes, R., 18, 32, 36, 37, 39, 44, 52, 56,
        72, 76, 89, 138, 145, 187, 224

Zarefsky, D., 335
Zavos, H., 48, 187-8, 190